BEYOND OUR MEANS

BEYOND OUR MEANS
Why America Spends While the World Saves

SHELDON GARON

PRINCETON UNIVERSITY PRESS   PRINCETON AND OXFORD

In the United Kingdom: Princeton University Press,
6 Oxford Street, Woodstock, Oxfordshire OX20 1TW

press.princeton.edu

Library of Congress Cataloging-in-Publication Data
Garon, Sheldon M.
Beyond our means : why America spends while the world saves / Sheldon Garon.
p. cm.
Includes bibliographical references and index.
ISBN 978-0-691-13599-1 (cloth : alk. paper) 1. Saving and investment.
2. Thriftiness—United States. 3. Thriftiness—Asia. 4. Capital movements.
I. Title.
HC79.S3G37 2012
339.4'3—dc23 2011023955

British Library Cataloging-in-Publication Data is available

This book has been composed in Goudy

Printed on acid-free paper ∞

Printed in the United States of America

1 3 5 7 9 10 8 6 4 2

To Sherrill, Claire, and Thea

CONTENTS

BEYOND OUR MEANS

INTRODUCTION

When I began researching this book several years ago, saving money was not the sexiest of topics—certainly not in America. Policymakers here have long emphasized *consumption* as the driver of the economy, while historians prefer to write about the rise of our vibrant consumer culture. But recently the issue of saving has become maybe too exciting. Despite a booming economy, household saving rates sank to near-zero levels by 2005. Three years later, the U.S. economy experienced a housing and financial meltdown from which we have yet to recover. Americans now contend with massive credit card debt, declining home prices, and shaky financial institutions. It has become painfully clear that millions lack the savings to protect themselves against foreclosures, unemployment, medical emergencies, and impoverished retirements.

As American families ponder their next move—whether to spend, save, or borrow—they might consider the very different ways in which other advanced capitalist nations behave. In Germany, where households sock away much more than Americans, saving *is* sexy. That's how we may translate *"Geiz ist geil!"* the wildly successful advertising campaign run by the electronics chain Saturn between 2002 and 2007. The message offended some because it could also be rendered, "Stinginess Makes Me Horny!" Yet for many Germans, the slogan playfully affirmed their frugal, often stodgy approach to consumption. In Japan, which until recently boasted the world's highest household saving rates, saving was rarely sexy. But it has been stylish. The pert, modern housewife demonstrates her cleverness by controlling the family's spending and boosting savings. Once while shopping in a Tokyo department store at the end of the year, a thought occurred to me. Americans would also be at the stores, each buying hundreds of dollars worth of Christmas presents. Mired in recession, Japanese shoppers demonstrated more restraint. What instead flew off the shelves were brightly colored "household account books," ledgers used for saving and economizing in the New Year. Some seven million were annually purchased at the time.

Americans first became aware they had a savings problem during the 1980s. The rise of Japan came as a shock to Americans. As the United States wallowed in stagnation, the economic juggernaut across the Pacific seemed poised to overtake us. Americans talked openly about their country's shortcomings. We'd lost our work ethic; high divorce rates were destroying families; and once-great cities rotted. The nation's low saving rate was the source of considerable handwringing. As people saved less, the U.S. economy suffered from a dearth of investment capital. Meanwhile, Japanese people not only worked incredibly hard, they saved huge portions of income. Accused of "excessive saving" and living in "rabbit hutches," they appeared frugal to the point of fanaticism. Japanese household saving rates reached 23 percent in the mid-1970s. This occurred during sky-high inflation, when economic theory predicts that people should save less, not more. Benefiting from the ready supply of low-cost capital, Japanese manufacturers ran circles around their American rivals. Japan would be followed by the rise of other high-saving economies in South Korea, Taiwan, Singapore, and Hong Kong. Then came the biggest one of all—China, which currently boasts a household saving rate of roughly 26 percent. By the first decade of the twenty-first century, those in charge of the U.S. economy spoke disapprovingly of a global "saving glut" exacerbated by Asians who oversaved and underconsumed.[1]

For the last three decades, economists have endeavored to explain why Asians save so much and Americans so little. High growth in Asia has surely been one factor. Consumption tends to lag behind sharp gains in household income. One would not expect such saving in a mature economy like the United States, economists reasoned. In addition, Asians recorded higher saving rates because they had younger populations hard at work and saving for the future. In Western societies, where larger portions of the population were older and retired, households presumably were spending down their accumulated assets. Another incentive to save in Asia was said to be the lack of welfare states. Knowing they could expect few benefits from the government, families engaged in higher levels of "precautionary saving" to deal with emergencies and old age. Some economists and political scientists further considered the impact of Asian institutions that single-mindedly mobilized popular savings—notably the mighty Japanese system of postal savings.[2]

It has also been tempting to fall back on "culture" as an explanation. Aren't Japanese, Chinese, and Koreans traditionally thrifty because of a shared Confucian-Buddhist heritage? None other than Alan Greenspan recently weighed in on the issue. The former Federal Reserve chairman blamed Asian savers for investing in America's catastrophic housing bubble. Chinese saving rates soared because "consumption restrained by culture and inadequate consumer finance could not keep up with the surge of income."[3]

Such cultural explanations have serious limitations. My colleague Nell Irvin Painter once observed that somehow only women have gender, and only black people have race. And apparently, I would add, only non-Western peoples have "culture." The fact is that Americans, too, are constantly shaped by culture and subcultures—those commonly held understandings of what's good or bad, prudent or reckless, savvy or stodgy. We must explain not only why East Asians save so much, but how powerful norms contribute to the free-spending propensities of Americans. Why not invert Greenspan's words? In the United States, consumption—stoked by a *culture of instant gratification* and fueled by *excessive* consumer finance—*surpassed* families' incomes and decimated savings.

It is equally problematic to assume that Americans are the standard-bearers of "Western" culture. Viewed from a global perspective, American thriftlessness is far from the norm. As indicated in table 1, several European nations have also saved at high rates over the last three decades. They still do, despite slow growth, aging populations, generous welfare states, and other factors that are supposed to *diminish* saving. In fact, leading European economies save larger portions of household disposable income today than the Japanese and South Koreans. American economists and business writers seldom refer to high saving

Table 1 Net Household Saving Rates, 1985–2008 (Percent of Disposable Household Income)

	Japan	USA	UK	France	Germany	Italy
1985	16.5	8.5	6.9	10.2	12.1	21.5
1990	13.9	6.7	5.6	9.2	13.7	21.7
1995	11.9	5.7	6.7	12.7	11.0	17.0
2000	8.8	3.0	0.1	11.8	9.2	8.4
2005	3.9	1.5	-1.2	11.4	10.5	9.9
2008	2.3	4.2	-2.8	11.6	11.7	8.2

Source: OECD. See appendix for notes and other countries' saving rates.

in Europe, perhaps because it so subverts our notions of a shared transatlantic culture and the triumph of Americanization.[4] An "Irresistible Empire" is how one historian describes American consumer culture and its supposed embrace by Europeans after World War II.[5] However, in their savings and consumption patterns, Europeans and East Asians resemble each other more closely than they do Americans over the past century. By nearly every measure, the United States jumps out as exceptional in its low saving and turbocharged consumption. Irresistible to itself no doubt, but not necessarily to others.

What brings together the high-saving societies of Europe and East Asia is not a common heritage, but rather a common modern history. This book tells the global story of how nations molded cultures of saving that have proven remarkably enduring in several advanced economies. Beginning around 1800, social reformers and governments became preoccupied with creating prudent, self-reliant citizens who saved their earnings. Nineteenth-century proponents called this "organizing thrift." To encourage "humble" folk to save, they established philanthropic savings banks and later post office savings banks. These institutions offered small savers safety, convenience, and attractive interest rates. Moral suasion figured prominently. To inculcate habits of thrift in the young, governments in the West and Japan next established school savings banks. Every week, pupils would deposit pennies, *centimes*, or Japanese *sen* in their special accounts. In the pantheon of virtues we term "Victorian," thrift occupied an exalted station. Many of the world's famous writers were unabashed champions of popular saving. We will encounter Daniel Defoe, Charles Dickens, Diderot, the Japanese writer Saikaku, and of course Benjamin Franklin. Samuel Smiles, the Victorian moralist who penned the best sellers *Self-Help* and *Thrift*, reached audiences throughout the world.

By 1914, the world's great powers regarded thrift as not simply good for the soul and society, but as a matter of national survival. During the two world wars, the belligerents ran highly intrusive savings campaigns to finance the unprecedented demands of protracted warfare. Populaces were harangued to curb consumption and deposit their earnings in "national savings"—small-denomination government bonds, national savings certificates and stamps, and postal savings. Although World War II ended in 1945, savings campaigns did not. With victory in sight in the war's final months, officials in Britain feared the public would stop saving. Exhorted to "Keep on Saving," Britons were told that saving and investment, not renewed spending, would be key to postwar recovery. From Europe to Japan, in war and in peace, savings campaigns formed an inescapable feature of everyday life during the 1940s and 1950s. Thereafter, entrenched cultures of thrift—in tandem with newer ideologies, notably environmentalism—continued to restrain the expansion of consumption and consumer credit in ways seldom seen in the United States. Elsewhere, states in East and Southeast Asia emulated Japan's successful developmental model, mobilizing domestic savings to finance rapid economic growth.

Beyond Our Means interweaves the history of savings promotion in Europe, the United States, Japan, and other Asian nations. It is more than a comparative study of disparate national cases. For that matter, this is more than a book about saving. I contribute here to the emerging field of transnational history. Although Japanese and Germans love to talk about thrift as part of their national character, nations do not save simply because of indigenous traditions. The similarities in savings institutions and campaigns across the globe are far from coincidental. They have resulted in large part from transnational or international exchanges of knowledge on how to organize prosperous, powerful, and stable nations. Notes Daniel Rodgers in his pathbreaking *Atlantic Crossings*, the mid-nineteenth century to the mid-twentieth was a time when nations systematically surveyed each other, emulating what we today call "best practice."[6] The encouragement of saving occupied a prominent place in transnational discussions of social and economic policy. The postal savings bank, we'll learn, was not a peculiarly Japanese institution, but one of the hottest social policy innovations of the nineteenth century. It began in Britain and Belgium before being adopted by Japan. Postal savings systems soon spread throughout Europe and European colonial empires.

Efforts at transnational history center on the Atlantic world. *Beyond Our Means* offers a more global narrative. The story of modern thrift unfolds on several continents—Europe, North America, and Asia— and energetically travels among them. The vectors of diffusion do not flow in one direction, from the so-called European core to the non-Western "periphery." Japanese, to be sure, avidly borrowed from the West. Yet Japan acted not only as a taker but also as a *maker* of transnational knowledge. In key instances, Westerners eagerly investigated Japanese models of national mobilization and savings promotion. So would other Asian nations. In this global marketplace of ideas and institutions, emulation was always a multidirectional phenomenon. European nations studied each other; Americans frequently expressed interest in European innovations; and postwar Europeans were alternatively fascinated and repelled by American consumerism. At times the United States (or at least parts of it) encouraged mass saving as much as Europeans and Japanese. Rather than assume that Americans by nature are "exceptional," we must therefore explain how the United States came to diverge from the concerted promotion of saving common elsewhere.

The encouragement of saving is very much a *modern* story. Historians generally write about thrift as a vestige of traditional morality— something that must be overcome before consumer revolutions can occur. In reality, the histories of saving and consumption are entwined. The rise of wage labor and a money economy in modern times permitted ordinary people both to spend and save. Indeed, concerns about mass consumption prompted reformers to urge the working poor to adopt "modern" habits—that is, to plan for the future and "rationally" budget their spending. By the late nineteenth century in Western nations and Japan, states and middle-class reformers regarded thrift as a

key marker of "civilization." Its inculcation would civilize colonial subjects, as well as people living in the slums and rural areas of one's own
country. There were also important gendered dimensions. Reformers
looked to the wife to play the role of the sober saver who would stop
her man from dissipating family wealth on drink and prostitution. From
Victorian England to twentieth-century East Asia, new norms envisioned the "housewife" as scientific manager of household finances. In
visual terms, too, the encouragement of saving increasingly relied on
modern, even modernist forms. War savings campaigns were at the
forefront of new techniques of mass propaganda. Everywhere, citizens
encountered radio spots, movie trailers, and the evocative color posters
that illustrate this volume.

Before we go further, let me clarify what I mean by "saving." This
is not a book about investment by wealthy individuals and businesses.
We are concerned here with the history of "small saving" and "small
savers." Small saving takes the form of deposits in banks, post offices,
savings bonds, or life insurance schemes. Small savers are the working,
farming, and middle-class people who make up the vast majority of any
society. "Small saver" may be an unfamiliar term to Americans today, yet
it was commonly used here before the 1980s. From a macroeconomic
perspective, a growing economy requires savings for capital formation,
but it is not particularly important how those savings are generated. A
nation's total savings are comprised of government savings, business
savings, and household (or personal) savings. If the government runs
surpluses and business saving rates are high, lower rates of saving by
households may not be a problem. In addition, foreign savings substitute in part for domestic small savings. Over the past three decades the
United States has attracted enormous savings from abroad at low interest rates. Currently the Chinese and Japanese central banks own
significant portions of U.S. Treasury securities.

Nonetheless, small saving has been vital historically for reasons
that go well beyond the economic. Politically, countries like Japan and
France regarded the small savings of their people as crucial to maintaining autonomy from foreign creditors and to investing in national
power. Their strategic approach gained wide acceptance by the time of
World War I. British war savings campaigns, for example, targeted the

"small investor"—liberally defined as every man, woman, and child. The equation of small saving and national independence resonates less today, unless we consider contemporary American anxieties about China. Low household saving, fear some observers, has made the United States financially dependent on an authoritarian regime that is hardly a strategic ally.[7]

Above all, the encouragement of small saving was, and is a *social* policy. Nineteenth-century champions of thrift believed that a working person with savings would be less likely to depend on public assistance, turn to crime, or engage in revolution. This overriding objective of social well-being explains why savings banks and postal savings systems were typically created as nonmarket institutions. Commercial banks generally discouraged small deposits because of perceived high transaction costs. By contrast, postal savings banks and savings banks in France and Britain for decades offered depositors fixed interest rates respectively of 3 and 2.5 percent, oblivious to money market rates. These were not profit-making banks, but rather state institutions capable of paying interest directly from national treasuries to promote small saving. In an American variation on the theme, the federal government permitted savings and loan associations to offer higher interest on savings deposits than commercial banks prior to the 1980s. Although small saving as a sociopolitical goal has largely disappeared in the United States, it may be making a comeback following the Great Recession of 2007–2009. Can a society—or an economy—be strong if the majority of households lack adequate savings for emergencies, retirement, and renewed consumption?

Defining small saving is only half the problem. How do we measure whether and how much ordinary people save? This is a challenge, historically and comparatively. Calculating a nation's household saving rates for periods before the twentieth century is of limited value. Such figures pick up the savings of wealthier investors at times when relatively few families saved money in modern financial institutions. As an alternative, I cite century-old international tabulations of the number of savings accounts per population. These numbers offer a fresh perspective on how many people actually saved in financial institutions, changes in savings behavior, and comparisons among nations. In the years preceding World War II, economists introduced the now-familiar household saving rate. In the United States, the government's National Income and Product Accounts (NIPA) became the standard measure. In their simplest terms, household or personal savings constitute the portion of aggregate personal income not spent on current consumption. The saving rate represents personal savings divided by after-tax personal disposable income. Nothing is simple, however. The saving rate is a national-level metric and does not necessarily tell us how much the typical household saved. Interview-based surveys of household saving and spending provide useful supplements. International standardization has moreover been difficult. What counts as savings and income varies by country. Major economies have adopted a new system of national accounts since 1993, but significant deviations persist.[8] To complicate matters, the U.S. government continually revises historical NIPA data. For example, the revised rates for the early 1980s now indicate much higher saving rates in America. Conversely, the new international standard (SNA 93) led to downward revisions of Japanese saving rates for the years since the early 1990s. This book uses the latest calibrations of saving rates, bearing in mind that people at the time may have had different understandings of how much their nations saved.

The biggest problem with saving rates, economists have long argued, is that they fail to measure increases in the value of household assets.[9] Essentially, saving rates reflect how much people put aside, rather than the appreciation of those savings and investments. Americans own homes and stocks in much greater proportions than Japanese and most Europeans. Accordingly, insist influential economists, American savers would rank higher internationally if the statistics took into account the higher returns they receive on their assets. Net worth (household assets minus debt) may be a better metric than household saving rates. On the other hand, household net worth fluctuates more than the value of one's small savings. What goes up often comes down, as we have seen in recent stock market volatility and the collapse of U.S. housing prices. Whether we rely on household saving rates or net worth goes well beyond statistical analysis. The question is fundamental to this book. Are households better off "investing" in homes and equities in anticipation of higher returns? Or should they systematically save larger portions of income in lower-interest bank accounts and savings bonds?

Clearly people do not come to these choices with a tabula rasa. This is a history about how human beings intervened to influence the economic choices of other human beings. Admittedly my approach will strike economists as unorthodox, even heretical. Academic economists have been reluctant to study moral suasion. It is difficult to measure, and most economists are skeptical that individuals could have been persuaded to behave in ways that do not appear to be in their rational self-interest. Economic theory is more willing to consider that institutions might affect savings behavior, although few empirical studies exist.[10] Did it make a difference in 1910 that savings banks and postal savings offices were widely accessible in Europe, Japan, and Canada, while institutions for small savers barely existed in many parts of the United States? Institutions not only influenced short-term savings decisions, but savings banks and school-savings programs also helped mold enduring cultures of thrift. These cultures in turn acted upon subsequent institutional developments. In Japan and continental Europe, for instance, political cultures long resisted American-style credit cards, fearing they would erode thrift.

I envision this book as broadening—rather than supplanting—economic analyses of saving. As specialists on international savings comparisons readily acknowledge, economic theory has not persuasively explained cross-national variations in saving.[11] For decades, the "life-cycle" hypothesis has held sway in American economic departments. Formulated by Nobel Prize–winning Franco Modigliani and Milton Friedman, this model posits that people calculate household income over a lifetime. As young adults, they "smooth" consumption by borrowing against future earnings to buy the things they need. Saving the most in middle age to provide for retirement, they spend down assets in their senior years.[12] American economists also broadly subscribe to Martin Feldstein's model of national pensions' negative impact on saving.[13] Later the chairman of the Council of Economic Advisors under President Reagan, Feldstein theorized that Americans' anticipation of Social Security retirement benefits depresses personal saving by 30 to 50 percent. A quick look at international saving rates severely challenges those grand theories. Here are just a few of what economists call "puzzles":

- Germans and other continental Europeans save at high rates despite generous national pensions and comprehensive welfare programs.
- Americans live in a less secure, free-market economy. Although Social Security and Medicare cover the elderly, the general populace receives few social protections against unemployment or home foreclosure while paying much more out of pocket for health care and higher education. "Rationally" they *should* be saving up; instead they spent down until recently.
- Germans, French, and other Europeans generally maintained high saving rates over the last twenty years despite rapidly aging societies.
- The proportion of elderly in the United States and Britain is lower than in continental Europe, yet the Anglo-Americans save little.
- German and Italian adults have positive saving rates at all ages, including the retirement years, whereas elderly Americans dissave.
- U.S. saving rates declined during the 1990s amid impressive *growth* in incomes, while several European nations maintained high saving rates despite slow growth.

These puzzles lead thoughtful specialists to fine-tune their models, considering such factors as variations in national pension schemes.[14] But do the economists protest too much? Could it be they've missed qualitative, normative elements that significantly shape saving and spending in each society?

Any analysis of why people have saved over the past two centuries must consider a multitude of motivations that go well beyond what economists can measure.[15] The American media imagines that households save almost entirely for retirement. That assumption underlies the life-cycle hypothesis, as well as tax breaks given for retirement savings plans but not for other forms of saving. In actuality, the concept of retirement—the long period between working and death—is only about a century old in the United States, and just a few decades old in

East Asia. Even today in advanced economies, households commonly save for shorter-term goals like unanticipated emergencies and purchasing consumer durables and homes. For millions of lower-income Americans, finding the money for car repairs is of more immediate concern than planning for the senior years.

Then there are the less tangible, yet powerful, motivations that have guided saving in modern times. Many save in part to achieve "independence" from creditors, employers, or relatives—much as Benjamin Franklin advised two and half centuries ago. Economists tend to study saving as an individual or household act, but we will also encounter numerous cases around the world in which people save to impress others. The Victorian gentleman was expected to be thrifty. A Japanese housewife improved her social status by prudently managing her family's finances while teaching other women in the neighborhood association how to keep household account books. In many times and places, the prosperous dared not consume too conspicuously or in environmentally wasteful ways lest the wrath of society fall upon them. Nationalism, too, has motivated saving, and not just in wartime. Untold numbers of Germans, Japanese, and Singaporeans will tell you they save because it's in their national character. Thrift forms an integral part of their identity—a defining trait they often invoke to distinguish themselves from consumption-addicted Americans. And of course savers have long regarded themselves as virtuous. In religious terms, the "Protestant Ethic" comes to mind, although other religions encouraged frugality as well. Likewise, the self-disciplined "millionaire next door" regards himself as morally superior to his hedonistic consumerist neighbors. Thrift moreover infuses secular environmentalism and Christian ideals of "stewardship." Adherents of both believe themselves ethically obligated to spend modestly and conserve resources for the greater benefit of humankind.[16]

To a certain extent these attitudes vary by individual. Some seem born to shop, others to save. Yet the episodes in this book suggest that individual motivations have themselves been shaped by larger cultural norms and social relations. Historically, governments, institutions, and groups worked hard to sell populaces on the virtues of saving. Subfields of economics have tackled sociocultural aspects of saving with varying degrees of success. Invaluable has been the work of development economists. Relying on extensive interviews, the best of these studies survey how poor people actually save and borrow in developing countries in Africa, Asia, and Latin America. Their findings mesh well with the historical evidence presented here from Europe and East Asia. Where formal financial institutions are absent or weak—then and now—villagers and neighbors often organize savings clubs, or savings and credit associations. In social terms, peer group pressure may result in higher levels of saving than individuals could achieve on their own. At the same time, depositing money with a group or in an institution enables individuals to *overcome* social obstacles to saving by safeguarding their money from husbands or relatives who might otherwise spend it. The development economics literature also demonstrates the importance of popular access to safe, convenient financial institutions. What was true in Japan one hundred years ago is true in South Africa today. People save more when they can trust that their money is secure in a nearby bank or post office.[17] Within the United States, social welfare experts have similarly deepened our understanding of saving by lower-income households.[18]

The emerging field of behavioral economics also offers fresh insights on the human dimensions of saving. Drawing on psychology and its experimental methods, the behavioralists provide a long-awaited corrective to mainstream economic models that assume people always make "rational choices." Households don't necessarily calculate lifetime income and save and consume accordingly. They may intend to save, but they succumb to procrastination and spend what they have. In the words of the economist, they exhibit "self-control problems." The key then is to devise schemes that make saving the default, not the last option after borrowing and spending. Like development economists, behavioral economists confirm many of the historical experiences in this book. People will save more when automatically enrolled in savings plans at the workplace or in groups. They are more likely to accumulate when engaged in "commitment saving" in Christmas Clubs or college savings accounts. Because one's level of financial literacy affects behavior, programs of financial education in high schools and workplaces appear to stimulate greater saving. Unquestionably, institutions matter. Individuals tend to spend cash more readily than savings in the bank.[19]

For all the promise, behavioral economics has its methodological limits. The discipline necessarily examines savings behavior but not how people *think* about saving. Subjects are assumed to have entered surveys and lab experiments with no preconceived notions that might have been formed by history, society, and culture. They are presented simply as human beings. Most behavioral economic research in fact occurs in the United States, often relying on unrepresentative subjects including students at elite private universities. Might not the results be different if we experimented on Belgians or Japanese who for generations have been exhorted to save? Indeed, behavioralists are no more likely to study the impact of moral suasion campaigns than are other economists. "Paternalistic libertarianism" is how Richard Thaler, dean of the behavioral economists, describes his position. He's a paternalist in devising schemes to encourage saving, yet libertarian in opposing efforts to tell citizens what might be good for them.[20] This strikes me as a bit disingenuous. Americans may save little not just because they are human beings. As we shall see, they have long been socialized *not* to save by legions of advertisers, finance companies, political leaders, and even neighbors. Elsewhere, moral suasion has been an important factor in molding cultures of saving. The United States, too, experienced successful campaigns that altered behavior, notably those that discouraged smoking and promoted seatbelts—not to mention the war bonds drives of World War II.

If we are to think creatively about the financial plight of American households and the possible remedies, why stop at the border? Why confine ourselves to the present? In this study, the global history of the past two centuries shall be our laboratory. When I talk to people from other nations, they are bewildered by everyday financial practices we take for granted. Recently a visiting Italian colleague had difficulty understanding that her American bank's ATM card was a debit card, not a credit card. We usually obtain credit cards independently of our local bank, I explained; we go online or respond to mailed solicitations. But how, she asked, do you pay your credit card bill each month? Well, I replied, we send a check or transfer funds to some address in South

Dakota or Georgia. "That makes no sense," said she. True, it wouldn't make sense to Italians or Germans, who rarely encounter an American-style credit card. Their "credit cards" are almost always issued by their bank, and are paid off each month from funds in one's bank account. But "what would happen," my colleague wondered, "if you didn't have enough money in your account to pay the credit card bill at the end of the month?" That'd be no problem, I assured her, because half of the country doesn't pay in full and borrows the balance from the card company; besides the companies encourage customers to go into debt because their profits lie in high interest charges. Again she shook her head, "That *really* makes no sense."

I was loath to tell my friend that to most Americans, neither she nor her country makes any sense. According to our economists, Italy is plagued by "imperfections" in its financial markets.[21] Far from helping people to save and avoid overindebtedness, the Italian system apparently punishes consumers by restricting their access to credit and denying them richer lives. So, who's right? When societies with such fundamentally different assumptions cohabit the capitalist world, surely we require a more historical understanding of how these rival cultures of saving and debt came to be. This book is dedicated to making sense of it all.

1

THE ORIGINS OF SAVING IN THE WESTERN WORLD

On a cold frosty day an Ant was dragging out some of the corn which he had laid up in summer time, to dry it. A Grasshopper, half-perished with hunger, besought the Ant to give him a morsel of it to preserve his life. "What were you doing," said the Ant, "this last summer?" "Oh," said the Grasshopper, "I was not idle. I kept singing all the summer long." Said the Ant, laughing and shutting up his granary, "Since you could sing all summer, you may dance all winter."

—"The Ant and the Grasshopper," *Aesop's Fable*[1]

So goes the world's best-known parable of thrift—a story taught to generations of children in the West and East alike. To this day, Japanese commonly identify with Aesop's ant in explaining their propensity to save. When it comes to putting aside for wintry days and encouraging others to save, humankind has been at it a long time. Aesop may not have been a real person, but the fable of "The Ant and the Grasshopper" dates back more than two millennia to ancient Greece. Likewise, the Bible overflows with injunctions to be prudential. In Proverbs, we meet again the farsighted ant: "Go to the ant, thou sluggard; consider her ways, and be wise: which having no guide, overseer, or ruler, provideth her meat in the summer, and gathereth her food in the harvest."[2]

To survive, human beings have always had to "save" in the sense of accumulating surpluses to prepare for times of want. As agricultural societies emerged, wise cultivators set aside part of their produce, lest like Aesop's grasshopper they perish in the winter or in bad harvests. Nor did hunter-gatherers fail to save, according to environmental historians. Although Puritan settlers in colonial New England denounced the natives for a lack of diligence and thrift, the Indians planned prudently for the lean winter months. They preserved meats and fish while purposefully eating little at the times of greatest scarcity. Native Americans also engaged in what scholars term "using nature as a bank." To conserve fish, game, or wild plants, aboriginal peoples consciously left such resources in nature so that they might be "withdrawn" later when needed.[3]

In many places and times, saving was a cooperative project. Rather than accumulate wealth solely for oneself or one's family, people commonly pooled their surpluses to distribute among group members who became destitute or ill. We would today call this social insurance. Members might form a savings group voluntarily, but degrees of compulsion were common. China's imperial state created the most extensive and venerable collective savings system in the form of the communal granary. At least as far back as the Song dynasty (960–1279), officials encouraged and invariably pressured local people to contribute to the granaries. Communities would then loan or grant grain to the poor and victims of famine.[4]

In medieval Europe, guilds of craftsmen routinely accumulated savings for mutual assistance. Members contributed small sums to a general fund that would aid them and their families in the event of sickness, unemployment, old age, or death. In many modern societies, including Japan, we shall encounter the legacies of group saving in the form of village and neighborhood savings associations. In early modern and modern Britain, guild-sponsored saving directly evolved into working-class "friendly societies." A fixture in most communities by the nineteenth century, friendly societies met regularly at pubs. While carousing, members also donated to the common fund. Often called "Box Clubs," friendly societies typically placed the savings in a lockbox. The box could be opened only after each of three officials inserted his key.[5] The American presidential candidate Al Gore evoked this tradition centuries later in the year 2000. He vowed to put all Social

Security funds in a metaphorical lockbox secure enough to withstand raids by his tax-cutting opponents.

Saving for the common good was nothing new in 1800. What was novel was the now-familiar practice of saving for one's own good by depositing money in a bank. As one banker-turned-historian put it, "the instinct to save is almost as old as human nature," but "organized thrift is a more recent development."[6] Its origins date only to the late eighteenth and early nineteenth centuries. Within a short span of time in Europe and North America, large numbers of individuals, groups, and public authorities began encouraging *all* strata of society to save money—a "radical innovation," in the words of one French scholar.[7] In the course of the nineteenth century, governments and reformers established savings banks, nationwide postal savings systems, and school savings programs. They also penned countless moral tracts. Suddenly states and societies became preoccupied with how ordinary people managed their assets.

The passionate encouragement of saving did not remain confined to Europe and its dominions. After 1868 when modernizing Japanese leaders set out to discover the secrets of Western might, they observed the "civilized" powers to be obsessed with creating patriotic, hardworking, and thrifty citizens. This now-forgotten Western world of character-building played a profound role in shaping the Japan we know today. It behooves us to comprehend an era—not so long ago—when the saver, rather than the consumer, was sovereign.

So What Ever Happened to the Protestant Ethic?

Why did societies become so avid about encouraging thrift some two centuries ago? It is tempting to single out one historical development that explains everything. For instance, some European scholars relate the emergence of savings banks to the Industrial Revolution. In their view, upper and middle classes moved to inculcate thrift in the rising working classes to fend off revolution. The problem with this interpretation is that the savings banks spread throughout Europe decades *before* mechanized industry took hold in most lands. Savings banks began operations as early as the 1780s in the old commercial centers of Germany, the 1810s in the rural parishes of Scotland, and the 1820s in the pre-industrial Scandinavian countries.[8]

Better known are theories that link the modern notion of thrift to the rise of Protestantism. The "Protestant ethic" has become part of everyday language. The term itself was coined by the German sociologist Max Weber in his book, *The Protestant Ethic and the Spirit of Capitalism* (1904–1905). Like many Europeans and Americans at the time and since, Weber argued that Protestants and Catholics approached economic life differently based on their religious beliefs. Catholics were prone to spend what they had. The humbler classes of Catholic France were "greatly interested in the enjoyment of life." Catholicism, explained Weber, tolerated occasional extravagance because humans were expected to sin, repent, and be granted absolution. Moreover, Catholics believed they would attain salvation by the gradual accumulation of "good works," which often meant donating one's surpluses to the Church.[9]

Weber's Protestants marched to the beat of a different drummer. In modern times, he observed, they achieved greater success than the Catholics. He highlighted the Protestants influenced by the doctrines of John Calvin (1509–1564). They lived in Scotland, England, Holland, the American colonies, and among France's Huguenot minority. Calvinism reputedly fostered a "spirit of capitalism." By this, Weber meant not a utilitarian approach to accumulating and investing money, but the intense desire to engage in hard work and frugality for their own sake. By exerting "systematic self-control" and resisting the "impulsive enjoyment of life," Calvinists convinced themselves and others that they would attain salvation or "election." Their "ascetic compulsion to save," concluded Weber, favored the development of a "rational bourgeois economic life" and stood at the "cradle of the modern economic man."[10] The formula was demanding, but straightforward. One saved, and was saved.

Scholars have roundly criticized the "Protestant ethic" thesis for failing to explain the development of the vibrant spirit of capitalism among Catholic merchants in Renaissance Italy or sixteenth-century Antwerp.[11] Yet few scrutinize Weber's arguments about thrift and Protestantism. As we shall see, thrift movements spread like wildfire across Europe oblivious to religious borders. We may conjure up images of frugal Scots and austere New England Puritans, but we must also reckon with the millions of prudential types in the Catholic lands of France, Belgium, Italy, and Austria. This is hardly to suggest that religion played no role. On the contrary, clergy often took the lead in propagating gospels of thrift in *both* Protestant and Catholic Europe.

Savings-promotion movements developed in too many places, within too many social structures, and at too many stages of economic development to reduce the phenomenon to the "Protestant ethic" or any other single explanation.[12] Rather, the origins of modern thrift programs lay in the interplay of several important developments in the late eighteenth and nineteenth centuries. Influential publicists began to think in new ways about the economy, society, and the individual. At the same time, living standards of the masses slowly improved to the point that ordinary people attained some margin to save. Needless to say, the general public could not save effectively until accessible financial institutions arose. Nor should we overlook the expanding networks of communication that enabled the pioneers of thrift to learn from successful experiments in other countries. Finally the growth of nation-states sparked new campaigns to encourage popular saving for the purpose of augmenting national power.

Overcoming Impediments to Popular Thrift

In today's advanced economies, we take it for granted that saving money is a vital means to increasing wealth. Yet just a few centuries ago, institutions and thought tended to *discourage* household saving in Europe and East Asia. Most people lived in self-contained villages and towns. Too much thrift and accumulation invariably threatened the rest of the community. Anthropologists confirm this in studies of relatively isolated villages today. Among peasants, observes George Foster in his classic essay on the "image of limited good," it follows that "an individual or a family can improve a position only at the expense of others." In this perceived world of finite resources, anyone who saves a bundle must be stealing from his neighbors. To restore village harmony in Latin America and elsewhere, those who amass wealth have been routinely obligated to dissipate their savings on costly festivals or lavish weddings and funerals.[13]

Back in medieval Europe, the teachings of the Church did much to hinder saving. The moral Christian put aside enough to tide his family over in bad years. But longer-term accumulation made one guilty of avarice, a cardinal sin. Ideally what little remained should be given to the parish and charity. Moreover, the Church condemned the very basis of modern saving—the payment of interest. Its ban on "usury" not only impeded lenders from charging interest, but also applied to paying interest on deposits. In Catholic France, both Church and civil law prohibited the payment of interest on savings—incredibly enough—until the end of the eighteenth century.[14]

Human beings are resourceful creatures, especially those engaged in commerce. While the Church's ban on interest inhibited a great many people from saving money, men of means devised ingenious methods of safeguarding and augmenting their surplus funds. The savings deposit has a long history, dating back to the rise of banking in late-medieval Europe. The word "bank" is thought to have originated in the Italian port of Genoa in the twelfth and thirteenth centuries. The first bankers were foreign-exchange dealers who sat at a table termed a *bancum*. In 1200 Genoese moneychangers were already accepting deposits and making loans. By the mid-fourteenth century, the famous Medici Bank of Florence had established numerous branches, some as far away as London. Taking in the deposits of prosperous Florentines at handsome interest, the Medici financed not only international trade but also several wars undertaken by European rulers. Over the next several centuries, bankers commonly offered rates of return on money deposited. Countless ruses arose to evade the Church's proscriptions. A depositor might receive shares of the profits of the invested monies. Typically bankers concealed interest on loans in complicated exchange transactions. Or a depositor bought a bill or commercial paper at a discount, receiving face value at a later date. The Protestant Reformation did much to weaken Catholic barriers to interest-bearing loans. Acknowledging the need for capital, John Calvin and his followers recognized the payment of interest as long as rates did not approach usurious levels. At roughly the same time in the seventeenth century, bankers in England, Scotland, and the Netherlands began to charge interest on loans more openly.[15]

Prior to 1800, however, few considered banks to be places where one saved money. Even in England, which saw the greatest advances in banking, the banks did not generally pay interest on deposits until well into the nineteenth century. European merchant-bankers like the Rothschilds and Barings concentrated on financing trade, kings, and national debt. Investing in their banks was not for humble folk or the faint of heart. Returns could be great, but so were risks. Merchant banking was a private, clubby world, in which merchants and the rich entered into transactions based on personal trust.[16]

While merchant bankers maintained a studied indifference to small savers, the Catholic Church and civic leaders in Italy and Spain founded a number of rudimentary banks for the general public during the fifteenth and sixteenth centuries. Known as a Monte di Pietà in Italian, this establishment was—first and foremost—a municipal pawnshop. Its philanthropic founders were motivated by the decidedly Catholic urge to eradicate the scourge of usury. Providing an alternative to the despised moneylender, the Monte di Pietà loaned money to the needy at minimal interest. Initially the capital for Monti di Pietà came from charitable donations and sometimes the not-so-voluntary contributions of Jewish moneylenders. Gradually the establishments assumed some aspects of savings banks in many Italian cities as the well-to-do deposited funds at interest. With regard to the poor, on the other hand, the Monti di Pietà remained institutions of credit, rather than saving.[17]

Nonetheless, in their concern for the financial well-being of the needy, the Monti di Pietà inspired reformers in Catholic Europe to contemplate genuine savings banks for the working poor. The earliest known proposal was put forward by Hugues Delestre—doctor of law, ambassador, and counselor to the king of France. In 1604, Delestre submitted his "Plan for a Bank." This bank would function alongside the local Mont de Piété (the French equivalent). Aiming to encourage providence among the poor, Delestre planned to restrict the bank's depositors to manservants, maidservants, and laborers. The individual would deposit "money that will be one's own, to assure tranquility in one's old age." Should emergencies arise, funds could be withdrawn at any time. To attract savers, the bank would pay interest amounting to 5.88 percent per annum. Delestre's proposal came to naught, but Europeans would adopt his strikingly modern vision of saving some two centuries later.[18]

The Founding Fathers of Frugality

To be alive in the Western world of the nineteenth century was to be exhorted. From clerics to civic leaders, from publicists to educators—men and women of influence urged people to live frugal and provident lives. The name of Benjamin Franklin (1706–1790) became synonymous with the encouragement of thrift in the United States and elsewhere. "A penny saved is a penny earned" is simply the best known of his maxims. By the 1910s, Franklin had taken his place as America's patron saint of saving. Supported by the YMCA and the American Bankers Association, organizations and schools commemorated Franklin's birthday every January 17 as the kickoff to "Thrift Week."[19]

Franklin's influence around the world has been enormous. Yet we would do well to place his adages within a longer global history of those who propagated the virtues of economizing. Over the previous centuries, countless authors of advice books instructed readers in the ways of curbing unnecessary expenditures. Rarely did they write about the more positive act of saving money in financial institutions. Nevertheless, these champions of frugality paved the way for Franklin and the modern apostles of thrift. Their advice helped form self-conscious middle classes, whose members not only identified themselves as thrifty, but increasingly sought to mold provident lower classes in their image.

Nearly one hundred years ago, the German economic historian Werner Sombart offered a compelling history of the modern idea of saving. He did so in the context of a contemporary debate with Max Weber and other German scholars who investigated the origins of modern capitalism. Whereas Weber traced the "spirit of capitalism" to the rise of the Protestant ethic, Sombart pointed to the development of "middle-class virtues" throughout Western and Southern Europe. Frugality figured prominently along with "industry" and fastidious bookkeeping. The conscious propagation of these virtues, he argued, began with the rise of the bourgeois in Renaissance Florence and culminated in the eighteenth-century writings of Franklin. Sombart highlighted the pioneering role of the Florentine scholar and architect, Leon Battista Alberti (1404–1472), whom he called "the most perfect type of the 'bourgeois' of those days." Influential among Florence's great mercantile families, Alberti's *Four Books on the Family* instructed readers in the art of managing the household. The way to wealth, he inveighed, was to control expenditures: "Do you know in whom my soul finds most pleasure? In those who spend their money on just what they need and no more, laying by the surplus; these I call thrifty, successful managers." Anticipating Franklin by three centuries, Alberti touted Diligence in no less fervent terms: "To lose not even one iota of that most precious good, Time, I follow this rule. I am never idle; sleep I flee from, and I lay me down only when weariness overcomes me." And much like Franklin, Alberti started each day by writing out a "time-table."[20]

To Sombart, the modernity of Alberti and his successors lay in their elevation of thrift to the core of bourgeois identity. In contrast to the extravagant feudal lord who spent first and then extracted what he needed from his subjects, the bourgeois defined his social worth by the ability to husband resources within the constraints of his income. Whereas the poor had long been forced by necessity to be thrifty, merchants and prosperous farmers began to practice frugality for its own sake: "But now rich men became thrifty, and this was the unheard-of thing. Before long, the original doctrine of not spending more than you were earning gave rise to its corollary of actually spending less than you were earning. The idea of saving thus came into the world; of saving not as a necessity but as a virtue."[21] In the ensuing centuries, moral tracts on diligence and thrift were published widely in Europe and North America. Sixteenth-century manuals for farmers in Spain, France, Italy, and elsewhere commonly employed the agrarian notion of "husbandry" to inculcate values of frugality, industry, and assiduous bookkeeping. The seventeenth century witnessed the publication of numerous "Books for Merchants" and "Commercial Dictionaries." These tracts likewise advised merchants to practice "economy" in its dual meaning of constraining expenses and putting aside the resulting surplus.[22]

By the early eighteenth century, there was serious money to be made in instructing the growing body of merchants and artisans in the wise use of money. The propagators of frugality included leading writers of the Atlantic world. Among them was England's Daniel Defoe (1660–1731). Better known for spinning tales about the adventurer Robinson Crusoe and the amorous Moll Flanders, Defoe was equally at home counseling merchants to lead frugal, industrious lives. In 1726 he published *The Complete English Tradesman*, which went through several editions and achieved popularity in North America as well. Defoe himself engaged in various commercial ventures, at one point falling into bankruptcy. Accordingly, his advice book brimmed with warnings to avoid debt and extravagance: "For a tradesman to borrow money upon interest, I take to be like a man going into a house infected with the plague; it is not only likely that he may be infected and die, but next to a miracle if he escapes." As for limiting expenses, Defoe admonished tradesmen to eschew the boorish lifestyles of the aristocracy: "When I see young shop-keepers keep horses, ride a-hunting, *learn dog-language*, and keep the sportsman's brogue upon their tongues ... I am always afraid for them." Mimicking those brutes would ruin the tradesman, whereas "prudent management and frugal living will increase any fortune to any degree."[23]

Defoe and other eighteenth-century writers helped persuade a stratum of society that prosperity and respectability flowed from hard work and sound financial management. Although Defoe did not invoke the modern term "middle class," he had Robinson Crusoe's father wax eloquent on the Temperance and Moderation of "the middle Station." This middling class neither succumbed to the "vicious Living, Luxury and Extravagances" of the upper class, nor suffered the "hard Labour, Want of Necessaries, and mean or insufficient Diet" of the lower orders. The shipwrecked Robinson Crusoe himself becomes an exemplar of self-discipline and prudence, husbanding the resources about him and laying up his "Stores of Provision."[24] And when in *The Farther Adventures of Robinson Crusoe*, five English mutineers become marooned on a desert island, Defoe pointedly relates their different fates to individual effort: "The Diligent liv'd well and comfortably, and the Slothful liv'd hard and beggarly; and so I believe, generally speaking, it is all over the World."[25]

It comes as no surprise that Benjamin Franklin devoured the works of Defoe.[26] The American proved an able student. No one sold thrift like Franklin. As scholars are quick to insist, there was more to Franklin than penny-pinching, hitting the sack early, and not sleeping-in. He was a man of impressive breadth and appetites—publisher, philosopher, inventor, and patriot. Franklin pursued wealth not as an end, but as the means to lead a useful and enjoyable life. Having become wealthy, he retired at the early age of forty-two and devoted his remaining forty-two years to public affairs and intellectual endeavors. As an American emissary to France from 1776 to 1785, he cheerfully reconciled his odes to frugality with a flamboyant, flirtatious life in the salons of Paris.[27]

Franklin, the man, had many faces. But to millions of readers around the globe, Franklin was *the* paragon of diligence and thrift, pure and simple. It was through *Poor Richard's Almanac* that his aphorisms first found their public. Franklin published the almanac from 1732 to 1758. Almanacs sold widely in England and North America during the seventeenth and eighteenth centuries. Bought by farmers, tradesmen, and fishermen, they offered readers practical information on the weather and holidays. As Franklin recalled in his autobiography, he bested rival publishers by making the almanac "both entertaining and useful." Adopting the pseudonym of Richard Saunders, he created the immortal "sayings of Poor Richard." Franklin "filled all the little spaces that occurred between the remarkable days in the calendar with proverbial sentences, chiefly such as inculcated industry and frugality, as the means of procuring wealth, and thereby securing virtue." The almanac sold nearly ten thousand copies annually. At the same time, Franklin was determined to educate his readers. He considered the almanac "a proper vehicle for conveying instruction among the common people, who bought scarcely any other books."[28]

Had Franklin stopped there, he would be remembered as a clever almanac-maker and one more writer in the centuries-long procession of peddlers of frugality. This "first American," however, was a singularly entrepreneurial moralist. In the twenty-sixth and final *Poor Richard's Almanac*, he gathered together one hundred of his catchiest maxims on frugality and industry from previous issues. He wrote a few new ones, too. Much as twentieth-century manufacturers would market familiar products as "New and Improved," Franklin titled this almanac "Poor Richard Improved." The centerpiece was the didactic tale of "Father Abraham's Speech." This established Franklin as the foremost spokesman for thrift over the next two centuries. Poor Richard tells the story of meeting up with Abraham, "a plain clean old Man with white Locks." Appropriately the setting is a site of consumption, a "Vendue" or outdoor market. As customers gather and ruminate about economic conditions, they call out to the old man: "Pray, Father Abraham, what think you of the Times? Won't these heavy Taxes quite ruin the Country? How shall we be ever able to pay them?" Abraham replies with a soliloquy on self-help ("God helps them that help themselves"). Taxes are heavy, he grants, "but *Idleness* taxes many of us much more," if one reckons all the time spent in "absolute *Sloth*" and in "idle Employments or Amusements." The solution, preaches Abraham, lies in Industry, Frugality, and Saving. "There are no Gains, without Pains."[29]

Franklin and his publishers saw to it that "Father Abraham's Speech" was widely reprinted and translated throughout the Atlantic world. The pamphlet was commonly titled *The Way to Wealth*. In France, where Franklin became particularly popular in the 1770s, the tract appeared as *La Science de Bonhomme Richard*. Remarkably, by the close of the eighteenth century—just ten years after Franklin's death—reprintings of the pamphlet numbered at least 145 in America, the British Isles, France, Italy, Germany, the Netherlands, and Sweden. Over the next century and a half, *The Way to Wealth* would be translated into nearly every major European language, plus Chinese, Japanese, and other non-Western tongues.[30]

In view of Franklin's global influence, it is worth examining his central precepts on the prudent use of money. Like Daniel Defoe, he advised readers to avoid debt at any cost: "*If you would know the Value of Money, go and try to borrow some; for, he that goes a borrowing goes a sorrowing.*" He worried about more than high interest charges. Franklin spoke of debt in the new language of individual liberty: *"The Borrower is a Slave to the Lender, and the Debtor to the Creditor*, disdain the Chain, preserve your Freedom; and maintain your Independency: Be *industrious* and *free*; be *frugal* and *free."*

Franklin also echoed Defoe in pitching "frugality" as the sober restraint of spending. He had little good to say about consumption, warning of ruinous Extravagances:

> Women and Wine, Game and Deceit,
> Make the Wealth small, and the Wants great.

Frugality required constant vigilance toward ordinary consumption as well: *"Beware of* little *Expenses; a small Leak will sink a great Ship."* Although he addressed "the Poor," Franklin—like Defoe—was really admonishing the middling strata against mimicking the lavish spending habits of the upper class: "'tis as truly Folly for the Poor to ape the Rich, as for the Frog to swell, in order to equal the Ox."

> Great Estates may venture more,
> But little Boats should keep near Shore.

For all his admonitions, Franklin understood human nature and the temptations of consumption. "Father Abraham's Speech" has a barbed end. After the old man finishes his oration, "The People heard it, and approved the Doctrine, and immediately practiced the contrary, just as if it had been a common Sermon; for the Vendue opened, and they began to buy extravagantly, notwithstanding all his Cautions, and their own Fear of Taxes." Only Poor Richard, in attendance, gives up thoughts of buying "Stuff for a new Coat." He decides to wear his old one a little longer and hopes readers will follow his example.

Franklin followed up with a series of injunctions to save money. It was not enough to work hard, he taught: "A Man may, if he knows not how to save as he gets, *keep his Nose all his Life to the Grindstone*, and die not worth a *Groat* at last. A *fat Kitchen makes a lean Will.* . . . *If you would be wealthy . . . think of Saving as well as of Getting."* In such pronouncements Franklin went beyond traditional frugality—the restraint of spending—to promote the act of saving for the future:

For Age and Want, save while you may;
No Morning Sun lasts a Whole Day, ...
Get what you can, and what you get hold;
'Tis the Stone that will turn all your Lead into Gold[31]

Much as Franklin and his predecessors propagated notions of frugality, they nonetheless fell short of instilling modern ideas of saving in
the masses. Even Franklin, who explicitly called on his readers to save,
said little about *where* individuals should deposit their savings. One
finds no mention of savings banks or any other institutional arrangement that might encourage popular thrift. Moreover, as Werner Sombart observed, the champions of frugality directed their bromides not at
the general public, but rather at the literate "middle class" of merchants, artisans, and well-to-do farmers. These were people who possessed the margin both to save money and to consume nonessential
goods. They were self-employed or at least could aspire to own their
businesses. The day had not yet arrived when publicists would encourage the working poor to save.

That day came soon enough. Franklin himself bridged the divide
between the promoters of frugality and those of popular saving. Although he consciously appealed to a middling stratum, his exhortations
to prudence would come to be addressed to *all* members of society. Ex-
changing ideas with reformers throughout the Atlantic world, Franklin
had a hand in this transformation. He corresponded regularly with the
Duc de La Rochefoucauld-Liancourt, who later cofounded the Paris Savings Bank for small depositors in 1818. To enlighten the people about
the advantages of the savings bank, the French reformer distributed
pamphlets written "in the persuasive simplicity of *The Way to Wealth*."[32]
It is to the proponents of institutional thrift that next we turn.

To "Banish Beggary and Poverty"

Walk down the main street of cities and towns in America's Northeast,
and you may still encounter financial institutions called savings banks.
Few Americans today could explain what makes a savings bank a sav-

ings bank. Nowadays one can open a savings account in any bank. But during the first half of the nineteenth century, contemporaries regarded the savings bank as one of the grand social experiments of the time—on par with public schools, public health measures, orphanages, prisons, and citizen-armies. Duc de La Rochefoucauld-Liancourt declared the savings bank to be "a moral institution, an institution of a healthy and great polity ... a monument to patriotism." Other French reformers termed the savings bank "the primary school of capitalism."[33] The savings bank, in short, was far more than a financial institution. It was where the authorities and public-spirited individuals endeavored to mold the humbler classes into self-disciplined members of the community and nation.

The use of institutions to promote popular saving reflected new European ideas that came together during the latter half of the eighteenth century. Many thinkers sought to encourage the poor to save for future needs, rather than rely on publicly funded poor relief. These advocates of self-help were particularly critical of England's Poor Law system, which had provided public assistance at the parish level since the sixteenth century. Just as he propagated frugality among the middling strata, Daniel Defoe pioneered schemes to promote working-class thrift. The author of *Robinson Crusoe* first achieved prominence with his political treatise, *An Essay upon Projects* (1697). In it, Defoe proposed the establishment of a "Pension-Office." Able-bodied laboring people, men and women, would pay an entrance fee of sixpence and thereafter one shilling per quarter. More than a bank, the Pension-Office would function as a mutual insurance scheme employing state-of-the-art actuarial assumptions of the time. Subscribers were to be entitled to free medical care if they became dangerously ill, or a lifetime pension for subsistence if sickness or injury prevented them from working. Although Defoe passionately believed in the power of individual effort, he was determined to persuade the poor to save by whatever means necessary: "I am indeed willing to think all Men shou'd have sense enough to see the usefulness of such a Design, and be perswaded [*sic*] by their Interest to engage in it; but some Men have less Prudence than Brutes, and will make no provision against Age till it comes; and to deal with such, Two ways might be us'd by Authority to Compel them." Poor parishioners would be warned that "they shou'd expect no Relief from the Parish if they refus'd to Enter themselves" at the Pension-Office. Second, the Church-Wardens in charge of the Poor Law were to bar delinquents from moving into their parishes. Defoe's plan was nothing if not ambitious. Were every person in England to pay four shillings per annum into "one common bank," their deposits would "in all probability Maintain all that shou'd be Poor, and for ever Banish Beggary and Poverty out of the Kingdom."[34]

Defoe's vision of organizing thrift to ameliorate poverty underlay numerous proposals associated with the Enlightenment. This intellectual movement swept France, Scotland, England, and much of the rest of Europe during the eighteenth century. Prominent thinkers sought to apply science and reason to solving a host of social problems. In 1755 a long entry on "Thrift" appeared in Diderot's *Encyclopédie*, the most widely read compendium of French Enlightenment thought. The author Joachim Faiguet recommended the establishment in every town of Monts de Piété (the pawnshop-banks of Catholic Europe). There ordinary people could "deposit, with confidence, sums that one has never before been able to invest usefully." These public offices would primarily serve laborers and domestic servants "who having saved small sums, ten pistoles, a hundred ecus ... worry with good reason about dissipating or losing these." They would be able both to deposit their money in safety and make withdrawals as they pleased. Availing themselves of such facilities, "most workers and domestics will become thriftier and more orderly in their lives."[35] The French Revolution inherited the Enlightenment project of improving society. At the height of the revolution in 1791, the National Assembly's Committee on Beggary investigated the possibility of establishing a "Savings Bank" in each department of France. In the words of the committee president, the ubiquitous Duc de La Rochefoucauld-Liancourt, "checking poverty is, without a doubt, the urgent work of society, but preventing it is no less sacred and necessary."[36]

Meanwhile in England reformers contemplated an array of savings institutions to combat pauperism and rising Poor Law costs. The Enlightenment philosopher Jeremy Bentham put forward the most scientific plan in 1797. As part of his proposal to employ the "burdensome poor" in Industry Houses, he recommended the institution of "Frugal-ity Banks," which would accept small deposits. For every pound saved in the Frugality Bank, the depositor obtained the right to an annuity that varied by one's age. Bentham designed the Frugality Banks to rem-edy the dearth of thrift institutions for ordinary people. The poor could neither deposit their earnings securely nor readily receive interest on their small sums, he observed. As such, they found it difficult to resist the "temptations afforded by the instruments of sensual enjoyment, where the means of purchasing them are constantly at hand." He criti-cized not only the commercial banks for refusing small deposits, but also England's working-class friendly societies. Group saving through the friendly societies suffered from improper calculations, embezzle-ments, and internal discord. Bentham expressed disgust at the friendly societies' practice of collecting members' savings at the local pub. En-couraging frugality at such establishments was "like choosing a brothel for a school of continence."[37]

New studies of political economy underpinned the encouragement of popular saving. To an extent seldom recognized, the pioneer econo-mists were influenced by the pro-thrift morality that swirled about them. In the seminal work of modern economics, *An Inquiry into the Nature and Causes of the Wealth of Nations* (1776), Adam Smith portrayed sav-ing as vital to the creation of wealth: "Parsimony, and not industry, is the immediate cause of the increase of capital.... [W]hatever industry might acquire, if parsimony did not save and store up, the capital would never be the greater." The Scottish economist also postulated that "consumption is the sole end and purpose of all production." By this he meant the interests of consumers should not be sacrificed to those of producers who worked to keep out cheaper foreign commodities. Yet Smith was no exponent of unbridled consumer spending. While casti-gating "the prodigal," he valued the "frugal man" whose savings gener-ated the capital that employed the "laborers, manufacturers, and artifi-cers, who reproduce with a profit the value of their annual consumption." Smith regarded saving, not immoderate spending, as normal, for "the principle which prompts to save, is the desire of bettering our condi-tion, a desire which ... comes with us from the womb, and never leaves us till we go into the grave."[38]

Here and there, iconoclasts warned against excessive thrift while extolling the economic advantages of mass consumption. The most audacious critic was Bernard Mandeville. A Dutch physician who emigrated to England, Mandeville penned the wickedly satirical *Fable of the Bees: or, Private Vices, Publick Benefits* (1714), an expansion of his earlier poem, "The Grumbling Hive: or, Knaves Turn'd Honest." Mandeville turned Aesop's fable on its head. Bees, like ants, had long been represented as models of thrift in European culture. They diligently produce wax and store up honey for the winter. Yet in Mandeville's allegory, the hive is "well stock'd with bees, That liv'd in luxury and ease." It was neither thrift nor private virtue that made the "whole mass a paradise," but rather fraud, extravagance, and other vices:

> The root of evil, avarice,
> That dam'd ill-natur'd baneful vice,
> Was slave to prodigality,
> That noble sin; whilst luxury
> Employ'd a million of the poor,
> And odious pride a million more:
> Envy itself, and vanity,
> Were ministers of industry;
> Their darling folly, fickleness,
> In diet, furniture, and dress,
> That strange ridic'lous vice, was made
> The very wheel that turn'd the trade.

This consumer-driven perfection was not to last. The bees grumbled about others' fraud, and the gods made the hive honest and temperate. In a flash, debtors repaid their creditors, lavish estates and stately horses were sold, and the temperate "paid their tavern score, Resolv'd to enter it no more." Women's fashions no longer changed at a whim, and the spendthrift Chloe now "wears her strong suit a whole year." As "pride and luxury decrease," the thousands who supplied those wants must leave the hive. The remaining bees "to avoid extravagance, They flew into a hollow tree."

In subsequent responses to outraged critics, Mandeville was unrelenting in the assault on frugality and saving. He characterized accumulation as avarice, arguing the "avaricious does no good to himself and is injurious to all the world besides, except his heir," whereas the "prodigal is a blessing to the whole society and injures no body but himself." Frugality is an "idle dreaming virtue that employs no hands." The prospect of popular saving irked him. What would happen, Mandeville asked, if all the people in Great Britain "shall consume but four-fifths of what they do now and so lay by one-fifth part of their income"? Not only would reduced spending harm producers, but the savers, too, would no longer work a full week because they would have money in their pockets. Individuals and families would be wise to be frugal, Mandeville conceded, "but it is the interest of all rich nations that the greatest part of the poor should almost never be idle and yet continually spend what they get."[39]

So familiar to us today, Mandeville's vision of a consumption-driven economy would not become mainstream economic thought for another two and a half centuries. Throughout the nineteenth century and well into the twentieth, political economists overwhelmingly favored saving over consumption for the purposes of fostering economic growth and social stability.[40] John Stuart Mill forcefully echoed Smith in *Principles of Political Economy* (1848): "All capital, with a trifling exception, was originally the result of saving.... Saving, in short, enriches, and spending impoverishes, the community along with the individual; ... society at large is richer by what it expends in maintaining and aiding productive labour, but poorer by what it consumes in its enjoyments."[41]

Among Britain's early political economists, one of the most impassioned advocates of creating popular savings institutions was, ironically, a man better known for his pessimistic views of human interventions into economic life. In his monumental *Essay on the Principle of Population* (1798), the clergyman-economist Thomas R. Malthus posited that populations tend to increase beyond their capacity to feed themselves. The result is "periodic misery" for laborers in town and country, and there is little that institutions and laws can do to make things better. If anything, by his dismal accounting, England's Poor Law made things worse. By encouraging the poor to reproduce more than they naturally would have done, parish relief ultimately lowered wages and raised food prices.

But it's not easy to remain a strict Malthusian, even if one's name is Malthus. By the time the second edition of his book appeared in 1803, Malthus had become less grim about prospects of escaping the population trap.[42] His change in outlook was no doubt influenced by British reformers' efforts to establish savings banks at the time. Malthus now counseled that the poor could improve their lives and relieve overall population pressures by exercising "moral restraint." By this he meant sexual abstinence before marriage, as well as the lengthy postponement of marriage until the man saved enough money to support a family. To Malthus, who condemned birth control, saving functioned as the virtuous alternative because it enabled men (and presumably women) to delay reproduction. As he elaborated in subsequent editions, young men should begin saving at the age of fourteen or fifteen and, on average, defer marriage until twenty-four or twenty-five—even later, if the man lacked sufficient savings. The reverend was not a man given to double-entendres, but clearly he imparted new meaning to the injunction of saving yourself for marriage.

To "encourage young labourers to economize their earnings" before marriage, Malthus in 1803 proposed the establishment of savings institutions that he termed "country banks." In these banks, "the smallest sums would be received, and a fair interest paid for them." The laborer should be able to withdraw his savings "whenever he wanted it, and have the most perfect liberty of disposing of it ... because the knowledge of possessing this liberty would be of more use in encouraging the practice of saving than any restriction of it in preventing the misuse of money so saved." As savings banks became reality in England and Scotland, Malthus expressed strong support. He elaborated on their promise in the 1817 edition of his *Essay*: "Of all the plans which have yet been proposed for the assistance of the labouring classes, the savings-banks ... appear to me much the best, and the most likely, if they should become general, to effect a permanent improvement in the condition of the lower classes of society. By giving to each individual the full and entire benefit of his own industry and prudence, they are calculated greatly to strengthen the lessons of Nature and Providence."[43] When it came to encouraging thrift, Malthus may have been more than a theoretician. In 1816, along with the economist David Ricardo, he was listed as a manager (trustee) of London's Provident Institution of Savings for the laboring classes, servants, mechanics, and tradesmen.[44]

Philosophers and political economists presented their ideas against the backdrop of sweeping social and economic changes. The encouragement of saving was predicated on the growing use of money in daily life. In several European countries during the eighteenth and nineteenth centuries, we see a shift from self-sufficient households to a money economy. Merchants and artisans routinely engaged in monetary transactions, and farmers increasingly sold their surpluses for cash. The era also witnessed a dramatic rise in wage labor. Founders of the first savings banks appealed to the many domestic servants, artisans, sailors, and laborers who flocked to the cities of Europe. Within Germany, nearly every one of the earliest savings banks originated in the prosperous commercial cities, primarily the ports. In France, too, the first savings banks appeared in Paris, with its huge population of artisans and domestic servants, as well as in ports like Marseilles and Bordeaux. Of the 800,000 people who lived in Paris in 1826, roughly 115,000 worked in domestic service in the homes of the well-to-do; some 71,000 of these servants were women and girls. Servants, male and female, generally comprised the largest group of depositors in Europe's early savings banks. Domestics held 44 percent of all accounts in the Lyons Savings Bank between 1836 and 1847. In Britain, household servants likewise constituted one-fourth to one-half of the savings banks' customers before the 1830s.[45]

To those who sought to organize thrift, the greater use of money made it all the more imperative to shape the spending and saving habits of the working poor. Were servants or sailors to squander their earnings, they would tax the limits of poor relief and endanger public order. Even when laborers attempted to save, remarked Jeremy Bentham, they lacked safe means of deposit and ended up simply hoarding. Worse, good savers were frequently punished for their virtue. Noted one writer in the early nineteenth century, "we find that persons in the lower station who acquire a reputation for the possession of hoards are almost always robbed."[46]

French and British reformers represented saving as a "vaccine" against all that ailed society.[47] In words that echoed Daniel Defoe's prescription from an earlier century, the *Sheffield Mercury* in 1818 declared: "As the practice of vaccination bids fair to eradicate the most loathsome and destructive diseases from the earth;—as the establishment of Houses of Recovery are likely in time to extinguish the infection of fever in our cities and large towns;—as the institution of the Bible Society tends to eradicate error and ignorance from the world;— so the establishment of Savings Banks may ultimately tend to *banish poverty and wretchedness from society.*" The establishment of savings banks, judged the newspaper, stood as "one of the greatest improvements which distinguish modern times."[48]

Acquiring a "Stake in the Country"

Savings banks sprang up in Europe and North America in a remarkably short span of time from the late 1700s to the 1830s. This was no coincidence. Transnational networks of communication enabled reformers to study one another's experiments aimed at encouraging thrift. Learned people read widely; they corresponded; and they crossed borders and sometimes oceans to view the innovations firsthand. An "international movement" is how one scholar describes the widespread introduction of savings banks.[49]

Although French and British intellectuals took the lead in drafting the visionary blueprints, civic-minded burghers in German cities were the first to establish savings banks. In 1778 the General Charitable Institution of the Hamburg Patriotic Society for the Promotion of Arts and Education founded the Savings Division (Ersparungsklasse). Other charitable associations sponsored savings banks in Oldenburg (1786) and Kiel (1796). Notables in the German-speaking Swiss city of Berne introduced the Servant's Interest Bank (Dienstbotenzinskasse) in 1782. German savings banks, or *Sparkassen* as they became known, have proven impressively resilient in their basic identity and mission. The publicly owned *Sparkassen* remain a fixture of everyday life today. German savings bankers still declare their primary task to be improving popular welfare and the "promotion of saving and of thrift by means of education and information."[50] Beginning in 1801, municipal governments replaced civic associations as the founders and managers of most savings banks. The authorities also introduced publicly administered *Sparkassen* at the district and state (Land) levels. In 1836 the German states counted approximately 280 savings banks, two-thirds of which were run by municipalities.[51]

The eighteenth-century German savings banks established institutional patterns that would appear elsewhere in Europe. One common feature was the central role played by philanthropic associations and individuals. Bourgeoisie in the neighboring Netherlands in 1784 formed the Society for Public Welfare (Het Nut), imbued with the Enlightenment project of improving and educating the lower classes. With the strong support of King Willem I, the society founded the first of many Dutch savings banks in 1817.[52] Most European savings banks embraced the mission articulated by Hamburg's pioneer Ersparungsklasse—to work "for the benefit of humbly situated industrious persons of *both sexes*, such as servants, day labourers, manual workers and seamen." By giving the working poor the opportunity to save "even trivial amounts" at interest, the Hamburg bank aimed to "encourage them, through diligence and thrift, to become useful and important to the [city] State."[53]

This quest to integrate the lower classes into the body politic emerged as another prominent aspect of modern thrift promotion. The late eighteenth century saw the rise of what contemporaries called "civil society" in the cities and towns of Europe and North America. Growing numbers of merchants and professionals identified themselves as "middle class" or "bourgeois," trumpeting their virtues of diligence and thrift. This middling strata joined clergymen and philanthropic aristocrats to organize moral reform groups and reading societies. Participants in the burgeoning civil societies not only engaged in *self*-cultivation, but also strove to "civilize" and make "citizens" of the lower classes by inculcating habits of thrift and sobriety.[54]

The British were not the first to organize thrift institutions, but the kingdom soon boasted the most extensive network of savings banks. As in German cities and the Netherlands, the impetus came from philanthropic organizations that arose to address poverty as a social problem, not merely an individual failing. The influential Society for Bettering the Condition of the Poor formed in 1796 to inquire "into all that concerns the poor" and to make the "promotion of their happiness a science."[55] Several members of the Society went on to promote lower-class thrift. Notable was Rev. Joseph Smith, who introduced the first of several "Sunday Banks." Smith encouraged poorer parishioners to bring pennies to his church in Wendover each Sunday. In return, at Christmastime they received the principal plus a bonus of one-third, which they were to spend on warm clothing or firewood.

England's first savings bank, the Tottenham Benefit Bank, owed its origins to a Quaker woman and social reformer, Priscilla Wakefield. Initially in 1798, Mrs. Wakefield organized the Female Benefit Club, in which subscribers contributed toward old-age pensions. She also founded the country's first Children's Bank. Every month the children deposited their pennies. They were permitted to make withdrawals to pay for apprentice fees, clothes for service, and other expenses deemed productive. The success of these savings schemes encouraged Mrs. Wakefield in 1804 to establish the Tottenham Benefit Bank for servants and the general poor. The bank accepted deposits as small as one shilling, paying an attractive 5 percent in interest on every complete pound. Needless to say, the early savings banks depended on philanthropy. To fund interest payments and guarantee deposits, the founders and other "respectable persons of property" dug deeply into their pockets.[56]

Besides establishing savings banks, British reformers encouraged workers to organize their own thrift activities. Requiring regular contributions from members, the friendly societies had long accumulated mutual-assistance funds for sickness, old age, and burial expenses. To expand working-class thrift and self-help, members of Parliament in 1793 introduced legislation that officially recognized the friendly societies and legalized their practice of group saving. Popular among skilled workmen, the friendly society evolved into a leading savings institution during the nineteenth century.[57]

The early English experiments were followed by rapid institutional advances in Scotland, which became a veritable laboratory for savings banks. Why Scotland? We could fall back on the stereotype of the stingy Scot (the object of English humor for generations to come). Yet the Scottish penchant for thrift was not necessarily an age-old national trait, but rather was forged by particular conditions and institutions. Unlike most of England, Scotland lacked a Poor Law system that required parishes to aid the destitute. Scots thus developed an earlier interest in persuading the poor to help themselves. In addition, savings banks in Scotland could draw on a broader customer base in town and country alike. Scottish agricultural laborers enjoyed greater real incomes than their English counterparts. And whereas English commercial banks were just beginning to pay interest on deposits, Scottish banks had been accepting deposits at interest since the early eighteenth century. This enabled Scottish savings banks to deposit their customers' money at 5 percent interest in the commercial banks—an avenue not open to most English savings banks. Many small traders and shopkeepers in Scotland had adopted habits of saving at interest even before the advent of savings banks.[58]

The pioneer in the Scottish savings bank movement was an erudite preacher named Henry Duncan. Rev. Duncan loathed the English Poor Law for bribing the "industrious to become idle." His "economical bank" would instead aid the laboring classes by providing "a means of ameliorisation dependent on no begrudged and degrading poor law subsidies— not even on the Christian charities of the rich and benevolent—but on prudent forethought and economy of the people themselves."[59] Only a system of secure savings banks, based in each parish, would deter the laborer from morally repugnant expenditures: "It is distressing to think how much money is thrown away by young women on dress unsuitable to their station and by young men on the debauchery of the alehouse and in other extravagant and demoralising practices."[60] In 1810 Rev. Duncan founded the Ruthwell Savings Bank in his rural parish in Dumfriesshire. The board of directors included local officials, philanthropic honorary members, and elected representatives of the depositors. An atmosphere of paternalism pervaded this and other savings banks. To encourage long-term saving, the Ruthwell Savings Bank offered a higher rate of interest on deposits of more than three years' duration. At the same time, spendthrifts were disciplined. Those who failed to deposit more than four shillings a year were fined, and the bank severely limited the opportunities to make withdrawals.[61]

The next five years witnessed a flurry of founding savings banks throughout Scotland. Some followed the Ruthwell model, but several others drew inspiration from the Edinburgh Bank for Savings. Founded in 1813 by the son of a prominent commercial banker, the Edinburgh bank was more of a business than Rev. Duncan's operation. It placed fewer restrictions on depositors while paying less generous rates of interest. Nonetheless, this savings bank, too, operated as a social and moral institution. It began life as a branch of Edinburgh's Society for the Suppression of Beggars. A savings account offered a plethora of advantages, insisted the Society, for "it leads to temperance and the restraint of all the disorderly passions, which a wasteful expenditure of money nourishes."[62]

English reformers followed the Scottish models to found a large number of savings banks in the mid-1810s. Unlike the Scots, they were not content to leave matters entirely to civic-minded individuals. In 1817 Parliament passed an Act to Encourage the Establishment of Banks for Saving in England. The measure was introduced by George Rose, the humanitarian politician who had earlier promoted working-class self-help through his Friendly Societies Act of 1793. Reflecting a long line of English thought, Rose confidently predicted that "savings banks would gradually do away with the evils of the system of poor laws."[63] The Savings Banks Act regulated all such banks in England and Wales, while a similar act applied to Ireland. The legislation lay behind the era's explosive growth in savings banks. Whereas only six savings banks had existed in all of England and Wales before 1816, some 62 appeared in 1817, 125 in 1818, and 32 in 1819. If one includes Ireland and Scotland, nearly 500 savings banks were operating in the British Isles by 1820.[64]

The Savings Banks Act created a legal framework that defined Britain's "trustee savings banks" until their restructuring in the 1970s. Their mission, as codified, aimed at the "safe Custody and Increase of small Savings belonging to the industrious Classes of His Majesty's Subjects." To inhibit wealthier individuals from taking advantage of the higher interest rates intended to encourage small saving, the laws set limits on annual deposits. In addition, the legislation mandated that savings banks operate fundamentally as philanthropic enterprises. They would be governed by trustees, who would derive "no Benefit whatsoever from any such Deposit or the Produce thereof." In practice, the bigger savings banks paid salaries to an actuary (chief administrator), and smaller banks paid token honoraria to the actuary, secretary, or treasurer. Nevertheless, the laws firmly established the principle of honorary management. Deposits and the interest earned on the deposits must be returned to the customers, minus the money necessary to manage the bank. No savings bank could be privately owned.[65]

Equally momentous for Britain and other nations that followed its lead, the Savings Banks Act of 1817 required savings banks to invest their deposits in a government-managed fund. Far from opposing this provision, England's savings banks welcomed the state's intervention. Previous attempts to establish savings institutions in England had been stymied by the problem of where to place the accumulated deposits. How would the savings bank safeguard customers' deposits and pay attractive rates of interest, when it could not invest its funds in English commercial banks? The new laws offered an elegant solution. The state became banker to the savings banks. This system soon governed all savings banks in the British Isles after it was extended to Scotland in 1835. Here's how it worked. The savings bank's trustees forwarded all surplus monies—minus the money needed to service withdrawals—to a special fund administered by the National Debt Commissioners. This governmental commission was comprised of the Chancellor of the Exchequer and other financial officials. Although the commissioners invested these funds in government stock, they were obligated to return to the savings bank's trustees the total sum of the deposits plus interest *as set by law*. The trustees then deducted operating expenses and paid the remainder to depositors. In essence, the state subsidized small savers, as the Treasury paid out at rates substantially above the prevailing return on government securities. By 1828, government losses amounted to a whopping 750,000 pounds. Despite two cuts in rates, savings bank customers were still receiving handsome, above-market interest rates of up to 3.04 percent in the mid-1840s.[66]

Within Parliament the paragons of fiscal probity repeatedly called upon the government to stop subsidizing the savings banks. Nonetheless, successive Chancellors of the Exchequer firmly defended the principle of the state encouragement of small saving. In 1818 Nicholas Vansittart declared that the benefits of elevating the "industry and morality of the people" was worth one hundred times the Treasury's losses of 6,000 to 10,000 pounds a year. Six years later Chancellor of the Exchequer Frederick John Robinson opposed demands to reduce the generous interest rates, reluctant to weaken public confidence in the savings banks. He termed these institutions "one of the greatest blessings ever conferred upon the Country."[67] Clearly the savings bank was no ordinary financial concern. It had become a vital national institution for improving the people's welfare and maintaining public order.

The government's determination to encourage saving had much to do with the upper and middle classes' fears of popular unrest. Between 1816 and 1820, England was rocked by a series of political demonstrations and mass meetings. Workers and others demanded enfranchisement and the fairer representation of urban areas in Parliament. In 1819 a demonstration of some sixty thousand at St. Peter's Fields in Manchester devolved into the "Peterloo Massacre" (a play on words referring to the recent battle of Waterloo). The local militia—sabers drawn—charged the crowd, killing eleven. Nine protest leaders were subsequently hanged, and one thousand others were transported as convicts to Australia.

In the face of what many Englishmen regarded as imminent social revolution, conservatives and reformers alike looked to savings banks to help contain the working-class challenge.[68] In a more positive sense, leading political liberals conceived of saving as an act of citizenship that would integrate the humbler classes into the national community. Indeed, liberals advocated savings banks in tandem with calls for expanded manhood suffrage. Nearly two centuries later in the 1990s, Britain's Prime Minister Tony Blair would refer to this concept of citizenship as "stakeholding." Interestingly enough, the rhetoric of stakeholding first appeared in the early nineteenth century—often in the context of efforts to promote thrift. Beginning with the Scottish political economist Patrick Colquhoun in 1806, British reformers argued that savings banks would convince the poor that they, like the rich, have "a stake in the country."[69] Added John Tidd Pratt, the barrister who oversaw the operations of the savings banks in 1830, "every person who has vested his savings in the public funds [the Treasury's fund for savings banks] has a stake in the security of the country ... and will be deterred from compassing the disturbance of his native land by a personal motive.... He who possesses property in a country is not interested in the stability of the administration for the time being, but in the perpetual stability of universal order and good government."[70]

The expansion of savings banks in Britain during the 1810s inspired reformers throughout the Western world. Over the next three decades, hundreds of savings banks were founded. The British soon transplanted the savings bank to their far-flung colonies, beginning with New South Wales (Australia) in 1819 and New Zealand in 1847. Patrick Colquhoun influenced American philanthropists to found several savings banks from 1816. On the European continent, nearly every society experienced upsurges in poverty and economic dislocation following the end of the Napoleonic wars in 1815. As in England, elites and middle-class liberals feared revolution from their hungry, politically awakened masses unless measures were taken to give the laboring classes a "stake" in the existing order.

European reformers learned of the British innovations almost as soon as they occurred. English or Scottish models informed the establishment of the first savings banks in the Netherlands (1817), France (1818), Austria (1819), Sweden (1820), Norway (1822), and Finland (1823). The Swedish state was particularly thorough in emulating best practice. In 1818, just one year after the passage of England's Savings Banks Act, the government dispatched a treasury official to the British Isles to survey the new savings banks and their role in ameliorating poverty. Carl David Skogman's widely distributed report lay behind the founding of Sweden's first savings bank in Gothenburg two years later. British precedents also lay behind the establishment of Vienna's first savings bank, which in turn served as the prototype for numerous banks throughout the vast Austrian empire. Some of the most vibrant of these banks appeared in northern Italy, then under Austrian control, beginning in 1822. In Spain liberal exiles returned during the 1830s. Influenced by British and French ideas, they founded the country's first savings banks.[71]

The English model was central to the creation of savings banks in France. Although Enlightenment thinkers of the eighteenth century had long championed the cause of popular thrift, their ideas had not resulted in introduction of savings banks under the French Revolution and Napoleonic rule. Together with fellow financiers and benefactors, Benjamin Delessert founded the Paris Savings Bank (Caisse d'Épargne de Paris) in 1818. An open admirer of British institutions and ideas, Delessert had spent his formative years in the 1780s studying manufacturing in Birmingham and new ideas of political economy at Edinburgh University. There he met Adam Smith himself. While laying plans for his own savings bank years later, Delessert freely acknowledged his debt to English institutions. Impressed by the "great advantages attending the Savings Banks which have arisen in England," he "procured the requisite prospectuses and information" and would soon imitate their "honourable and useful example."[72] Savings banks spread rapidly in the 1830s. By 1847 France counted 364 savings banks.

The French state similarly channeled savings banks' deposits into a centrally managed fund. French savings banks had even fewer opportunities than English counterparts to invest deposits in commercial banks. The overall banking system remained poorly developed. Savings banks thus filled the void, becoming by midcentury the principal site of saving for well-to-do farmers and townspeople, as well as the *petits gens* (little guys). To protect popular savings, savings bankers cited English precedent when they successfully lobbied the finance minister to permit savings banks to place their funds under the Treasury's management in 1829. This became mandatory in 1852. The government's Caisse des Dépôts et Consignations (Bank for Deposits and Consignations) assumed responsibility for the funds in 1837.[73] As in Britain, the state's custody of savings banks deposits did much to persuade the populace to entrust their savings to the new institutions.

The practice of saving money—once the province of the rich and commercial classes—was fast becoming part of national and local life in much of the Western world. No longer simply a moral virtue, "thrift" was represented as the key to escaping poverty and improving oneself. Self-confident middle classes embraced the new mission of helping the laboring classes to help themselves. Charles Dickens, arguably the best-known writer of early Victorian England, was also a champion of popular thrift. His novel *Martin Chuzzlewit* (1843–44) captured Dickens's faith, and indeed the era's faith, in savings banks. The profligate Chuzzlewit runs short of cash while traveling in America. Martin's manservant Mark Tapley comes to the rescue with a little bag of money withdrawn from his own savings bank account before leaving England. Questioned by his master as to the amount, the steadfast Tapley replies: "'Thirty-seven pounds ten and sixpence. The Savings' Bank said so, at least. I never counted it. But *they* know, bless you!' said Mark, with a shake of the head expressive of his unbounded confidence in the wisdom and arithmetic of those Institutions."[74]

2

ORGANIZING THRIFT IN THE AGE OF NATION-STATES

The promotion of economical habits amongst the people is indeed so much a matter of national concern, that we cannot conceive any direction in which the powers of Government could be more beneficially exercised than in giving effect to a scheme calculated to produce such valuable social results among the humbler classes of the people.
—Samuel Smiles, in support of post office savings banks, 1861[1]

November 12, 1859, was an extraordinarily good day for the London publisher John Murray. On that date he announced the publication of not one, but two, of the greatest sellers of their time. Charles Darwin's *Origins of Species by Means of Natural Selection* would transform how people around the world thought about life and society. But so, too, would Murray's other blockbuster, Samuel Smiles's *Self-Help, with Illustrations of Character and Conduct.* Between 1859 and 1905, an estimated 258,000 copies of the latter were published in Britain alone. Smiles became the Benjamin Franklin of his era. Yet if Franklin aimed his messages at the commercial classes, Smiles wrote that all men could improve themselves by exercising perseverance, honesty, diligence, and self-denial. Thrift figured prominently among these virtues, and Smiles would follow up with the best seller *Thrift* (1875). His ideas on character-building and saving profoundly influenced social reformers and national leaders throughout the world. In addition to numerous reprints in the

United States and other English-speaking countries, *Self-Help* was translated into more than twenty languages—nearly every major European tongue, plus Japanese, Chinese, Siamese, Turkish, Arabic, Armenian, Pali, Hindi, Gujerati, and Bengali. *Thrift*, too, went through numerous reprints and translations in Europe, North America, South America, and Japan.[2]

Samuel Smiles' notions of self-help and thrift strike us today as quaint relics of a Victorian mentality that interventionist governments and welfare states would soon supplant. That, however, would be a gross misreading of Smiles and the nineteenth century's many other paragons of popular saving. Smiles was no proponent of rugged individualism. He coupled his injunctions to individual thrift with calls for the state and society to provide institutions that would enable the populace to save. Throughout Europe and beyond, the champions of thrift cooperated with increasingly powerful states to create orderly, self-reliant citizens whose small savings would strengthen the nation. Governments introduced innovative institutions to promote saving, notably post office savings banks and school savings programs. If the early nineteenth century was marked by local, philanthropic efforts to persuade the poor to save, thrift in the latter half of the century became a measure of national progress and its encouragement a national mission.

Character-Building and Nation-Building

In his pamphlet *Friendly Advice to Industrious and Frugal Persons* (1817), William Davis, a manager of Bath's Provident Institution, counseled: "Saving is as necessary to be taught as reading or writing, for it would be absurd to suppose, that Economy is an intuitive faculty of the mind."[3] Throughout much of Europe, reformers encouraged thrift as part of a grand vision for creating an educated populace. In 1834 Benjamin Delessert, founder of the Paris Savings Bank, likened the expansion of savings banks to France's recently enacted law for public elementary education.[4] A visit to a European savings bank typically involved more than a simple deposit or withdrawal. Customers could expect instruction in how to live a life of economy and proper conduct.

During the latter half of the nineteenth century and early twentieth century, exhortations to practice thrift became a feature of daily life in the West and some parts of the non-Western world. The local savings bank was joined by an array of institutions and media that urged people to save money and exercise self-reliance. Schools played a central role in instilling habits of thrift in the young. Adults, too, encountered a myriad of injunctions, seemingly at every turn. A common sight in Victorian Britain was the allegorical statue of Thrift or Prudence.[5]

In the realm of literature, the virtues of thrift and the pitfalls of extravagance appeared as standard themes. Robert Louis Stevenson's *Treasure Island* (1883) ends on a decidedly moral note. Five men returned home with "an ample share of the treasure, and used it wisely or foolishly according to our natures." The sober seaman "Gray not only saved his money, but, being suddenly smit with the desire to rise, also studied his profession; and he is now mate and part owner of a fine full-rigged ship; married besides, and the father of a family. As for Ben Gunn, he got a thousand pounds, which he spent or lost in three weeks, or to be more exact, in nineteen days, for he was back begging on the twentieth."[6] In the popular novels of Charles Dickens, whom we have already encountered, the delicate balance between saving and spending meant the difference between respectability and wretchedness—a point not lost on the hapless Mr. Micawber in *David Copperfield* (1850). After settling with creditors and leaving his debtor's cell, Micawber instructs young David in words that would reappear in British savings-promotion propaganda for the next century: "Annual income twenty pounds, annual expenditure nineteen nineteen and six, result happiness. Annual income twenty pounds, annual expenditure twenty pounds ought and six, result misery."[7] Putting his money where his mouth was, Dickens actively encouraged thrift in poor individuals. He would deposit start-up sums in their names in the savings banks, as he did for one Bertha White in 1845.[8]

Samuel Smiles both reflected and fed the growing movement toward popularizing thrift. Historians commonly discuss his ideas as quintessentially "Victorian" and the embodiment of liberal British values. Nonetheless, the virtues Smiles promoted—diligence, thrift, self-reliance—traveled remarkably well around the world, to lands liberal and not so liberal. Mottos from *Self-Help* adorned the walls of a palace built by the Khedive of Egypt in the 1870s.[9] In early-twentieth-century Japan, officials of the powerful Home Ministry—in charge of both savings campaigns and the national police—devoured *Thrift* as they devoured socialists. What was it about Samuel Smiles that made thrift so internationally attractive?

To begin with, Smiles was not simply peddling age-old homilies to frugality. He offered distinctly modern responses to the new challenges arising from industrialization, urbanization, and popular demands for democratic inclusion. In his long and varied career as physician, radical journalist, and railway manager, Smiles (1812–1904) was a keen observer of social problems. Like many middle-class reformers, he developed his ideas in the context of improving the condition of Britain's burgeoning working class or, as he phased it, of elevating "the mass into the full communion of citizenship."[10]

Publication of *Self-Help* in 1859 marked Smiles's first efforts to propagate thrift. The book tells the inspirational stories of famous men—businessmen, politicians, inventors, and artists—whose self-discipline and character enabled them to rise from humble origins. The tone shifts in the chapter "Money: Its Use and Abuse." There the author addresses workers who would remain workers. "Simple industry and thrift," he wrote, "will go far toward making any person of ordinary working faculty comparatively independent in his means." If the worker were to save his pennies and "watch the little outlets of useless expenditure," the "healthy spirit of self-help created amongst working people would more than any other measure serve to *raise them as a class*." Saving not only ennobled the soul, but enriched the national economy. Quoting the liberal reformer Richard Cobden, Smiles popularized the economic knowledge of his time: "The building of all the houses, the mills, the bridges, and the ships, and the accomplishment of all other great works which have rendered man civilized and happy, has been done by the savers, the thrifty; and those who have wasted their resources have always been their slaves."[11]

Although *Self-Help* is best remembered for its emphasis on individual improvement, Smiles recognized that few people would develop habits of saving on their own. In subsequent writings, he urged society and state to adopt concrete measures to encourage thriftiness in the working class. These recommendations first appeared in a small book, *Workmen's Earnings, Strikes, and Savings* (1861), and then in his tome *Thrift*. Smiles clarified that better access to savings institutions would help the masses to help themselves: "Were greater facilities provided for saving, and greater encouragement given by the more intelligent classes to the formation of provident habits, we believe the habit of economy would spring up in many quarters where at present it is altogether unknown." In 1859, he observed, Great Britain was home to 152,222 licensed pubs, but only 606 savings banks: "Thus thriftlessness finds abundant openings for gratification, whilst thrift has perhaps to travel a mile or more to a savings-bank, which opens its door, it may be, for only a few hours once or twice a week."[12]

Smiles cast saving as the worker's best defense against exploitative employers. He took a dim view of strikes, contending they seldom succeeded and often lowered wages. Nonetheless, Smiles argued that savings bolstered the bargaining power of workers. When strikes did become necessary, "the man who has a store of savings to fall back upon, is always in a far stronger position to resist an unfair demand on the part of his employer than he who has nothing." Thrifty workmen could retire from hard work in old age and escape "being beaten down into the lower-paid ranks of labour."[13] The accumulation of a small sum may prove a "man's passport to future independence," and a young woman's, too. Ten pounds in savings would "keep many a servant-girl from ruin," as she regained her health and awaited a suitable position.[14]

Ultimately workers' thrift would redound to the benefit of a stable political order, predicted Smiles echoing earlier reformers who sought to give the masses a stake in the country. This was no small concern in Britain as the growing labor movement agitated for better working conditions and the rights to vote and organize unions. He assured middle-class readers that workers who saved would go on to purchase real property and thereby gain the right to vote. But "this is a kind of universal suffrage which no man need fear," for the practice of Economy is "evidently conservative" and makes men "lovers of public order and security."[15]

Of course to save properly, households would have to discipline their consumption. Like other Victorian reformers, Samuel Smiles sought to distinguish healthier forms of consumption from wasteful spending. Midcentury Britain and other industrializing societies were experiencing the beginnings of mass consumption. Working-class families spent money on goods and services as never before, thanks to rising wages and falling food prices.[16] The problem, as Smiles saw it, was that skilled workers dissipated their new wealth on unproductive consumption—especially drink. Frequent visits to the pub diverted money from more wholesome expenditures on behalf of their families.[17] Accordingly, temperance movements in Britain and elsewhere often made common cause with crusaders for thrift. Witness one handbill printed by the Liverpool Temperance & Band of Hope Union in the 1870s. Calculating the daily spending on filling one's pint jug over five years, the flyer asked, "Now what could a Working Man do with this amount?" The answer: he could put nearly half in the "Savings Bank for a rainy day" and still be able to buy five suits, a good silver lever watch, a good overcoat and top it off with "two weeks' holiday in London."[18]

Smiles left little doubt where workers should properly spend their money. It ought to be on "the Home," the only institution in which men could be "really and truly humanized and civilized" and where children were taught "their best and worst morality." Here, too, Smiles reflected the emerging gender norms and scientific knowledge of the British middle class. He exhorted workers to spend *more* on healthier, well-ventilated housing. Saving money by crowding into "foul neighborhoods" was "not economy; it is reckless waste."[19] The key to both healthy homes and healthy spending would be the "thrifty, cleanly woman," the "manager of every family and household." She should be taught how to spend money "wisely."[20] Smiles's ideal was the full-time "housewife." This woman was just emerging within the growing middle class yet she would have been scarce among working-class families.

Smiles's exhortations coincided with a spate of advice books aimed at middle-class women, notably Isabella Mary Beeton's *Book of Household Management* (1861). This best seller sold nearly two million copies in less than seven years. Smiles was in fact a friend of her family, and his son later married her younger sister. Mrs. Beeton admonished house-wives to practice "Frugality and Economy." Women were instructed to keep a "Housekeeping Account-Book" with precision and punctuality: "write down into a daily diary every amount paid on that particular day, be it ever so small; then, at the end of the month, let these various payments be ranged under their specific heads of Butcher, Baker, &c."[21] Popularizing the practice of household account-keeping, Victorian writers reformulated gender roles in ways that would make women central to the global history of saving (figure 1).

In the world of the late nineteenth century, writers and national leaders promoted thrift as a core element of "civilization." Saving for the future, Smiles remarked, "forms no part of the savage economy." Thrift "began with civilization: we might also have said that thrift produced civilization." Even among civilized peoples, he theorized, Northern Europeans and North Americans were more prosperous than Mediterraneans and Mexicans because colder winters made northern people save during the summer. Smiles did not dwell on the need to transform tropical peoples into thrifty, civilized beings, although others would (see figure 2). Instead he spotlighted the mission of inculcating thrift and "*civilizing the people*" right in the heart of England. In London's East End, the population resembled the world's "savage tribes," mired in "improvidence, dirt, and their secondaries, crime and disease."[22]

But by what means should citizens be made thrifty and civilized? This paragon of self-help was surprisingly unwilling to leave matters to individual effort. What enhanced Smiles's popularity around the world was that he entrusted the task of inculcation in large part to the secular state. In this he exemplified the innumerable middle-class professionals and social reformers who looked to emerging modern institutions to "normalize" popular behavior and create self-disciplined subjects. The phenomenon has been described by Michel Foucault, the influential French social theorist.[23] Foucault focused on the disciplinary role of the army, schools, factories, and hospitals, yet he could just as persuasively have included those institutions aimed at normalizing thrift and sobriety. Smiles himself envisioned a comprehensive set of institutions to teach thrift. In addition to savings banks, he campaigned for a post

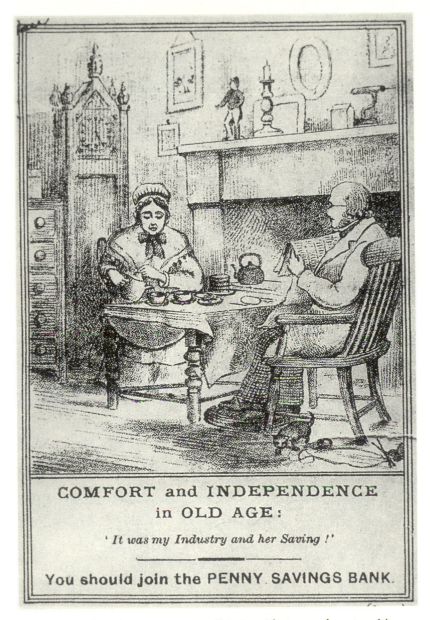

Figure 1. Extolling the woman as saver, Britain, mid-nineteenth century. Moss and Russell, *Invaluable Treasure*, 66.

Figure 2. "Saving Brings Well-being," 1936. A young Fascist "civilizes" an Ethiopian boy by teaching him how to save in this Italian poster commemorating the 15th annual World Thrift Day. Italy invaded and occupied Ethiopia the previous year. Talamona, *I Manifesti della giornata mondiale del risparmio*, 33. Courtesy of Acri—Association of Italian Foundations and Savings Banks.

office savings bank and he advocated penny banks in all elementary schools. Like Foucault's protagonists, Smiles supported the extension of military discipline to all members of society. Having observed that ordinary British soldiers saved more than well-paid workers, he ascribed the enlistees' frugality to the "magic of Drill." Were Britain to adopt military conscription and compel the populace to "pass through the discipline of the army, the country would be stronger, the people would be soberer, and thrift would become more habitual than it is at present."[24]

Smiles's embrace of disciplinary mechanisms was not unusual. In many lands, governments were devising new institutions to help citizens help themselves and thereby strengthen the nation. Reflecting the great-power rivalries of the day, he bemoaned the improvident habits of Englishmen while envying the frugality of the French and the sobriety of the Germans.[25] If saving were vital to national well-being and it did not occur naturally, then the state would have to intervene to encourage thrift. In the new world of powerful nation-states, character-building and nation-building made their debut as two sides of the same coin.

Saving at the Post Office

When Samuel Smiles remarked upon the inadequacies of savings banks in encouraging thrift, he joined a growing chorus of critics that reached far beyond the British Isles. Throughout Europe, reformers proceeded to create government savings banks that employed local post offices as branches. The advent of postal savings signaled a new stage in the modern efforts to persuade ordinary people to save. No longer would organized thrift remain the preserve of well-intentioned clergymen and philanthropists. The economic habits of the populace became a matter of state.

Britain inaugurated the world's first post office savings bank in 1861. The idea itself can be traced back to 1807. Samuel Whitbread, Member of Parliament, introduced legislation that would establish "one great national institution in the nature of a bank," to be operated by the Post Office.[26] The bill failed, but several developments over the next five decades would make postal savings a reality. Despite its image as the land of laissez-faire, nineteenth-century Britain steadily embraced doctrines of state responsibility for extending public services that the market did not readily provide. The government responded to the problems of urban poverty and working-class assertiveness with an array of social policies. These included regulation of working conditions, public health measures, and public education. Offering the working poor a secure, convenient place to deposit small savings, the Post Office Savings Bank represented one of those ambitious social policies. As one contemporary gushed, "Next, perhaps to the repeal of the Corn Laws, this is the greatest boon ever conferred on the working classes of this country."[27]

The most important precondition for postal savings was, quite simply, a nationwide system of accessible post offices. Britain had developed the world's most advanced postal services by midcentury. High postal rates had previously discouraged usage by those of modest means. All that changed after 1840. A civil servant named Rowland Hill persuaded the government to introduce the Penny Post. According to Hill, complex and expensive rates not only limited the Post Office's customer base and revenues, but also impeded trade and the nation's cultural progress. Henceforth, mail could be sent anywhere in the United Kingdom at a uniform rate for as little as one penny. The Penny Post became immensely popular. The increased business led to the rapid establishment of post offices at the village level during the 1840s and 1850s.[28] In an age when central governments had minimal presence at the grass roots, the "state" in Britain—and elsewhere—frequently entered everyday lives as the friendly face of the mailman, clerk, or postmaster. Britain's Post Office became, in the words of one historian, "the bureaucracy of bureaucracies." Beginning the era in 1839 with 10,000 employees, it ballooned to nearly 250,000 personnel by 1914, accounting for nearly one-third of all civil servants.[29]

Nor by midcentury did British politicians think it strange that postmasters might act as bankers to the people. Local post offices were already handling considerable sums of money as part of the thriving business in selling money orders. Money orders offered the populace a new inducement to save. Rather than squander one's earnings, enthused Charles Dickens, the itinerant young man could now send home remittances to relieve the "wants of the recipients, or to be prudently invested for himself."[30] Money orders could be cashed at any post office. Around 1840, the Post Office assumed control of private money-order offices and significantly reduced fees. Money orders proved popular among workers and small proprietors alike. The British Post soon became "the largest Banking Establishment that was ever carried on in the experience of mankind," observed an official at the time. By the late 1850s, the Money Order Department of the Post Office handled nearly seven million money orders annually.[31]

The growth of the Post Office permitted Britain's political leaders to imagine a more systematic means of encouraging thrift. In 1859 Charles Sikes, Member of Parliament and friend of Samuel Smiles's, proposed that customers be able to make deposits and withdrawals at postal money order offices. Such a system, he argued, would remedy the inadequate coverage of the existing savings banks. Together with the old savings banks, the new postal savings offices would bring savings institutions "within less than *an hour's walk of the fireside* of every working man in the Kingdom."[32] Reformulating the Sikes plan, civil servants in the Department of the Post Office drafted legislation for the establishment of the Post Office Savings Bank (POSB). In 1861 the bill sailed through Parliament with the enthusiastic support of William Gladstone, then Chancellor of the Exchequer and the foremost Liberal statesman of his time.

The unwieldy title, "An Act to Grant Additional Facilities for Depositing Small Savings at Interest with the Security of the Government for Due Repayment Thereof," nonetheless telegraphed the POSB's many advantages over the old savings banks. The government guaranteed postal deposits in full. To mollify the savings banks and commercial banks, Gladstone set the interest rate at 2.5 percent, below those of the existing banks yet attractive because of the greater security and convenience. Targeting the small savings of the "humbler classes," the POSB established caps on deposits and balances, and it accepted deposits as low as one shilling (one-twentieth of a pound). Withdrawals were permitted at any time, subject initially to ten days' notice. In terms of convenience, customers could make deposits and withdrawals at any post office bank in the United Kingdom.[33]

Gladstone and postal officials trumpeted the virtues of the Post Office Savings Bank in tandem with a blistering critique of the existing savings banks. For the purposes of encouraging thrift, they charged, the savings banks had proven insufficient, inconvenient, and insecure. The poor, claimed Gladstone, were saving at rates less than those of twenty years previously, notwithstanding recent increases in wages. Surveying the United Kingdom (including Ireland) in 1861, officials reported the absence of savings banks in 3,500 towns and villages above the level of hamlets, and in 150 towns with populations exceeding ten thousand. As many as fifteen counties were without a single savings bank. Access was not much better for those customers who could walk to the bank. Of the kingdom's 638 savings banks, the majority (355) opened their doors only once a week, 54 once a fortnight, and 10 once a month. A mere 20 savings banks were open daily.[34] Small wonder that the authorities emphasized the advantages of saving at the 2,481 postal money order offices, conveniently located throughout the British Isles and open for six to eight hours *each day*.[35]

Supporters of the Post Office Savings Bank directed their harshest criticisms at the insecurity of the savings banks. The government guaranteed postal savings to rebuild depositors' trust after a series of well-publicized frauds roiled savings banks during the 1840s and 1850s. One of the more spectacular cases involved the Rochdale Savings Bank. George Haworth, Quaker and upstanding citizen by reputation, served as the bank's longtime actuary. He had succeeded his philanthropic father. For more than a decade, Haworth falsified the bank's records with the knowledge or acquiescence of his handpicked trustees. Upon his death in 1849, audits revealed the lion's share of the bank's assets to have disappeared. The many instances of fraud by officers and trustees exerted an "evil influence" on the "spread of provident habits," claimed critics of the savings banks. Defrauded depositors reportedly took to hard drinking, insisting "We will spend our money rather than a George Haworth shall have it."[36]

The champions of the Post Office Savings Banks were interested in far more than remedying the shortcomings of savings banks. Their support of a state-managed savings institution rested on a broader liberal critique of the paternalism underlying the savings banks and private philanthropy. The working poor, they argued, would be more inclined to deposit earnings in the post office, a *public* institution, than in the local savings bank run by sanctimonious clergymen and philanthropists. *The Times* looked forward to the day when "these 531 fallible Savings-banks will all cease to exist."[37]

Proponents delighted in retelling stories of meddling actuaries and trustees. Take the case of the Manchester Savings Bank. In this hub of the Industrial Revolution, the setting of Charles Dickens's *Hard Times*, workers toiled long hours, six days a week. Yet for years the savings bank opened for withdrawals a mere two days every month. The reason? To the day of his death in 1847, Archdeacon Brooks insisted on paying all depositors himself.[38] Then there was the Reverend Alexander Silver, actuary of the Stonehaven Savings Bank in Scotland's Kincardineshire. When a young woman sought to withdraw 2 or 3 pounds of her own savings, the reverend was heard to ask:

"Fit are ye needin' the siller for, lassie?"
She: "A new jacket."
Rev: "Yer jaiket's gweed eneuch. G'wa home wi' ye."[39]

If lectures by clerical busybodies were not enough, workers reportedly avoided the savings banks because their masters often served as trustees. Workmen, argued the advocates of postal savings, did not want employers to know how much they saved, lest their wages be cut. Samuel Smiles told the story of one worker who wished to deposit in the savings bank, yet he ended up waiting at the door for several weeks until he felt certain that his master, a director, was not there.[40]

To Gladstone and the civil servants, the Post Office Savings Bank provided the self-evident solution to the savings banks' insecurity and irritating paternalism. The Post Office supervised its nationwide bureaucracy to detect neglect and fraud, explained one official. Officers were "pecuniarily responsible for every penny they receive." The Post Office Savings Bank would thus grant depositors a "feeling of perfect security," greatly increasing the "means afforded to the humbler classes of the country for depositing at interest their little savings."[41]

Postal savings also offered depositors the confidentiality necessary to encourage saving. Confronting the savings banks' partisans in

Parliament, Gladstone concealed neither his sarcasm nor disdain for paternalism. One class of depositors who desired "secresy in their investments" would prefer the post offices, while "another class, who wished to act under the immediate view of their local superiors" would prefer the existing savings banks.[42] Gladstone articulated the mid-nineteenth-century liberal view of the state. He sought not to create a welfare state that would guarantee citizens a certain standard of living, but rather—like his admirer Samuel Smiles—to use state power to encourage self-help. Individuals would be persuaded, not compelled, to save. The POSB, he later boasted, resulted in a "very great growth in the provident habits of the people," precisely because it offered laboring men the "liberty of choice," "perfect security," and convenience.[43]

The creation of the Post Office Savings Bank powerfully stimulated saving among the general populace. The number of POSB accounts soared from 46,643 at the end of 1861 to more than 11 million in 1908. Unquestionably, widespread access to postal savings offices induced more people to open accounts, and the increased business led to the opening of more offices. During those same years, post offices offering postal savings expanded from 301 to 15,239 offices. Although some depositors transferred their savings from the existing savings banks, the POSB attracted the vast majority of its early customers from those who had never before deposited in a bank. It soon surpassed the old savings banks (henceforth known as Trustee Savings Banks or TSB) as the most popular savings institution among lower- and middle-income Britons. The POSB raced ahead of the TSB in numbers of accounts in 1872, and in total deposits in 1887.[44]

Besides offering safety and convenience, the Post Office Savings Bank enrolled new categories of savers. Women and children represented the largest bloc of postal depositors. In one survey of 1879, female servants constituted 14.8 percent of all depositors, married women another 10.1 percent, and minors 14.0 percent. In a survey taken in 1896, half (50.4 percent) of the new accounts were opened by "married women, spinsters, widows, children."[45] Unmarried female servants, it is true, had long deposited in the old savings banks. However, the influx of *married* women into the POSB reflected new ways of thinking about gender relations.

In 1870 Parliament enacted the Married Women's Property Act. This revolutionary measure revised English common law, under which women had surrendered to husbands all rights to property upon marriage. The new law recognized a wife's rights to her own wages, inheritance, insurance policies, and rents and profits from real estate. Yet what most affected married women were the provisions by which they gained property rights over their deposits in savings banks (whether POSB or TSB). The origins of the Married Women's Property Act lay not so much in abstract principles of women's rights, but rather in pragmatic efforts to safeguard wives' savings from the "rapacity of bad husbands." Some 800,000 married women—most of them poor—earned money in England, estimated one parliamentary committee. The bill's supporters, including the conservative Earl of Shaftesbury, spoke highly of the "thrift, skill, and industry" of these working-class women; their wages were "the very existence of themselves and their children." Guaranteeing the married woman's legal control over her savings would "encourage providence."[46] Under the existing legal regime, men who "lived in idleness upon the earnings of their wives" commonly withdrew their wives' money from the savings bank, "squandering it in dissipation." The effect on working women was "demoralizing," with many a wife complaining, "What's the use of a body striving?"[47]

Upon passage of the Married Women's Property Act, POSB officials moved aggressively to encourage married women to open their own accounts. Pledging to maintain confidentiality vis-à-vis husbands, the authorities cooperated with women to send correspondence about their accounts to the post office branch rather than home. Despite Parliament's original focus on working-class women, large numbers of middle-class and lower-middle-class women also began depositing small savings at the post office. The Married Women's Property Act undoubtedly contributed to the doubling of postal savings accounts during the 1870s.[48] This marked a new stage in the history of thrift, as women, too, became accustomed to saving in modern financial institutions.

The Post Office Savings Bank similarly helped to institutionalize habits of saving among children. Although social reformers increasingly recognized the virtues of cultivating thrift in younger people, the transaction costs of accepting very small deposits remained prohibitive even for the POSB. The Penny Banks, of course, accepted sums as small as a penny, but only because philanthropists heavily subsidized the tiny deposits. In 1880 the Post Office hit upon a cost-effective method of organizing thrift among children. Under the dynamic leadership of Henry Fawcett, renowned as the blind postmaster-general, the POSB introduced several innovations aimed at expanding the customer base. Relying on mass-distributed pamphlets and a troop of public speakers, Fawcett vigorously marketed the benefits of the POSB to the general public. Among his successful measures Fawcett inaugurated the "stamp slip deposit." In schools and at home, children were taught to convert their little savings into one-penny postage stamps, which they pasted onto stamp slips. When they filled up the sheet with twelve stamps (totaling one shilling), their savings would be deposited in a postal account. The stamp slip system resulted in thousands of new accounts, contributing significantly to the more than eight million postal savings accounts by the end of the nineteenth century.[49] Thus was born a practice known to millions of twentieth-century children, who grew up pasting savings stamps or inserting coins in the pockets of savings books.

While the propagators of thrift cheered the rise of postal saving among women and children, Samuel Smiles and others complained that working men had not taken full advantage of the system specifically designed for them. Surveys of depositors offered conflicting evidence as to whether workers widely saved in the POSB. In Birmingham during the early 1870s, artisans constituted only one-tenth of all depositors, ranking below domestic servants, women, and minors.[50] However, in another survey in 1896, working-class people accounted for 90 percent of all postal depositors. Whatever the case, few *unskilled* laborers accumulated enough to save regularly in the POSB and TSB. Skilled workmen, on the other hand, became accustomed to making regular deposits. Measured by both the number of accounts and deposited funds, workers were most likely to save in the POSB. Yet they also held accounts in the savings banks, building societies, and cooperative societies. In addition, better-paid workers often contributed to the expanding friendly societies, whose accumulated funds helped insure workers against unemployment, sickness, old age, and funeral expenses.[51] By the early twentieth century, skilled workmen touted thrift as evidence of their self-discipline.

The Post Office Savings Bank did not by itself transform the savings habits of the British people, but this massive institution exercised what economists would term a multiplier effect on popular thrift. Other forms of saving became more secure as the authorities encouraged friendly societies, provident and charitable societies, trade unions, and penny banks to deposit their funds in the POSB as a safe haven at attractive interest rates. In its first year alone, 821 friendly societies and 68 penny banks invested their funds in postal deposits. Nor, contrary to the fears of the old savings banks, did the POSB eliminate the philanthropic movement to promote thrift. Clergymen of various denominations avidly propagated the virtues of postal savings in the government's early publicity campaigns. The creation of the POSB also "induced many benevolent persons" to establish penny banks, according to officials.[52] The Trustee Savings Banks, too, managed to survive the onslaught of the POSB.[53] Yet perhaps the greatest impact of the Post Office Savings Bank was as a model for the rest of the world.

The Globalization of National Thrift

In the increasingly interconnected world of the nineteenth century, there was nothing like the Post Office to spread the word. Beginning with the Paris congress of fourteen national post offices in 1863, postal officials met routinely to institute the international exchange of mail services that today we take for granted. Their cooperation resulted in the creation in 1875 of what became known as the Union Postale Universelle.[54] These forums afforded national post offices opportunities to compare notes on the latest innovations. Britain's Post Office Savings Bank was prominent among them. In June 1861, even before post offices accepted their first deposits, British officials were already packaging the virtues of the POSB for international consumption. The Post Office's George Chetwynd presented a paper on the topic to the Congrès International de Bienfaisance (International Congress of Charities,

Table 2 Major Postal Savings Banks, 1904–1906

	Year of Origin	Accounts	Total Deposits (US$)	Average Account Balance (US$)
Austria[a]	1883	1,900,194	42,536,862	22.59
Belgium	1870	2,316,633	155,646,121	67.19
Canada	1868	164,542	45,736,489	277.96
France	1882	4,577,390	246,703,726	53.90
Great Britain	1861	9,673,717	721,819,296	74.62
Italy	1876	4,689,669	233,735,421	49.84
Japan	1875	6,658,758	33,713,037	5.06
Netherlands	1881	1,259,681	56,153,000	44.58
Sweden	1883	567,032	14,648,559	25.83

[a] Savings accounts, excluding checking accounts.
Source: *To Establish Postal Savings Depositories*, 60th Cong., 1st sess., 1908, S. Rep. 525, 138.

Correction, and Philanthropy) then meeting in London.[55] The British went on to publicize the POSB in other international forums, including the era's frequent international expositions (world's fairs). At the Paris Exposition of 1900, the Post Office Savings Bank's exhibit boasted that the total number of postal depositors in the United Kingdom would fill five large cities on the continent.[56]

The British model of state-sponsored thrift was an idea whose time had come. Post office savings banks sprang up throughout the far-flung British empire, beginning with New Zealand (1867) and Canada (1868), followed by New South Wales (1871). They spread to the Straits Settlement (Singapore, 1877), India (1882), Cape of Good Hope (1884), and Ceylon (1885). Within two and a half decades, nearly every major Western country—plus Japan—had adopted a nationwide system of postal savings (see table 2).

It was no small thing for so many governments to create mammoth state savings banks. Unquestionably more was involved than providing new facilities for saving. Discourses on thrift had become part of far-reaching transnational debates over how best to build powerful nation-states.[57] There was a strong element of international cooperation in this. The late nineteenth century witnessed efforts at formulating international law, the widespread adoption of the metric system and the gold standard, and international congresses of scientists and other specialists. At the same time, emulation was propelled by profound anxieties about threats from within and without. Great-power rivalries boiled over into a series of conflicts. A short list would include the Crimean War (1854–56), Austro-Prussian War (1866), Franco-Prussian War (1870–71), Russo-Japanese War (1904–1905), and World War I (1914–18). Nations felt compelled to study their competitors' sources of strength, from military organization to public education. On the home front, elites and reformers appeared equally anxious about the rise of socialism and anarchism. They met regularly with counterparts in other countries to exchange ideas on social policies aimed at ameliorating working-class discontent.

The national encouragement of saving loomed large in transnational discussions of social policy. State savings institutions remained a major topic at the periodic meetings of the International Congress of Charities, Correction, and Philanthropy. At the Paris Exposition of 1889, the French government sponsored a special exposition of "Social Economy" in conjunction with several international congresses of specialists. The section on "Savings" emphasized national and postal savings banks, school savings banks, and other savings institutions. Participants also shared information on private savings societies, employers' encouragement of thrift, and mutual insurance schemes. The focus on savings and insurance institutions continued on a grander scale at the Paris Exposition of 1900.[58]

Although Britain's Post Office Savings Bank ranked as the leading model, experiments in Belgium attracted nearly as much international interest. A small country with less than seven million people in 1900, Belgium would seem a surprising object of emulation. Yet in the late nineteenth century, Belgium impressed observers the world over as the Little Country that Could, the plucky place that molded an entire people into a thrifty and industrious nation. The French as early as 1867 drew inspiration from Belgium's national savings bank in formulating their own postal savings system.[59] British reformers wrote admiringly of the "great thriftiness of the Belgian people." In a book subtitled *Lessons from Belgium*, B. Seebohm Rowntree effused that in "this relatively poor country, where wages are extraordinarily low, often not more than half as high as in England, the sum saved in the National Savings Bank is so much greater per head of the population than in Great Britain."[60] Equally admiring was a U.S. diplomat who summed up the thrift of Belgians in Darwinian terms as "adaptation to their environment." In this densely populated land, had the government not acted to "stimulate these habits of thrift and saving," the people's condition would "soon become insupportable, and a change, either by famine or revolution, or maybe both, would ensue."[61]

What captivated the international champions of thrift was the Belgian state's Caisse Générale d'Épargne et de Retraite (General Savings and Pension Bank). Established in 1865, the CGER transformed Belgium into a nation of savers more thoroughly than any other national savings bank in Europe. Prior to the adoption of the system, few saved in any bank. Yet by 1913, an extraordinary 1 in 2.4 Belgians held a deposit in the CGER alone. Already in 1890, the CGER accounted for 94.5 percent of the nation's savers and 90.7 percent of the aggregate savings deposits.[62]

Of the world's national savings banks, the CGER held the distinction of having originated independently of the British postal savings system. Proposals for a state-run, state-guaranteed savings bank surfaced in Belgium as early as 1848, amid the economic dislocations and widespread bank runs of that revolutionary year. Belgium was becoming the most industrialized society in Europe after Britain, yet commercial and municipal savings banks remained inaccessible to most industrial workers and the rural populace. As in Britain, proponents of economic liberalism spearheaded the creation of the national savings bank. Though generally opposed to state intervention, Belgian liberals similarly looked to the government to organize thrift. The private sector and Christian philanthropy were not up to the task, they insisted. State encouragement of saving afforded working people the self-help means of improving their lives, while reducing public welfare expenditures and preempting revolution. In the words of one supporter, the most effective ways to combat poverty lay in "teaching, public education, work, and thrift."[63] Advocates of the CGER also played upon nationalist anxieties that Belgium was falling behind its thriftier neighbors. Walthère Frère-Oban, the liberal finance minister who proposed the CGER in 1859, extensively surveyed savings institutions in Europe and the United States. Whereas only 1 in 137 Belgians reportedly held a savings account, the ratios were 1 in 15 in England, 1 in 34 in Prussia, and 1 in 36 in France. While savings banks in neighboring countries had expanded remarkably, "*we alone have remained stationary* since 1840, and, I must confess, we have slid backward."[64]

In the fast-paced world of international emulation, the creation of the CGER in 1865 established Belgium as a leading model in thrift promotion. But it was not long before Belgians, too, incorporated key elements of British postal saving. Initially the CGER gathered small deposits at its own branches, as well as those of the National Bank of Belgium (the central bank). Coverage of rural areas remained spotty until 1870, when the government additionally employed the nation's post offices as local agents. Within a few years, CGER customers could bank at any of 629 post offices. In 1881 the CGER emulated the recent British innovation of permitting deposits by means of sheets of postage stamps. This practice enabled schoolchildren and the poor to make small, but regular, deposits. The number of savers grew rapidly during those years, particularly among children and the lower middle classes. Workers and agricultural laborers, who initially were underrepresented, flocked to the CGER in the 1890s and especially after 1900. In addition, farmers and workers saved through credit and savings cooperatives, notably the German-style Raiffensen banks.[65] A culture of thrift had come to pervade working-class society, as captured in this popular Flemish ditty:

Een man die spaart drinkt niet!	A man who saves drinks not!
Eene vrow die spaart verkwist niet!	A wife who saves wastes not!
Een kind dat spaart snoept niet!	A child who saves won't a sweet tooth have![66]

Looking back, the director of the CGER in 1935 saw nothing natural about Belgian thriftiness. Thanks to the unceasing efforts of the national savings bank and the schools, "thrift has *become* in Belgium not only a habit, but much more: a tradition."[67]

Inspired by Belgian and British innovations, neighboring France instituted one of the world's largest postal savings systems, the Caisse

Nationale d'Épargne, in 1882. Unlike its models, however, France's national savings bank originated under conditions of national emergency. Not simply a vehicle to improve oneself, saving became an act of patriotism. The French suffered devastating defeat in the Franco-Prussian War (1870–71). The Second Empire of Napoleon III collapsed, and a provisional government took power. By treaty the victorious Germans extracted from the French government the extraordinary sum of 5 billon francs. German troops would occupy the country's northern provinces until the French paid the indemnity in full. In what became one of France's great national myths the people—from bourgeois to peasants—invested their savings in the National Defense Loan in such large numbers that the state quickly financed the indemnity. France had been liberated from foreign occupation, saved—as it were—by saving. To Samuel Smiles, France's patriotic workers and peasants joined their Belgian counterparts as the "most thrifty and prudent people in the world." Ordinary Frenchmen emerged from defeat accustomed to entrusting their savings to the state. One in every eight individuals held shares in the national debt. [68]

Postal savings soon joined bondholding as French traditions. In 1875 the provisional government gave way to the Third Republic. The new French government decreed that postmasters and tax collectors could handle savings deposits in those localities lacking savings banks. In 1881 the national assembly enacted legislation that extended state-guaranteed postal savings to all locales. The government's brief echoed British and Belgian rationales, albeit in republican France's distinctive language of citizenship. Postal savings involved the use of public authority to "remedy an insufficiency," in the words of the parliamentary commission's rapporteur Monsieur LeBastard. Of France's 36,000 communes surveyed in 1878, some 34,000 lacked a savings bank. This situation struck LeBastard as "contrary to justice because all French have the right to equal treatment . . . and the little communes whose inhabitants pay their taxes . . . are justified in making demands on the State." [69]

Like British and Belgian counterparts, French liberals embraced postal savings as the public, secular counterweight to philanthropy. The Third Republic went further to imbue the post office savings bank with a key role in the civilizing mission. The French middle classes looked to the nation-state to overcome the parochial hold of local notables, Catholic priests, and outmoded customs—to make "peasants into Frenchmen."[70] In 1881 the government embarked on Europe's most ambitious program of mass elementary education, which would be compulsory, free, and defiantly anticlerical. The enactment of postal savings legislation that same year sprang from similar impulses to modernize and standardize savings habits throughout France. The nation's schools would be mobilized to teach thrift as one of the republic's leading "civic virtues," an alternative morality to religion itself.[71]

From the start, the Ministry of Posts, Telephones, and Telegraphs aggressively promoted postal savings throughout France. At six thousand post offices, clerks threw themselves into drumming up business, stimulated by the offer of a bonus for every new account opened. Within the first seven years, customers opened one million accounts. By 1907 there were five million postal accounts, approximately one for every ten inhabitants. These years, noted one official history, witnessed the "democratization of thrift." Particularly in the countryside, savings habits were transformed as families took gold coins out of the proverbial "wool sock" (bas de laine) and deposited them at the post office. Workers constituted a large portion of postal depositors. The working class had already become used to depositing in savings banks and buying government securities. In the 1870s the French workman saved ten times as much as his English counterpart, claimed Samuel Smiles. In addition, the rapid growth in the number of postal savings accounts owed much to two new groups of savers: married women and children. Emulating Britain's Married Women's Property Act of 1870, the postal savings law of 1881 permitted married women to open postal accounts without approval from their husbands.[72]

Postal savings did not supplant France's existing savings banks. Over the next three decades, both types of savings institutions experienced sustained growth. In 1912 postal savings deposits totaled approximately 1.8 billion francs, while the local savings banks maintained their lead with 4 billion francs. To the French authorities as well as the public, postal savings and the savings banks formed twin pillars of one system of popular saving. They were governed by similar regulations, and deposits in both institutions were entrusted to the government's venerable Caisse des Dépôts et Consignations (Bank of Deposits and Consignations). On the eve of World War I, nearly one in two citizens possessed a *livret* (passbook) in a savings bank, whether postal or local. The *livret* became an icon of French life, still revered a century later. The French passbook, waxed one popular magazine in 1979, has been woven into the "social fabric, into tradition. It is the cherished wool sock, nourishing and protective, enmeshed in our customs. It's tantamount to religion."[73]

Throughout Europe, organized thrift spread to the hinterlands. In nearly every country, states directly encouraged modern saving at the post office. The circumstances under which postal savings developed—and the precise mix of state and nonstate savings institutions—varied by nation. In Italy the postal savings bank was bound up with the birth of a unified nation-state in 1861. At the time, local savings banks operated in northern and central Italy. One province, Lombardy, held more than half of the total savings deposits. No savings bank existed in the southern half of Italy before 1860. The new state inaugurated the postal savings bank in 1876 in large part to modernize popular habits in the south and the countryside in general. Spurred by nationwide coverage, state guarantees, and bonuses to clerks, the Italian post savings system surged in the late nineteenth century. By 1913 total deposits in the post office roughly equaled those in the commercial banks and fell just short of those in the local savings banks.[74]

Founded in 1883, Austria's postal savings bank occupied a prominent, if complex, place on the urban and political landscape of the Austro-Hungarian Empire. The Postsparkasse strikingly embodied modernity. Modeled after the British, Belgian, and new Dutch and French systems, it aimed to bring uniformity and rationality throughout the Austrian half of the empire (the Hungarian postal savings bank began operations in 1886). Vienna's leading modernist architect, Otto Wagner, designed the Postsparkasse's headquarters, an imposing structure of aluminum, marble slabs, and glass floors that opened in 1906 (figure 3). However, Austrian postal saving also became identified with the populist nationalism and virulent anti-Semitism of the Christian Social Party led by Karl Lueger, mayor of Vienna from 1897 to 1910. The Christian Socialists championed the postal savings bank as the state's program to

Figure 3. Main banking hall of the Austrian Postal Savings Bank, Vienna. Photo by Luzia Ellert. Courtesy of WAGNER: WERK Museum Postsparkasse.

help the "little man" improve himself while pooling his savings with others to rival the power of the Jewish banking houses.[75]

By 1900 the post office savings bank had become a familiar feature of everyday life in much of Europe. Nonetheless, state-managed institutions in Germany and northern Europe never dominated popular savings to the extent seen in Britain, Belgium, France, and the Netherlands. In general, postal savings systems encountered resistance where alternative modes of small saving thrived and where nonstate savings institutions were well organized. One such rival was the cooperative bank, which sprang up among farmers, craftsmen, small merchants, and workers. Founded to provide loans to those who had little access to commercial credit facilities, the cooperatives also gathered the savings of their members. Many were associated with the rural Raiffeisen cooperative movement. Friedrich Wilhelm Raiffeisen founded the first cooperative bank in 1864. The Raiffeisen-type banks spread throughout rural Germany and Austria, and later to other European countries, North America, and even East Asia. By the mid-1880s, Germany alone claimed 1,072 Raiffeisen banks.[76]

The most potent resistance to postal saving appeared where communally owned savings banks abounded. In predominantly rural Sweden, the savings banks achieved impressive density by the mid-1870s with 325 banks and 550 branch offices. Aided by their communities, the fiercely autonomous savings banks opposed government legislation to institute postal savings during the 1860s. Sweden eventually instituted the Postsparbanken in 1883, primarily to supplement the network of the local savings banks and provide state guarantees for deposits. Not until the period between 1925 and 1950 did postal savings become a major player, increasing its share of Sweden's total deposits from 2.5 to 16.8 percent.[77]

Among major European nations, Germany alone chose not to create a national postal savings bank during the nineteenth century. Not unified until 1871, Germany remained a federation of historically autonomous states. It also was home to Europe's most extensive network of municipal savings banks, numbering 2,685 by 1900. Like postal savings banks, the *Sparkassen* were public institutions dedicated to encouraging thrift. In 1884 the local savings banks allied to form a powerful national association, which stopped all efforts to establish a rival postal savings system. It required Hitler's Third Reich to overcome regional opposition and centralize the promotion of saving. In 1939 Germany adopted the Austrian model of postal saving. The emulation was hardly peaceful. When the Nazis annexed Austria the previous year, they also annexed its Postsparkasse.[78]

Saving at School

The post office was not the only public institution marshaled to encourage thrift. The state's promotion of saving coincided with the rise of mass education in Europe. Reformers jumped at the new opportunity to inculcate habits of thrift in the youngest, most malleable citizens—and to do so, not urchin by urchin, but by the hundreds of thousands.

The focus on children developed gradually during the first half of the nineteenth century. Britain's many Penny Banks were one such initiative, but they remained philanthropic ventures. Typical was the Gloucester Penny Bank, whose Honorary Secretary harangued working-class children to save rather than spend their coins on "gingerbread and humbugs."[79] In France and Belgium, on the other hand, public authorities intervened earlier in efforts to universalize habits of saving among children. France's first school savings program dated back to 1834. The elementary school director in Mans encouraged pupils to deposit small savings in a school bank until amounts totaled enough to start accounts in the town savings bank. Schools in other French towns followed suit. To cultivate prévoyance (planning for the future), French authorities also introduced the practice of opening and depositing small sums in savings accounts for children. In 1820 King Louis XVIII celebrated his son's birth by presenting savings accounts to every poor child born that day in Paris. The Duke of Orleans, eldest son of the succeeding king, rewarded 1,760 meritorious elementary school students throughout France with passbooks on the occasion of his marriage in 1837.[80]

Neighboring Belgium took center stage as the internationally recognized leader in school savings during the mid-nineteenth century. The same impulses that prompted the ruling Liberal Party to launch the national savings bank (Caisse Générale d'Épargne et de Retraite) lay behind its crusade to instill thrift in Belgian schoolchildren. Liberals strove to create secular public institutions that circumvented the Catholic Church's control of education and philanthropy. In the 1860s and again after 1878, Liberal governments expanded the state-supervised network of communal schools. François Laurent, law professor and pioneer in school savings, was notorious in Catholic circles for his anticlericalism. He envisioned thrift as the "new charity" by which the "worker will never have need of the Bureau of Welfare and the hospitals" except in the event of grand misfortunes.[81] Laurent instructed teachers to incorporate thrift throughout the curriculum until it "becomes an habitual idea and enters, so to speak, into the very blood of your pupils."[82]

The Belgian government's creation of the CGER in 1865 proved indispensable to the spread of school savings in Belgium. Aided by Professor Laurent, the city of Ghent had been teaching thrift in the schools since 1858. Laurent won the support of the CGER and Ministry of Interior to extend Ghent's school savings program to the rest of the country. School savings were a boon to the national savings bank. Schoolchildren's deposits were transferred to CGER branches, and to no other bank. By 1908, 40 percent of children in the nation's elementary schools saved in the classroom, and by the mid-1920s three-fourths of the elementary schools administered such programs (see figure 4). Once a week, Belgian teachers collected pupils' coins, recorded the amounts, and maintained their passbooks in the CGER. The schools endeavored to teach both children and parents the "necessity of saving."[83]

It fell to the highly centralized French state to nationalize school savings. Impressed by the Belgian experiment, Augustin de Malarce oversaw the government's introduction of school savings banks from the 1870s. The subsequent adoption of free, compulsory, and secular education for children permitted the Ministry of Education to implement savings banks in every elementary school. Some 23,000 schools administered these banks by the end of the 1880s. Ministry directives also resulted in the inclusion of thrift education within the standardized curriculum. Although pupils' savings might be deposited in the local savings banks, the inauguration of French postal savings in 1882 greatly

Figure 4. "Let's Be Prudent," Belgium, 1906. An earnest schoolgirl urges the other children to stop wasting money at the candy store and instead deposit their centimes in the national savings bank branch (CGER) to the right. Illustration by André Mathy. Archives of the CGER, courtesy of BNP Paribus Fortis collection, Brussels.

stimulated school savings. Post offices accepted smaller deposits than the savings banks, and like British and Belgian counterparts they offered stamp slips (*bulletins d'épargne*). Children would buy 5 centime postage stamps, pasting them on sheets until they reached the minimum deposit of one franc. [84]

Britain, home to the first Post Office Savings Bank, nonetheless developed school savings programs later than Belgium and France. Samuel Smiles gazed enviously across the Channel. All French, he observed, were "thrifty, saving, and frugal, because they are educated in economy from their earliest years." Like others, Smiles was captivated by Belgium's Ghent model, where savings programs operated in every school in the city.[85] In his own country, school savings evolved more slowly, dependent on the gradual adoption of mass education and impeded by a more decentralized educational system. Elementary education became compulsory in 1872 in Scotland and in 1880 in England and Wales, but it did not become free until 1891. Nevertheless, Britain, too, entered the twentieth century with an extensive network of school savings banks. The POSB embarked on a nationwide campaign to introduce children to the "advantages of thrift" in 1891. Post office clerks were dispatched to local schools where they sold savings stamps, opened accounts, and collected deposits. By the 1930s, most British schools operated savings programs.[86]

The practice of school savings spread rapidly in Europe and beyond. The pioneers were followed by Italy, the Netherlands, Sweden, Finland, and many others. Postal savings banks and centralized educational systems advanced these programs nationwide, but local initiatives could also be effective. In Germany, municipal savings banks and the authorities actively promoted school savings at the grass roots from the 1880s.[87] By the early twentieth century, the school savings bank had become an integral part of daily life. In a truly transnational moment, once a week around the globe—from Munich to Melbourne to Minneapolis—millions of schoolchildren tendered their pocket money to teachers who deposited the sums in savings or postal savings banks (figure 5). Seldom did the centimes or pennies add up to big savings, and it could be costly to collect the tiny deposits. But that was not the point, insisted proponents the world over. In "forming the habit of thrift," observed one prominent Scottish savings banker, educators were "laying the basis of character" and "building up a type of citizen which will carry our nation forward to still greater prosperity."[88]

From Social Policy to National Savings

Character and citizenship remained at the heart of nineteenth-century European efforts to encourage thrift. The goal was to produce self-reliant citizens who would neither revolt nor require poor relief. Like school savings programs, savings banks and postal savings systems were predominantly *social* rather than financial institutions. They gathered small deposits to bring stability to people's lives, not to generate investment capital for industry or government. When the British introduced postal

Figure 5. "The Weekly Thrift Parade," school savings in Melbourne, Australia, ca. 1930. Alexander Cooch, *The State Savings Bank of Victoria* (Melbourne: Macmillan, 1934), 132.

savings, the economy had little need for small savings. London was awash in capital, furnished by the great merchant banks and wealthy investors. When the state needed to borrow, it too turned to the big savers. To pay for the balance of the Crimean War in 1855, the government sold the entire war loan of 16 million pounds to the London house of Rothschild.[89]

Little by little, European governments discovered that small savings deposited in post offices and savings banks became vast pools of capital. There arose a new motivation for encouraging the people to save. The masses' savings might also finance national power. Between 1894 and 1913, military budgets more than doubled in Britain, Germany, Austria, and Italy, and nearly doubled in France. Moreover, European states rapidly increased their social spending on urban infrastructure, education, health, and welfare. To finance these expenditures, governments raised taxes but also issued bonds as never before.[90]

The extent to which states employed the people's savings to purchase national debt depended on the disposition of deposits in each country. In Germany, which lacked a postal savings bank, most small savings remained at the local level. The municipal savings banks were free to invest their funds, and they generally made loans to local enterprises and local governments. Autonomous savings banks in Italy, Sweden, and Austria similarly drew on deposits to advance loans within their regions. At the same time, savings banks and commercial banks often invested heavily in government securities, thereby playing important though indirect roles in financing national debt.[91]

The link between small savings and national finance was far more direct in countries where nearly all deposits flowed into government coffers. In Britain and France, state agencies served as custodian for deposits from both the new postal savings banks and the older savings banks. Administered by finance officials, the National Debt Commissioners and the Caisse des Dépôts et Consignations invested the everincreasing deposits in national debt. By 1890 France's Caisse des Dépôts placed fully 85 percent of its assets in long-term government securities. British and French centralization of small savings enhanced both nations' ability to borrow more easily than their rivals.[92]

Belgium, at best a minor military power, similarly deployed small savings to advance national projects, albeit with less emphasis on the central state. Although the Caisse Générale d'Épargne et de Retraite, the national savings bank, enjoyed a near monopoly over the nation's savings, the state's financial officers did not control investment choices. The CGER's autonomous Administrative Council decided where to invest its funds subject to loose statutory guidelines. The largest portion of the assets went toward servicing the national debt. The CGER also invested heavily in the obligations of the provincial and communal governments. What further distinguished the CGER's investments were the bank's commitments to financing Belgium's economic and social development. Mindful of the instability of other financial institutions in Belgium, economic liberals founded the national savings bank in part to accumulate industrial capital. The CGER advanced credit to many commercial ventures, particularly in the first twenty years. Beginning in the 1880s and 1890s, the bank loaned substantial portions

of its funds to agricultural credit cooperatives and toward the construction of workers' housing. Most remarkable for a national savings bank,
the CGER purchased the debt of *foreign* governments—amounting to
23 percent of the portfolio in 1885. Recalling previous crises in their
small economy, the founders had encouraged the bank to diversify across
national boundaries.[93]

French officials, by contrast, explicitly related popular saving to
the power of the central state. On the eve of World War I, France was
considered the world's most indebted nation in both absolute and per
capita terms. During the century before 1914, governmental expenditures soared while revenue sources proved inadequate. Luckily for the
French, the state could rely on the savings of citizens to finance en-
demic deficits at low cost. As it did in 1871 to end the German occupation, the state frequently issued *rentes* (bonds) in conjunction with
nationalistic campaigns.[94] When making the case for the enactment of
postal savings in 1881, government spokesman trumpeted its potential
to provide capital for the "grand enterprises" that "augment our machinery, develop our industry, our commerce, our agriculture, and place
us in the position to compete internationally." The accumulated sums
would advance the "grandeur and prosperity" of France.[95]

Nor should we overlook the politics of organizing thrift under the
French state. By encouraging citizens to deposit in postal savings and
the savings banks, officials strengthened their own position vis-à-vis
parliamentary and provincial interests. Financial bureaucrats exercised
broad powers over the investment of the enormous savings funds lodged
in the Caisse des Dépôts. To finance their agenda, they sometimes by-
passed the National Assembly by simply appropriating monies from the
state's deposit bank. Among the Third Republic's ambitious projects,
the Caisse des Dépôts underwrote bonds for national railway construction and the adoption of universal elementary education. As a proportion of France's monetary resources, the combined deposits in postal
savings and the savings banks grew rapidly from 8 percent in 1870 to an
extraordinary 27 percent in 1900 (rising further to 33 percent in 1938).
The state bureaucracy successfully resisted all efforts to permit the local
savings banks to invest their own deposits. The French people, for their
part, generally accepted the government's messages that their thrift

contributed to the strength of the nation-state. They enthusiastically purchased bonds. And when they deposited at the post office—called the "*National* Savings Bank"—they were reminded that their savings supported the Republic's borrowing. The French visualized aggregate savings as a key measure of national wealth and power. Supporters of the Third Republic celebrated the surge in savings to 418 million francs in one 1881 cartoon captioned: "Never before has popular saving attained such proportions, a sure sign of public prosperity."[96]

The British government was less aggressive about mobilizing small savings to finance specific national projects. Thanks to modest spending and an efficient income tax, Britain's national debt actually declined between 1857 and 1914.[97] Small investors could buy government bonds at the post office or the Trustee Savings Banks, but popular bondholding in Britain never approached French levels prior to World War I. Still, the Treasury's holdings of postal savings and savings banks deposits constituted a strategic resource that could be tapped when needed. Nineteenth-century chancellors of the exchequer were no less emphatic than French finance ministers in asserting their freedom to invest the funds. In 1859 Chancellor of the Exchequer William Gladstone thought it a "gross delusion" that depositors would think of the funds held by the National Debt Commissioners as their own. The chancellor insisted he could do with the funds as he wished. Earlier in 1854 Gladstone circumvented Parliament to use the savings bank fund to help finance the Crimean War. After creating the Post Office Savings Bank, he regarded it, too, as a vital source of cheap capital because postal depositors lent their money to the state at below-market interest rates.[98] Treasury officials later borrowed from the savings fund to finance military and naval works, Suez Canal bonds, Pacific cable and telegraph development, and various investments in the expanding British Empire.[99]

Despite the trends, Western European states remained ambivalent about promoting saving primarily to enhance national power at the turn of the twentieth century. Even France's financial officials attempted to slow the growth in savings deposits, concerned that an oversupply of savings would encourage greater national indebtedness and lower the value of bonds.[100] Nonetheless, with a European-wide war looming, nations possessing postal savings and school savings programs recognized that thrift had become more than a personal virtue. Speaking in 1908, Lord Rosebery, former British prime minister, nervously remarked on the greater frugality of the French and Germans. Thrift, he concluded, "is the surest and the strongest foundation of an empire—so sure, so strong, and so necessary that no great empire can long exist that disregards it."[101]

3

AMERICA THE EXCEPTIONAL

The great lesson our people need to learn is that of economy. The American people are apt to earn but are not wise to save.

> —T. O. Howe, Postmaster-General, in support of postal savings, 1882[1]

Little Ja-pa-nee Save-a-his money.
Never waste a cent like A-mer-i-can;
He can live so cheap But he save a heap.
Ne-ver-be-broke like A-mer-i-can.

> —School savings song, 1917[2]

Politicians and historians often talk of "American exceptionalism." What each regards as distinctive about the American experience varies, but generally they highlight freedom, individualism, egalitarianism, risk-taking, and laissez-faire.[3] There is, to be sure, something self-congratulatory and insular in this selection. Curiously, few Americans consider what has struck so many *foreign* observers as exceptional about the United States over the past 150 years. To an uncanny degree, travelers remark upon American abundance, excessive consumption, and the weak spirit of thrift.

It matters little whether these visitors hailed from Europe or East Asia, from the nineteenth century or the present day. When Japanese emissaries of the shogun set foot on American soil in 1860, their San Francisco hosts attempted to dazzle them with feats of modern engineering. Fukuzawa Yukichi, a translator and later a famous publicist, was not impressed. He had already studied Western science in Japan. He recalled being more surprised by the "enormous waste of iron everywhere. In garbage piles, on the seashores—everywhere—I found lying old oil tins, empty cans, and broken tools. This was remarkable to us, for in Yedo [Tokyo], after a fire, there would appear a swarm of people looking for nails in the ashes."[4] A half-century later among Europeans, reported the *New York Times*, it "has passed almost into an axiom" that "Americans are an extravagant people," an observation confirmed by statistical evidence. The United States, where wages were roughly three times those of France, nonetheless ranked fourteenth in savings banks depositors per thousand inhabitants—far below the French, but also behind the "poverty-stricken" countries of Italy and Japan.[5] A French family, it was commonly said, could "live on what an American family throws away."[6]

Belgian observers were no less appalled than the Japanese by the thriftlessness and "waste of America." In 1914, while visiting the United States to appeal for aid against the invading Germans, one Belgian commissioner complained—not so tactfully—of seeing "hundreds of miles of fertile lands lying fallow," "orchards and fields with ungathered products rotting on the grounds," and everywhere wooden fences containing "enough lumber to build the homes of an empire." If "any country in Europe had such bounteous natural wealth, such limitless land-area fit for cultivation, and such unused labor energy, it would be quickly transformed into prosperity beyond dreams. Why, in Belgium even our dogs work."[7]

A comparative measure of canine diligence is beyond the scope of this book. But the Belgians were on to something. Modern America has differed sharply from other industrializing societies in its approach to saving and consumption. This is not to say that Americans lack a history of personal saving. Yet somewhere, somehow the United States diverged from the concerted promotion of thrift by states and local governments that developed in Europe and Japan. In this respect, American exceptionalism was apparent by the time of World War I and it became clearer still in the decades following World War II. When and why did Americans become less inclined than other nations to encourage popular saving? We run the risk of caricaturing the entire American experience as one sustained burst of consumerism and extravagance. Instead I consider several historical junctures at which the United States, little by little, diverged from other advanced economies.

A Transatlantic World

In the beginning, the United States was far from exceptional. Nineteenth-century European visitors to the eastern seaboard observed much that was familiar. Like many other ideas, discourses on thrift traversed the Atlantic nearly as fast as schooners plied the seas—and in both directions. At the end of the previous century, Benjamin Franklin inspired Europeans with maxims on frugality. Just a few years later, European reformers transformed these ideas into a social movement that encouraged thrift among the masses. In turn they exported blueprints for savings institutions back to their American cousins.

Philanthropists in New England and the Mid-Atlantic states founded savings banks at the same time and for much the same reasons as British counterparts. In 1816 civic-minded individuals and officials held meetings in New York, Boston, and Philadelphia with the object of establishing savings institutions for the poor in their respective cities. Before year's end, one group had organized the Philadelphia Saving Fund Society and another secured the incorporation of the Provident Institution for Savings in the Town of Boston. The Bank for Savings in the City of New York opened in 1819. The three pioneer institutions survived well into the latter half of the twentieth century. Other savings banks followed, particularly in Massachusetts towns, where twenty-three additional "institutions for saving" were incorporated before 1834.[8]

As in England, American reformers encouraged saving to ameliorate urban poverty and reduce the rising costs of poor relief. "It is not by the alms of the wealthy, that the good of the lower class can be generally promoted," declared the trustees of Boston's Provident Institution for Savings. Rather, "he is the most effective benefactor to the poor, who encourages them in habits of industry, sobriety, and frugality."[9] The object of savings banks, elaborated New York City's Society for the Prevention of Pauperism, "is to encourage and promote industrious and provident habits among the poor; and to bring within the reach of every industrious person, the great advantage of PUBLIC SECURITY and INTEREST for small sums of money, without much expense of time, or trouble."

The savings banks, explained one Boston savings banker, targeted "humble journeymen, coachmen, chamber-maids, and all kinds of domestic servants and inferior artisans, who constitute two-thirds of our population." And like their English counterparts, civic leaders coupled their benevolence with anxieties about popular disorder. The Society for the Prevention of Pauperism remarked that savings institutions in England had not only benefited the poor, but also the "higher ranks in society," for the latter's "comfort and happiness" depended "in a measure on the economy, prudence, honesty, and sobriety" of the lower ranks. Savings banks might produce even "greater good in the United States, than in any other part of the world," predicted some reformers. The "proportion of suffering" was considerably smaller than in most countries because of greater opportunities, yet America's poor "squandered" an estimated one-sixth of what they earned.[10]

It was no coincidence that savings banks sprang up in the United States when they did. Although Americans had fought two wars against the British (most recently the War of 1812), civic leaders in the Northeast belonged to a transatlantic world that eagerly exchanged knowledge on how to confront problems of social change. America's paragons of thrift remained inspired by innovations in England and Scotland. James Savage took the lead in founding Boston's Provident Institution for Savings after plans for London's Provident Institution for Savings "fell accidentally" into his hands.[11]

The most influential mediator between British and American developments was Thomas Eddy, the man behind the establishment of New York's Bank for Savings. Eddy faithfully corresponded with Patrick Colquhoun, the Scottish political economist and longtime champion of savings banks. After Colquhoun informed Eddy in 1816 of his plan to found a savings bank in London, the New Yorker sprang to action. As Eddy later explained to Colquhoun, "Immediately on receiving from thee an account of the Provident Institution in your metropolis, I proposed to a number of my friends to establish a similar one in this city."[12] The systematic encouragement of thrift in America, as in Europe, arose as part of a broader social movement to create social institutions aimed at inculcating self-discipline in the poor and the dispossessed. Savings banks took their place alongside orphanages, schools, prisons, hospitals, and asylums. Thomas Eddy is best remembered as the penal reformer who founded the model Newgate prison in New York. The founding fathers of savings banks included the penal reformer Roberts Vaux, the poor-law reformer Josiah Quincy, and the socially minded New York governor DeWitt Clinton. Together they comprised what one historian has termed the "trans-Atlantic community of the benevolently inclined."[13]

Savings banks in the northeastern United States operated as philanthropic enterprises on the English model. Although these institutions came to be known as "mutual savings banks," this was a misnomer. Depositors had no voice in management. The mutual savings banks were governed by boards of trustees comprised of civic-minded men who drew no pay nor owned stock. Savings banks paid interest, accepted small savings, and invested the funds so as to maximize safety rather than seek high rates of return. This single-minded promotion of popular saving was as novel in America as it was in England. As late as 1900, commercial banks in the United States rarely paid interest on deposits, aside from large time-deposits. In the New England states, trustees retained considerable discretion over investment, though they generally placed surplus funds conservatively in securities of governments, mortgages, and corporate stocks and bonds. Savings banks in New York State more closely resembled the essentially public Trustee Savings Banks in Britain. By charters and law, trustees invested nearly all surplus funds in bonds of the U.S. government and New York State and its locales.[14]

Where savings banks existed, they encouraged ordinary Americans to adopt modern habits of saving over the course of the nineteenth century. In the Northeastern states, the American story was decidedly *unexceptional*. The cities between Baltimore and Boston were well served by mutual savings banks. In the county encompassing New York City alone, twenty-six savings banks were in operation by 1900. Statistics reveal only the number of savings accounts, not the number of depositors. For comparative purposes, I equate the number of accounts with the number of depositors. The New England states boasted the greatest density of accounts. Half the population held a savings bank account in Massachusetts in 1900 (one per 1.9 people). Connecticut followed closely behind with one account per 2.3 people. Even in rural, sparsely populated New England states—notably Vermont and Maine— one in every 2.8 and 3.8 people, respectively, saved at the savings bank. Savings banks did not cover the Mid-Atlantic states as thoroughly, although 29 percent of residents of New York State possessed a savings account (one per 3.5 inhabitants).[15] These were levels of account holding on par with the thriftiest nations of Europe.

Who were the savers of nineteenth-century America? True to their original intent, savings banks drew heavily from the laboring classes. In the fast-growing manufacturing city of Newburyport, Massachusetts, unskilled workmen commonly had savings accounts. Of 410 laboring families in the 1870 census, 154 opened accounts in the local Institution for Savings. At the mammoth Philadelphia Saving Fund Society, working-class depositors constituted a substantial majority of the bank's customers. Of those adult males opening accounts in the 1850s and 1860s, 33 percent were skilled craftsmen and another 30 percent were semiskilled workers. Contrary to what we might expect, the rise of housing credit tended to encourage greater saving among workers. Because most nineteenth-century mortgages required repayment in a lump sum— rather than by installments—workers typically used savings banks to accumulate sizable sums toward the purchase of homes. In the United States overall, an estimated 37 percent of non–farm families owned homes by 1890. Of that cohort, 29 percent carried a mortgage, while the rest had either paid in full or repaid mortgages.[16]

Savings banks stimulated thrift among the urban middle classes as well. While many middle-class households availed themselves of other financial institutions, savings banks offered greater security, attractive returns, and tax benefits in some states. At the Philadelphia Saving Fund Society, professionals and businessmen constituted 17 percent of male depositors during the 1850s and 1860s, well above their share of the city's population. Middle-class and affluent depositors often kept large balances. States occasionally attempted to enforce caps on deposits, but it proved difficult to stop prosperous customers from opening accounts in fictitious names or at other savings banks.[17]

In popular literature, thrift infused the American myth of the self-made man. Samuel Smiles enjoyed less influence in the United States than in Europe or East Asia, perhaps because he disassociated his successful men from ruthless competition and moneymaking. Far more appealing to Americans were Horatio Alger's best sellers about poor boys who clawed their way to the middle. *Ragged Dick* (1868) tells the story of a young bootblack determined to rise but beset by those who wish to keep him down. Applying for a job as errand boy in a fashionable store, Dick encounters several rivals, including "a rather supercilious-looking young gentleman, genteelly dressed," who sneers at our hero,

> "I've seen you before."
> "Oh, have you?" said Dick, whirling round; "then p'r'aps you'd like to see me behind."

But it's more than pluck or luck that enables Dick eventually to become a clerk. Like Samuel Smiles's characters, he begins his climb only after opening a savings bank account, giving up his entertainments in the Bowery, and saving more than $100. Whenever he reflected upon his new bank book, "it was wonderful how much more independent he felt" and "with what an important air of joint ownership he regarded the bank building in which his small savings were deposited."[18]

The virtues of saving became apparent to many American women as well. At the Philadelphia Saving Fund Society, females comprised roughly half of all new account holders throughout the nineteenth century. From the start, savings banks like the Provident Institution for Saving in Boston welcomed "young women, who may expect to change their condition."[19] As in Europe, female domestic servants constituted one of the largest groups of depositors in the early savings banks. They opened nearly one-quarter of the new accounts at the Philadelphia savings bank in 1850. Men and women apparently saved in different ways. Whereas men typically held their accounts for a few short years with the goal of saving to acquire property, women methodically accumulated large nest eggs over many years. Limited in their ability to acquire property, obtain insurance, or borrow money, working women embraced savings banks to safeguard themselves against emergencies and the perils of old age.

The nineteenth century was also a time when married middle-class women, like their English sisters, became associated with management of the "domestic economy." In her popular guide, *The American Frugal Housewife* (1829), Lydia Child advised young wives to "keep an exact account of all you expend." Budgeting would discipline spending and enable "your husband to judge precisely whether his family live within his income."[20] By the late nineteenth century, wives were regularly exhorted to keep household accounts to advance "planning" and "rationalization" in the home. Housewives' magazines, notably the *Ladies Home Journal* (established 1883), propagated the new norm of woman as the family's financial watchdog. Increasingly they featured stories of housewives who assisted in saving money. In 1903 *Ladies Home Journal* ran the popular series, "How We Saved for Our Home."[21] As in England, common law had prevented wives from holding assets independently of their husbands. From the 1830s, however, savings banks quietly accepted deposits from married women. Midcentury state legislatures affirmed the separateness of wives' savings deposits by passing Married Women's Property Acts.[22]

Wives were expected to exercise a thrifty, sober influence over profligate husbands. In one magazine story from the 1850s, the young wife urges her husband (a bank employee, no less) to acquire the "habit of saving" so that they may build a house. "Women don't understand these things," Charles feebly replies, only to discover that she has diligently recorded every household expense in her "small account book." Charles, she reveals, has spent $300 beyond "our necessary expenses." The shamed husband learns to curb his spending on expensive "segars," ice creams, oysters, and sherry cobblers. She also gives him a circular from the People's Savings Bank, demonstrating how small sums accumulate when deposited regularly. Soon he's saving $100 each quarter, enough to buy and furnish a house in four years. Charles becomes one of thriftiest young men in the town, thanks to the "beneficent influence of the Savings Bank" and his "sweet accountant."[23]

The Unevenness of American Thrift

Frugal housewives, prudent workers, thrifty clerks, and savings banks. The central players in the global story of thrift all made their appearance in the United States. When Americans saved, they saved as few others. In 1910, aggregate deposits in the savings banks of America exceeded those in the savings banks and postal savings banks of every other country (table 3). Deposits in the savings banks of New York State *alone* surpassed those of every nation but Germany.[24]

These figures do not necessarily demonstrate that a sizable proportion of Americans were systematically saving money. But this hasn't stopped economic historians from asserting that personal saving rates in the United States around 1900 were "historically and comparatively high," based on examinations of national income and individual family budgets. Already in the mid-nineteenth century, concludes one study, depositors with active accounts at the Philadelphia Saving Fund Society saved an estimated 10 to 15 percent of income.[25] We must be wary, however, of relying on either microstudies or data on aggregate domestic savings to measure the savings habits of Americans nationwide. Growing assets of the commercial banks rested largely on the capital of shareholders, not the deposits of small savers. Microstudies necessarily limit themselves to people who had active savings bank accounts or maintained the discipline to keep family budgets. We learn not about saving in America, but about subcultures in which good savers were good savers.

What about the remarkably large majority of Americans who had *no* savings accounts? Table 3 reveals the exceptional state of American thrift. If we equate the number of accounts with the number of depositors, only 10 percent of Americans possessed a savings bank account in 1910. In stark contrast, 30 to 39 percent of the population had savings bank or postal savings accounts in Japan, Germany, France, Britain, Belgium, Sweden, and the Netherlands.

How could the wealthiest nation on earth be home to the lowest percentage of people with savings accounts among the major nations? The most compelling explanation is institutional. As late as 1910, most Americans lacked access to safe, convenient savings institutions

Table 3 Savings Banks (Including Postal Savings Banks) by Country, 1909–10

	Year	Accounts	Total Deposits (US$)	Average Account Balance (US$)	Accounts per Population (%)
Austria	1909–10	6,324,998	1,207,773,130	190.95	22.1
Australia	1909–10	1,483,573	258,496,304	174.24	33.1
Belgium	1910	2,808,549	186,180,990	66.29	37.4
Canada[a]	1910	184,907	57,411,249	310.49	2.5
France	1908–1909	13,491,251	1,026,712,474	76.10	34.3
Germany	1910	21,534,034	3,993,775,184	185.46	33.4
Italy	1910	7,421,235	786,921,337	106.04	21.5
Japan	1908–10	17,518,142	121,008,109	6.91	34.9
Netherlands	1909–10	1,943,242	107,758,077	55.45	32.7
Sweden	1909–10	2,115,804	228,923,251	108.20	38.6
Switzerland	1908	1,963,147	307,342,077	156.56	55.2
United Kingdom	1910	13,659,636	1,076,265,509	78.79	30.2
United States[b]	1910	9,192,908	4,070,486,246	442.79	10.2

[a] Includes only postal savings and Dominion government savings banks. Excludes special private savings banks ($32,156,708 in deposits) and the highly accessible chartered banks, in which a large percentage of Canadians held savings deposits totaling $534,432,054.

[b] Includes only mutual and stock savings banks.

Source: Adapted from United States, Office of the Comptroller of the Currency, *Annual Reports*, 1910–12.

that accepted small savings and offered attractive rates of return. They may have saved in the mattress or invested in land. Yet such modes of saving were either highly insecure or relatively illiquid when one faced pressing needs.[26] Nothing encourages popular saving, the European experience shows, more than the availability of reliable savings institutions.

The American history of thrift becomes extremely uneven as we move beyond the Northeastern states. The mutual (trustee) savings banks were heavily concentrated in New England and the Mid-Atlantic states. Those two regions were home to 617 of the nation's 638 mutual savings banks in 1910. The Midwest accounted for a few more (eight in Minnesota, five in Indiana, and three each in Ohio and Wisconsin). The rest of the country claimed the remaining *two* mutual savings banks. People outside the Northeast could and did save in other types of savings institutions. Yet these, too, were concentrated in certain regions. Joint-stock or "stock savings banks" widely appeared in the Midwest from the 1880s. Although stock savings banks distributed profits to shareholders, they functioned as savings banks inasmuch as they paid interest on small savings and invested funds more conservatively than commercial banks. Of the 1,121 stock savings banks reporting in 1910, most (734) were in the Midwest with an additional 156 in California, Oregon, and Washington State. Depositors were best served in agricultural Iowa, where an impressive 663 stock savings banks did business. By contrast, only 149 stock savings banks existed in the thirteen Southern states and a paltry 59 in the inland Western states.[27]

Building and loan associations offered Americans another venue for saving. Modeled on Britain's building societies, they also resembled credit and savings cooperatives found in Germany and other continental countries. First established in Pennsylvania around 1840, building and loan associations spread rapidly. By 1910 the federal government counted 5,737 associations and two million members. The building and loan associations enabled people to save in order to purchase a home. Members would pay regular dues into a pool, from which they as homebuyers could borrow at interest. As borrowers repaid their loans, the assets of the association grew. Building and loan associations evolved into permanent financial institutions, permitting easy membership and departure. Later known as savings and loan associations, they met the needs of small savers in areas less covered by the savings banks, especially in Pennsylvania, Ohio, Louisiana, and North Carolina. Nevertheless, like savings banks, these associations largely remained an urban phenomenon. They scarcely existed in most of the South and West in 1910.[28]

What about the thousands of commercial banks doing business in areas not served by savings banks or building and loan associations? The banking industry insisted that commercial banks encourage small saving. Many commercial banks, it is true, established savings departments during the late nineteenth and early twentieth centuries. In general, however, commercial banks remained poor substitutes for savings banks. "Bankers' hours" have become synonymous with a cushy job, but one hundred years ago the term was no joke to small savers. Commercial banks typically opened for business from 9:00 a.m. to 2:00 p.m., very inconvenient times for wage earners. Workers and farmers tended to distrust the banks, and for good reason. Between 1880 and 1910, a total of 361 federally regulated national banks and 1,649 state and private banks failed or suffered insolvency. Whereas the savings banks invested deposits conservatively, commercial banks often invested savings deposits in riskier ventures with higher returns. In Southern and Western states, observed a local banker in 1900, most commercial banks did not accept small sums at interest.[29] Speaking to a well-heeled gathering of the Minnesota State Banking Association, one prominent Chicago banker proudly admitted his disinterest in depositors of modest means: "the bank with which I am connected not only does not invite savings deposits but imposes a prohibitory charge upon all accounts which average less than $300 for the express purpose of *driving them away*."[30]

Surely, ordinary Americans had access to some type of savings institution? In fact, shockingly large numbers did not. We have only to read the National Monetary Commission's report of 1909. In the most comprehensive study of savings institutions to date, the commission surveyed all national, state, and private banks, plus savings banks and loan and trust companies. Within the continental United States, 57 percent of commercial banks reportedly accepted savings deposits. Furthermore, of the commercial banks that reported details on minimum deposits on which they offered interest, 33 percent paid no interest on accounts of $25 or less. Some 15 percent went out of their way to drive away small savers, for they paid interest only on deposits exceeding the hefty sum of $500.[31]

Nothing reveals the unevenness of saving in America more than the National Monetary Commission's breakdown of savings depositors by state and region (table 4). Significant portions of the populace saved money in banks in the Northeast, the Midwest, and on the Pacific Coast. In the South and inland West, on the other hand, astonishingly few people possessed savings accounts. If we include *all* banks carrying savings accounts in 1909, the percentage of savings depositors (accounts) in the population ran as high as 53.5 percent in the New England states.

Table 4 Savings Accounts in Savings Banks and Other Banks by Region and State, U.S., 1909

Region and State	Savings Banks			All Banks Carrying Savings Accounts[a]			Accounts per Population (%)
	Number	Savings Accounts	Total Deposits (US$1,000s)	Number	Savings Accounts	Total Deposits (US$1,000s)	
NEW ENGLAND	413	3,178,040	1,258,180	650	3,504,482	1,392,171	53.5
Maine	51	226,166	87,410	131	322,687	118,779	43.5
New Hampshire	51	174,341	77,693	72	197,757	84,060	45.9
Vermont	21	104,620	39,471	74	178,585	65,894	50.2
Massachusetts	187	2,002,010	728,497	244	2,049,137	747,150	60.9
Rhode Island	18	130,231	69,298	31	192,415	116,570	35.5
Connecticut	85	540,672	255,811	98	553,901	259,718	49.7
MID-ATLANTIC	233	3,843,048	1,778,322	1,971	5,620,477	2,480,274	26.6
New York	137	2,760,343	1,405,240	551	3,238,890	1,595,040	35.5
New Jersey	27	297,200	98,131	245	641,868	208,548	25.3
Pennsylvania	11	452,487	166,095	967	1,270,023	520,489	16.6
Delaware	2	25,380	9,135	29	35,668	11,628	17.6
Maryland	44	243,569	88,425	162	346,317	125,677	26.7
District of Columbia	12	54,069	11,296	17	87,711	18,893	26.5
MIDWEST	548	815,877	277,853	3,980	3,781,262	1,123,044	14.6
Ohio	41	295,222	97,854	523	861,516	274,282	18.1
Indiana	5	32,039	10,975	333	271,221	68,885	10.0

Illinois	—	—	—	663	821,203	258,315	14.6
Michigan	14	74,178	30,490	443	606,989	174,438	21.6
Wisconsin	3	6,249	1,145	396	324,965	79,027	13.9
Minnesota	11	92,544	21,770	461	257,267	64,937	12.4
Iowa	474	315,645	115,619	841	419,546	153,980	18.9
Missouri	—	—	—	320	218,555	49,181	6.6
SOUTH	154	280,388	66,843	1,907	883,325	223,254	3.4
Virginia	20	32,212	9,257	135	126,867	43,119	6.2
West Virginia	10	28,681	5,652	155	91,628	23,454	7.5
No. Carolina	21	37,967	6,231	235	103,744	18,201	4.7
So. Carolina	22	27,129	8,502	159	66,553	18,701	4.4
Georgia	16	31,953	7,117	250	99,236	19,816	3.8
Florida	4	6,295	955	97	38,380	8,573	5.1
Alabama	7	12,271	1,861	95	50,725	7,811	2.4
Louisiana	8	46,474	12,540	113	80,733	21,356	4.9
Texas	—	—	—	127	34,484	9,158	0.9
Arkansas	4	2,406	534	85	14,187	2,933	0.9
Kentucky	9	9,368	1,080	183	59,594	21,374	2.6
Tennessee	21	37,992	11,111	148	85,643	21,327	3.9
Mississippi	12	7,640	2,003	125	31,551	7,432	1.8

(continued)

Table 4 *Continued*

| Region and State | Savings Banks | | | All Banks Carrying Savings Accounts[a] | | | Accounts per Population (%) |
	Number	Savings Accounts	Total Deposits (US$1,000s)	Number	Savings Accounts	Total Deposits (US$1,000s)	
WEST	56	86,140	21,814	1,853	385,314	123,801	4.6
North Dakota	—	—	—	259	23,774	13,006	4.1
South Dakota	10	3,024	684	256	43,012	13,073	7.4
Nebraska	11	16,846	2,618	355	67,673	24,177	5.7
Kansas	13	16,031	2,836	379	61,220	14,936	3.6
Montana	3	4,067	3,368	58	21,076	9,772	5.6
Wyoming	—	—	—	43	6,819	2,387	4.7
Colorado	8	14,185	3,193	93	62,804	20,087	7.9
New Mexico	4	1,575	415	37	3,930	1,747	1.2
Oklahoma	—	—	—	194	10,507	2,475	0.6

Idaho	4	1,217	160	75	11,263	1,972	3.5
Utah	3	29,195	8,540	71	63,901	16,503	17.1
Nevada	—	—	—	19	4,657	2,400	5.7
Arizona	—	—	—	14	4,678	1,266	2.3
PACIFIC COAST	136	413,720	230,927	621	698,501	331,315	16.7
Washington	8	12,355	3,793	184	135,729	35,045	11.9
Oregon	6	3,339	1,011	78	37,284	15,042	5.5
California	122	398,026	226,123	359	525,488	281,228	22.1
U.S. TOTAL[b]	1,540	8,617,213	3,633,939	10,982	14,873,361	5,673,861	16.2

[a] The National Monetary Commission stated that what constitutes "savings deposits" was "not carefully considered by the bank officials in all instances, as certificates of deposit, both time and demand, appear to have been included in savings deposits."

[b] Excludes Alaska and island possessions.

Sources: Adapted from National Monetary Commission, *Special Report from the Banks of the United States*, April 28, 1909, pp. 44-46, 54-56; E. W. Kemmerer, "The United States Postal Savings Bank," *Political Science Quarterly* 26, no. 3 (September 1911): 468-71. U.S. Bureau of the Census, *Thirteenth Census of the United States*, 1910 (Washington, DC: Government Printing Office, 1912).

Massachusetts topped the charts at 60.9 percent. In the Mid-Atlantic states, accounts amounted to 26.6 percent of the population. At 14.6 percent, inhabitants of the Midwestern states apparently had less, but nonetheless significant, access to savings institutions. The same could be said for those in the three Pacific Coast states (16.7 percent). In stark contrast, only 3.4 and 4.6 percent held savings accounts in the thirteen Southern states and thirteen Western states, respectively. In Texas, the percentage of accounts stood at a mere 0.9 percent of the population. Incredibly, more than 99 percent of Texans lacked a savings account in 1909.

The figures cast doubt on commercial bankers' claims to have promoted popular thrift effectively. Bankers drew selectively on the National Monetary Commission's survey to assert that if savings accounts in all banks—not simply savings banks—were included, the total number of American savings depositors would rise to roughly 16 percent of the population. If we added in members of the building and loan associations, the total might rise another 2 percent. Such calibrations, however, distort meaningful comparisons with other countries, several of whose savings figures would also rise substantially if depositors in cooperative banks and commercial banks were included.

How do we explain the unevenness of institutional thrift in America? Many at the time invoked the presence or absence of Puritanism, akin to Max Weber's theory of the Protestant Ethic. According to the contemporary expert James Henry Hamilton, mutual savings banks thrived in New England thanks to its "stern, Puritan sense of simple living, industry and providence."[32] Yet Puritanism alone cannot explain why savings institutions sprang up in some places but not in others. For instance, mutual savings banks also flourished in predominantly non-Calvinist cities like New York, Philadelphia, and Baltimore. And by the turn of the twentieth century, large numbers of depositors in Northeast savings banks were Catholic immigrants.[33]

We would do better to consider transatlantic influences, conceptions of community, and socioeconomic structure. The English model of philanthropic trustees directly inspired the formation of savings banks in the Northeast. Although religion played a role, the founders of savings banks strove to create secular institutions to ameliorate pov-

erty. Underlying the trustees' mission was the vision of modern citizenship by which upper classes felt obligated to improve the habits of the
community's poorer members. Transatlantic norms likewise shaped the
establishment of savings institutions in Midwestern and Mid-Atlantic
states. Building and loan associations, Hamilton observed, were heavily concentrated in areas of Ohio and Pennsylvania where German-
Americans drew on the model of cooperative banks from the old
country. Urbanization and industrialization constituted another set of
factors. Savings banks did well in some agricultural areas—notably
northern New England and Iowa—but generally they were located in
cities and manufacturing centers where wage earners congregated.[34]

Conversely, how do we explain the glaring weakness of institutional thrift in the South and West during the early twentieth century?
Both regions lacked the levels of urbanization and industrialization
conducive to savings institutions elsewhere. Because Southern commercial banks catered overwhelmingly to business concerns in the large
retail and wholesale centers, entire counties in some states had "no
banking facilities of any kind," remarked Hamilton. In addition, most
Southern and Western states failed to enact laws that would effectively
regulate savings institutions and protect depositors. In the sparsely
populated Western states, huge distances further impeded the development of banks serving small savers.[35] The South was of course much
poorer and less industrialized than the North, and in parts more moun-
tainous. Nonetheless, large percentages of poor peasants managed to
save in many European countries, and mountains did not stop thrifty
villagers in Switzerland or Japan from making deposits. Nor did the
South want for potential depositors. In 1910 fully 28 percent of the nation lived in the thirteen Southern states.

Viewed comparatively, the weakness of Southern thrift reflects the
upper class's indifference to establishing institutions aimed at improving conditions of the general populace.[36] Unlike counterparts in the
Northern states or Europe, few Southern elites stepped forward to organize savings banks. Their disinterest in moral uplift was bound up with
the distinctive politics of race and class governing the South in the
decades following the Civil War. Southern elites felt little obligation
to help fellow citizens, especially when so many of these citizens were

freedmen—former slaves freed by the federally imposed Reconstruction after 1865. In 1900 African Americans comprised 32 percent of the Southern population; in Mississippi and South Carolina they formed more than half the population. The sharecropping system, which re-placed slavery, left black farmers with little money that might be saved. Moreover, white planters seldom volunteered to serve as trustees of savings banks for blacks, judged Hamilton, because of their "unfortu-nate prejudices and suspicions."[37] Southern states proceeded to strip African Americans of citizenship itself, beginning with disenfranchise-ment and severe cutbacks in schooling.

Southern elites were not much more inclined to help poor *whites* help themselves. The region's tiny percentage of savings accounts high-lights that the vast majority of whites did not save, either. In the North and in Europe, mass education and savings institutions typically de-veloped together as "public" projects to create a modern citizenry. By reverse logic, the paucity of savings banks in Southern states appears closely associated with rudimentary public education and minimal pub-lic services. In 1900, when all but two states in the rest of the nation had adopted compulsory education, Kentucky—a border state—was the only Southern state to have done so.

In some respects, the unevenness of thrift in America was *not* ex-ceptional. Hadn't this also been the story in England, France, and Italy, where local savings banks served cities while often neglecting the countryside? Indeed, spotty coverage in Europe had been the single most important reason for state intervention in the form of postal sav-ings systems. American reformers would propose a similar solution, yet the outcome would be very different.

Learning from the "Civilized World"

Constrained by a constitutional structure emphasizing states' rights, the federal government generally lacked the centralized authority under which European nation-states organized thrift. Prior to the 1870s, the U.S. government made only one effort to encourage thrift on anything approaching a national basis. This initiative targeted not the masses of working people or farmers, but rather one racial group. As Union victory in the Civil War loomed, a group of Northern businessmen and abolitionists met to plan the establishment of a savings bank for Negro soldiers and freed slaves. In March 1865 Congress voted to charter the Freedman's Savings Bank. The bank soon dubbed itself a "national savings bank," resting on an interstate network of branches. By 1870 thirty-seven branches operated throughout the South, as well as in New York and other Mid-Atlantic cities with large African American populations.

Unlike European national savings banks, the Freedman's Savings Bank was neither owned nor managed by the central government. Nonetheless, the bank's trustees took advantage of a unique moment in U.S. history when the federal government exercised unprecedented powers vis-à-vis the defeated Southern states under the Reconstruction authority. The Freedman's Savings Bank operated much as a federal agency. In the South, the Freedman's Savings Bank worked closely with the federal government's Freedmen's Bureau, which provided financial support and sometimes personnel to the bank's branches. Pamphleteers promoted the Freedman's Savings Bank as "Abraham Lincoln's Gift to the Colored People.... He gave *Emancipation*, and then this Savings Bank."[38]

Trustees of the Freedman's Savings Bank applied the lessons of savings banks elsewhere to the uplift of newly freed slaves. The bank's missionaries taught the habits of saving to enable freedmen to acquire property, withstand the hostility of Southern whites, and avoid depending on poor relief. In the words of the abolitionist Rev. John W. Alvord, "Pauperism can be brought to a close.... That which savings banks have done for the working men of the north it is presumed they are capable of doing for these laborers."[39] To teach by example, the bank officials employed a large number of educated African Americans as cashiers and placed many others on the branches' advisory committees. The number of open accounts rose rapidly from 23,000 in 1870 to 61,000 in 1874. Touted as testimony to the "prudent thrift" of the "colored people," the bank had become a national institution—symbolized in 1871 by the construction of its four-story headquarters facing the U.S. Treasury.

Praise for the Freedman's Savings Bank proved short-lived. In 1874 the bank closed its doors forever. The institution had fallen victim to several problems—including overextension of the branches, weak central supervision, and high operating costs. Worst of all, a handful of trustees had assumed control over investment policy. Departing from the bank's original mandate to invest deposits in government securities, they made risky loans to cronies and speculators. The financial Panic of 1873 precipitated the bank's demise. Although a government-appointed commission oversaw the partial reimbursement of depositors over a nine-year period, the majority of depositors lost their entire savings.

The collapse of the Freedman's Savings Bank profoundly influenced the history of American thrift. The bank's failure dealt a devastating blow to the cause of savings promotion in the South. Few wealthy Southern whites had been enthusiastic about the Freedman's Savings Bank in its heyday, and even fewer stepped in to support new savings banks for freedmen once the externally imposed institution failed. African Americans, for their part, became wary of entrusting money to savings banks and banks in general. The failure of the Freedman's Savings Bank "not only ruined thousands of colored men, but taught to thousands more a lesson of distrust which it will take them years to unlearn," observed sympathetic charity workers in New York.[40]

In addition, the fiasco fueled a raging debate about federal activism in the encouragement of saving. To American bankers who opposed the introduction of a European-style postal savings bank, the failure of the Freedman's Savings Bank was evidence of the folly of government intervention.[41] Others drew the opposite conclusion. The ill-fated institution, observed New York's *The Independent* in 1874, was never truly a national savings bank, but merely a trustee savings bank. Had it been a government-guaranteed postal savings bank, "not a dollar would have been lost to the depositors."[42]

The Freedman's Savings Bank soared and crashed just as Americans began debating the merits of a nationwide postal savings system. If the Freedman's Savings Bank were a peculiarly American story revolving around the abolition of slavery, the question of postal savings was very much part of global history. Cosmopolitan Americans became interested in Britain's innovative Post Office Savings Bank within months of its creation in 1861. Detailed accounts appeared in American newspapers throughout the decade.[43]

Officials in the U.S. Post Office Department took the lead in lobbying for the enactment of a postal savings law. Postal authorities were ideally suited to this task. Within the federal government, the Post Office was uniquely national and international. Administering thousands of post offices in every state, the Post Office Department functioned as the one truly nationwide civil bureaucracy in an otherwise decentralized polity. Moreover, at a time when American officials rarely investigated conditions abroad, the U.S. Post Office actively gathered information about other nations as part of the growing internationalization of postal services. In December 1861 the postmaster of Pittsburgh learned of the Post Office Savings Bank from an English immigrant. He forwarded the British materials to his superiors in Washington with the strong recommendation that a similar system be adopted in the United States. A few months later, to "bring our postal system up to the English and French standard of excellence," Postmaster-General Montgomery Blair dispatched John A. Kasson to investigate European postal systems and attend the European Postal Convention in Paris. Acting on Kasson's report, the U.S. Post Office introduced a nationwide money order system in 1864. Three years later, according to the *New York Times*, "the great success which has attended our experiment of postal money orders, copied after the English system" persuaded influential Americans that the Post Office was capable of adopting other British postal services—first and foremost, postal savings banks.[44]

As European parliaments considered postal savings systems during the 1870s and 1880s, so too did the U.S. Congress. The staff of Postmaster-General John A. J. Creswell drafted the first such legislation, which Congressman Horace Maynard introduced in 1873. Citing the popularity of post office savings banks in Britain, the Australian colonies, and Canada, the postmaster-general championed government-guaranteed postal savings in terms heard throughout the English-speaking world. Creswell's "postal savings depositories" would accomplish "perfect security" and the "utmost facilities for deposits, withdrawals, and transfers." The system would "encourage economy and habits of saving" of all who earned small sums of money—particularly among the "industrial classes ... in time merging the workman into the capitalist." Every postal depositor would gain a "direct interest in the stability of the Government"—a vital consideration in the aftermath of the Civil War. Other proponents similarly related the inculcation of savings habits to "better citizenship," repeating the British refrain that depositors in government banks acquire a "stake in the country." In addition, Creswell highlighted the financial advantages of secure postal savings banks in attracting new deposits that would circulate throughout the economy. Foremost on his mind was the recent Panic of 1873 in which large numbers of banks failed. The postmaster-general blamed the panic on the national money shortage resulting from massive hoarding as depositors withdrew their savings from the banks.[45]

From the start, one argument distinguished the American proponents from their British counterparts. Whereas the British founded the Post Office Savings Bank primarily to encourage popular thrift, American supporters openly promoted postal savings as a means of financing the federal government. During the late 1870s, several postal savings bills featured in their titles the objective of refunding the national debt. The U.S. government at the time suffered high levels of indebtedness as the result of the Civil War.[46]

Confronting deep-seated notions of laissez-faire in the United States, advocates for postal savings vigorously defended the need for government intervention. Congressman Edward Lacey declared in 1882: "private enterprise alone does not, and cannot, in this respect, meet the necessities of the industrious poor in any country, and least of all in the United States."[47] Officials marshaled evidence to demonstrate the lack of savings banks outside the Northeast, Midwest, and a few Western states. During the early 1890s, Postmaster-General John Wanamaker, the philanthropic Philadelphia businessman, forcefully advocated postal savings banks because private savings banks were not serving the large mass of wage earners outside of the large cities. In "one portion of the country containing twelve millions of population," he remarked alluding to the South, "there are not as many places of deposit for the saving of small sums as exist in a single city of 80,000 people in a New England State." Even in the big cities, he observed, most banks offered working people inconvenient hours and did not "care to deal with small sums." Wanamaker could discern no reasonable objections to the adoption of postal savings banks, for Americans had the "experience of nearly the whole civilized world" from which to learn.[48]

The frequent invocation of the "civilized world" suggests this was more than a debate over postal savings. The United States confronted the same challenges as European nations in dealing with the problems of industrial society, agrarian dislocation, and regional disparities. Although some Americans placed their faith in homegrown solutions, others systematically studied foreign models.[49] The U.S. government gathered data about postal savings systems in more than a score of countries—including Britain and her dominions, Italy, the Netherlands, Belgium, France, and Japan. On three occasions between 1881 and 1907, the secretary of state also received detailed reports from consular officials charged with investigating postal savings systems in their host countries.[50]

The champions of postal savings unapologetically portrayed their country as the laggard among civilized countries. The American people "know how to make money, but not how to save it," declared Postmaster-General James A. Gary in 1897. In Europe, he continued, postal savings banks taught millions how to save from the time they were children. The Japanese postal savings system, too, was singled out for remarkable growth since its creation in 1875. By the late 1890s congressional committees reported that the United States and Germany were the only two major nations that had not adopted postal savings. Yet in the German case, they recognized, the ubiquitous municipal savings banks promoted small saving so effectively as to render a national savings bank unnecessary.

Neighboring Canada loomed large. Post office savings banks dotted the vast reaches of the western provinces, and farmers constituted the largest single group of postal depositors. Proponents drew on the Canadian example to refute the exceptionalist arguments of critics who insisted the United States was too large to sustain the postal savings services found in compact European nations. Postmaster-General Gary minced no words about how the United States ranked against other sparsely populated lands: "While the frontier settlements of Finland, Algiers, South Africa, India, Ceylon, South and West Australia, Tasmania, New Zealand, Hawaii, and British Columbia are enjoying the blessings of banks of exchange and of interest-paying [postal] depositories, private enterprise in this country has left the people of many old communities, and in a few cases of almost entire States, without any facilities whereby they may protect and invest their hard-earned savings."[51]

Historians of the United States commonly depict the supporters of postal savings legislation as conservative because most congressional backers were affiliated with the business-oriented Republican Party.[52] From a comparative perspective, however, American advocates more closely resembled the midcentury *liberals* who established postal savings in Western Europe. On both sides of the Atlantic, proponents sought to fashion nations composed of thrifty, productive, and self-reliant citizens. Similarly the American champions of postal savings belonged to a broader alliance of Republican politicians and reformers who—in the wake of the Civil War—favored the creation of national institutions that would overcome sectional divides and ameliorate social problems. In 1871, for instance, the Post Office Department proposed to establish not only postal savings banks, but also a nationwide network of postal telegraph lines as in Britain.[53]

Postal savings appealed as well to influential thinkers and social workers known as "progressives." In 1884 the State Charities Aid Association of New York began lobbying Congress for such legislation. This soon led to a nationwide effort among charitable organizations. Seeking to aid the poorer classes in forming "habits of saving and thrift," the New York association argued that bank failures and lack of access to the existing savings banks discouraged the very poor from saving. Charity workers noted the success of postal savings systems in Britain, Japan, and a host of European nations.[54] At the dawn of the twentieth century, proponents included the most famous social reformers of the time. Jane Addams, founder of the Hull-House settlement in the Chicago slums, campaigned for postal banks as a "boon to the poor." Having established a branch post office in Hull-House to help neighbors send money orders back to Europe, she witnessed "one perplexed immigrant after another turning away in bewilderment when he was told that the United States post office did not receive savings."[55]

The cause was further advanced by a number of political economists and social policy specialists within American universities. A rising generation of academic progressives studied in Britain, Germany, and other European countries, where they were captivated by critiques of laissez-faire and the case for state intervention. In 1902 sociology professor James Henry Hamilton published *Savings and Savings Institutions*, an influential analysis of foreign savings institutions and their application to the United States. Condemning his country's "voluntary system" of savings banks for not reaching the "most improvident classes" and "backward" sections, Hamilton recommended postal savings banks as the most effective solution.[56]

At the level of mass politics, too, postal savings legislation enjoyed considerable popularity. In 1897 the daily *Chicago Record* mounted a nationwide petition drive that gathered 662,257 signatures. Two other national petitions each garnered more than 100,000 names. Popular support tended to be strongest in those regions inadequately served by savings institutions—the Midwest, West, Pacific Coast, and to a lesser extent the South. The burgeoning social movements took center stage in agitation for a government-guaranteed national savings bank. Beginning in the 1880s, nascent labor unions led by the Knights of Labor supported the adoption of postal savings banks to encourage workers to save for emergencies and strikes. The American Federation of Labor in 1905 likewise campaigned for enactment, recognizing the "well-known fact" that postal savings banks in foreign countries benefited all the people.[57]

America's farmers formed the most potent mass lobby for postal savings. This may seem odd. Historians tell the story of agrarian protest in terms of debt, not saving. Beset by falling crop prices, farmers in the Midwest and South organized a series of political movements between the 1870s and 1890s. These culminated in the formation of the People's Party or Populists. While demanding governmental solutions to rising indebtedness, farmers' organizations also campaigned for the federal protection of small savings. In 1892 the People's Party platform urged the establishment of postal savings banks. Populist members in Congress introduced six such bills, albeit with an agrarian twist. Populists detested the commercial banks for starving farmers of credit. The farmers' movement thus proposed a postal savings system that not only accepted and secured deposits but also loaned funds to cultivators at the same low interest rate of 2.5 percent.[58]

When Postmaster-General Creswell first proposed postal savings banks in the early 1870s, he posed the following rhetorical question. Considering the experiences of postal savings banks in the English-speaking world, "how can the success of similar institutions in the United States be doubtful?"[59] As it turned out, the grounds for doubt were ample. From 1873 to 1908, some ninety postal savings bills were introduced to Congress. *Not one* would be reported out of committee, despite support by four presidents and nine postmasters-general. Asked one Senate committee in 1898, "Shall we wait fifty years, or one hundred years, or one thousand years, until countless generations are born and dead, until private capital will see fit to establish a sufficient number of savings banks conveniently located to the people?"[60]

Postal Savings in America: A Most Forgettable Story

To explain America's exceptional resistance to postal savings is to confront much of what made the United States different from most other modern societies. We begin with the singular power of American private capital. Most other nations adopted postal savings systems when commercial banking was weak. Moreover, postal savings legislation in Europe encountered little opposition from the savings banks, which in Britain and France had themselves become quasi-governmental institutions required to deposit all their funds in the national treasury.

In the United States, commercial banks became a forceful presence in the economy by the 1870s. Throughout the four decades of debate, commercial and savings bankers allied to oppose postal savings legislation. The American Bankers Association went on the offensive soon after its formation in 1875. In 1907 the association set up a Postal Savings Committee, which rallied regional, state, and local bankers asso-

ciations against the administration's renewed efforts to enact legislation. In cities and towns across America, businessmen who depended
on the kindness of bankers pressured congressmen to vote no. Testify-
ing before Congress, the American Bankers Association's Lucius Teeter
disputed the need for postal savings banks on the grounds that 18,245
banks were already "doing a savings business." This figure was greatly
exaggerated, as we have seen.[61]

Bankers blasted proponents of postal savings for seeking to introduce European-style "paternal government." Unimpressed by global
trends, George Gibson in 1877 retorted that just because "England
receives and guarantees deposits or issues [postal] insurance policies—
because some Continental nations own and control railroads—it does
not follow as a logical sequence that we, with a different social and
political system, should follow their example."[62] Speaking to the Wyoming Bankers Convention, the banker E. R. Gurney accused the advocates of postal savings of forcing the government to abandon protection of the individual and instead "plunge into the frightful slough
of socialism."[63]

Postal savings legislation also ran up against Americans' reverence
for localism. Opponents warned that a mammoth national savings bank
would transform the federal government into another European centralized state. Aware that European governments had drawn on ever-
increasing postal deposits to finance ambitious national projects, critics
warned that postal savings would drain rural communities of desperately needed capital. Bankers opposed federal plans to invest the deposits in government securities, insisting the banks best served popular
needs by loaning money to local businesses. As the United States rapidly retired national debt in the late nineteenth century, bankers further argued that the government would have no place to invest postal
deposits because the United States—unlike European nations—lacked
a permanent national debt.

The bankers' attacks forced the federal government to make an
extraordinary concession in 1890. Funds saved at post offices would
not be forwarded to Washington; rather they would be deposited in
the national (commercial) banks located within that state. No other
postal savings system so decentralized the investment of deposits. Among

opponents and advocates alike, commented one contemporary economist, the desirability of keeping "the money at home" became "almost a fetish."[64] Populist agrarians, for their part, charged that the Republican Party's legislation would end up transferring the people's savings to Wall Street and the "rich bankers of New York."[65]

These suspicions bottled up postal savings legislation for decades. In 1910 Congress finally voted to establish postal savings depositories. The financial Panic of 1907 was critical in breaking the impasse. Banks failed in large numbers. Promising to protect worried depositors, both of the major parties endorsed postal savings legislation in their 1908 platforms. William Howard Taft, who handily won election that year, lobbied for postal savings as had no previous president. Though best remembered for his corpulence, Taft fit the mold of the cosmopolitan statesman who believed America should "look abroad frequently to learn lessons" in finance and administration. At the Wisconsin State Fair, he reeled off the names of some twenty nations and territories that already enjoyed the benefits of postal savings. Taft was uniquely familiar with postal savings banks, having himself set one up in 1906. As governor-general of the Philippines, he commissioned Princeton economist Edwin W. Kemmerer to devise a postal savings bank for America's recent acquisition.[66]

What clinched the passage of postal savings was the new focus on immigrant depositors. Immigrants poured into turn-of-the-century America. For all the nativist hoopla about Protestant thrift, immigrants—great numbers of whom were Catholic, Jewish, and Japanese—generally saved higher percentages of their income than native-born Americans. Therein lay a problem, which the proponents of postal savings cleverly exploited. As Postmaster-General George von L. Meyer explained to Congress, immigrants sent much of their savings back to the old country rather than depositing in America's banks. Banks often discouraged deposits by the foreign-born. And immigrants tended to distrust the banks because of recurrent fraud and failures—particularly among the poorly regulated immigrant banks. In 1907, reported the postmaster-general, residents sent postal money orders abroad totaling $90 million, of which $20 million went to Italy, $15 million to the Austro-Hungarian Empire, nearly $9 million to Russia, and $4.5 million to Japan. Immigrants were said to have deposited substantial amounts of this money in the secure postal savings systems back home because the United States lacked government savings banks. If, reasoned Meyer, "we had postal savings banks, with the workings of which they are familiar, a great deal of this money would remain in the country and be led back into the channels of trade." As evidence, supporters observed that foreigners sometimes purchased postal money orders payable to themselves, just to secure a government guarantee for their earnings.[67]

Not everyone accepted this logic. Scoffed one savings banker before Congress, "what we need, gentlemen, is to Americanize our immigrants, not to *Italianize* our Post-Office Department."[68] Yet to many of the legislation's supporters, postal savings made sense as an institution primarily for "foreigners." President Taft himself assured bankers that the postal savings depositories would offer no competition. Besides attracting foreigners' money "secreted in stockings and mattresses," postal savings would appeal "only to those timid persons who are afraid to trust the ordinary banks and who would rather get the 2 per cent. or less interest than to place the money in the regular savings banks, where it would draw from 3 to 4 per cent."[69] Once in effect, postal savings became widely known as the bank for "provident, ignorant, timid foreigners," in which "no intelligent American will deposit under present restrictions."[70]

Ultimately, America's restrictive system of postal savings bore little resemblance to the postal savings banks of other countries.[71] The act of 1910 reflected years of compromises in the face of relentless opposition from bankers and others. During its fifty-five years of operation, rarely did the U.S. government employ the post offices to promote saving on a truly nationwide basis. In Europe, state officials had ample incentives to expand postal savings among the populace. Not only did those systems create self-reliant citizens, but the pooled deposits financed an array of national projects. By contrast, the decentralized postal savings system in the United States kept the money in the locales and out of the hands of government. The law required only 5 percent of deposits to be forwarded to Washington to constitute a reserve. As for the remainder, each postmaster was instructed to deposit the funds in banks located in that city, town, or village, or—should a qualified bank not exist—in a bank in the nearest locality. Because the receiving bank paid a below-market interest rate of 2.5 percent on the deposits, many banks reaped huge profits from the legislation they had so fervently opposed. Washington seldom invested substantial portions of postal savings in government bonds. Such investment occurred briefly at the end of World War I, during World War II, and in the mid-1930s to refinance Liberty Bonds from World War I.

From the depositor's perspective, legislators had crafted a singularly unattractive system of postal savings. The interest rate was set at 2 percent, the lowest of any postal savings bank in the world, and well below rates offered by private savings banks. Because postal savings paid no interest on deposits held less than *one year*, the effective rate of interest was estimated at just over 1 percent. Nor for most of its life did postal savings offer the mobile American population one of the chief selling points elsewhere: the opportunity to draw upon (or deposit into) one's account at another post office. In terms of access, the federal government severely limited the number of postal savings branches, and it would not permit letter carriers to handle deposits and withdrawals—a common feature in other nations. Excepting the first few years when fourth-class post offices accepted postal savings, only seven or eight thousand post offices offered savings services from 1916 to 1967. France operated roughly the same number of branches and Britain nearly twice as many, notwithstanding their smaller populations and compact sizes. To those who expected the government to encourage thrift nationwide, the paucity of postal savings in the countryside must have been the greatest disappointment. The U.S. Post Office abandoned the rural South without a fight.

Small wonder that few Americans ever banked at the post office. The Taft Administration sold postal savings as a bank for the "timid" and the foreigner, and that's just what they got. In 1916 the foreign-born accounted for 60 percent of all postal depositors and roughly three-quarters of total deposits. As a percentage of total postal deposits at the end of fiscal year 1915, those born in Russia led the way (21 percent) followed by depositors born in Italy (14 percent), Britain and Austria (9 percent each), and Hungary and Germany (4 percent each). Most depositors lived in big cities or in Midwestern and Western mining and lumbering towns where immigrant laborers clustered. Relative to postal savings in Europe and Japan, the number of depositors in the United States grew slowly during the 1910s and 1920s. However, the banking crisis of the early Depression years prompted many native-born Americans to seek the safety of the postal savings banks. The number of depositors rose from a mere 466,401 in 1930 to 2,816,408 in 1940. These trends continued during World War II, as soaring wages, patriotic appeals, and postal savings for military personnel swelled the numbers to 4,196,517 in 1947.

Thereafter postal savings declined for several reasons—the most important being widespread access to safe private banks resulting from the expansion of the Federal Deposit Insurance Corporation (established 1934). At its peak, the U.S. postal savings system had far fewer depositors than either the French, British, Japanese, or Italian postal savings banks had had *forty years earlier*. By the early 1950s, postal savings was widely believed to have outlived its usefulness. Supported by the administration, Congress abolished the postal savings system in 1966. The last deposits were liquidated in 1970. Few mourned its passing. It is a rare American who remembers that postal savings banks ever existed.

The School Savings Movement

On the other hand, quite a few Americans recall saving their pennies and nickels in the schoolroom. Here, too, the United States took part in the global history of thrift, but with all the unevenness that marked other organized efforts to encourage the populace to save. America's school thrift programs did not spring up spontaneously in the bastions of traditional Puritan frugality. School savings banks developed rather late in this country, modeled directly on innovations in Belgium and France. The prime movers were rarely hind-bound conservatives, but typically cosmopolitan philanthropists and academic progressives who sought to emulate the Europeans' encouragement of saving through mass education. In 1876 the superintendent of the Beloit, Wisconsin, schools introduced the first known school savings bank in America after learning of Belgium's Ghent system at the Vienna Exposition three years earlier.

The most impassioned champion of saving for schoolchildren was—appropriately—a former teacher from Belgium, John H. (Jean Henri) Thiry. Acquainted with Belgian and French practices, Thiry was appalled by the extravagance of American children and the schools' lack of countermeasures. Upon retiring from a successful business career in his adopted land, he persuaded fellow trustees on the school board of Long Island City, New York, to establish school savings banks in 1885. School banking, he argued, trained the young in lifelong habits of thrift while fostering morals: "a better manhood is inseparable from a frugal life." Until his death in 1910, Thiry tirelessly coordinated the movement to disseminate savings programs to other schools. He was assisted by Sara Louisa Oberholzer who headed the Women's Christian Temperance Union's department of school savings banks from 1890 to 1923.[72]

The U.S. school savings bank movement grew slowly before World War I, lagging far behind those in European nations (see chapter 2). In 1910 Thiry counted only 160,488 school depositors and 530 participating schools.[73] The existence of thousands of local school systems impeded the sorts of national initiatives that ministries of education spearheaded in Europe. An even bigger problem was that most schools lacked access to a secure local bank willing to handle the small deposits of children. The philanthropic mutual savings banks were the most sympathetic and safest, but they did not exist in most parts of the country. The American banking community did not play a major role in establishing school savings banks before the 1910s. This state of affairs prompted advocates of youth saving to urge the immediate enactment of postal savings. In Europe, they observed, post offices worked closely with schools nationwide to promote children's saving. Post offices there processed very small deposits by permitting schoolchildren to paste stamps onto sheets until they accumulated the minimum deposit. Were the United States to adopt postal savings, reasoned James Henry Hamilton in 1902, a "competent corps" of postal clerks would serve as "missionaries," visiting schools, homes, and factories to encourage and collect savings.[74]

The United States implemented the postal savings system in 1911, but the post offices never systematically promoted children's saving.

They accepted no deposits from children under ten, preventing elementary schools from forwarding younger children's deposits. Nor by law could parents establish trustee postal accounts for their small children. Congress inserted these restrictions for a reason. The last thing the banks wanted was a nationwide cadre of postal missionaries eager to cultivate loyal depositors in the schools.[75]

Instead, school savings banks developed ad hoc under the auspices of a loosely connected movement. Replacing Thiry was the philanthropist Simon W. Straus, founder of the mortgage-banking firm S. W. Straus and Company and the son of a thrifty immigrant from the German Rhineland. In January 1914 Straus organized the American Society for Thrift, according the highest priority to teaching saving and economy to the children of America. A few months later he returned from a European tour, impressed by school savings banks in France and Belgium. Americans were the "most wasteful of all people," Straus concluded. "Notoriously thriftless," they squandered money and they ate too much. After World War I broke out in Europe in 1914, Straus found receptive audiences among educators and bankers who agreed that national preparedness required education in saving, reduced spending, and conservation of resources. In 1915 he persuaded the National Education Association to form the National Committee on Thrift Education.[76]

School savings banks received a major boost after the Savings Bank Division of the American Bankers Association announced its support in 1912. Why it took the banking community nearly thirty years to endorse school savings is unclear. The timing was likely related to the enactment of postal savings. Advocates of postal saving had harshly criticized bankers for doing little to encourage small saving, especially among youth. Bankers also feared competition from the new postal savings banks. Whatever the motivation, the ABA increasingly cooperated with the National Education Association's thrift education initiative. Member banks assisted local school savings programs. According to the ABA's statistics, school savings banks grew rapidly during the 1920s. The number of student depositors rose nearly tenfold, from 462,651 in 1919–20 to 4,222,935 in 1928–29.

Nonetheless, America's school savings programs suffered from the usual unevenness. They relied, above all, on the public-spiritedness of

Figure 6. School savings program sponsored by Farmers and Mechanics Savings Bank, Minneapolis, Minnesota, 1920s. Photo by Charles J. Hibbard. Courtesy of the Minnesota Historical Society.

local banks. Take the state of Minnesota, where school savings banks thrived in urban school districts from the 1910s to the 1950s. Minneapolis's only mutual savings bank, Farmers and Mechanics, assumed all the expenses for running the city's school savings banks (figure 6). Every week, the bank sent young female employees, whose sole job it was to encourage and collect the children's stamp deposits. Farmers and Mechanics—and nearly every other bank that managed successful school savings banks—incurred deficits when handling such small deposits at interest. Yet they carried on, imbued with the mission of "encouraging habits of thrift and economy."[77]

Few other banks proved willing to launch—much less sustain—school savings banks. Even the American Bankers Association's leading expert on school saving complained of the participating banks' "financial sacrifice."[78] School banks, like other savings institutions, were concentrated in the urban areas of a small number of states—notably New York, New Jersey, Pennsylvania, California, and the New England

and Midwestern states. Of the more than twenty-five million school-children nationwide in 1924, just over two million participated in school banks. In Mississippi, Texas, Arizona, Idaho, Montana, Utah, and North and South Dakota, not a single city reported a school bank in operation. Only one or two cities reported any in Tennessee, Arkansas, New Mexico, Florida, Alabama, Nevada, Delaware, Oregon, and South Carolina. Singling out the "backward" South, an American Society for Thrift spokesman felt obliged to quote General Robert E. Lee: "When to the intelligence of Southern men we have added the wholesome instinct of saving, no race will equal us."[79]

During the Depression years of the 1930s, student-depositors plummeted from more than 4.5 million to less than 2.8 million. Participating schools dropped by nearly half from 14,629 to 8,483. The decline did not simply reflect bad times. In Depression-era Britain, school savings programs advanced. It had more to do with American banks, whose widespread failures or shakiness forced schools to discontinue their savings programs without being able to turn to the postal savings system. The vast majority of American children had yet to experience the thrift programs so common elsewhere.

In a country as diverse as the United States, how does one sum up the story of popular saving before World War I? Contemporary images of the "Thriftless American" or the "Spendthrift Nation" are not particularly helpful.[80] Urban savings banks were doing a booming business; aggregate savings exceeded those in every other nation; and American reformers competed with Europeans in the fervor of their thrift-promotion movements. Nor had Americans reached the point—familiar to us today—when the lure of consumer goods overpowered impulses to save. What distinguished the United States was the weak commitment of government and society to establishing the institutions that promoted small saving in Europe: accessible savings banks, a national postal savings system, and school savings banks. In these and in so many other respects, America had become "exceptional." Ironically, on the other side of the globe, a rising "Oriental" people embraced European methods of thrift with a tenacity that survives today.

4

JAPANESE TRADITIONS OF DILIGENCE AND THRIFT

There lived in the town of Sakura-machi a mat-maker,
Genkichi by name, who was patronized by the sage
[Ninomiya Sontoku].* Though he was a clever speaker
and a talented man, he was always in needy circumstances,
because he was excessively fond of drinking in addition to
being lazy. One year end, he called on the sage and asked
for the loan of some glutionous [sic] rice in order to have it
made into *mochi* (rice-cake). The sage said to the man:
  "It is wrong of a man like you, who neglects his occupation all through the year and spends whatever money he
happens to have on drinking, to desire to eat *mochi* on
New Year's Day like decent people who have worked hard
during the past year.... You till land next spring, sow seeds
of rice in it and make them grow with the manure you
have made. Obtain rice in this way and eat *mochi* on New
Year's Day of the year after next. Meanwhile go without
mochi, but eat the fruit of repentance."[1]

Centuries of Japanese children grew up without Aesop's fable "The
Ant and the Grasshopper," but they did not lack for comparable

* Following East Asian practice, Japanese, Korean, and Chinese surnames in this book precede
given names, excepting when cited as authors of English-language works. Macrons in Japanese
words have been omitted for well-known terms and familiar place names such as Tōkyō, Ōsaka,
and Kyōto.

parables. In the story above, Japan's legendary apostle of thrift, Nino-miya Sontoku (1787–1856), lectured the profligate Genkichi with the sternness of the Ant. The parallels in cultivating thrift are all the more remarkable considering Japan's isolation from Western developments before the mid-nineteenth century. For more than two centuries the Tokugawa shoguns secluded the archipelago from the outside world, permitting only limited trade and exchange with the Dutch, Koreans, and Chinese. Contact with the West did not resume in earnest until 1854. In that year Commodore Matthew Perry and his flotilla of "black ships" forced the shogun to open Japan to commerce and diplomacy with the United States. Relations with the European powers soon fol-lowed. The Tokugawa shogunate itself fell in the Meiji Restoration of 1868, replaced by a new regime intent on modernizing institutions and practices along Western lines.

Japan thus occupies an anomalous position within the global his-tory of modern saving. The Japanese did not participate in the earlier transnational movement to create thrifty citizens that swept Europe and parts of North America at the beginning of the nineteenth century. The first savings banks—whether postal or private—did not appear until the 1870s. The Japanese quickly made up for lost time. Within a few short decades they emerged as the only non-Western people to oc-cupy the ranks of the great powers and modern industrial societies. By 1910 the nation boasted the second largest number of postal savings depositors in the world and one of the highest proportions of savings accounts per population.

The Japanese people's adoption of modern savings practices raises some obvious questions. To what extent had the Japanese traditionally been good savers? Conversely, how important was the introduction of Western institutions and thought in creating one of the world's thrifti-est populations? The answers depend on whom you ask. Most Japanese today will tell you that thrift is at the core of their national character, and it *always* has been. According to Japanese public opinion surveys in recent decades, significant majorities agree with the statement, "The Japanese are said to be frugal people who love saving, and that's an admirable thing."[2] At the height of U.S.-Japanese trade tensions two decades ago, there seemed no end to popular books in Japanese that boasted of the nation's superior savings habits. Some traced thrift to the country's distant past. In one widely read book of the late 1980s, Toyama Shigeru, chairman of the government's savings-promotion council, grudged that not all Japanese are "incarnations of diligence and thrift, nor are Americans a people entirely lacking in diligence and thrift." "America is a big country," he conceded, "and in certain states I hear they work no less hard than Japanese." However, "on average, Japanese people work harder and save more than other peoples." These exceptional traits, Toyama explained, originated in the thought and customs prevailing at the time of the Tokugawa shoguns (1603–1868).[3]

Not so fast, reply the economists. Long-term statistics on rates of household saving tell a very different story. Japanese saving rates from 1906 to 1937 were volatile and generally low. If we exclude the years when the country was at war, saving rates ranged from *negative* 5 percent to 12 percent—well below the rates Japanese would achieve in the decades after World War II. These figures, concludes savings specialist Charles Horioka, suggest that postwar Japan's high saving rates "are *not* due primarily to cultural factors." Prewar statistics "do not support the view that the Japanese have always been thrifty and that their high propensity to save has its origins in the prewar period."[4]

Most Japanese leaders at the turn of the twentieth century would have agreed with the economists. Soeda Juichi, president of the Japan Industrial Bank, declared himself dissatisfied with the "small amount of thrift which prevails at present, and much must be done to encourage the habit of saving among the public."[5] A century ago when Japanese compared their nation's sense of thrift to that of Western peoples, the Japanese invariably came out at the bottom. In 1904 a prominent social reformer noted that the British saved twenty-four times as much as the Japanese despite having ten million fewer people.[6]

The problem, contemporary observers concurred, was Japanese tradition itself. Laborers in the shogun's capital, Edo (Tokyo), were legendary for their spendthrift ways. "Never sleep overnight on your money" was said to be the creed of the salt-of-the-earth artisans (the so-called Edokko). Japanese businessmen would mock their workmen for lacking diligence and thrift. After visiting workplaces in the United States, one factory director in 1908 reported that American workers had no "idiotic saying" like "never sleep overnight on your money." Every American laborer, "no matter what his income, works hard and tries to save."[7]

Japanese farmers did not fare much better in the eyes of officials. The pages of the government's journal on local administration were filled with disparaging comments about reckless spending in the countryside. In the words of one specialist in 1913, "Japanese farmers—compared to the farmers of Germany, Denmark, and France—live extravagantly, and haven't the slightest idea of how to keep accounts.... What bad habits have the Japanese!" Those with an annual income of ¥1,000 "buy watches for ¥200 and swagger in a manner not befitting their social status."[8]

So, which is it? Were the Japanese traditionally profligate or innately thrifty? Neither image is particularly helpful. Their savings behavior in premodern times is more complex and certainly more interesting. Two points must be made. Japanese, no less than Europeans, possessed powerful traditions of diligence and thrift. Second, however much the Japanese people actually saved, political authorities and private reformers for centuries intruded into the lives of ordinary Japanese to shape their spending and saving habits. To grasp how modern Japan's culture of thrift came to be formed, we must first examine inheritances from the past.

Frugality under the Old Regime

There was no shortage of Japanese Benjamin Franklins to encourage thrift during the two centuries before the formation of the modern nation-state in 1868. What instead distinguished Tokugawa Japan from early modern Europe and the American colonies was the extraordinary degree of *government* intervention into the economic lives of humble folk. Prior to the late eighteenth century, European rulers had not generally concerned themselves with how laborers and farmers spent their incomes. In Japan, however, the authorities relentlessly exhorted their subjects to practice frugality. By "frugality" (*ken'yaku*), officials meant restricting or regulating one's consumption. They were less interested in promoting saving. The shogunate and the self-governing domains generally frowned upon popular saving, even if they tolerated it in practice. If commoners saved too much, their wealth might challenge the authority of their lords. And if farmers grew too rich, they might consolidate large landholdings at the expense of poorer peasants. By exhorting the populace to regulate consumption, the overlords hoped to tax away most of the surplus wealth for themselves. Peasants were to be left with only enough to sustain their productivity and a minimum standard of well-being.[9]

Financial considerations motivated the frugality measures in part. The shogun and many daimyo (domain lords) found themselves perennially strapped for cash by the early eighteenth century. To control the daimyo, the Tokugawa shoguns required the provincial lords to maintain mansions in Edo and, along with large retinues, to alternate their residence between the capital and local castles on a regular basis. The daimyo incurred enormous expenses. Then there were the huge costs of paying the legions of hereditary military retainers, the samurai. On the revenue side, rulers proved incapable of effectively taxing the productivity gains made in agriculture. If things were not bad enough, the latter half of the Tokugawa era witnessed three major famines. These disasters not only reduced land tax revenues, but also required rulers to open their granaries to prevent starvation.

Plagued by indebtedness and insolvency, shoguns and daimyo increasingly called on their subjects to reduce spending. Many of these injunctions were directed at the samurai, whose monthly stipends drained the lords' treasuries. In his edict to middle-ranking retainers (*hatamoto*) in 1657, the shogun Ietsuna adopted the tone of supreme schoolteacher. Ietsuna ordered the retainers to discuss among themselves methods of practicing frugality. They were then to write their thoughts down, turning in their papers to the shogun himself.[10]

The best known advocate of samurai austerity was Matsudaira Sadanobu, who spearheaded the shogun's thoroughgoing retrenchment program between 1787 and 1793. Matsudaira believed that rulers and samurai must serve as models of personal economy to the common people. He displayed his own frugality by conspicuously postponing castle repairs and cutting back on servants. As daimyo of Shirakawa at the height of the famine of the 1780s, he had previously halved samurai stipends. Matsudaira further ordered officials to serve as exemplars by eschewing luxuries and learning to live on less. Retainers and commoners alike received detailed warnings against spending too much on food, clothing, and festivals.[11]

These attempts to control spending represented more than economic responses to fiscal problems. The authorities obsessively regulated consumption with an eye toward maintaining the political and moral order. Tokugawa-era rulers divided society into legally defined, hereditary status groups.[12] The samurai or warrior aristocracy topped the hierarchy. They were followed in descending order by peasants, artisans, merchants, outcastes, and those not ethnically Japanese. Peasants were not to move to the towns; samurai could not engage in commerce; and prosperous merchants were prohibited from affecting the manners of the ruling status group. Nothing more visibly marked one's status than the clothes one wore or the food one ate. To reinforce boundaries between statuses, those at the top devoted considerable energy to mandating what each group might and might not consume. Frugality was less an absolute virtue than an injunction to avoid aping the ways of one's superiors.

This mentality resulted in a steady stream of sumptuary regulations from the late seventeenth to the mid-nineteenth century. These remarkably detailed edicts reveal a loathing of certain types of consumption that would influence Japanese thrift campaigns well into the twentieth century. Peasants bore the brunt. Regulations commonly forbade them to wear clothes made from anything but cotton. Village headmen were allowed to dress in silk or undyed pongee silk, but only on official occasions or for festivals. Peasants were forbidden to smoke. "Tobacco is no substitute for food," decreed one edict in 1649, "on the contrary, it causes illness."[13] The authorities further exhorted farmers to eat rougher, more affordable grains. Millet was acceptable, whereas peasants should refrain from consuming rice—finer-grained and costlier. Officials intended not only to protect cultivators from living beyond their means, but also to ensure they would tender rice crops to the overlords. In messages repeated for centuries, rulers harangued villagers to curb expenditures on weddings, funerals, and festivals. At wedding and New Year's banquets, instructed one edict of the 1640s, the menu must be limited to one soup, one choice food, and one side dish.

Nor were townspeople immune from the micromanagement of consumption. Sumptuary regulations imposed excruciatingly quantifiable limits on urban spending. This was perhaps because of merchant culture's greater familiarity with figures, as well as the relative abundance of goods in the cities. In 1683 the shogunate issued no less than seven laws regulating the clothing of urban dwellers. One edict in 1724 set the maximum price for gold-embroidered robes at 300 *me* (in silver coins), while the price of robes containing dyed patterns should not exceed 150 *me*. Another regulation in 1713 banned the sale of women's combs and hairpins adorned with gold lacquer, gold inlay, or silver inlay; the sale of any combs or hairpins costing more than 60 *me* was prohibited outright. Of course, people—being people—devised elaborate stratagems to evade the controls. A common subterfuge was to conceal consumption by wearing fancy undergarments. But the ever-vigilant shogunate was not about to be tricked. In 1648 officials prohibited male servants from wearing any loincloth made of velvet or silk.[14]

Sumptuary regulations rested on highly gendered assumptions, as would the later thrift campaigns. When it came to assigning blame for conspicuous consumption, authorities singled out urban women in aspiring commoner households. The identification of women with ruinous spending reminds us of contemporary European discourses about female extravagance. Or as Mandeville put it in *Fable of the Bees*, "The Haughty Chloe; to live Great; Had made her Husband rob the State."[15] In Japan, too, wrote the popular writer Ihara Saikaku (1642–1693), townspeople's wives and daughters "are satisfied with nothing but finery, with nothing but what is beyond their station or purse." Such women undermined not only husbands, but the entire status hierarchy. To "forget one's proper place," cautioned Saikaku, "is to invite the wrath of heaven."[16]

Japanese rulers were hardly unique in attempting to regulate consumption according to class or status. The ancient Greeks, Romans, and Chinese governed by elaborate sumptuary laws. As late as the fifteen and sixteenth centuries, authorities regulated clothing and ceremonial expenditures in France and England and in Italian, German, and Swiss city-states. John Calvin's puritanical rule in sixteenth-century Geneva is a notorious case in point.[17] Nonetheless, Japanese regulations stand out in certain respects. While the importance of sumptuary regulations waned in European societies, such edicts mushroomed in Japan during the eighteenth century and first half of the nineteenth century. Sumptuary laws became all the more pervasive as villages promulgated their own regulations on consumption. Imposing finer and finer status distinctions on villagers, peasant elites introduced village codes to maintain domination over lower-status neighbors.[18]

In the long run, Japan's overlords were more successful than European counterparts in constraining popular consumption. To be sure, townspeople and peasants frequently ignored sumptuary laws. Occasionally commoners possessed such an abundance of officially banned commodities as to make a mockery of the laws. Still, most people appear to have complied in the early stages of each campaign.[19] Whether sumptuary regulations worked perfectly or not, argues Herman Ooms, they "created ideals and norms that, for the first time in Japanese history, tried to structure peasant life."[20] Indeed, the Tokugawa era was formative in the nation's long history of encouraging frugality and saving. Japanese became accustomed to governments and communities vigorously intervening to shape their economic behavior.

Popular Thrift

From their lofty perch, Tokugawa-era rulers occupied themselves with regulating consumption while doing little to encourage popular saving. Yet on the ground, Japanese took it upon themselves to save for emergencies, posterity, and investment opportunities. As they did, a more positive ethic of thrift evolved in the two centuries prior to the Meiji Restoration. Although modern banks did not exist before the 1870s, people saved in a variety of ways. Many simply placed their wealth in drawers or pots. Hiding money in the proverbial mattress was less of an option in a culture that rolled up futons each day.[21]

Others turned to loan-making institutions that resembled banks. In the great cities of Edo, Osaka, and Kyoto, merchants deposited major portions of their liquid capital with "money changers" (*ryōgae*) by the 1640s. These accounts rarely paid interest, yet merchants could draw upon them to make payments to others by means of deposit notes or checks. In some cases merchants effectively borrowed from the money changer by drawing out more than their deposited funds. The growth of commerce and manufacturing in the countryside resulted in new wealth and the rising demand for credit. Mechanisms for small saving emerged toward the end of the Tokugawa era. Peasant moneylenders, who had lent primarily from their own houses' savings or entrepreneurial profits, began tapping new pools of capital. One source consisted of loans from expanding networks of fellow moneylenders. Local financiers also solicited interest-bearing deposits from well-to-do commoners. One way or another, some rural people were saving substantial sums. Among commoners in the agricultural domain of Chōshū, by one recent estimate, the overall household saving rate approached 7 percent in the 1840s. Wealthier merchants, landlords, sake brewers, and fishing boat owners amassed the bulk of the savings.[22]

The nascent banks remained beyond the reach of most Japanese. Nonetheless, humbler peasants found ways of putting aside small surpluses. In Tokugawa Japan as in premodern China and Europe, many people engaged in collective forms of thrift. Villagers often saved through the communal granary. Depending on one's financial resources, each household was expected to contribute a portion of its harvest or earnings to the granary. Community elders frequently lent out the common rice or money. They used the earned interest and repaid principal to relieve the needy, particularly in times of crop failures. From our perspective today, placing one's wealth in a common pool may not seem much like saving. However, in an age when destitution and starvation might be one bad harvest away, communal thrift met one of the primary objectives of saving—to put aside for life's emergencies. And like insurance, it pooled risk.

Closely related to the granaries were the confraternities known as *kō*.[23] These may have been the most widely used institutions for small savings from the latter half of the eighteenth century. They were variously termed *mujinkō* (unlimited trust associations) or *tanomoshikō* (mutual assistance associations). Buddhist in their origins, the *kō* first appeared in ancient China. The associations studied sacred texts, evolving into communities of worshippers throughout East Asia. Gradually many of the confraternities became economic in orientation and common-place in Tokugawa villages.

The economic *kō* combined attributes of insurance companies, credit associations, and savings banks. Accordingly, the confraternities resembled English friendly societies and continental Europe's credit and savings cooperatives. Villagers deposited rice and money in the *kō* just as they contributed to the communal granaries. The accumulated grain and cash would in part be redistributed to victims of famines and other disasters. In 1756 a local Confucian scholar, Miura Baien, organized one of the best known of these, the "unlimited compassion confrater-nity" (*jihi mujinkō*). As credit institutions, the *kō* also offered peasants an alternative to the profit-seeking moneylender. Those who contrib-uted to the association were entitled to borrow from it. Most groups required collateral and charged some interest. The custodians of the *kō* increasingly drew on surpluses to make loans to farmers, merchants, and manufacturers. Borrowers were occasionally outsiders who purchased the right to receive funds from association members. Following the Meiji Restoration, some of the better endowed *kō* transformed them-selves into loan companies and unlicensed banks.

Although scholars focus on the credit side of the *kō*, the associa-tions played an equally important role in developing Japanese habits of thrift. At first blush the confraternities appear an odd mode of saving. Members were obliged to make regular contributions, but they could not withdraw funds at will. To recover their deposits, they usually had to bid, or win a lottery, for part or all of the pool. Once a member won, he was expected to resume depositing until all others had won. For all their differences with modern saving, the *kō* shaped how many Japa-nese approached the act of saving well into the twentieth century. Vil-lagers were contractually obligated to deposit a set amount of rice or money on a regular basis. Those who did not were subject to various sanctions, for their delinquency threatened the association's solvency and communal harmony. The confraternities also advanced the notion of "trust" in the custodians who managed the collected deposits. It was easier to entrust one's savings to neighbors or fellow temple parishioners than to total strangers. Above all, the *kō* bequeathed the legacy of saving as a highly *social* act that communities encouraged and managed.

Parsimonious Merchants

Although official Confucianism took a dim view of accumulating private wealth, the gospel of thrift gained a large following among Japanese commoners. Merchant houses trumpeted the virtues of economy. So did popular literature read by ordinary townspeople. The seventeenth century witnessed intense urbanization. A vibrant commoner culture appeared in the big cities and in the daimyo's castle towns. A mere fishing village in the sixteenth century, Edo held more than one million souls by the 1720s, vying with London for the distinction as the world's largest city. Osaka—home to more than 400,000 inhabitants—emerged as the country's preeminent commercial center teeming with the newly wealthy. One of the greatest publishing industries on earth developed to meet the needs of the burgeoning urban populace.[24]

Just as in early modern Europe and colonial America, Japan's mercantile culture devoured books on how to get rich. Guides to bookkeeping and household management sold well. One of the earliest tracts, *The Millionaire's Gospel* (Chōja kyō), was published in 1627. The way to wealth lay in hard work, moderation, and providence. "The man who makes money by normal economies, saving one copper at a time, is the steady man whose present and future alike are assured."[25] There was, however, a darker subtext in such advice. The "how to" books may also be read as warnings against what *not* to do. We recall Daniel Defoe's advice to English tradesmen to eschew the financially ruinous life of the aristocracy.[26] Within the highly stratified status society of Tokugawa Japan, thrift served not simply as a bulwark against bankruptcy, it constituted the merchant's defense against capricious warrior rule. In 1716 the head of the now-famous Mitsui house made the following observation. Of the forty-six defunct merchant houses he examined, most failed because of bad loans made to daimyo. Whereas the daimyo might lead lives of luxury with impunity, observed Mitsui Takafusa, the merchant's fortunes were ever-threatened. Prudent management offered merchants the surest means of preserving and building wealth over the generations.[27]

The best-known, and certainly most entertaining, spokesman for merchant thrift was Ihara Saikaku, the prolific writer of townspeople fiction. He is better remembered for lurid stories of amorous women, sodomized boy-actors in kabuki, and townsmen who dissipate themselves in the brothel quarters. Yet to Saikaku, saving—no less than sex—was a keystone of urban culture. In 1688 he published *The Japanese Family Storehouse* (Nihon eitaigura), a collection of thirty stories based loosely on the lives of famous merchants of the past half-century. While Saikaku wrote to amuse his readers, he also strove to educate. He offered parables to future generations, placing them in a metaphorical "storehouse to serve each family's prosperity." A former merchant himself, Saikaku praised those commercial houses that survived in the precarious environment of warrior rule. They thrived for having avoided ostentation and admirably conserved their earnings for coming generations. "Birth and lineage mean nothing," he declared. "Money is the only family tree for a townsman."

Saikaku's merchant heroes prosper because of hard work, fastidious bookkeeping, and levels of self-denial that appear comical at times. In one story, Fuji-ichi amassed a fortune but lives in a tiny rented house. He wears only a thin undervest under a simple cloth kimono. Fuji-ichi is "not a miser by nature," the author tells us; he simply wishes to serve as "a model for others in the management of everyday affairs." Once at the height of New Year's festivities, neighbors sent their sons to Fuji-ichi's home to seek guidance on getting rich. The young men hear the grinding sounds of a mortar coming from the kitchen. Naturally they offer opinions as to which New Year's delicacy would be served. Their host then appears and recites story after story on ways to eliminate unnecessary expenditure. Hours pass and stomachs growl. Finally Fuji-ichi announces wryly: "it is high time that refreshments were served. But not to provide refreshments is one way of becoming a millionaire. The noise of the mortar which you heard when you first arrived was the pounding of starch for the covers of the [new year's] account-book."

At the same time, Saikaku scorned true misers who saved simply for the sake of saving. Saving must have a purpose, either for posterity or for enjoyment in one's old age. Take the case of Chopstick Jinbei. In the tale "A Dose of What the Doctor Never Orders," Jinbei makes his appearance as a poor man who asks a wealthy gentleman for a cure to poverty. The prescribed "Millionaire Pill," contains the following ingredients: "Early rising, 5 parts. The family trade, 20 parts. Work after hours, 8 parts. Economy, 10 parts. Sound health, 7 parts." The rich man also warns him to abstain from "certain noxious things"—expensive foods, brothel quarters, the tea ceremony, preoccupation with the next world, and "giving too generously to temple funds." Jinbei heeds the advice. Gathering cypress wood carelessly dropped by those working on the mansions of the extravagant daimyo, he sells the bigger pieces and carves the scraps into chopsticks. Wasting nothing, he soon becomes a successful timber merchant. In only forty years he accumulates the enormous sum of 100,000 ryō. Upon turning seventy, Jinbei loosens his purse strings at last. Dressing only in silk, he attends kabuki and throws himself into flower arranging. The moral of the story might have been written by Benjamin Franklin himself: "Save in youth and spend in old age. It is impossible to take your money to heaven."[28]

Saikaku and the merchant house codes presented thrift as a practical means of attaining wealth. Other Japanese proponents of saving elevated thrift to a spiritual act. The leading figure was Ishida Baigan (1685–1744), founder of the ethical movement known as Shingaku. From the time of his first lectures in 1729 until the mid-nineteenth century, the charismatic Ishida and his disciples reached a broad audience that included merchants but went well beyond them. No other popular movement in Tokugawa Japan gained as extensive a following among the urban lower strata and peasantry. Shingaku preachers spread the word through their writings, public lectures, sermons, and charitable acts. They also organized adherents into religious confraternities (kō), which gathered savings and advanced credit. Shingaku combined elements of Buddhism, Confucianism, and Shinto. Its mass appeal lay in straightforward, this-worldly teachings. Anyone could achieve goodness and enlightenment through hard work.

The sociologist Robert Bellah has compared Shingaku to Max Weber's Protestant Ethic. In Europe as we have seen, the spirit of capitalism and virtue of thrift were by no means confined to Protestants. Yet one can readily understand why Shingaku appears so "Protestant" to Western observers. Whereas warrior rulers denigrated commercial activity, Ishida taught that the merchant's profit "is like the samurai's stipend" from his daimyo. Both were "gifts" from Heaven. According to Shingaku, the moral-political order rested not only on "the Way of the samurai" (Bushido), but just as firmly on "the Way of the merchant." Here we have a *Japanese* religion that legitimized the making and saving of money in the name of attaining salvation.[29]

In Ishida Baigan's cosmology, frugality provided the key to both goodness and profit. He expounded on this theme in the published tract, "Frugality and Managing the Household" (*Seikaron*, 1644). Ishida adapted traditional Buddhist teachings, which made a virtue of suppressing one's desires, to the thriving merchant culture around him. Frugality became a means to commercial success, rather than an end in itself. For the merchant to maximize his profit, Ishida preached that "the first principle is to practice economy" in household consumption: "For the necessities that previously cost you 1 *kanme* [1,000 *me*], you should now spend only 700 *me*." He further warned followers of the "evils of luxury." Those who did not keep good accounts would invariably succumb to temptation and impoverish their households. Frugality, on the other hand, would enable families to save. In an image repeated in coming centuries, Ishida envisioned the thrifty merchant as one whose savings "mount up as high as Mt. Fuji."

Like Saikaku before him and later Samuel Smiles half a world away, Ishida distinguished thrift from greedy individualism and miserly behavior. He represented frugality as a virtue meant to benefit the greater community, sometimes at the expense of the merchant himself. The "customer is master," declared Shingaku's founder, and the buyer would best be served when the merchant cuts his own living expenses and reduces his profits. Ishida further linked frugality to compassion toward subordinates. By moderating his family's expenditure on luxuries, a master could afford to treat servants kindly and avoid overworking them.[30]

A Peasant Saint

Most Japanese no longer remember Ihara Saikaku as a paragon of thrift. Nor is Ishida Baigan's role in popularizing frugality well known beyond scholars. Yet every schoolchild knows of Ninomiya Kinjirō (referred to in this book by his posthumous name Ninomiya Sontoku). An agrarian reformer who died in 1856 on the eve of Japan's modern era, Ninomiya revived the fortunes of many an impoverished village. His ardent disciples would elevate the man and his teachings to mythic heights. In the decades before 1945, statues of young Kinjirō adorned school yards throughout Japan and its empire. As a moral exemplar for Japanese children, Kinjirō appeared more often in prewar textbooks than any individual other than the Meiji emperor (r. 1868–1912).[31] Whether statue or illustration, his image is always the same. The peasant boy Kinjirō carries home a bundle of gathered firewood, earnestly reading a book as he walks (figure 7). For more than one hundred years Japanese have looked upon Ninomiya as not only the model student, but also their most famous spokesman for "diligence, thrift, and saving" (*kinken chochiku*)—a phrase he is thought to have created. "Work hard, spend little. Gather much firewood, but burn little," the plain-spoken sage advised his countrymen.[32]

Rarely has one Japanese been claimed by so many. To Japan's powerful bureaucrats after 1868, Ninomiya Sontoku became the embodiment of a very useful myth. Embarking on industrialization and military expansion, officials eagerly harnessed his teachings in the service of the state. The new public schools and nationwide savings campaigns systematically invoked Ninomiya in their efforts to inculcate diligence, thrift, and self-sacrifice. Japan's defeat in World War II temporarily tainted the image of Ninomiya, whose acolytes had so closely associated with the imperial state. In more recent years, the captains of Japanese industry enthusiastically proclaimed their intellectual debt to Ninomiya's ideas of thrift and economic planning.[33] The founders of Toyota Motors and Matsushita Electric were noted admirers of the sage.

More remarkable has been Ninomiya Sontoku's extraordinary appeal to less conservative Japanese, and even to Westerners. While Japanese capitalists extolled the agrarian reformer, other devotees dubbed

Figure 7. Bronze statue of Ninomiya Kinjirō (Sontoku), the Japanese paragon of diligence and thrift, ca. 1920. Hundreds of these figurines were distributed to schools at the time. Photo by John Blazejewski. Courtesy of Cotsen Children's Library. Department of Rare Books and Special Collections, Princeton University Library.

Ninomiya an "early Japanese socialist"—in the words of European and North American members of the Asiatic Society of Japan in 1894. His efforts to encourage cooperation and credit associations among villagers, reported one member, left Ninomiya ill disposed to "the wretched individualism that characterizes our nineteenth century."[34] Americans have long regarded Ninomiya as something of a cross between Johnny Appleseed and Honest Abe. In the late 1940s, when U.S. forces occupied a defeated Japan, American officials did their bit to mythologize the man. Ninomiya became "Japan's Abraham Lincoln," a democratic model to postwar Japanese youth. Here was a hero who had grown up poor but achieved success by hard work and simple living. Equally noteworthy was the reverence in which Japanese Protestants held Ninomiya, a non-Christian. In Ninomiya they found a kindred spirit who preached the work ethic and value of thrift. To Uchimura Kanzō, the nation's best-known Christian at the turn of the twentieth century, Ninomiya Sontoku was, quite simply, Japan's "Peasant Saint."[35]

Saint or socialist? Conservative moralist or efficiency expert? These are images of the mythic Ninomiya. But the real Ninomiya was no less important in conveying the gospel of thrift to modern Japan. He and his followers created an enduring organizational network for promoting saving at the grass roots. Ninomiya's success as an agrarian reformer lay in the fact that he himself was a man of the soil. A peasant by status, he stood apart from samurai officials who exhorted the people from on high. Ninomiya was born in 1787 to a prosperous peasant household, whose luck quickly turned. A flood decimated the family's lands when Kinjirō was four. His father and mother died when he was in his early teens. That he and the rest of the family escaped from poverty owed much to Kinjirō's determination to conserve resources. When not toiling in the fields, he scoured the mountainside for firewood and straw, which he sold in the nearby town. At night he augmented the household's income by making rope from the remaining straw. Little by little, Kinjirō restored the family fortunes. Word of Ninomiya's diligence spread. In 1811 officials of his domain of Odawara turned to the young commoner to help restructure the finances of the chief minister's indebted household.[36]

Ninomiya soon joined the ranks of what one historian calls the "technologists" of the Tokugawa era. Akin to those who wrote agrarian manuals in early modern Europe, these farmers and merchants offered practical advice on how to increase productivity. Often higher authorities or wealthy peasants hired the technologists to rehabilitate destitute villages. Since the mid-eighteenth century, the shogunate and domain governments had grown concerned about rural poverty and the peasantry's large-scale abandonment of fields. Uncultivated fields meant dwindling land tax revenues. The itinerant technologist was part agricultural extension worker, part preacher. Many in fact associated themselves with religious movements—including the established Buddhist sects, new religions, Ishida Baigan's Shingaku, and the pro-emperor "national learning" school (Kokugaku). Besides introducing farming techniques, they lectured the populace on the virtues of filial piety, obedience, honesty, and, of course, diligence and thrift.[37] Ninomiya Sontoku emerged as the most influential technologist. In 1816 the daimyo of Odawara commissioned him to work on rehabilitating indebted villages in the domain. Ninomiya went on to direct a series of rehabilitation projects until the end of his life. All told, he took part in twenty-three village reform efforts, affecting hundreds of villages. Eventually this man of humble birth rose to the exalted rank of a retainer of the shogun.

Ninomiya left an indelible mark on Japanese thought as well as methods of encouraging thrift. Like Ishida Baigan and Christian clergy in the West, the rustic philosopher encouraged saving not simply as the way to wealth, but as a deeply spiritual act. As Robert Bellah observed of Ninomiya's writings, "salvation in the religious sense and economic recovery seem to be conceptually fused."[38] Ninomiya distilled his teachings to the principle of "repaying virtue" (hōtoku). Human beings, he explained, were fortunate to receive "virtue" from heaven in the form of soil, water, ancestors, and the community. When people made the best of these endowments by working hard and planning carefully, they repaid the virtue. Ninomiya's philosophy was fundamentally optimistic. It was in the "Way of humans" to overcome constraints of nature. A diligent farmer may reclaim an abandoned field. Or by controlling spending, humans could "manage to influence Heaven's will by [their own] efforts."[39] Conversely, nature defeats those who are lazy or extravagant (*ogori*). "Wealth and poverty both exist in human society," remarked the sage. "One might think this is accidental, but it is not.... Wealth resides with a frugal man; it disintegrates if it resides in an extravagant man."[40]

To Ninomiya, thrift was not merely a choice people might make. The capacity to save was what separated humans from all other creatures. "A man who does not follow the Way of putting aside today's goods for the sake of tomorrow is not a man," he declared. Animals, he insisted, were incapable of storing surplus food for times of scarcity. Unlike future generations of Japanese, Ninomiya did not extol the virtues of the industrious ant as in Aesop's fable. No, extravagance was tantamount to bestiality: "To never sleep overnight on one's earnings, that is the Way of the birds and beasts, not the Way of humans."[41]

Unlike modern economists, Ninomiya did not envision saving as an act aimed at maximizing one's wealth. Quite the opposite. Villagers were exhorted to save for the sake of others. In Ninomiya's metaphysics, saving involved the individual's "concession" (*suijō*) or transference of wealth. When a farmer put aside part of his crop or money for the next year, he engaged in transference. The surplus might be used to buy fields or build a house, and the accumulated wealth would eventually be bequeathed or transferred to descendants. In addition, Ninomiya expected households to "concede" some of their savings to friends in need, to one's community, and to the domain. The rich man should learn to live without needless luxuries, he inveighed, and thus accumulate enough wealth to concede to less fortunate villagers. In short, one saved not only for one's family, but to relieve poor and sick neighbors, contribute to communal granaries, and pay taxes to one's lord.[42]

Although Japanese officials would invoke Ninomiya's teachings in twentieth-century campaigns to restrain popular consumption, the man himself disparaged the preaching of austerity for its own sake. He seldom urged frugality (*ken'yaku*), which implied cutting back on daily expenses. Instead Ninomiya emphasized the desirability of saving (*chochiku*) a portion of income with specific goals in mind. He scorned those who hoped to enrich the realm by getting people to consume less rice. It would be far better, he retorted, to encourage poorer peasants to work harder by allowing them to eat as much as they wanted. Undeveloped lands would thus be cultivated, more goods would be produced, merchants and artisans would prosper, and the realm itself would thrive.[43]

Nor did the propagators of spiritual asceticism escape his derision. Once he heard a charismatic Shinto priest hold forth on the moral goodness of frugality. "Be frugal, be frugal," the man exhorted the crowd. Ninomiya was not impressed. "Frugality by itself is not very interesting," explained the sage, "and it does nothing for the realm." If one intends to cut back on food, clothing, and shelter, he cautioned, such frugality must serve useful purposes. The kind of frugality that he admired generated savings that "build capital, enrich the realm, and relieve the people."[44]

Ever the practical reformer, Ninomiya systematically applied his principles to rehabilitate insolvent communities. He devised detailed programs, complete with diagrams that stipulated how much peasants should save and work. His daily production schedules divided up the workday, right down to the timing of the lunch break. With respect to thrift, the first step was to calculate the income (*bundo*) that a peasant, village, or domain could reliably expect. His elaborate calculations have impressed modern Japanese statisticians. Indeed, in 1936 one management consultant published a monograph titled "Ninomiya Sontoku, Efficiency Engineer."[45]

Once income capacity was determined, Ninomiya instructed villagers and daimyo alike to live within their means. His regimen of saving was tested most extensively in the revitalization of Sakuramachi in modern-day Shizuoka prefecture. At one time a thriving town, Sakuramachi by 1820 had become a veritable Sodom or Gomorra, if one believes the chroniclers. Idleness and gambling left the people in debt, the fields uncultivated, and taxes unpaid. Enter the sage. Undeterred by the protests of many locals, Ninomiya prescribed that inhabitants set aside a predetermined proportion of their harvest. The savings were placed in a collective capital fund that financed reclamation of new land. Little by little, applied doses of diligence and thrift expanded production and restored Sakuramachi's prosperity.

With Sakuramachi as the springboard, Ninomiya and his followers transformed methods of communal saving into a full-fledged Hōtoku (repaying virtue) movement over the course of the nineteenth century. In village after village, reformers organized Hōtoku societies that resembled the existing confraternities (kō), yet strove to aid the community as a whole. Savings were accumulated and deposited in the society's Hōtoku fund (hōtokukin). For the fund to remain solvent, all members were expected to deposit—without interest—a certain amount of money or percentage of income. In some cases, members or nonmembers could deposit additional sums for a fixed term and draw interest.

In contrast to modern financial institutions, the Hōtoku societies employed the funds in accord with Ninomiya's communitarian teachings. The amassed money and grain served as an emergency fund, which would relieve the victims of famine and natural disasters. Much like agricultural cooperatives, Hōtoku societies also invested the monies in repairing roads, buying fertilizer, and making other improvements that served the common interest. Finally the Hōtoku fund provided a vital source of capital for members who required capital for productive purposes. Borrowers repaid the loans in annual installments, paying an additional one-year sum as an offering of "gratitude." This final payment amounted to a substantial interest rate, even though Ninomiya represented the loans as interest free and the societies as emphatically nonprofit.[46]

To what extent did reformers like Ninomiya Sontoku influence the savings habits of ordinary Japanese? Lacking mass media and centralized government, they confronted formidable obstacles in their quest to reach a wider audience. Nonetheless, one cannot help but be impressed by Ninomiya's ability to energize his supporters into a vibrant, politically savvy movement. The sage cultivated numerous acolytes in the two decades before his death in 1856. Several devotees returned to rehabilitate their own villages, inspiring other local reformers with the master's teachings. Already in the 1840s Hōtoku societies sprang up in villages throughout what is today Shizuoka prefecture near Tokyo. The movement steadily expanded following the Meiji Restoration of 1868. By the turn of the twentieth century, more than three hundred of these societies (now called hōtokusha) operated in Shizuoka prefecture alone.

Ninomiya's disciples did not stop at local organization. Although they had been lowly peasants in the old status system, local reformers gained influence within the highest reaches of the new central regime after 1868. One protégé, Okada Ryōichirō, became a member of parliament. His sons, Okada Ryōhei and Ichiki Kitokurō, served as elite bureaucrats in the Ministry of Education and Home Ministry, respectively. From those positions they actively promoted the Hōtoku movement. Both eventually rose to the rank of cabinet minister, Okada Ryōhei as minister of education, and Ichiki as minister of education and then home minister.

Other followers got the ear of the Meiji emperor himself. Tomita Kōkei wrote the canonical account of Ninomiya's reform work, the *Hōtokuki* (Chronicle of repaying virtue). In 1880 his former daimyo presented the chronicle to the emperor, who reportedly was so moved he ordered the Imperial Household Ministry to publish the *Hōtokuki* and distribute it throughout the government. Five years later the Ministry of Agriculture and Commerce mass-produced the pamphlet for dissemination nationwide. Another disciple, Fukuzumi Masae, recorded the sage's "evening talks." This tract, too, was presented to the Imperial Household Ministry and then widely circulated by the government. In 1893 the Ministry of Education certified the first of many elementary-school textbooks featuring the boyhood Ninomiya Kinjirō as paragon of diligence, thrift, and filial piety. After a well-known sculptor in 1910 cast the first bronze image of Kinjirō carrying home the firewood, officials saw to it that one graced the emperor's desk. The desktop Kinjirō soon appeared in elementary schools, where pupils would sing out, "Ninomiya Sontoku, he's our role model." By the 1930s when life-size statues sprang up in school yards throughout Japan and its colonies, nearly every Japanese associated Ninomiya with the imperative to save.[47]

That gets us ahead of our story. In the initial stages of Japan's modernization, some doubted that Japan's indigenous traditions of thrift would survive in a rapidly changing society. In 1894 one of Ninomiya's Western admirers pronounced the Hōtoku societies a touching anachronism, "adapted not to modern but to feudal times." The present, he regretted, "is hardly a time for a rapid advance of such an institution. Our century is a time of individual enterprise, of self-interest and the desire for wealth." Referring to Ninomiya's communitarian approach to saving and credit, he judged it highly unlikely that the Hōtoku movement would achieve much success.[48]

As it turned out, the skeptics were wrong. Quite wrong. Japan's modern era would see banks, battleships, and big businesses. The new environment transformed traditional modes of saving and thrift promotion, but it hardly destroyed them. Thrift, already accepted as an individual and communal virtue, would be mobilized for the nation's good as well.

5

SAVING FOR THE NEW JAPAN

Yet if you compare [our savings] to England and America,
Or Germany, Belgium, and Holland,
The civilized countries, that is,
We're way behind.
So keep on saving,
Don't let up.
We'll catch up.
And the day'll come when we pass them all.
—"The Savings Song," compiled by a local postmaster, 1901[1]

In history as in sports, timing is everything. Following the Meiji Restoration of 1868, Japan became a modern nation-state at a peculiar moment. In the world of great-power rivalries, Western nations were hard at work managing and mobilizing their own peoples. They no longer regarded thrift as simply an individual virtue, but as a vital ingredient in the making of national power and social order. In 1909 Ichiki Kitokurō, Japan's influential vice minister for home affairs, declared: "Nothing can be as positive, and nothing increases the nation's wealth nor contributes to the advance of the nation as much as thrift."[2] He made no claim to originality. Ichiki cribbed from Lord Rosebery, who just months before had called thrift the "surest and the strongest foundation of an empire."[3] Japan's encounter with the intense nationalisms of the West profoundly shaped its path of development. Throughout the *twentieth* century, Japan would behave much as late-nineteenth-century European states, haunted by a sense of national vulnerability and determined to rally its populace behind a national purpose.

Japan rapidly emerged as one of the central players in the global history of saving. By 1910 its people held 17.5 million savings accounts, the second highest in the world. Savings accounts per population totaled 35 percent—surpassing Britain, France, and Germany (refer to table 3). These were remarkable achievements for a country that in 1868 lacked modern financial institutions in which ordinary people could save. The concept of thrift itself had been transformed. The needs of the new nation required more than simply restraining consumption or burying one's wealth in the ground. Thrift in the true sense, insisted Vice Minister Ichiki, occurred when people cut *wasteful* spending and converted the savings into "the capital and atoms of all production."[4] Over the course of the Meiji emperor's reign (1868–1912), Japanese officials and reformers introduced the institutions, organizations, and thinking that would guide the modern promotion of saving during the twentieth century. To a remarkable degree, the Japanese married indigenous traditions of "diligence and thrift" with Western discourses of "character" and "civilization." Samuel Smiles became as popular in Meiji Japan as he was in Victorian Britain. From Confucians to Christians, Japanese envisioned a thrifty populace as a cornerstone of the modern nation.

Japan's exuberant participation in the international exchange of ideas and institutions was crucial to savings promotion. Despite a meager treasury, the new Meiji regime devoted enormous resources to hiring more than 2,400 foreign consultants, who informed the regime of Western trends in military, economic, social, legal, and political affairs.[5] Japanese officials, for their part, were dispatched to survey institutions in Europe and North America. The Japanese embraced the emerging international norms of the late nineteenth century as no other non-Western state. They took their seats at nearly every world forum—conferences, treaties, and expositions.[6] It was in this transnational environment that Japan became a nation of savers.

Postal Savings at the Stroke of a Pen

Japanese commentators often remark—with no hint of irony—that what makes their nation incomparable is a knack for borrowing from others.

In 1875, just seven years after the Meiji Restoration, the young regime adopted the British model of postal savings. The institution became the linchpin in the promotion of saving. Excluding the British dominions, Japan took its place as the third nation to institute postal savings— behind only the British (1861) and the Belgians (1870). The speed with which the government incorporated the foreign system was soon the stuff of legend. By dogged investigation, reminisced the postal savings official Shimomura Hiroshi in 1910, Japan in just forty years assimilated the "civilization" of the West more quickly than had the Western powers themselves. Japanese officials, he boasted, introduced postal savings in "not much more time than it took to do the translations."[7]

The system was born not of extraordinary prescience, but through the nation's chance encounter with a foreign model. Historians often praise the Meiji-era government for its genius at "selective borrowing." Japanese officials supposedly scoured the world for the leading models, selecting those that could be best "adapted" to native conditions. In many accounts, we see Japanese leaders cleverly modeling the army and constitution after imperial Germany, the navy after Britain, and the police after France. In reality, notes sociologist Eleanor Westney, the process of transnational emulation was more haphazard. During the formative era of the 1870s, Japanese were hampered by less than perfect information. Travel to the United States and Europe required time and considerable expense. Generally only those sponsored by the state could afford the passage. Japanese officials commonly selected models from a particular nation simply because they had visited that nation, or because they knew enough of the language to translate the basic information. Emulation was often cumulative. Once the Japanese chose a model and established regular communication with the country of origin, they were more likely to borrow other institutions from the same country.[8]

Westerners themselves often preselected the menu of choices available to Japanese investigators. Nowhere was this more evident than in the famous Iwakura Mission. For twenty-two months between 1871 and 1873, some fifty top leaders from the Japanese government toured the world, visiting the United States, Britain, Germany, France, Austria, Russia, and several smaller European powers. Although the Japanese observed differences among the Western nations, they appear more struck by how each nation showcased similar institutions as hallmarks of "civilization." Like any tourist on a package tour, the mission's scribe Kume Kunitake expressed occasional irritation. In each country, he re-marked, "most of the events their respective governments invited us to observe were to do with preparations for war.... It was as though each government saw it as almost the whole of its duty to make a show of the nation's prestige and a display of its military strength."[9] In nation after nation, the hosts also took the Japanese entourage—no doubt a sight in itself—on field trips to elementary schools, national telegraph offices, and post offices. The visitors were informed repeatedly that Western governments after 1800 intervened to improve their people, integrate their nations, and communicate with the world. The Japanese were im-pressed by the growing commitment to public education of all children, boys and girls, rich and poor. And they marveled at Britain's General Post Office, where "we saw an unending stream of postmen, one every five or six seconds, arriving from all directions with sacks of mail"; some envelopes "would go as far as Hong Kong and Yokohama; others would travel only a few hundred yards."[10] The emissaries arrived home unsure about which models to adopt, yet eager to introduce a broad array of institutions said to have made Western nations wealthy and strong.

Postal savings was among those new institutions, thanks in large measure to one determined official. Maejima Hisoka personified how Meiji Japan, despite a scattergun approach, successfully emulated so many state-of-the-art Western organizations. Maejima (1835–1919) was one of several officials who had studied things Western in the waning years of the Tokugawa shogunate. He started early. At age twelve, his family sent him to Edo (Tokyo) to study "Dutch medicine." For more than two hundred years, the Dutch had been the only Westerners permitted to trade and reside in Japan. In 1853 when the U.S. Navy's Matthew Perry sailed into Tokyo Bay demanding to "open" Japan, young Maejima journeyed to see the American fleet. The experience changed his life. "Holland is dull and in decline," one daimyo lectured Maejima; henceforth "all men of determination" must learn English— the language spoken in America, much of Asia, and Britain, a country "peerless among the civilized nations."[11] Maejima embarked on the study of English, a decision that would predispose him to British models.

As supervisor of the posts in the new Meiji government, Maejima set about to Westernize the Tokugawa-era system of post stations. Initially he knew little, if anything, of the new phenomenon of postal savings. That changed in the course of a yearlong stay in England in 1870 and 1871. His primary mission was to arrange a large government loan from London financiers. In his spare time, he investigated the operations of the British Post, then considered the world's leading model. Before long, Maejima stumbled upon the recently established Post Office Savings Bank. This social innovation was already attracting the interest of governments in Europe and the United States. Maejima sensed the international excitement. Curious about the POSB's inner workings, Maejima opened a postal savings account, experimented with withdrawals, and sent money orders to himself.[12] What the British Post had developed in three distinct stages—mail delivery, money orders, and postal savings—Maejima imported in one fell swoop. Postal savings came to Japan part and parcel—as it were—of the British Post.

Upon returning to Japan, Maejima threw himself into formulating plans that resulted in the inauguration of postal savings and money orders in 1875. In contemporary Europe and the United States, postal savings legislation often encountered formidable resistance from political and economic interests. How do we explain Japan's speedy adoption of the system? First off, Meiji Japan was a technocrat's paradise. Leaders and elite bureaucrats governed with few challenges from the rest of society. No national parliament existed until 1890. Transnational models became enshrined in law as soon as cabinet-level authorities signed off on bureaucratic proposals. Equally important, Japan's early postal savings system faced no opposition from rival banking interests. Local savings banks had yet to be established, and Japanese commercial banks were in their infancy. The Tokugawa era's "money changers" did not rise to the new tasks of financing industry and stabilizing the currency. In their place, the Meiji government hastily adopted the American model of national banks in 1872. Undercapitalized and plagued by mismanagement, only four national banks functioned in 1876.[13]

Japanese authorities unabashedly emulated the British Post Office Savings Bank. They, too, initially envisioned postal savings not as a financial institution but as a social policy to prevent poverty and improve the habits of the masses. Their language was emphatically Victorian. The government, announced Maejima in 1875, created postal savings for the benefit of the "humble folk" (*shōmin*) to "elevate the ways of thrift" among them. The director of the posts conjured up Dickensian images of such people living in "squalid back alleys." The typical individual in the "lower orders" does not "plan in the morning for the night; he just spends all he has." Were he to save some of his earnings at the post office, Maejima counseled, he would not only stave off the calamities of starvation and the cold, but also "build up his industrial capital and allow a life of independence to flower."[14]

As Maejima would soon discover, not everything British could be readily transplanted in Japanese soil. He had hoped, for example, that Shinto and Buddhist priests would play the role of Christian clergy in spearheading the first savings campaign. The priests responded unenthusiastically, woefully ignorant of the basics of modern saving. For all the talk of reforming the humble folk, the early postal savings system scarcely affected the masses. After ten years in operation, the number of postal accounts amounted to less than one percent of the population. The minimum deposit was beyond most artisans. Savings services spread slowly to rural post offices. The authorities moreover made little effort to attract the small savings of women, unlike the British and French post offices. Although Maejima originally proposed that females be able to open accounts nearly as freely as males, conservative Justice Ministry officials overruled this challenge to patriarchal authority. According to the finalized regulations, any customer who did not legally head a household—including sons and all women—required the family head's approval to make deposits and withdrawals.[15]

Despite the uncertain start, what began as a modest experiment to encourage popular thrift soon evolved into the state's principal *financial* mechanism for funding economic growth and national power. The Meiji regime desperately needed capital to support its nation-building agenda. Japan was a classic late developer of the time, except in one major aspect. Russia, Argentina, Australia, and Egypt all borrowed heavily from

Western financiers. After the Japanese government floated two loans in London in 1870 and 1873, incredibly it eschewed all foreign loans for the next twenty-four years. The Meiji oligarchs were loath to continue borrowing at the high interest rates the City of London charged nations with shaky finances.[16] Yet anxieties ran deeper. Japanese leaders were keenly aware of what happened to non-Western countries that could not repay their foreign debts. Europeans regularly intervened in, and sometimes occupied insolvent nations. The cases of Egypt, Mexico, and Turkey were among the better known. Ulysses S. Grant happily stoked Japanese fears when he visited the emperor in 1879. There was nothing "Japan should avoid more strenuously than incurring debts to European nations," advised the former president of the United States. The Egyptian khedive had been allowed to "borrow right and left" until Egypt became a "dependency" of British and French creditors in 1876. It was better, judged Grant, for a government to borrow from its own people.[17]

Japanese leaders firmly agreed. In lieu of foreign capital, the state did its utmost to mobilize the meager surpluses of the people. Taxation furnished the largest part of the government's extractions. But it did not take officials long to eye the growing pool of postal savings, too, as a rich source of national finance. In 1884 a powerful group of bureaucrats seized control of postal deposits. One hundred twenty-seven years later, Japan still lives with the consequences. Finance Minister Matsukata Masayoshi arranged for all postal savings funds to be transferred to the Ministry of Finance. The ministry's Deposit Bureau managed these monies following its creation the following year. Henceforth, Ministry of Finance officials invested the country's postal savings with nearly total discretion. Governments in Britain and France likewise required postal savings banks to forward deposits to institutions run by finance bureaucrats. The French connection was notable. Much has been made of the increasing influence of German ideas on Meiji Japan.[18] Institutionally, however, Japanese bureaucrats were more drawn to the centralized French state than to the federal system of Germany. Japan's Deposit Bureau closely resembled its French namesake, the Caisse des Dépôts et Consignations. Matsukata had investigated French and Belgian financial administration firsthand a few years earlier.[19]

Like their French counterparts, Japanese bureaucrats gained ready access to the expanding assets of postal savings—piles of cash they could invest in national projects without budgetary approval by the parliament. The Deposit Bureau financed government bonds for the Sino-Japanese War (1894–95) and the Russo-Japanese War (1904–1905). To spur economic development, the Deposit Bureau channeled substantial sums to the government's "special banks"—notably the Hypothec Bank (est. 1896) and the Industrial Bank of Japan (est. 1900). Both were modeled after the French state's special banks. The Deposit Bureau also invested hefty sums in the development of the new colonies of Taiwan and Korea and later in the South Manchurian Railway. Besides lending to agriculture, the special banks made low-interest loans to modern industries.[20]

As in France, local notables and businessmen accused national officials of using the people's savings for their own political schemes. The postal savings system removed scarce capital from the locales in which it was deposited. The "Nishihara loans" ranks as the most notorious abuse of the system. To strengthen Japan's influence in China, the government in 1917 arranged for the special banks to extend ¥145 million to Duan Qirui's tottering regime in Beijing. After Chinese officials squandered the money, Japanese leaders milked the Deposit Bureau's postal savings funds to repay the special banks.[21]

Officials did all they could to fatten their cash cow. They privileged postal savings while inhibiting the development of private savings banks. The state initially welcomed the establishment of philanthropically minded savings banks. Inspired by his studies in America and Britain, Hara Rokurō founded the first licensed savings bank, the Tokyo Savings Bank, in 1880. The bank pledged to place the interests of "ordinary people" ahead of shareholders. In practice, few of the early savings banks adequately protected depositors, plagued by insufficient reserves and occasional malfeasance. Ministry of Finance officials concluded that small savers would be better served by expanding postal savings offices nationwide. From 1884 to 1890, the ministry refused to authorize any new savings bank. In the meantime, the government lowered minimum deposits, simplified withdrawal procedures, and maintained above-market interest rates on postal deposits. Surging postal savings dwarfed deposits in the savings banks. The savings banks resumed growth during the 1890s. By 1910 roughly one-third of all savings-banks accounts were in private savings banks and two-thirds in postal savings.[22] However, official obstruction had given the postal savings system a huge head start in the competition for small savings. The savings banks declined precipitously following the 1927 financial panic, and all but disappeared by 1945.

Like contemporary France and Britain, Japan experienced the logic of state-led savings promotion. Between 1900 and 1910, fueled no doubt by interventionist national campaigns, the number of postal accounts rose from two million to eleven million (22 percent of the population). Japan rivaled Britain and the Netherlands in the proportion of the population saving at the post office, behind only Belgium. Control of postal savings funds had given the central bureaucracy more and more reason to encourage the people to save.

◆

Confucian Victorians and the New Middle Class

The encouragement of saving involved more than the creation of savings institutions. As in the West, "thrift" in Meiji Japan was at the core of the vast ideological project to create a nation of self-reliant individuals. The New Japan demanded new Japanese. In a veritable cultural revolution, reforms in the 1870s abolished the hereditary status system of the Tokugawa era. New laws recognized the freedom to choose one's occupation and move freely about the country. Under the emerging capitalist order, former samurai became entrepreneurs, and peasants sent sons to be educated in the cities. The old exhortations to "frugality" would have to be revised, for they acted to discourage the accumulation of savings that enabled people to move up.

It was in this fluid environment that Samuel Smiles made his Japanese debut. Smiles crystallized the new thinking on thrift in far-off Japan, much as he had in Britain. *Self-Help* appeared in Japanese in 1871, just three years after the Meiji Restoration. Rendered as *Saikoku risshi hen* (Lofty Ambitions in Western Countries), it was one of the most widely read books of the Meiji era. Boasted translator Nakamura

Masanao (Keiu) in a letter to Smiles, "almost all the high class of our fellow-countrymen know what *Self-Help* is."[23] Nakamura proceeded to translate *Character*, which also sold well. How do we explain Smiles's enormous appeal to the Japanese? As elsewhere, ambitious youths— suddenly freed of the status system—savored *Self-Help*'s stories of self-made men.

Yet the messages of self-help and thrift, as Smiles often remarked, were about more than individual success. His emphasis on "character" and the "gentleman," notes historian Earl Kinmonth, resonated with the Confucian upbringing of Japanese readers, many of whom had been samurai.[24] Nakamura Masanao, a former Confucian scholar himself, deftly translated Smiles's precepts into traditional Japanese virtues. The secrets of Western wealth and power came across as traits readers already revered: self-control, self-cultivation, perseverance, diligence, and honesty. *Self-Help*'s advice on thrift, too, accorded well with Tokugawa-era ideals of frugality prevailing among samurai, merchants, and rich peasants. The translated chapter on "Money—Its Use and Abuse" warned readers to live within their means, keep out of debt, and avoid useless expenditures on present gratifications. Even as they reinforced traditional values, however, Smiles's books helped modernize Japanese thinking on saving during the 1870s. *Self-Help*, the translation, com-municated that all the people—regardless of their status under the old order—were capable of improving their family's comfort by working hard and saving.[25]

Japanese leaders, who numbered among *Self-Help*'s greatest fans, also agreed with Smiles that thrifty populaces beget powerful, wealthy nations. As the Iwakura Mission traveled the length and breadth of Europe in 1872–73, officials related the economic habits of each people to national progress. Germans were thrifty and hard-working, observed senior oligarch Ōkubo Toshimichi.[26] British husbands and wives re-portedly kept fastidious accounts of their businesses and households. Britain became the world's richest country due to "its people's industri-ousness," whereas in Spain, "simply taking a short siesta is enough to gain one a reputation for hard work." Were the thrifty Dutch to culti-vate the rich plains of China, mused the scribe Kume Kunitake, "who knows how many hundred Hollands could be born in the East?" Could the Japanese compare themselves to the Dutch in diligence, "or are we, from the outset, more akin to the indolent Chinese?"[27]

That was of course a rhetorical question. To catch up to the West, the oligarchs resolved they too must inculcate diligence and thrift in the masses. At the time, literate Japanese society was caught up in the frenzy of "civilization and enlightenment." In 1873 officials joined intellectuals to form the influential Meiji Six Society (Meirokusha), whose founders included Self-Help's translator Nakamura Masanao. The primary goal, he insisted, was to "change the character of the people and to elevate them to the level of the most advanced peoples of Europe and America." Japanese needed to learn perseverance, diligence, and the "value of money." Following the creation of the Ministry of Education in 1871, "ethics" (shūshin) emerged as a vital part of the national system of compulsory elementary education. While in America and Europe, the Iwakura Mission frequently noted the centrality of ethics instruction in the elementary schools, where children were taught how to become orderly, productive members of society.[28]

Thrift took its place among the core values propagated in Japan's ethics curriculum. Many ethics textbooks were in fact translations of popular moral tracts from the West. Smiles's Self-Help was one of the Ministry of Education's first approved texts in 1872 (see plate 1). Aesop's "The Ant and the Grasshopper" has a remarkably long history in Japan. Introduced by Portuguese Jesuit missionaries, Aesop's Fables first appeared in Japanese translation in 1593. Nearly three centuries later Japanese readers rediscovered the Fables, thanks to a new translation in 1873. Aesop's Fables became one of the best-known moral texts in ethics courses before World War II and again in the postwar decades. Generations of Japanese children were taught to identify with the ant and his fellow ants (see figure 8 and plate 2). These insects worked hard in the summer, cooperated for the greater good, and above all saved for the future. To this day, when asked why postwar Japanese saved so much, informants typically compare themselves to Aesop's ant. In some postwar textbooks, the ants are kind enough to give the thriftless grasshopper a morsel. But in the prewar translations, the grasshopper served as a stark reminder of what happens to children who don't save. As in the Victorian version, the grasshopper was sent away to starve. Equally

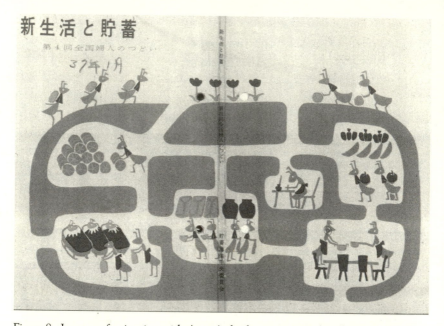

Figure 8. Japanese fascination with Aesop's thrifty ant persisted well beyond World War II, but postwar images sometimes took on gendered tones reflecting the rise of the housewife as saver. In this cover of the proceedings of the 1962 national women's meeting on "New Life and Saving," males work on the outside, while female ants manage the home and keep household accounts (center-right). *Shin seikatsu to chochiku: Dai 4-kai zenkoku fujin no tsudoi kiroku.*

disturbing to Japanese pupils must have been his humiliation at the hands of the group. "You better work hard and earn money while you're young," read the moral in one edition, "so when the winter of old age comes, you won't be laughed at by ants."[29]

The Meiji state's expansion of thrift programs mirrored developments in the contemporary West. Samuel Smiles himself had shifted from emphasizing individual cultivation in *Self-Help* to institutional encouragement in his book *Thrift*. Japanese translations of *Thrift* never enjoyed the commercial success of *Self-Help*, but they powerfully influenced elite bureaucrats. In 1885–86, the Bureau of Posts translated *Thrift* to learn more about Britain's Post Office Savings Bank and European school savings programs. A new translation of *Thrift*, appearing at the height of the Russo-Japanese War savings campaign, appealed to a broader audience of social reformers, educators, and bureaucrats.[30] Paul Mayet, a German agricultural economist working for the Japanese government, first proposed a nationwide system of school savings banks in 1886. Some years later a rising Home Ministry official, Kawamura Takeji, made an impassioned plea for emulating Belgium's highly regarded school savings banks.[31] Small as it was, Belgium fascinated Japanese officials as a model for catching up to the major powers by mobilizing one's human resources. In just forty years, this once impoverished nation had become an export powerhouse fueled by abundant capital, they observed, because Belgians had learned to save at school. Everyone knows that saving benefits the individual, Kawamura declared, but it is also "one's duty to the State."[32]

The task of school saving was made easier by the spread of postal savings offices, which handled most deposits from the classroom. In 1900 post offices introduced "stamp savings," adopting the British innovation of stamp slip deposits. Henceforth Japanese children, too, would buy and paste postage stamps onto sheets until they added up to the minimum postal deposit. By 1906 Japan boasted one of the highest rates of school saving in the world. One-quarter of the nation's elementary students, nearly two million children, held postal savings accounts.[33] Thrift education—mixed with large doses of economic nationalism— became part of growing up Japanese (see figure 9).

Some of Japan's leading progressives took part in encouraging the populace to save. Particularly active were members of the self-styled "middle class," or what sociologists term the *new* middle class. The category included educators, lawyers, journalists, health professionals, social welfare specialists, and white-collar employees in government and business. Their status rested not on wealth per se, but rather on the acquisition of Western knowledge. Many middle-class activists— including several notable women—were converts to Christianity, especially Protestantism, who maintained regular contact with moral and social reform movements in North America and Britain.

Among the Victorian values they imbibed, Japanese reformers seized upon diligence and thrift to assert the superiority of the "middle ranks." "Work, frugality, thrift, and activity" characterized the productive middle class, explained one women's magazine in 1904. By contrast, the

Figure 9. School savings, Japan, 1936. Savings campaign poster commemorating annual Diligence, Thrift, and Savings Day. Yūsei Kenkyūjo, *Modanizumu no jidai*, 13. Courtesy of the Communications Museum, Japan.

upper class lived lives of "idleness and debauchery," while those in the lower class succumbed to "laziness, wasteful spending, and immorality."[34] Beginning in the 1880s, progressives waged spirited campaigns to bring middle-class morality and financial self-discipline to rich and poor alike. Middle-class investigators conducted the first surveys of urban poverty. Some became socialist and labor leaders. Yet sympathy for the poor did not prevent them from frequently complaining that laborers spent recklessly on *sake*, gambling, and whoring with little thought of saving.[35] Middle-class figures thus had their own reasons for encouraging saving, and those reasons differed from the state's. As Christians, many suffered discrimination and sometimes persecution. Protestant and secular progressives also attacked Meiji legal codes for subordinating the married woman to the patriarchic head of the household. They looked instead to Anglo-American norms of the woman as mother, thrifty manager of household finances, and equal partner with her husband.

Despite tensions with the state, the middle-class quest to "civilize" the habits of the lower classes motivated prominent reformers to cooperate with government officials in encouraging popular saving. The partnership proved irresistible. Higher civil servants turned to Christian specialists for help in the areas of education, charity work, and moral uplift. Reformers, for their part, jumped at the chance to use state institutions—schools, campaigns, welfare programs—to instill middle-class virtues in the entire nation. The powerful Home Ministry soon employed several Protestant social workers and clergymen as temporary commissioned officers. Kanamori Michitomo, former head of the Protestant academy Dōshisha, emerged as the government's leading spokesman in savings campaigns. Commissioned by the Home Ministry and Ministry of Finance, Kanamori wrote several primers on the encouragement of thrift and children's saving. From 1900 to 1913, the well-known missionary crisscrossed the country, exhorting local groups to save.[36]

American-educated Protestants preached thrift to villagers, while conservative bureaucrats extolled Samuel Smiles, and ethics textbooks featured Benjamin Franklin's homilies on industry and frugality. The line between Victorian and indigenous notions of saving certainly had

blurred. Cosmopolitan Protestants in fact had a large hand in inventing Japan's indigenous "traditions" of thrift. Ninomiya Sontoku, the
Tokugawa-era village reformer, would seem a surprising object of Christian adoration (see chapter 4). He couched his messages of diligence
and saving in the Buddhist language of "repaying virtue" (hōtoku).
Confucianism, too, pervaded his thought. The Meiji regime resurrected
Ninomiya as the model Japanese subject who embodied self-sacrifice
and obedience toward parents and, by extension, the emperor and his
state. Curiously, foreign missionaries and Protestant converts claimed
Ninomiya as their own, casting the sage as the Japanese who best personified the "Christian" morals of hard work, frugality, and even indi-
viduality. In 1894 Uchimura Kanzō, Protestant cleric and famous victim of anti-Christian persecution, compared Ninomiya's Hōtokuki to
the "Christian bible itself."[37] To Tomeoka Kōsuke, another influential
Protestant, this canonical text stood as the "Orient's Self-Help."[38]

Ironically, the figure most responsible for formulating the official
cult of Ninomiya was Tomeoka, the Christian social worker. Commissioned by the Home Ministry, he became a familiar presence at the
government's diligence and thrift rallies throughout Japan. With his
assistance the Home Ministry established the Central Hōtokukai in
1906. The state-run federation oversaw the massive effort to organize
Hōtoku societies in every village.[39] Tomeoka was captivated by Ninomiya's teachings on "self-reliance" (jiriki). Whereas the peasant sage
had encouraged villagers to work together to revitalize the community
as a whole, Tomeoka understood self-reliance as the means to achieve
individual independence. The Japanese state advanced yet another understanding: self-reliance meant villagers should work hard and economize, so they could pay high taxes, deposit in postal savings, and avoid
relying on public assistance. Whatever their understandings, Japan's
educated elites united to encourage thrift in the masses.[40]

Organizing Thrift at the Rice Roots

Little by little, the Japanese state established the world's most intrusive
system of savings promotion. Officials organized entire villages into what

became known as savings associations (*chochiku kumiai*). Many savings associations based themselves on village groups that had thrived since the late Tokugawa era. These ranged from credit and savings confraternities (*kō*) to Ninomiya Sontoku's *hōtokusha*. The associations also incorporated aspects of the old communal granary system in which peasants collectively saved surplus grain to cope with emergencies.

But there was also much that was new. Instead of contributing crops to the communal granary as before, Meiji-era farmers were told to deposit money in individual postal savings accounts. The Ministry of Agriculture and Commerce relied on the advice of Paul Mayet, the German agricultural economist. Mayet recommended the establishment of "Rural Savings Unions," modeled after the savings societies that abounded in German communities. Savings associations would encourage farmers to save in two important ways. They significantly improved access to financial institutions at a time when postal savings offices did not exist in most villages. Members tendered their savings to the association representative, who then deposited the money in the member's account at the nearest post office. Second, savings associations would teach peasants the utility of "*regulated* saving," argued Mayet. Members promised to contribute a set sum on a weekly or monthly basis. Farmers would thus become accustomed to "regular" saving and "regular economy." In Mayet's liberal scheme, deposits would be voluntary. Delinquents would simply earn no interest or lower interest on their balance.[41]

Voluntary saving, however, was not high on the Japanese state's agenda. Over the next several decades, officials and local elites advanced a system of regulated saving that administered heavy doses of compulsion. As revealed in local reports from the 1880s, all households in the village or hamlet were expected to join the savings association. Regulations further limited members' ability to make withdrawals. Associations imposed harsh penalties on those who failed to make regular deposits— the most extreme being expulsion from the savings group and cutting the household off from interaction with the community. The government counted on local hierarchy and group pressure to induce peasants to save more than they would have on their own. Those in charge of the savings associations were typically village headmen or one's landlord.[42]

At the dawn of the twentieth century, the Japanese government embarked on nationwide savings campaigns unprecedented in fervor and thoroughness. Whereas the authorities had previously encouraged peasant thrift to stave off destitution, the new campaigns promoted saving mainly to finance Japan's soaring military and economic ambitions. The Sino-Japanese War had been a dazzling success. After handily defeating China in 1895, Japan forced the Qing court to pay a massive indemnity that helped finance a veritable industrial revolution in Japan. Two years later, Japan adopted the gold standard, paving the way for the immediate resumption of foreign borrowing after a twenty-four-year moratorium.

The outbreak of the Russo-Japanese War in 1904 saw the Bank of Japan's vice governor racing off to New York and London to secure war loans. Initially Anglo-American financiers were dubious that this upstart Asian nation could defeat the Russian bear. But the New York Jewish banker Jacob Schiff—outraged by Russia's anti-Semitic pogroms—rushed to finance his enemy's enemy. Anglo-American concerns put together hefty loans that enabled Japanese forces to fight on to victory. Japan continued to borrow heavily from abroad after the end of hostilities. From 1904 to 1914, capital imports generated fully one-sixth of the Japanese government's revenues and one-fifth of productive capital formation.[43]

For Japanese leaders, the Russo-Japanese War was a moment of truth. Had the nation bitten off more than it could chew? Japan suddenly became a great power while remaining one of the industrial world's poorest societies. The government immediately confronted the postwar costs of servicing rising foreign debt, improving infrastructure at home, maintaining a formidable military, and administering its expanding colonial empire. Already in control of Taiwan, Japan added Korea, half of Sakhalin Island, and territory in southern Manchuria. Officials worried whether the populace would continue to bear the crushing burden of high wartime taxes and national saving. Ominously in September 1905, thousands in Tokyo engaged in violent protests after the Japanese government failed to extract an indemnity from the defeated Russians. The ramifications were clear to officials and ordinary subjects alike. This time, unlike the aftermath of the Sino-Japanese War, the Japanese people would have to pay the full costs of what the state called "postwar management." To achieve "a grand victory in the coming peacetime war" with Western commercial and military powers, warned one Home Ministry bureaucrat, the fifty million Japanese would have to keep on saving.[44]

Such anxieties prompted the government to mount the first sustained drive to encourage saving and economy. At the height of the Russo-Japanese War, patriotism motivated many Japanese to save at record levels in post offices and banks. But from the start of hostilities, officials also adopted new measures to make the "spirit of saving" permanent.[45] No sooner had the Russo-Japanese War broken out than the Home Minister directed prefectural governors nationwide to extract savings from the communal savings associations and establish such associations wherever they did not exist. Working with local elites, officials admonished villagers against squandering money on "pleasures" and "wasteful expenditures." The resulting savings should be deposited in post offices and sound savings banks. Rural Japanese encountered a barrage of wartime exhortations from "diligence and thrift" associations to avoid luxury, increase production, and pay ever-rising taxes.[46]

National leaders aggressively promoted saving long after the Russo-Japanese War ended. On the ideological front, the state issued the Boshin Imperial Rescript of 1908. Combining indigenous and Western discourses, the Rescript served as the canon of savings campaigns for the next two decades. There was no mistaking the "Japanese" parts of the message. The emperor instructed his subjects to be "frugal in the management of their households ... to abide by simplicity and avoid ostentation, and to inure themselves to arduous toil without yielding to any degree of indulgence." At the same time, official interpreters likened their exhortations to contemporary Western efforts to advance national prosperity. Diligence, thrift, and production—the Rescript decreed—would enable Japan "to keep pace with the constant progress of the world, and to participate in the blessings of its civilization."[47] Home Minister Hirata Tōsuke explained the benefits of combining diligence and thrift. Because "we're poor in capital," working hard and cutting useless expenditures would generate "capital, enrich the nation, and put our homes in order." Although cabinet ministers lambasted extravagance in the cities, their real target was the countryside. Ōura Kanetake, minister of agriculture and commerce, expressed shock at the extent to which the "winds of luxury" had reached even the formerly "steady" rural areas where people now dreamed of getting rich quick. Anticipating the slogans of World War II, he labeled luxury the "enemy of the nation."[48]

The ensuing Local Improvement Campaign saw the government massively intruding into the everyday lives of the rural populace. Officials left little doubt about what they meant by "improvement." In lieu of technological and capital inputs from the outside, villagers were expected to generate savings for the nation by sheer effort, austerity, and cooperation. Improvements in farm yields would result from pooling resources through officially sponsored agricultural cooperatives and *hōtokusha* credit societies. The state also strove to reduce spending on the locales by encouraging residents to engage in mutual assistance and "group saving" to pay for community improvements. As one prefectural governor put it, "If the entire nation works longer and thereby saves one sen [one-hundredth of a yen] per additional day, the extra savings—they say—would add up to ¥182,500,000 the first year ... and in the *fiftieth* year to ¥38,900,000,000."[49]

In many communities, officials went to extraordinary lengths to coax those surpluses out of the locals. Typical was Kashimo in Gifu prefecture where the mayor and postmaster stimulated saving by means of the village savings association. Once a month, headmen in the ten subdivisions gathered savings from households and deposited the monies at the post office. Lest they flag, the mayor routinely harangued headmen to increase their neighborhoods' totals from the previous month.[50] Another common practice was to convert "diligence" to "thrift." Senchō village in Kumamoto prefecture adopted the following regulations. Every month in their spare time, all men were to make three lengths of rope, "each weighing 10 *kan*" (82 pounds); women would weave one mat. A committee in each subdivision then sold the rope and mats, depositing the proceeds at the post office in the name of individual households. To ensure things happened as planned, the mayor annually inspected every passbook.[51] In the wake of the Russo-Japanese War, officials moreover worked with unit commanders to encourage veterans to deposit their meritorious service awards in postal savings and keep them there. Most ex-servicemen were induced to join the savings associations, whose regulations empowered mayors to refuse withdrawals for anything other than investments deemed productive.[52]

Savings promotion piggybacked on long-standing campaigns to "rectify morals" (kyōfū) in the countryside. This was something upon which bureaucrats, urban progressives, and provincial elites could agree. The rustics, they believed, would save more money if they stopped spending so much on weddings, funerals, and other forms of social interaction. Officials—no less than the Japanese Women's Christian Temperance Union—decried wasteful expenditures on drink and tobacco. Allegedly inspired by the governor of Ibaraki prefecture, residents of one hamlet established the Moral Rectification and Savings Society. Every household agreed to deposit at least ten sen (one-tenth of a yen) monthly in their postal savings account, to be left unredeemed for ten years. The savings association further issued a long list of prohibitions on gift-giving, summertime drinking by the kō confraternities, and all use of tobacco. Members were required to snitch on anyone seen smoking. Savings rose, the association proudly reported. No one in the hamlet any longer smoked, nor did children dare sport toy cigarettes.[53]

Economists are skeptical about the capacity of campaigns to persuade people to save. But the interventions of the Japanese state described above offer compelling evidence in support. Small savings surged between 1903 and 1910 precisely when the regime barraged people with messages to save while it expanded savings associations, postal savings, and school savings. The number of postal savings accounts leapt from 3,562,000 to 11,266,000. Aggregate postal deposits increased more than fivefold. More than any other factor, conclude Japanese scholars, the government's highly intrusive campaigns introduced habits of small saving to millions of small farmers and working people. In particular, the ubiquitous savings associations—encompassing more than 1.2 million members in 1914—demonstrated their worth in encouraging, and often compelling, practices of regulated saving.[54]

Great Japan: A Model of National Efficiency

The degree to which people saved became a common index of national strength among the great powers in the decade leading up to World War I. Japanese bureaucrats tended to highlight the country's relative *weaknesses*. They employed cross-national indices to prod the country to work harder and save more, while seeking increased appropriations for their own ministries. Agencies commonly released international tables listing Japan's high rates of death, suicide, divorce, and imprisonment, and its low level of saving. In 1908–1909, according to one chart, Japanese saved a mere ¥5 per capita, compared to ¥172 by both Americans and Germans and ¥110 by Britons.[55] The authorities took particular pleasure in disparaging the profligate habits of Japanese farmers vis-à-vis French or German cultivators. Many Japanese farmers, claimed one governor, spent their work time "humming a tune or engaged in idle chit-chat. When you come right down to it, their mouths and hands don't work at the same time."[56]

Ironically, at the moment Japanese bureaucrats were ridiculing the populace's spendthrift ways, Westerners took notice of Japan's singular success in mobilizing its citizens. While fighting the Russo-Japanese War, Japan became the first nation to conduct a war savings campaign. In Britain, the world's only Asian power gathered a cult-like following as it went from victory to victory against the Russians. Feelings of national decline gripped the British at the time. Germany challenged the nation's economic and military hegemony. In 1899–1900 Her Majesty's forces suffered humiliating setbacks against the mangy Boers in South Africa. Among political leaders and intellectuals, the call went up for making Great Britain great again by pursuing "national efficiency." Many studied German efficiency, but Germany loomed as the enemy. Japan, on the other hand, had become Britain's closest ally as the result of the Anglo-Japanese Alliance of 1902. From Conservatives to Liberal imperialists to Fabian Socialists, eminent Britons trumpeted Japan as the leading model of national efficiency.[57] To be efficient, all agreed, the state and its people needed to work as one in war and peace.

In 1906 the journalist Alfred Stead published the provocatively titled *Great Japan: A Study in National Efficiency*. Former Liberal prime minister Lord Rosebery wrote the laudatory foreword. Beset by partisan squabbles, Britain had "muddled through," he observed, while the "old State machine creaks on." Fortunately the country was furnished with the stimulating example of Japan. Here was a "nation determined on efficiency" led by what Rosebery could only envy: a "directing and vitalizing Government that shall do and inspire great things." Stead himself portrayed Japan as the land where the state molded a patriotic, frugal people prepared to sacrifice for the country's good on the battlefield and at home. In the Russo-Japanese War, Stead reported, Japanese saved prodigiously at post offices and banks to finance the war: "The farmer, labourer, the tradesman, and the servant eagerly handed in their savings. The very school-children, hoarding up their small pocketmoney ... also carried their offerings to the Treasury department." In Japan "no one Atlas is left to bear up the skies—every man, woman, and child is ready and proud to share the task." From whence came their self-sacrifice and frugality? Stead was unequivocal. It was Bushido, literally the "Way of the samurai." Even poor shopkeepers and milkmen, he insisted, "retain all the instincts of the samurai."[58]

Why would Britons propose emulating the ways of an Oriental nation rooted in the ancient warrior code? Curiously they found in Bushido a vitalizing force that transcended Japan. As Henry Dyer wrote in *Dai Nippon: The Britain of the East*, the newest Power combined "a large share of Anglo-Saxon virility" and "Eastern thought." H. G. Wells, himself an apostle of national efficiency, wrote *A Modern Utopia* at the height of the Russo-Japanese War. His utopian state was staffed by talented, austere administrators who ruled a society built on "self-sacrifice" and the rejection of "extravagances." He called his guardians the *samurai* (figure 10) The British craze for samurai was sparked by the much-reprinted *Bushido, the Soul of Japan*, first published by Nitobe Inazō in 1899. Nitobe's samurai had little time for killing. Instead they bore a distinct resemblance to Victorian gentlemen, embodying the virtues of self-control, honesty, thrift, and a manly distaste for luxury. And small wonder. The author was no nativist, but a cosmopolitan Japanese Quaker. Nitobe wrote the book to explain to foreigners (and his Philadelphia wife) how Bushido provided Japanese with a form of moral education equivalent to the religious instruction in European schools.

Figure 10. The austere Samurai as model for Britain, 1905. Frontispiece by Edmund J. Sullivan, in H. G. Wells, *A Modern Utopia*. Courtesy of the Rare Books Division, Department of Rare Books and Special Collections, Princeton University Library.

British writers fixated on Nitobe's observation that since the Meiji Restoration, Bushido "permeated all social classes," infusing the nation with loyalty and patriotism.[59]

Japan was not the only model available, but this other island empire provoked Britons to imagine new ways of mobilizing the home front to save for national power. As the Russo-Japanese War raged, *The Times* urged readers to adopt the self-denial of their Japanese allies. The daily reported on the intrusive frugality campaigns at the village level as evidence of the "single-minded devotion with which the Japanese people endeavor to meet their country's needs at the present crisis."[60] Japanophiles would go on to play prominent roles in establishing Britain's own national savings campaign in World War I. In 1912 the gentlemen reformers of London's Agenda Club received a bejeweled sword from the Japanese Chargé d'Affaires as a symbol of the "self-sacrificing spirit" of the samurai who made the New Japan. Seven years and one world war later, that sword was presented to Sir Robert Kindersley, director of the war savings campaign. The National Savings Movement, he declared, "could never have been the living force which it has proved itself to be unless it had been placed upon the same foundation as that of the Samurai—the spirit of self-sacrifice and of personal service for the State.... [It] was this spirit *permeating the whole country* which won the war for us."[61] Britain, the home of Victorian thrift and an inspiration for Meiji Japan, now claimed to have learned a thing or two from Japan's statist model of national saving. The history of thrift truly had become global.

6

MOBILIZING FOR THE GREAT WAR

Saving is now a national duty, because if we spend our
money we cannot lend it to the Government which wants
it for the costliest war that ever was waged.
> —Britain's National Organizing Committee for
> War Savings, 1916[1]

𝔚e must 𝔅eat 𝔈nglan∂!

NOT WITH WEAPONS ONLY—BUT WITH MONEY
TOO! ...
Therefore LEND ALL YOU HAVE beyond the bare
necessaries of life, LEND it to your Fatherland the safest
Debtor in the World.
> —German leaflet for the Sixth War Loan, 1917[2]

Nineteenth-century wars were short. In the hundred years after the
Napoleonic wars, hostilities between the great powers typically
lasted one or two years. When fighting broke out in Europe in August
1914, both sides again expected a brief war. The Schlieffen Plan called
for the German army to take Paris just thirty-nine days after mobilization. The Kaiser's troops marched through Belgium, believing they'd be
home before the "leaves dropped from the trees."[3] After the German
advance stalled in September, the French and British likewise predicted the war would be over by Christmas. And for one of the belligerents, that's exactly what happened. Allied with Britain, the Japanese
overwhelmed German forces at Qingdao in northern China after only

eight weeks of fighting and essentially sat out of the rest of the war (aside from some naval assistance against German submarines in the Mediterranean). Europeans were not so lucky. The Eastern Front saw several more years of offensive and counteroffensive, while the Western Front devolved into the unimaginable. By November 1914 the Allied and German armies were mired in trenches that stretched 350 miles from Switzerland to the Belgian coast. That grim line would barely move over the next three years.

Few anticipated this protracted war, in large part because few believed it could be financed. The staggering costs of modern warfare would make conflict among the major continental powers nearly "impossible," predicted the Polish banker Ivan Block in 1899. Moreover, nations had financed recent wars—notably the Japanese against the Russians—by borrowing heavily from investors in an array of countries from Britain and America to France and Germany. How, commentators wondered, would Europeans fight one another when they no longer could borrow from one another?[4] The two remaining financial options would be taxation and domestic borrowing. Yet in World War I, the belligerents resisted paying for more than a fraction of war costs from revenue. Taxation financed at most one-quarter of war expenditures in the United States and Britain, less than 17 percent in Germany, and almost nothing in France. Instead, each government relied on borrowing from its own people at levels never before seen.[5] Intrusive savings campaigns became a striking feature of daily life in World War I. Citizens were relentlessly exhorted to buy war bonds or otherwise place their savings at the service of the state.

Some twenty years later, savings campaigns again dominated the home front in the century's second total war. Taken together, World Wars I and II imparted new meanings to saving and consumption. People continued to save in banks and post offices, but millions more learned habits of systematically investing in government bonds or national savings certificates and stamps. Citizens were admonished to save not simply out of self-interest, but as their patriotic duty to the nation and its fighting men. Everywhere "war savings" involved more than lending money. Savings drives also harangued citizens to practice "economy" in consumption as a vital weapon in the struggle for national survival.

Only if civilians engaged in a "general reduction in the consumption of commodities," insisted Britain's war minister Lord Kitchener in 1916, would the nation be able to contain inflationary pressures and free up labor and capital for military needs.[6] Chancellor of the Exchequer Reginald McKenna was blunter still: "Extravagance and waste are treason in war time."[7] In Germany the planner and industrialist Walther Rathenau warned countrymen to overcome their "crazy hunger for commodities," describing consumption as "not a private affair but an affair of the community, the state, ethics and humanity." Historians commonly write about the twentieth century in terms of the rise of "the consumer" and "consumer society." But the experiences of the two world wars should give us pause. Interestingly the word "consumption" first gained wide currency in Europe and Japan during World War I in the context of drives to persuade consumers not to spend, but to *restrain* desires in the name of the greater good.[8]

Persuasion was indeed the name of the game. The same techniques that sold soap would "sell" saving. Savings campaigns occupied center stage in the unprecedented use of propaganda during the two world wars. Ultimately the capacity to wage protracted war depended on maintaining the entire nation's willingness to contribute lives, labor, and savings. States harnessed several new technologies of mass communications. Besides placing countless newspaper ads and distributing handbills, war savings campaigns spread the word through motion pictures, sound recordings, and later radio.

Nothing captured the public's attention more than posters. Color lithography burst forth as a mass medium in the late nineteenth century. Although posters began life in the service of art and commercial advertising, governments in World War I seized upon their potential to rally popular support. Posters were soon reproduced in mind-boggling quantities—plastered onto kiosks, public buildings, and billboards. In the United States, nineteen million posters were printed for just two campaigns, the Third and Fourth Liberty Loan drives of 1918. War loan campaigns in Germany and Austria-Hungary employed the most visually arresting posters. Despite their overall conservatism and militarism, the Central Powers recruited leading avant-garde designers, including artists from Vienna's Secessionist school. British placards tended to be stodgier, while American war bond posters made up in mass appeal for what they lacked aesthetically.[9]

Savings campaign posters traveled well. Minimal in text but powerful in image, they transmitted methods of savings promotion throughout the world from the 1910s to the 1950s. National styles developed, but we also see remarkable similarities in the visual messages to save, economize, and buy war bonds. This was no accident. To surpass the enemy in propaganda, states systematically collected posters of other nations. Britain's state-run Imperial War Museum amassed some twenty thousand war posters, cartoons, advertisements, and pamphlets in 1917 and 1918. Following World War I, Japan's Foreign Ministry collected more than six hundred wartime posters from America, Britain, France, Canada, India, and Italy. Propagandists in Britain and the United States cooperated closely, sharing posters in both world wars. In the postwar eras, too, governments frequently exchanged savings posters. Posters in one nation invariably reflected themes seen elsewhere. Sometimes they simply plagiarized (see figures 11 and 12). America's most famous recruiting placard, "Uncle Sam Wants You," was actually a knockoff of the 1914 poster, "Britons, [Lord Kitchener] Wants You."[10] The Canadians produced yet another variation (see plate 3). Whatever the inspiration, war posters helped standardize appeals to save around the globe.

Unleashing the Armies of Saving

Despite similarities in propaganda, belligerents in World War I organized their savings campaigns in different ways. The French were quick off the bat, turning to small savers to fund a substantial portion of war spending. The state could rely on time-tested mechanisms to finance national projects from mass savings. Deposits in the local and postal savings banks had long been placed in government's Caisse des Dépôts et Consignations, which in World War I digested a major part of the national defense loans. To encourage savings bank accounts and postal savings in wartime, the state doubled the maximum amount allowed in each account, raised the interest rate, and exempted all interest from taxation. In even greater numbers the French flocked to buy national

Figures 11 and 12. Transnational appeals to women as savers, 1918. Although the United States emulated many aspects of Britain's war savings campaign, in this instance British propagandists copied the American poster—and crudely so. Joan of Arc was the rage in America following the release of Cecil B. DeMille's pro-French film, *Joan the Woman* (1916). The poster played less well among the English, for whom Saint Joan was anything but a hero—having led French forces against them in the Hundred Years War.
Poster on left by Bert Thomas. Reproduced by permission of TNA, NSC 5/8.
Poster on right by Haskell Coffin. Reproduced by permission of the Robert D. Farber University Archives & Special Collections Department, Brandeis University.

bonds, as they had in times of crisis since the aftermath of the Franco-Prussian War (see plate 4). The government sold enormous quantities of war bonds in denominations as low as 100 francs (about US$20) and national defense notes as small as 5 francs. The French citizen, reported envious U.S. Treasury officials, "neither had to be taught to save nor trained to invest his savings in government securities."[11] Patriotism reinforced traditional thrift, as countrymen answered the appeal to join the *armée de l'épargne* (army of saving).[12]

Nor did the thrifty Germans require training in saving. But because Germans of modest means lacked the French tradition of directly owning government bonds, Reich officials adopted a two-pronged approach to stimulate war saving. Local authorities and bankers encouraged the middle classes and workers to keep on saving in the familiar municipal savings banks (*Sparkassen*). Although the savings banks historically preferred to make loans within their locale, the wartime regime pressured savings banks into investing deposits in the Reich's war loans in ever-increasing amounts. The assets of the savings banks soared by 11 billion marks in 1914–18, substantially contributing to war finance. At the same time, the German government began to market bonds directly to small investors. Businesses, banks, and the wealthy bought well over half of each war loan, yet millions of ordinary Germans bought small-denomination bonds for the first time. The number of subscribers to smaller bonds (up to 200 marks) leaped from 231,000 in the first war loan drive to more than 4 million in the final campaign. In late 1916 the Reichsbank established a special office that advertised the bond drives and linked up with a voluntary network of 1,300 head agents and 100,000 regular agents nationwide.

If one believed British propaganda, the German war machine mobilized the home front with near perfect efficiency. The reality was very different. The Reich's savings campaigns did not keep up with the skyrocketing costs of war. There were limits to how much domestic savings could finance total war. While the British borrowed heavily from the Americans, wartime Germany cut itself off from most sources of international finance. German war loans developed aspects of a Ponzi scheme. Expecting a short war and eager to maintain the supply of credit to the civilian economy, the Reichsbank's "loan bureaus" lent many investors the cash they then used to buy war bonds. By autumn 1916 the public's purchase of long-term war bonds no longer financed short-term treasury bills. As shortfalls worsened, the government simply printed more money. Prices soared, culminating in the Great Inflation of 1923.[13] Germany had become anything but the "safest Debtor in the World." Military collapse in 1918—coupled with postwar economic chaos—rendered Germany's war savings campaigns a singularly unattractive model.

The nation that developed the most intrusive war savings campaigns was ironically Europe's most liberal. Prior to 1914 few regarded

Great Britain as a model of "national efficiency." The state's capacity to wage total war appeared enfeebled by traditions of individualism, laissez-faire economics, and local autonomy. Nor in the first months of World War I did the British quickly adapt to the new age of mass conscript armies and mobilized home fronts. "Business as usual" was a common refrain. Yet as the reality of protracted war sunk in, the British state leapfrogged Germany and Japan to carry out perhaps the most thorough mobilization of civilians to date. Besides introducing military conscription in 1915, the state established an array of institutions that channeled production, labor, and money toward the war effort.

In April 1916 His Majesty's government established the National War Savings Committee, charged with overseeing a nationwide network of local organizations in England and Wales. A separate War Savings Committee coordinated Scottish savings campaigns. Their origins lay not only in immediate wartime needs, but also in the national-efficiency thinking of the prewar years. Public figures had long envisioned ways of persuading the civilian populace to contribute to national strength. Several were devotees of the Japanese people's samurai-like spirit of "self-sacrifice" and broad participation in war savings drives (see chapter 5). One of their numbers, investment banker Robert Kindersley, would become the first chairman of the National War Savings Committee. Proposals for a national savings campaign moved closer to fruition following the first war loan of 1914, which relied on big investors. Influential Britons worried that American loans and the wealthy could not alone support the war's soaring costs. In June 1915 the financier Robert H. Brand, Kindersley's associate at the investment house Lazard Frères, urged the government to "bring home to every man, woman, and child" that they must economize and save as vital sacrifices for the nation.[14] Convinced, the government convened the Committee on War Loans for the Small Investor to devise the best methods for attracting the savings of working people.

Based on the committee's report of early 1916, officials recast the state's historic approach to small saving in Britain on several fronts. First, they pioneered the popular War Savings Certificate. The authorities continued to encourage deposits in postal savings and savings banks, whose funds flowed into the Treasury to be invested in the national debt. But the government decisively shifted to promoting the direct owner-ship of war debt by a broad swath of the public. Bank deposits might be withdrawn at short notice and reserves needed to be maintained, whereas the people's investments in longer-term government securities could be used in full to finance war spending.[15] War Savings Certifi-cates served these goals exquisitely. They were simple and accessible, available for purchase at post offices, official vendors, and War Savings Associations. The most popular denomination sold for less than 1 pound at the price of 15 shillings, 6 pence (20 shillings = 1 pound; 12 pence = 1 shilling). Unlike French, German, or U.S. war bonds of the time, the Certificates did not pay interest until redeemed. They could be cashed at post offices at any time, although their value would increase only after twelve months and then by a penny a month until they rose to their final value of 1 pound at the end of five years. From 1916 to 1918, more than 76 million 1-pound Certificates were issued. Typically households would own many Certificates up to the legal maximum of five hundred. The War Savings Certificate was commonly termed the "small investor's Treasury Bill."[16]

In a second innovation the British organized small savers into War Savings Associations. Leaders questioned the value of "mere propa-ganda" and slick posters, preferring "personal persuasion man to man."[17] Established as intermediaries between "the small investor and the State," War Savings Associations became the principal vehicle for selling War Savings Certificates to those of humble means. Associations sprang up in workplaces, schools, churches, friendly societies, and other social groups. At the end of World War I, more than four million people be-longed to 41,301 War Savings Associations in England and Wales and nearly 4,000 associations in Scotland. British organizers were hardly the first to discover the benefits of collective saving. Individuals tend to save more when prodded to make regular contributions by their peers and local notables. This had long been the experience of savings and credit cooperatives from Europe to East Asia. Nonetheless, British officials—like Japanese bureaucrats since the Russo-Japanese War—did not sim-ply utilize existing savings groups; they systematically organized savings associations throughout the country. Members of War Savings Associations would weekly tender small sums that accumulated toward the purchase of War Savings Certificates from association treasurers.[18]

Wartime Britain gave the world the first model of a dedicated national savings agency. The National War Savings Committee undertook propaganda work at the central level while administering a hierarchical structure of savings-promotion organizations reaching down to the village. All boroughs, county boroughs, and urban districts with more than twenty thousand inhabitants set up war savings committees known as Local Central Committees; rural and less populous urban districts established County Committees and below them Local Committees. There was something very "English" about the arrangement, insisted campaign organizers. This would not be some top-down campaign but rather the War Savings Movement: "a huge voluntary organization with almost complete freedom of action by the Committees and Associations." Just as "our Anglo-Saxon forefathers used to 'organise' themselves," reported one county committee secretary, each village dispatched "two discreet and true men" as representatives.[19]

The war savings "movement" was in fact a highly centralized operation. The staff of the state-funded National War Savings Committee swelled to 391. Claims to independence from the state rang hollow. In 1917 the government summarily deputized the War Savings Movement to run nationwide campaigns to induce Britons to subscribe to the war loan and practice "Food Economy." Tens of thousands of volunteers were commandeered in that most English of ways. The Chancellor of Exchequer politely asked Lord Kindersley if he would "be good enough to ask the War Savings Committee to place at my disposal their organization, both at Headquarters and throughout the country."[20]

"A Permanent Feature of English Life"

War savings in Britain meant much more than lending money to the war effort. Campaigns sought to shape popular thought and behavior in ways that would endure beyond the war as "a permanent feature of English life." The encouragement of saving, the government's top planners readily admitted, was at least as important as accumulating savings for the state.[21] The cultivation of enduring habits was also at work in the drive to restrain consumption. Officials excoriated arguments by merchants that mass spending, not saving, would better sustain the wartime economy. They countered with the doctrine of Goods and Services. If civilians reduced consumption of goods and services, they would not only save money for personal investment and finance the state, they would also release scarce materials, food, and labor for the war. Decreased demand in turn would lessen inflationary pressures. Christmas itself was fraught with treasonous potential. Admonishing the populace not to give presents, savings campaigners asked whether the festival was to "aid Germany or our own men in the trenches and the North Sea?"[22] Following the Allied victory in 1918, the renamed National Savings Committee continued to preach the virtues of personal economy and "wise spending" in the interwar years.[23]

Although the national committee commonly related thrift to patriotic sacrifice, officials added that saving and economy need not lower living standards. Even in the midst of war, they often identified saving with improvements in the people's welfare. Harking back to the immediate prewar years, campaigns trumpeted "efficiency" in consumption. If the populace eliminated "waste" and "luxuries," citizens could increase savings while leading healthier, prosperous lives at the same or lower levels of consumption. Specifically the war savings movement propagated methods of improving nutrition and clothing, particularly for children.[24]

The campaigns moreover appealed to rising democratic sentiments for inclusion in society and the nation. Britons commonly regarded saving and economizing as crucial means of diminishing social inequalities. Britain was rife with class tensions at the start of World War I. The propertied dominated politics, even as the burgeoning trade unions and Labour Party challenged their hold. Total war required enormous sacrifices of the working masses. Workers were called upon to eschew strikes, produce at greater levels, and ultimately offer their lives on the battlefield. Would they also—officials wondered—reduce consumption and save for the nation at the very moment they earned record-high wages in war industries? Initial signs were discouraging. In Warrington, the Trades and Labour Council shunned the local savings committee, protesting that those "who are making big war profits" shouldn't be "preaching to the wage-earning classes on the matter of economy." Accordingly, savings campaign organizers enlisted the cooperation of the labor movement's top leadership. Encouraged by the Trades Union Congress, union representatives joined war savings committees in many locales.[25]

Indeed, the war savings movement tapped into workers' desires for social leveling. By creating the War Savings Certificate, the state offered the so-called small investor the same high interest and ease of withdrawal enjoyed by wealthy bondholders. Workers delighted in the campaigns' penchant for disciplining upper-class "extravagance" in the name of shared sacrifice. Agricultural and urban laborers found themselves praised for saving their meager earnings and doing "their bit" far more than the "better-to-do." In tones recalling Daniel Defoe, war savings officials demanded the wealthy classes stop spending on "hunting, shooting, horse-racing," unless the rich actually ate what they killed.[26] The National War Savings Committee pressed the well-to-do to "set a good example" for the poorer classes. Posters denounced extravagant dress in wartime as "not only unpatriotic—it is bad form." Other placards admonished the affluent not to "ride a motor-car for pleasure." If motorists persisted, recounted one Treasury official, they faced the wrath of "the indignant and patriotic proletariat."[27]

Aiming to democratize war saving, campaigns further targeted the nation's proverbial other half. Women had been objects of nineteenth-century efforts to encourage thrift, but rarely the agents. World War I marked their dramatic entry into public life in Britain and elsewhere. With so many men at the front, large numbers of women went to work in war production or served in home-front activities ranging from nursing to savings campaigns. The National War Savings Committee enlisted the support of national women's organizations and the wives of prominent politicians. Nationwide the NWSC instructed local committees to appoint women members, including a special Women's Deputy who would work with women's groups to form War Savings Associations. Local committees were also directed to identify "well-to-do women" who could be deployed to persuade other women. War saving represented enfranchisement of a sort. Increasingly recognized as citizens, women now participated in the affairs of the state just as men did their duty in the trenches. The organizations that had agitated for women's suffrage played prominent roles in the war savings movement, along-side antisuffragist women's associations. Their patriotic service on the home front, more than any other factor, convinced Parliament in 1917–18 to enact suffrage for women aged thirty and older.[28]

The National War Savings Committee propagandized all women, yet differentiated by class. Women working in war production were regarded as savers. The authorities eyed their rising wages as an important source of war finance. As for middle- and upper-class families, the authorities assumed that husbands made the financial decisions while wives did the spending. Campaigns thus deputized nonworking women to teach wives how to economize on food and other household ex-penses. Nor could organizers resist the time-honored practice of chid-ing wives for extravagance. Chancellor of the Exchequer McKenna instructed better-to-do women to stop spending money on expensive furs and other "trifles"; they should instead set an example for the working-class families who were "patriotically saving." Prominent wom-en's organizations, too, exhorted women to "deny themselves" regard-ing changes of fashion. They canvassed neighborhoods and ran hundreds of household economy demonstrations, warning that needless expen-ditures were tantamount to sacrificing "our fighting men" in "blind ingratitude."[29]

How much moral suasion affected actual saving is never easy to gauge, but organizers pronounced the campaigns a smashing success. While big investors provided the lion's share of war finance, small sav-ings financed more than 10 percent of all war borrowing from 1914 to 1918 by official estimates. This was not an insignificant figure, consid-ering the war's enormous total cost. War Savings Certificates, small-denomination war bonds, and increases in savings bank and postal sav-ings deposits totaled 433,000,000 pounds.[30] War Savings Certificates alone accounted for 218,000,000 pounds, or half of wartime small sav-ings. Prior to World War I, only a few hundred thousand individuals, mostly wealthy, owned government securities, whereas some fifteen million people would purchase War Savings Certificates; an additional two million held various government bonds. Many, reported the National War Savings Committee, acquired the "habit of saving" for the first time.[31]

Those habits would endure. Over the next several decades ordinary Britons systematically accumulated National Savings Certificates to save for housing, education, apprenticeships, and marriage. Commentators noted the democratic benefits of widespread government-bond holding. As the poorer classes became "stockholders" in the national debt, they contributed to the war effort and also to the state's welfare spending after the war. In addition, Britain's war savings movement bequeathed a new international model. War Savings Certificates and national savings committees spread rapidly throughout the English-speaking world—to India, Canada, Australia, New Zealand, even to the colossus across the Atlantic that had so resisted earlier models of savings promotion.[32]

America Joins the Campaign

The bond drives of the two world wars occupy a special place in U.S. history. Remembered for mass rallies and movie stars, they appear so "American" that few historians or filmmakers would think of inserting them into the larger global story.[33] Back in 1917 Americans knew better. When the United States entered World War I in April, the country experienced transnational currents more intensely than ever before. The prospect of fighting a protracted war against highly mobilized adversaries changed the nation's view of itself and the world. Mainstream politicians and businessmen no longer touted the exceptionalism of American ways. Most agreed the federal government would have to intervene to a degree not seen since the Civil War.[34] The pressing needs of the wartime economy sent policymakers scrambling to adopt facets of European war savings campaigns. Following the lead of all the other cash-starved belligerents, the U.S. government floated the first of four Liberty Loans in June 1917. Treasury Secretary William McAdoo hoped to finance the war half from taxes and half from bonds, but business and banking opposition persuaded him to seek no more than one-third in taxation. The Liberty Loan drives targeted larger investors with bonds denominated in amounts from $50 to $100,000.

To appeal to the vast majority of small savers, Treasury officials launched a parallel "war savings movement" modeled on the campaigns of their British ally. In July, the National War Savings Committee in London dispatched its highest-ranking civil servant, Basil Blackett, to Washington. Adopting his recommendations, the U.S. Treasury Department inaugurated its own National War Savings Committee in October. The sale of War Savings Stamps and Thrift Stamps commenced two months later. The War Savings Stamp was a virtual copy of Britain's War Savings Certificate. The stamp cost approximately $4.12; held to maturity in five years it paid $5.00, at 4 percent interest. Aimed at schoolchildren and the poor, Thrift Stamps cost 25 cents. Once sixteen stamps were pasted on a Thrift Card, they could be exchanged for one War Savings Stamp.[35]

Resemblances to Britain's war savings movement did not stop there. The National War Savings Committee oversaw a nationwide campaign organization administered by six federal directors, one for each Federal Reserve district, and directors in every state. Assisting them were State Committees of War Savings, county chairmen, and local committees of volunteers. Emulating the British War Savings Associations, American campaigners created War Savings Societies in workplaces, schools, and clubs in an effort to sell more War Savings Stamps. Like his European counterparts, President Woodrow Wilson urged every man, woman, and child to "enlist" in War Savings Societies, forming a "great volunteer army of production and saving here at home." Americans heeded the call in droves, and U.S. Treasury officials boasted that Americans had surpassed their English mentors.[36] By the war's end, the government counted 151,361 War Savings Societies and estimated membership at more than six million, compared to 41,301 associations and some four million members in England and Wales.

The U.S. war savings movement took several additional pages out of the British playbook. Washington embraced the Goods and Services doctrine. All Americans were harangued to save and economize. Such behavior would dampen inflation and release goods, labor, and money to the war effort. Campaigns chided the populace to curb the unnecessary use of cars, make shorter phone calls, conserve electricity, and save "tin foil, bottle tops and tubes, old rubber articles, newspapers, wrapping paper, and twine." There were, however, limits to the calls for austerity. Only in America could the government be seen as demanding sacrifice when it advised the people to turn the heat in their homes down to a still comfortable 68°F.[37]

Like the British, campaign organizers insisted that war savings would cultivate long-term habits of thrift. And God knows Americans needed them, according to speaker after speaker. In the words of the National War Savings Committee's chairman Frank Vanderlip, the most important goal of the War Savings Stamps program was not to raise money, but to "teach us a lesson of thrift." Americans had become "a spendthrift people, careless, prodigal, wasteful, luxurious." They saved much less per capita than Swedes, the Swiss, and a host of poorer nations, he continued. President Wilson went so far as to declare that "if this country can learn something about saving out of the war it will be worth the cost of the war." For the first time, the U.S. government aggressively marketed small saving to the entire nation. War Savings Stamps, Treasury Secretary McAdoo noted, offered the "most direct incentive to economize and save ever offered to the people of the country."[38]

To sell War Savings Stamps and Liberty Bonds, the government launched a public relations offensive unprecedented in American and world history alike. Both campaigns were tightly coordinated by the Committee on Public Information headed by the newspaperman George Creel. Ironically, the nation most apprehensive about strong federal power ended up creating the most centralized propaganda agency of World War I. The country may have been decentralized politically, but culturally America's mighty advertising industry reached national audiences as nowhere else. The CPI struck observers as a "gargantuan advertising agency." And for good reason. The president of the American Association of Advertising directed the CPI's all-important Advertising Division, and nearly every advertisers' and publishers' association cooperated with the Committee in the Liberty Loan and War Savings campaigns. Publishers and advertisers donated free space for War Savings advertising in 1,130 newspapers and magazines. While Europe's

Central Powers often employed avant-garde designers in savings campaigns, George Creel preferred commercially successful artists with
proven appeal to the general public. Charles Dana Gibson, America's
most famous illustrator and creator of the statuesque "Gibson Girls,"
was put in charge of the Division of Pictorial Publicity. Staffed by well-
known painters, lithographers, and cartoonists, the division designed
hundreds of posters and advertisements for the savings and bond drives.

Another of Creel's innovations was the "Four-Minute Men," a play
on the Revolutionary War heroes. In an era before radio, this cadre of
some seventy-five thousand volunteers broadcast the CPI's messages
in bite-size speeches of four minutes throughout the nation. Unless an
American "lived the life of a hermit," wrote two of Creel's admirers, "it
was impossible to escape the ubiquitous Four-Minute Men." War Savings Stamps and the Liberty Loans were recurrent topics. The Four-
Minute Men (and some women) attracted their largest audiences at
movie houses and theaters. They spoke also at churches, synagogues,
clubs, colleges, even lumber camps.[39]

As in Europe, the U.S. government used savings and bond campaigns not simply to raise cash, but also to cultivate feelings of citizenship particularly among previously marginalized groups. The National
War Savings Committee established the Division of Labor Organizations, whose staff worked with individual unions and the American
Federation of Labor to promote the "doctrine of thrift and a spirit of
loyalty and patriotism" among workers. Central labor unions generally
proved cooperative, and unions formed large numbers of War Savings
Societies. Women, as well, became a major focus of national appeals to
save and economize. Assisted by the National Woman's Liberty Loan
Committee, women's groups in most states played a large role in selling
Liberty Bonds. The National War Savings Committee oversaw the ap-
pointment of women to the executive committees of state war savings
committees while employing women's associations and women school-
teachers to promote War Savings Stamps.[40] As in Britain, the government mobilized women in their emerging capacity as saver-citizens who
were expected to make sacrifices on the home front. In Charles Dana
Gibson's iconic drawing in *Life*, a fetching "House Manager" marches
alongside the troops.[41] And in Howard Chandler Christy's much-viewed

Figure 13. Gendering women as saver-citizens, U.S., 1917.
Poster by Howard Chandler Christy. Library of Congress.

poster, the gendered charge to Americans could not have been clearer:
"Fight or Buy Bonds" (figure 13).

If U.S. war savings campaigns resembled European efforts in incorporating women and the working class, they were distinctive in appealing to the diverse ethnic groups that made up America at the time of
World War I (figure 14). One-third of the population were foreign born
or children of immigrants. Immigrants were known as excellent savers

Figure 14. Saving in the service of Americanization, 1919.
Poster by Howard Chandler Christy. Library of Congress.

who craved the safety of government-guaranteed financial instruments, and they would surely be prime customers for Liberty Bonds and War Savings Stamps. Officials also used savings drives to inculcate patriotism in communities suspected of harboring loyalties to the old country, particularly those identifying with Germany or the Austro-Hungarian Empire. The Foreign Section of the Committee on Public Information organized no fewer than twenty-three ethnicities into patriotic organizations. Working with the Foreign Language Division of the Treasury

Department's War Loan Organization, the CPI translated numerous handbills and pamphlets for war savings and Liberty Loans into German, Italian, Polish, Hungarian, Croatian, Czech, Yiddish, Swedish, Spanish, German, Italian, even Chinese. In performances that would have no doubt startled the original Minute Men of 1776, hundreds of Four-Minute Men addressed New York City audiences in Yiddish and Italian.[42] Nearly half of the subscribers to the Fourth Liberty Loan, the most successful bond campaign, were of foreign birth or parentage.

The American Small Saver: Lingering Problems

By most accounts the Liberty Loan campaigns transformed the savings habits of Americans. Many who previously lacked access to banks became accustomed to saving by purchasing government securities. After the war, writes Lizabeth Cohen in her study of Chicago, banks aggressively sought the savings of ethnic workers who had accumulated war bonds. A mere forty-five thousand investors owned government bonds before the war. By the end of hostilities, an estimated twenty to twenty-five million individuals (20–23 percent of Americans) possessed either Liberty Bonds, War Savings Stamps, or Thrift Stamps.[43]

Nevertheless, the U.S. savings and bond drives of World War I did less to create a nation of small savers than the many celebratory accounts suggest. The mobilization of small savings took a backseat to selling bonds to big investors. Given its wealth, the United States could easily finance the war without selling "these little savings certificates," admitted Chairman Vanderlip of the National War Savings Committee. The savings stamp program aimed primarily to "build character," not fund the struggle. The wartime Liberty Loans brought in $17 billion, whereas the War Savings and Thrift Stamps raised just under $1 billion—well short of the target of $2 billion.[44] What's more, the campaigns did little to stimulate small saving in areas ill served by savings institutions. Few War Savings Societies formed in the Southern and Western states. Eight states accounted for half of all societies in mid-1918. With the notable exception of populous Texas, they were the Mid-Atlantic and Midwest states that had long boasted a density of small savers: Pennsylvania, Illinois, Wisconsin, New York, Minnesota, Ohio, and Indiana.[45]

What of the small investors' share of Liberty Bonds? Although millions of Americans purchased a bond, relatively few adopted the habit of systematically saving by accumulating Liberty Bonds. The lowest-denomination bond was a pricey $50. Moreover, the bond drives were of short duration and confined to wartime and early 1919. Most small savers bought bonds in just two campaigns, the Third and Fourth Liberty Loans of 1918. According to one contemporary study of Philadelphia workers, the average worker in these drives subscribed to one $50 bond but could not be persuaded to buy more (see figure 15). Workers often purchased that bond by installments, and many subscribers were unable to complete their payments. In the recession that followed World War I, large numbers of workers sold their bonds, sometimes at considerable loss.[46] War bonds remained the domain of affluent and institutional investors.

The bias toward big investors pervaded wartime campaigns. The $50 and $100 bonds accounted for only 20 percent of total receipts, while 70 percent came from bonds in amounts of $1,000 and more.[47] Britain's Basil Blackett advised U.S. officials to avoid creating a gigantic "bond-selling" operation, but instead to encourage saving and economizing among the entire populace.[48] The Americans, however, were in a hurry to raise funds. Besides, for the admen who organized the campaigns, salesmanship was what they knew. Liberty Loan drives were intense affairs lasting about three weeks. At rallies and on foot, bond salesmen lined up subscribers as fast as they could. The larger the subscription the better. More surprising, the same psychology governed drives to sell War Savings Stamps ostensibly intended for small savers. By law no individual could own more than $1,000 in saving stamps so that the affluent could not take advantage of the higher interest rates. Yet faced with high quotas levied on each state, many war savings committees concluded—as Treasury officials admitted—that it would be "quicker and more economical to raise $1,000 from one individual than to raise $50 each from twenty individuals."[49] The most brazen examples occurred in the numerous "Limit Societies." Wealthy men pledged to buy $1,000 in stamps, the legal limit. Former president Taft

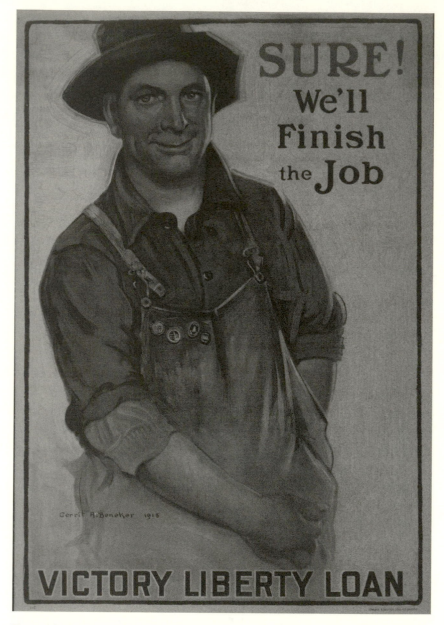

Figure 15. In reality, American workers found it difficult to keep buying the high-priced Liberty Bonds. Poster by Gerrit A. Beneker, 1918. Library of Congress.

served as president of the Connecticut War Savings Limit Society, while former secretary of state Elihu Root presided over New York City's society. Club members promised to generate the $1,000 by practicing "real economy from day to day," rather than drawing on their ample investment funds. In reality, much of war saving—by large and small investors alike—did little to increase net saving but simply involved the transfer of funds from other forms of investment to government securities.[50]

The public's enthusiasm for savings campaigns was further diminished by coercive methods at the local level. Savings promotion in Britain or Japan also involved group pressure, but in wartime America, pressure tactics against noncomformism often degenerated into vigilantism. Quotas for the Liberty Loan were assigned to counties and municipalities. Local committees typically assessed each household a "fair subscription." Those who failed to buy the requisite number of bonds or savings stamps were denounced as "slackers." People who failed to purchase any bonds commonly had their names recorded on "yellow cards." In extreme cases, homes were painted yellow. One family in an Iowa town suffered mightily. Neighbors scattered their cattle; local banks forced them to sell their shares; and residents erected in the town's center a yellow monument with the names of the entire family inscribed. To pressure those unmoved by vaguer threats, communities in Iowa and elsewhere organized "slacker courts." Reported one such court in Pottawattamie County, "We have redeemed and dedicated to Americanism 447 slackers and pro-Germans." In the nation's schools, too, teachers and fellow pupils goaded poorer children into purchasing savings stamps in amounts beyond their families' meager resources. These tactics struck many social workers and journalists as excessive. "Prussianization" was how one writer in the *Atlantic Monthly* described the campaign in Wisconsin, while the *Iowa Homestead* dubbed the campaign period a "reign of terror." [51]

The U.S. savings drives of World War I never achieved the legitimacy of European and Japanese campaigns. Britain's war savings movement easily swept aside the arguments of "business as usual." In America, by contrast, business interests launched a full-throated assault on Washington's thrift campaign with proconsumption arguments that resonate to this day. The famed inventor Thomas Edison denounced the "hysterical" ideas of those who urged consumers to cut back on nonessential purchases. The best way to win the war, he insisted, was for Americans to *increase* spending on luxuries—among which his phonographs rated particular mention. The desire for luxuries induced people to work harder and would do more to speed up war production "than all the prize contests, bonus plans, and proclamations."[52]

Thomas Nixon Carver, a prominent Harvard economist and champion of war saving, was flabbergasted by the intensity of business opposition. In nearly every city he visited on a nationwide tour in summer 1917, he observed storefront placards warning customers against economizing too much. Many proclaimed "Business as Usual" or "Beware of Thrift and Unwise Economy." Others asserted "Money Breeds Money," based on a popular theory that wealth was created when money circulated rapidly. Reliant on advertising, newspapers and magazines adopted hostile positions toward the government's thrift campaign throughout the first year of the war, observed Carver.[53]

The U.S. government's savings campaigns would not survive more than a few months into the postwar era, in sharp contrast to Britain's National Savings Movement. Treasury officials had hoped to build on wartime momentum and persuade the millions of "temporary investors" to continue saving, rather than return to the prewar "habits of thriftlessness, extravagance and waste."[54] They soon realized they were fighting a losing battle. In peacetime, many banks no longer volunteered to sell War Savings Stamps, which competed with them for the small saver. Merchant groups once again protested that thrift campaigns damaged business. The government moreover lost much of its capacity to mount publicity drives on behalf of savings. Accused of "Kaiserism" and partisan censorship, the Committee on Public Information was shut down by Congress in early 1919. Most telling, a great many small savers stopped saving. Sales of War Savings Stamps plummeted after January 1919. Large numbers of Americans cashed their stamps three or four years before maturity. Resigned to the flight of small savers, the Treasury Department in 1919 introduced Treasury Savings Certificates in denominations of $100 and $1,000 for higher-income investors. Pressures from the banking industry forced the government to stop selling savings certificates of any type in 1924. Excepting the limited postal savings system, Americans of modest means no longer had access to government-guaranteed savings instruments until shortly before World War II.[55]

Efforts to encourage saving did not cease during the 1920s, but the project fell almost entirely to banks and nongovernmental organizations. The YMCA and National Education Association teamed up with the American Bankers Association to expand school savings programs. The number of Americans with savings deposits in banks increased substantially during the decade. Continuing prewar trends, commercial banks stepped up appeals to workers, immigrants, and other small savers. Building and loan association membership exploded, albeit within the borders of a few states.[56] By the late 1920s, it appeared that the United States had finally become a nation of savers—not by means of European-style national savings banks, but by virtue of largely unfettered financial markets. Just a few years later, thousands of banks and building and loan associations no longer existed. It would require new government policies and a second world war to instill sustainable savings habits in much of the nation.

International Thrift

As America privatized efforts to encourage thrift after 1918, other governments refitted national savings campaigns to peacetime needs. Contrary to the predictions of prewar critics on both the Right and Left, the rise of European welfare states between the two world wars tended to reinforce rather than supplant household saving. Increasingly national savings financed vital social programs. Belgium's national savings bank (CGER) and the French government's Caisse des Dépôts et Consignations invested heavily in subsidized "social housing" for workers.[57] In interwar Britain, too, saving became a fixture in governance, deemed more important than consumption to advancing social welfare and economic growth. The National Savings Movement was embraced by the major parties, including the Labour Party, which came to power in 1924. Campaigns encouraged saving and "wise spending" on the grounds that saving "adds to the volume of employment and increases the consuming power of the community," according to the Labour Party's former Chancellor of the Exchequer Philip Snowden. Savings generated industrial capital, whereas spending on "luxuries and extravagance" made the country poorer, Snowden noted, because those things "do not tend to the reproduction of capital and to the constant employment of productive labour."[58]

Britain's National Savings Committee remained a well-funded operation with a national network of local organizations. It promoted all forms of national savings, from ordinary postal savings and savings banks deposits to the popular National Savings Certificates. Campaign organizers later boasted that the preponderance of state-guaranteed small saving protected Britons from the worst ravages of the Great Depression. As an official history of the National Savings Committee smugly observed, the U.S. national savings campaign—"run entirely on publicity"—had shut down as soon as World War I ended. While American depositors would watch helplessly as commercial and savings banks collapsed in the early 1930s, the British public "remained steady"—having deposited their savings "with the State on the disinterested advice given voluntarily by our Group and Committee workers whom they trusted."[59]

It was during the interwar decades that saving achieved international respectability as well. In 1924 the Savings Bank of the Lombard Provinces convened the first International Thrift Congress in Italy. Greeted by Fascist leader Benito Mussolini, delegates from twenty-seven countries voted to establish the International Thrift Institute headquartered in Milan. The organization continues to this day as the World Savings Banks Institute in Brussels. It's best known for having established World Thrift Day (later called World Savings Day). From Italy and Germany to Senegal and Japan, October 31 has been the annual occasion for governments and savings banks to mount special campaigns in schools. The original International Thrift Institute brought together two distinct constituencies. There were paternalistic local savings bankers from places like Germany and the United States, plus officials responsible for the mammoth postal savings and national savings banks of Britain, France, Belgium, and Japan. What they shared was a fierce desire to encourage small saving as a social and moral mission. Speakers at the International Thrift Congresses presented thrift as a fundamental solution to several problems confronting the globe in the wake of World War I. Wartime and postwar inflation had badly eroded people's savings in many lands, especially Germany. The first congress worked to formulate "thrift propaganda" to combat "new incessant enticements to squander" and "thrift-disparaging political theories."[60]

The International Thrift Institute played a critical role in transmitting models of savings promotion throughout the world. Organizers singled out Britain's National Savings Committee, inspiring other nations to study the model closely. The Institute devoted considerable effort to expanding savings programs for schoolchildren and the working and middle classes. The staff also facilitated the exchange of numerous savings posters among member governments and savings banks. The worldwide Great Depression did little to dampen internationalist sentiments among the members. A record number of delegates from thirty countries attended the Third International Thrift Congress in Paris in 1935. The next congress was to meet in Berlin in 1940, but that was not to be.[61] The peacetime brotherhood of savings bankers would soon be fractured by the Second World War and with it the most intensive savings campaigns ever seen.

7

SAVE NOW, BUY LATER:
WORLD WAR II AND BEYOND

The tall man with the high hat and the whiskers on his chin
Will soon be knocking at your door and you ought to be in
The tall man with the high hat will be coming down your way
Get your savings out when you hear him shout "Any bonds
today?"
  —Irving Berlin, "Any Bonds Today?" 1941, theme song of
    the National Defense Savings Program[1]

Axis or Allies, the parties to the Second World War shared some
critical assumptions. Financial planners were determined not to
repeat the mistakes of the previous world war. They all planned for a
lengthy struggle, obsessed with preventing the sort of inflation that had
traumatized postwar Germany and weakened other economies. Rather
than rely overwhelmingly on borrowing as before, belligerents resolved
to pay for the war to a much greater degree by tax increases. To finance
the balance, the warring states launched new waves of savings campaigns. At no other time in world history, to paraphrase Winston
Churchill, would so many be encouraged to save so much.

In Nazi Germany, small saving occupied center stage in war finance.
Hitler took the ordinary depositor quite seriously. Imperial Germany
lost World War I, he remarked, because inflationary policies destroyed
the confidence of "small savers and housewives."[2] To contain inflation,
the Third Reich raised taxes substantially in the early years of the new
war. Nonetheless, Nazi leaders eschewed steeper tax increases in favor
of savings campaigns. Their reasons were in large part political. Ever-

increasing taxation, they feared, would erode popular support for the regime. The Nazis likewise rejected war bonds drives, unlike predecessors in World War I and certainly unlike their American adversaries. Bonds campaigns carried the risk of becoming a "financial plebiscite" that Hitler might lose. Instead the regime engaged in what scholars call "silent war finance." Propaganda campaigns exhorted citizens to deposit rising earnings in the savings banks (Sparkassen) and other banks. The state in turn compelled these institutions to invest more and more of their assets in government securities. Financial institutions absorbed 67 percent of government debt, with the savings banks alone holding 27 percent.[3]

Nazi war finance was a grand bargain of sorts. Germans endured sharp declines in consumption resulting from the stringent rationing of goods; their unspent marks indirectly financed the war machine. In exchange, many believed themselves to be saving not only for the war, but also for a brighter consumer life after the war. Propaganda exploited this mentality. Even after most Germans abandoned hopes of victory in 1943, the leading building society, Wüstenrot, attracted large numbers of new customers who saved for postwar home purchases. In February 1945, with Allied bombers pulverizing German cities, aspiring homeowners still responded to the building societies' slogan, "Save in Wartime—Build Later."[4] Hitler's famous promise of consumer happiness, the Volkswagen, was in fact a form of war saving. In the late 1930s, more than a quarter of a million Germans entered into four-year installment plans to buy the "people's car." The catch was they agreed to receive the auto at the end of the payment period. Once industry shifted to war production, few ever did—their savings flowing straight to the Reich.[5]

Despite the abnormal nature of Nazi rule, the wartime system reinforced Germans' long-standing habits of making regular deposits in local savings banks. Between 1939 and 1941, savings banks deposits rose from 2.6 billion to 14.5 billion Reich marks. Germans also learned how to save at the post office. They continued to do so after the war. Hitler, it will be recalled, extended the Austrian postal savings system to Germany in 1939. From the regime's standpoint, the savings campaigns were a big success. Massive savings drained purchasing power, helping to contain inflation for most of the war. Yet as in World War I,

Germany reached the point in 1943 when neither taxes nor savings could sustain the soaring costs of its military ambitions.[6] The ensuing inflation decimated savings, but not savings habits themselves.

The Savings Commandos

Called up to serve in its second world war, the veteran National Savings Movement achieved an iconic presence on the British home front. According to the opinion research organization Mass-Observation in 1941, the National Savings Committee mounted the "most active and vigorous propaganda of this war," spending more to persuade the public than "most other Government departments put together." That propaganda produced a "general atmosphere in which it is the 'done thing' to save."[7] By 1943 Britons saved roughly 25 percent of disposable income—a staggering rate considering the high levels at which they were also being taxed.[8] The National Savings Certificate remained the small saver's investment of choice, although the Trustee Savings Banks and especially the Post Office Savings Bank also experienced sharp increases in deposits during the war. If we include these and the new Defense Bonds, small savings in World War II raised an estimated 4 billion pounds, or roughly 40 percent of total war savings.[9]

Among the impassioned advocates of war saving was the economist best known for explaining the importance of *spending*. Americans commonly regard John Maynard Keynes as the father of a revolution that held mass consumption to be the engine of economic growth. Within Britain's policy community, however, Keynes was a more complex figure. In *The General Theory of Employment, Interest and Money* (1936), he challenged the classical economists' notion that saving automatically translates into robust investment. Worse, too much saving might starve a slowing economy of the consumer demand it needs to keep production humming.[10] Writing in the depths of the Depression, he advised governments to stimulate aggregate demand by spending at extraordinary levels. Yet Keynes was hardly hostile to saving per se. Nor was he averse to using state power to *increase* saving under certain circumstances. The outbreak of World War II raised the specter not of too little investment, but of an overheated economy and inflation.[11]

In a series of articles in 1939 and 1940, Keynes went well beyond the National Savings Movement to call for "compulsory savings" in wartime.[12] Although he also urged the government to raise taxes rapidly, it would not be "just and wise" to pay for the war entirely from taxation. Workers needed an incentive to produce more, and it made "all the difference in the world" to individuals whether their surplus income were taxed, or saved for future consumption. Under Keynes's plan, a portion of everyone's excess income over a stipulated level would be deposited in a Post Office Savings Bank account (the percentage rising with income, from 20 to 80 percent). With some exceptions, these savings could not be withdrawn for the duration of the war. Opposition to Keynes's scheme was deafening. Labor leaders, financiers, and the National Savings Committee all denounced the use of compulsion, even after Keynes tactfully renamed it the "deferred pay" plan.[13] The economist sympathized with the National Savings Movement, which he believed rightly appealed to small savers—the ones who accounted for the bulk of aggregate consumption. But this voluntary savings campaign could not fully close the gap between revenues and war spending, he estimated. The resulting inflation would rob the working and middle classes of their purchasing power. Which would it be, he asked, "compulsory savings or compulsory inflation?"

The revolutionary implications of Keynesianism notwithstanding, Keynes, the man, echoed the Goods and Services thinking of World War I. To critics who argued "business as usual requires spending as usual," Keynes shot back that in wartime almost no act of spending could be "innocent." Any expenditure usually set up "a series of subsequent expenditures" that would lead to a "harmful exhaustion of resources." Here was "our old friend the 'multiplier' principle," he observed wryly, but in wartime it was saving, not spending, that multiplied the gain to the economy. Keynes's compulsory savings plan failed, yet his wartime expositions on behalf of expanding saving and curbing spending did much, observed The Times, to further the success of the voluntary savings campaign.[14]

The organizational reach of the wartime National Savings Movement vastly exceeded that of the World War I campaign. Individuals who saved nothing for the war found fewer and fewer places to hide. Volunteers who worked in the Local Savings Committees and the Savings Groups numbered more than 500,000 in England and Wales during the war's later years. These volunteers also staffed the five hundred Savings Centres, which sold National Savings Certificates to Savings Group secretaries and the public. The Centres were established in populous areas as the post offices became inundated with customers wishing to buy certificates.[15]

Expansion of Savings Groups (formerly War Savings Associations) proved to be the campaign's most effective measure. Although these groups accounted for less than 20 percent of total small savings in wartime, the Committee singled them out for having extracted "genuine saving out of weekly income" while withdrawing mass purchasing power. Savings Groups crested to 292,850 by October 1943. More than twelve million people, or fully 32 percent of the population of England and Wales, belonged to a Savings Group. Quite a few successful groups formed in air raid shelters and even pubs. Nearly every school housed Savings Groups, in which three million children purchased savings stamps weekly. Covering more than four million members, workplace Savings Groups netted the most small savings. People saved more when the money was deducted from wages before they could spend it. The General Council of the Trades Union Congress supported workplace saving, but only after the government guaranteed that workers who saved would not be disadvantaged. Officials promised to disregard wartime savings when means-testing applicants for unemployment assistance and other government aid. Employers, for their part, pledged not to deny wage hikes because workers possessed savings. The upshot was that the Labour Party strongly identified with the National Savings Movement in wartime and beyond. Former TUC leader George Gibson became a vice-chairman of the National Savings Committee, and Labour ministers in the government—notably Ernest Bevin—exhorted workers to save.[16]

The fastest growing savings groups were known as Street Groups. Like other home-front agencies in wartime Britain, the National Savings Committee made a concerted effort to organize residential life.

More than 125,000 Street and Village Savings Groups operated in England and Wales. With able-bodied men at the front or in factories, Street Groups were notable for the large proportion of married women as members and leaders. The group secretary or collector became a familiar, if not always welcome, presence. She regularly called on each home armed with National Savings Certificates (figure 16). Shortly after D-Day, the National Savings Committee encouraged Street Groups to stage "Commando raids." In one locale, leaflets warned that the following week "Savings Commandos will raid this street, and 'attack' your house," if a link chain proving membership in the Street Group wasn't displayed. It must have been an awesome sight. Matrons wore red, white and blue "Recruiting Sergeants" flashes, replete with armlets bearing the words "National Savings Commandos."[17]

The National Savings Committee supplemented person-to-person persuasion with propaganda on a much grander scale than in World War I. Officials solicited favorable news coverage and saturated newspapers with war savings ads—so much so that the NSC created its own press office on Fleet Street staffed by veteran journalists. Among the new media deployed were sound trucks, gramophone records, and radio broadcasts by Committee members, cabinet ministers, and celebrities. Every Sunday the public was treated to the "Weekly Savings News." The NSC commissioned some forty films, shown at movie houses and special events. In an illustration of transnational Technicolor, it adapted four animated shorts that Disney Studios produced to promote war savings certificates in neighboring Canada.[18] The NSC printed one million posters displayed nationwide, plus ten million leaflets. In addition, the office ran special campaigns that related individual acts of saving to the war effort. During "Warship Weeks" in 1941–42, each local savings committee "adopted" a ship that its savings would ostensibly build. While propaganda generally appealed positively to one's patriotic duty to save, messages occasionally warned Britons of the treasonous consequences of doing otherwise. The NSC's most memorable posters were of the "Squanderbug," an all-consuming vermin and "Hitler's Pal" (figure 17). In yet another variant, campaigns sometimes appealed to self-interest. War savings, proclaimed one poster, would make "dreams" of postwar consumption come true (figure 18).

Figure 16. In this 1946 British poster, the family welcomes the local savings collector. But to many, she was the neighborhood busybody who invaded homes and pressured families to buy National Savings Certificates. Reproduced by permission of TNA, NSC 5/211.

Figure 17. One of several wartime Squanderbug posters, Britain, 1943. Reproduced by permission of TNA, NSC 5/104.

Figure 18. Propaganda in many countries appealed to people to save in wartime and buy later. Note the modest dreams of consumption in this British poster, 1943. Reproduced by permission of TNA, NSC 5/110.

Were the savings drives effective? World War II witnessed the first applications of public opinion research to measuring the impact of home-front propaganda and mobilization. The British did this with particular thoroughness. Commissioned by the government, Mass-Observation in late 1941 surveyed savings behavior among the working classes in three sample localities, as well as among middle-class people nation-wide. One of the more surprising results concerned how individuals responded to the incessant blandishments to save. Opinion was "mostly exceptionally favourable" to National Savings Committee propaganda, even among nonsavers. Seventy percent pronounced it "very good" or "good," and only 10 percent found it "bad." Many commented that "we'd never have saved without it," or "it's brought the nation to understand we're all in together." Respondents generally liked savings posters, films, broadcasts and surprisingly the loud-speaker vans, although some complained about uninspiring repetition. What they most agreed upon was the importance of Savings Groups and personal contact in moti-vating them to save. Typical was a female munitions worker who re-ported that she never saved before the war, but "then we had a Savings Group, and now it's nice to feel you've got something behind you." Several praised the interventionist Street Group collector: "the lady comes round the house every Monday, so people will save."[19]

Mass-Observation provided additional data on what factors moti-vated people to save more. Many respondents internalized the govern-ment's patriotic appeals. A third of working-class people surveyed men-tioned patriotic motives, more than any other factor. "So long as we keep on saving we keep on winning the war," one explained. Large numbers mentioned personal motivations *in combination* with patriotism. They saved "to help the war effort, and to help ourselves." A fair number of working people saved with the intent of going on a vacation or even a "spree" after the war. Nonetheless, many more saved out of pessimism about the future. The rainy day they feared would be a postwar eco-nomic slump and unemployment. Recalling the recession after World War I, a good number agreed with the following reply: "We'll want some-thing after the war. After the war there won't be nothing, will there?"

The World War II savings campaign reinforced long-standing hab-its of thrift among many Britons, but went further to create hordes of new savers particularly among the working class. Mass-Observation's mid-1940 survey of three sample communities bears this out. Already high in prewar times, the proportion of middle-class families saving in National Savings or bank accounts increased to about 90 percent. Those of skilled-worker families surged to about two-thirds (dramatically in Bristol from 48 to 71 percent). Few unskilled-worker households saved in National Savings or banks before the war, but, they, too, increased such saving significantly—in Bristol from 21 to 49 percent and in Blackburn from 27 to 38 percent. By late 1941 Mass Observation estimated that two-thirds of the working-class population was saving.[20] Overall, the wartime National Savings Movement did an extraordinary job of organizing and propagandizing the British people. Yet as victory approached, many wondered if Britons would continue saving.

America's Golden Age of Saving

Americans speak nostalgically about the savings mentality of parents and grandparents who grew up in the Depression. It was not, however, the Depression experience per se that transformed many Americans into regular savers, but key interventions by the U.S. government during the 1930s and World War II. Thanks to federal guarantees and new government securities, it became safer and more convenient to save. American depositors came to inhabit an environment attained by Europeans and Japanese decades earlier.

The first of these innovations was federal deposit insurance. The Banking Act of 1933 created the Federal Deposit Insurance Corporation in the wake of a market failure of catastrophic proportions. Rocked by plummeting real estate values and prices of high-yield bonds, more than nine thousand banks failed between 1930 and 1933. Millions of depositors lost their savings. Millions more lost the basic confidence in banks that makes systematic saving possible. The FDIC moved to shore up remaining banks. By assessing annual premiums on member banks, the independent government corporation insured deposits in banks up to $5,000 initially. The FDIC grew to encompass nearly all commercial banks and mutual savings banks. The Federal Savings and Loan Insurance Corporation insured deposits in savings and loan associations (formerly, building and loan associations). To address the universal challenge of assuring small savers of the security of deposits, other nations had instituted accessible postal savings banks and other state-guaranteed savings institutions. The FDIC system proved to be America's answer.[21]

The newly created FDIC did not instantly send distrustful small savers back to the banks. Not until after World War II would a majority of households possess a savings account in a bank.[22] Few people of modest means were able to save during the rest of the economically sluggish 1930s. The U.S. National Resources Committee calculated savings based on income group for 1935–36. The most striking finding was that families earning less than $1,250—or 59 percent of all households—on average saved nothing or spent more than they earned. The next 10 percent (earning $1,250–$1,500) saved only 1 percent of income.[23]

Vital as the FDIC was in the long term, the war bonds campaign of World War II marked the government's most successful effort at popularizing habits of thrift in U.S. history. Much attention focuses on the patriotic spectacle and morale-boosting aims of the sales drives. Treasury Secretary Henry Morgenthau Jr. was said "to use *bonds* to sell the *war*, rather than vice versa."[24] Yet beneath the hoopla, the bonds campaign was in large measure about getting Americans to save. U.S. Savings Bonds originated not in wartime, but in an earlier Depression-era initiative. The inspiration was anything but American. On a trip through Europe in 1934, Morgenthau was taken by national savings programs in Scandinavia, France, and Britain. The following year the Treasury issued the first U.S. Savings Bonds aimed at small savers as well as larger investors. For Morgenthau, savings bonds offered several benefits long appreciated by European officials. Broadening the holding of public debt would provide new sources of finance for the Roosevelt Administration's ambitious New Deal. Equally important, Morgenthau envisioned government-guaranteed bonds as a vital means of inducing ordinary Americans to save in the wake of rampant bank failures.[25]

The peacetime savings bonds of 1935–41 did not attract as many small investors as had been hoped. Nonetheless, the prewar Series A bond represented a breakthrough in U.S. savings promotion and the precursor of the popular Series E bond of World War II. Morgenthau designed these bonds to remedy the shortcomings of the previous war's Liberty Bonds. The Liberty Bonds had been priced too high ($50) for small savers, fluctuated in value, and sent the bondholder periodic interest payments. Like the later Series E bonds, Series A bonds were nonnegotiable and administratively simple. The customer bought them at 75 percent of face value, receiving accrued interest—2.9 percent per annum—at the time of redemption. They were affordable and easy to accumulate. Dubbed "Baby Bonds," the $25 Series A bond could be purchased for as little as $18.75, maturing to the face value in ten years. If the Series A bond looked like an American copy of Britain's National Savings Certificate, that was hardly a coincidence.

From Baby Bonds to War Bonds was but a step. With Europe and East Asia already at war, Morgenthau unveiled the National Defense Savings Bonds program, including the Series E bond, in May 1941. Once again, Treasury officials modeled the small-denomination bonds on Britain and Canada's war savings certificates. Appealing to schoolchildren and poorer individuals, they also reintroduced Savings Stamps (10 cents to $5). The stamps were based on U.S. and British precedents from World War I. Following the Japanese attack on Pearl Harbor in December 1941, National Defense Savings Bonds were renamed War Savings Bonds. The United States thus fought the Second World War with a far more coherent savings campaign than in the previous war. Instead of running competing drives for small savers (stamps) versus large investors (Liberty Bonds), the war bonds campaign of 1941–45 united the two. Like the British, U.S. leaders financed the war roughly half from taxes and half from borrowing, a large portion of which came from people's savings.[26]

Besides improving war finances and inculcating patriotism, the bonds campaign operated as a "long-range effort to encourage thrift by systematic, regular, and continuous purchase of defense savings securities by every American," according to Treasury Department spokesmen.[27]

The payroll savings plan took its place as the war's most effective con-tribution to regular saving. Beginning with AT&T in 1936, a few large companies before the war offered employees plans to allocate a set por-tion of each paycheck toward purchasing U.S. savings bonds. Treasury's War Savings Staff pushed hard to universalize payroll savings plans in all large and medium companies. By October 1942, some twenty-two million employees—more than 22 percent of the adult population—participated in payroll savings plans. Eventually more than twenty-seven million people enrolled. Among payroll savings firms, average participation reached 76 percent, and bond purchases rose to 11 per-cent of total wage payments.[28] The wartime workplace was where mil-lions of Americans first learned to save systematically.

The War Savings Staff opened a second front in the nation's schools. Prewar school savings programs had thrived in some districts of the country but were absent in most. The Schools at War initiative, noted one banker, achieved "overnight" what had stymied the champions of school savings banks for the past fifty years. No longer did school sav-ings depend on the solvency and altruism of local banks. Once a week on Stamp Day, pupils throughout the nation purchased U.S. savings stamps until they attained $18.75 to buy an E bond. Schools with sav-ings programs shot up from a mere 8,500 in 1938 to more than 200,000 by the war's end. Lessons on thrift and conservation became standard parts of the curricula in arithmetic, social studies, and civic education. An important goal was to educate children to continue saving as post-war adults. From 1941 to early 1946, schools accounted for an impres-sive $2 billion in stamps and bonds.[29]

It was a greater challenge to instill systematic saving among farm-ers, the self-employed, and other adults not enrolled in payroll savings plans. After vowing not to repeat the high-pressured sales drives of World War I, Morgenthau resigned himself to mounting eight short, intense bond drives that punctuated the continuous campaign to sell bonds and stamps. Some 500,000 volunteers worked for local bonds committees and civic organizations on an ongoing basis. Altogether some five to six million "Minute Men" could be called up during the drives. Many actually were "Minute Maids" or "Molly Pitchers." Women attired in "attractive attention-getting costumes" sold bonds in public places. Women were also central in door-to-door drives to solicit subscriptions from neighbors.[30]

Reinforcing personal solicitations was the greatest advertising blitz ever mounted by the U.S. government. Messages to buy bonds and save were everywhere—on radio, posters, and in ads that filled the pages of newspapers and magazines. Irving Berlin's "Any Bonds Today?" was a popular song of the era. The distinction between entertainment and sacrifice was sometimes difficult to appreciate. Bonds sold Hollywood as much as Hollywood sold bonds. The movie industry not only made numerous trailers shown to millions before its regular films, but also produced several feature-length movies for the drives. "The All Star Bond Rally" presented Betty Grable and her pretty "bondbardiers." The Stars over America bond tour had the entire nation talking. Marlene Dietrich, Humphrey Bogart, Gary Cooper, Clark Gable, Judy Garland, Cary Grant, and other cinematic idols visited an incredible 360 cities and towns.[31]

The war bonds campaign of World War II revolutionized savings behavior in the United States. Personal savings rates, which in the 1930s ranged between *negative* 1.7 percent and 6.2 percent, soared to 26 percent in 1944.[32] In lieu of the government's campaign, some might argue, Americans would have naturally saved at high levels because wartime production spiked employment and incomes, and the diversion of goods to the war effort left consumers little to buy. Perhaps, but doubtful. Institutions matter, as we have seen. Would most Americans, whose past access to banks had been limited, have saved as much in the absence of U.S. savings bonds? Unquestionably the bonds' unprecedented safety and nationwide availability—aided enormously by payroll and school savings plans—introduced habits of systematic saving to millions. From 1941 to the end of the war, a staggering 85 million individuals came to hold E bonds in a population of roughly 132 million. Ordinary Americans were far more likely to place wartime savings in bonds than in banks. Sixty-three percent of households surveyed in early 1946 owned U.S. savings bonds, whereas remarkably 61 percent had *no* savings account.[33]

The wartime campaign helped persuade a great many Americans of the long-term benefits of saving. As in Britain's war savings campaign, patriotic appeals motivated people to buy bonds, but often in combination with personal considerations. Named after Rensis Likert, some forty Likert surveys measured the effectiveness of the Treasury Department's campaign. Beginning with the first survey in May 1942, respondents generally offered two salient reasons for purchasing bonds: they helped the government win the war, and they provided safe, attractive means of saving for the future. Accordingly, the government frequently marketed bonds as an investment in one's children and family. "For Their Future Buy Bonds," proclaimed one poster, while another advised: "Nest Eggs Won't Hatch Unless You Set on Them! Hang On to Your War Bonds."[34]

If in several respects the U.S. government during World War II adopted European methods of promoting saving, there was one essential difference. American savings propaganda combined injunctions to save with enticements to spend. German and British authorities also attempted to convince citizens that war savings would make their "dreams" of postwar consumption come true. American dreams, however, were considerably more vivid than the Englishman's hopes for a hand-powered lawn mower or the holiday at a shabby seaside resort (refer to figure 18). We see this in a color poster sent to the nation's schools in 1943. Pupils were encouraged to buy war stamps and bonds not just to hasten victory, but as "your down payment on the exciting new things of 1953" (see plate 5). You might save up for a futuristic "private air car," radio-television sets, or plan to fly off for the vacation in Madagascar, Alaska, Hawaii, Venezuela, or just "weekend" in Mexico City or Newfoundland. In the postwar world, "the good things of life are there for the buying" and everyone could "buy his share." Children should save to "start staking out your claim to our post-war production."[35]

War bonds ads often suggested Americans might start spending *before* the war ended. This was an unintended consequence of the Treasury Department's decision to rely almost entirely on companies and private individuals to pay for bond advertising in newspapers, magazines, and on radio. As a result, charged critics, the U.S. government lost control of the message, whereas the British and Canadian states designed most advertisements for national saving.[36] Some American advertisers were content to place the company's name at the bottom of war bonds ads. Increasingly, firms unabashedly marketed their products under the rubric of war saving. Typical was an ad by Cannon Mills. "For Victory, Buy U.S. War Bonds and Stamps" appeared in fine print, and women were instructed to "buy *only* things we really *need!*" Still, the overpowering message was to buy "lovely" Percale Sheets. And "if we can't find exactly the size we want in Cannon Percale Sheets, we'll scowl at Tojo," the Japanese leader, and "ask to see Cannon *Muslin* Sheets—well-made, long-lasting, a real value!"[37] Indeed, real consumption *rose* in wartime America, while it significantly declined in Britain. Although consumer durables were generally diverted to war, Americans spent more on food, clothing, and entertainment than before.[38] Here was another of those exceptions. Americans in wartime learned to save, yet with little sacrifice—anticipating postwar abundance of which others could only dream.

"Keep on Saving"

Allied bombers scored a direct hit on the Milan palace housing the International Thrift Institute in 1943. To dispirited savings bankers following the war, it seemed that thrift itself had been blown to smithereens. They shuddered at the growing popularity of Keynesianism, appearing as it did to privilege spending while denigrating the virtue of saving.[39] Certainly in the United States, victory gave rise to the age of mass consumption that has lived with us ever since (see chapter 11).

In the rest of the world, few experienced anything like the American consumer revolution. Observed Japan's Ministry of Finance in 1947, it didn't particularly matter whether countries emerged from the war "victors or vanquished." Nearly every nation mounted savings and austerity campaigns in the early postwar years. Often it felt as if the war had never ended. States throughout Europe continued to harangue citizens to save and curb spending. The goal was no longer to support war efforts but to finance the daunting tasks of reconstruction and recovery. Much of Europe lay in ruins. From London to Stalingrad, cities had suffered devastation from aerial bombardment and advancing armies. Factories and transportation networks were in shambles. Reconstruction required extraordinary levels of finance. Yet private capital markets barely functioned. As in wartime, governments necessarily invested on a massive scale.[40] States did what they could to raise taxes, but national saving offered the quickest means of tapping the meager wealth of the greatest numbers.

And it did not particularly matter whether nations lay in Western Europe or Soviet-occupied Eastern Europe. Capitalist or Communist, governments envisioned saving, investment, and production—not consumption—as key to economic recovery. Poland's Communist state employed draconian measures to increase personal savings and invest them in the socialized industrial sector. Established as a compulsory savings scheme in 1948, the Social Savings Fund required citizens to make regular deposits at progressive rates based on income or land-tax assessments. The depositor could withdraw no more than 5 percent of the balance except under special circumstances. Compulsory savings constituted a significant source of revenue, amounting to approximately 4 percent of Poland's central budgets up to 1950. East German planners likewise promoted saving to finance reconstruction and development of the socialist economy. Much of the saving occurred at recognizably "German" savings banks (*Sparkassen*), which the regime reestablished in towns under direct state supervision. In the German Democratic Republic and elsewhere in the Eastern bloc, aggressive savings campaigns further aimed to soak up purchasing power and diminish popular demand for consumer goods.[41]

Leaders in capitalist West Germany looked more kindly on the expansion of consumption. Nonetheless, they, too, remained fiercely committed to encouraging saving after 1948. Economic officials steadfastly rejected Keynesian advice to stimulate domestic demand by deficit financing. Haunted by memories of hyperinflation in the early 1920s and plagued by acute capital shortages following World War II, the authorities regarded small savings as essential to investment in production for export markets. The model citizen was a saver first, and consumer second. For the most part, the Federal Republic promoted saving indirectly—by containing inflation and granting tax exemption to depositors who participated in contractual plans to save regularly. Retaining the prewar mission to promote saving and thrift, local savings banks quickly reestablished themselves as the sites where most Germans saved. By 1956 there were 856 *Sparkassen* and nearly 8,000 branches in West Germany. Citizens also saved increasingly in the government's postal savings banks. Household savings skyrocketed during the 1950s, helping to fuel West Germany's "economic miracle."[42]

Saving likewise achieved mythic importance in the revival of postwar France. The government appealed to large and small investors alike to buy "Liberation bonds" following the end of German occupation in 1944 (figure 19). In addition, the French state retained control over the nation's small savings deposited in postal savings and local savings banks. Those savings played an indispensable role in financing the government's plans for the reconstruction and modernization of the French economy. Drawing on the savings fund, the Caisse des Dépôts et Consignations and related state-owned banks made loans for public housing, roads, rural electrification, agricultural machinery, and other infrastructure. As in West Germany, rising incomes led to steadily rising rates of household saving—from 9 percent in 1950 to 13.5 percent in 1956.[43]

Unapologetic thrift promotion pervaded postwar European culture. In 1955 the Swedish government regarded it as perfectly proper to subsidize saving for the explicit purpose of "restricting consumption" in a heated economy. Depositors received a whopping 20 percent premium on increases in their accounts. European campaigns commonly targeted women and children. Governments in Sweden and the Netherlands brought together postal savings banks, savings banks, and educational authorities to inculcate habits of saving in pupils and those who had recently left school. Belgium's national savings bank, the CGER, reinvigorated the late-nineteenth-century practice of encouraging savings accounts for newborns. If parents or others opened an account for the baby with at least 50 francs, municipal officials would deposit an additional 50 francs.

Also, the mid-1950s marked the time when the home joined the workplace and school as the primary sites for promoting saving. With

Figure 19. "France is Free. Buy Liberation Bonds," 1945. Poster by [Bernard] Villemot. Caisse des Dépôts, *Livret A*, 219. Poster held by the Archives Départementales des Côtes d'Armor, 25 Fi 112 (collection of Dr. Lejeune).

economic growth, women became identified as "housewives" in charge of family finances. Emulating innovations in the Netherlands and Sweden, savings banks associations and public authorities in several nations established family budgeting centers in cooperation with housewives' organizations. West Germany's Advisory Center for Efficient Family Budgeting instructed housewives in "thrifty housekeeping and the sensible handling of money." Holland's Institute for Advice on Family Budgeting taught people how to save by spending "rationally."[44]

Britain was no exception to these postwar developments. The venerable National Savings Movement roared into peacetime. In August 1944 the National Savings Committee unveiled the new campaign slogan, "Keep on Saving." The message was deliberately ambiguous. The war-weary populace was to keep saving for victory over Germany and Japan, but also not to let up once the war ended (see plates 6 and 7). Continued self-denial would build a "new and better Britain."[45] This was a far cry from wartime America's promises of postwar abundance. Material life failed to improve following victory over the Axis. Britons experienced acute shortages in food, fuel, and clothing. Wartime rationing continued on many necessities including milk, eggs, meat, and soap. By 1948 individual food rations actually declined to below the wartime average. Even bread, which had *not* been rationed in wartime, became rationed between 1946 and 1948. Rationing of some commodities persisted until 1953–54. Pessimism, as it often does, buttressed appeals to save. In "these days of shortage," advised Chancellor of the Exchequer Hugh Dalton, "put your money by, so that you may have it still to spend when the days of abundance come." Remarking on the "dark cloud" hanging over the nation, organizers aptly named the 1947 savings drive the National Silver Lining Campaign.[46]

Founded in 1916, the National Savings Committee administered savings campaigns, incredibly enough, until 1978. Although grassroots activism slackened once the national emergency passed in 1945, the postwar National Savings Movement operated on a far grander scale than before World War II. In 1950 some 300,000 volunteers and 170,000 Savings Groups functioned in England and Wales. For millions in workplaces, schools, neighborhoods, and social organizations, National Savings campaigns remained a fixture of everyday life during the first fifteen years of the postwar era. Quaint practices from the war lived on. Women commando teams, including the celebrated "Ulster Commandos," still attacked neighborhoods in canvassing efforts to sell National Savings Certificates in the late 1940s and 1950s. One survey in 1948 found that 86 percent of the adult population in England and Wales possessed savings, and 59 percent held National Savings including certificates, bonds, and deposits in postal savings or savings banks. In 1956 the National Savings Committee introduced one of its biggest draws—literally. Instead of paying interest, new Premium Bonds offered holders the chance to win tax-free cash prizes at monthly drawings. "The more you buy, the more you save," announced the government. A room-sized computer affectionately known as ERNIE (Electronic Random Number Indicator Equipment) chose the winners. One of his descendents still does. Combining incongruously the qualities of thrift and gambling, this savings lottery proved immensely popular. There are today twenty-three million Premium bondholders.[47]

National Savings thrived because it offered solutions to several problems besetting postwar Britain. Officials promoted saving not simply to finance reconstruction and check inflation, but to restore British might itself after a half-century of decline. In 1945 the country was in desperate financial straits. It had fought World War II on a shoestring, propped up by America's Lend-Lease Program. After Washington abruptly ended Lend-Lease in September, British leaders were forced to rely on the U.S. government for a mammoth loan of $3,750,000,000 to pay for essential imports until export trade revived. In a reversal of fortunes, Canada the former dominion provided an additional $1,250,000,000 in loans. Missing several payment deadlines, Britain did not repay the U.S. loan in full until 2006. Amid heated negotiations over the Anglo-American loan, the Liberty Party's Anthony Eden declared the National Savings Movement to be vital to the "continued assurance of our financial stability as a nation and the maintenance of British credit."[48]

Recovery, according to early postwar British governments, depended not on stimulating consumption, but rather on increasing savings and exports. Theirs was an "island nation," which they argued must export manufactured goods to pay for the massive imports that provided food

Figure 20. Promoting saving to finance exports while diminishing demand for manufactured imports, Britain, 1946. Reproduced by permission of TNA, NSC 5/199.

and work for forty-eight million people (figure 20). With exports falling to less than one-third of their prewar volume by 1947, policymakers
encouraged saving to finance industrial expansion while restraining
spending on imports and exports alike. Stafford Cripps, Labour's abste-
mious Chancellor of the Exchequer, expressed the logic behind diminishing the "demand for goods in our home market." If "we consume too
many of the goods which we produce ourselves, we cannot export
them; and if, in the process, we force up our costs and so our prices, we
shall lose our export markets."[49] Some Conservative politicians evinced
less enthusiasm for savings campaigns. Still, after Winston Churchill
and his Conservatives returned to power in 1951, Chancellor of the
Exchequer Richard A. Butler promoted saving to solve balance of payments problems just as ardently as his Labour predecessors. Lukewarm
in his Keynesianism, Butler was running National Savings campaigns
for "Restraint in Spending" as late as 1955. That campaign cast "excess
of demand" as the main cause of the overheated economy, resulting in
"higher imports, lower exports and the drain on the reserves."[50]

Prime Minister Churchill himself urged greater national savings to
shore up Britain's fading great-power status amid the Cold War. Embarking on an ambitious rearmament program in 1951, his government
inaugurated the "Lend Strength to Britain" campaign. The hard-hitting
rhetoric recalls savings campaigns of the two world wars and appears
strangely out of synch with the "consumer society" that historians
imagine to have developed in postwar Britain. National Savings Movement speakers explained that rearmament required sacrifices in terms
of fewer consumption goods and a lowered standard of living. Britons,
Churchill insisted, must save more to contain price increases that
would otherwise follow from arms spending. Churchillian in war and
peace, the prime minister admonished that his defense program "requires a diversion of goods and services from the consumer—that is *from*
you and me—to the national needs—that is *for* you and me."[51]

The rival Labour Party took a particularly dim view of personal
consumption while advancing National Savings. During the nineteenth
and early twentieth centuries, the trade union movement had been
ambivalent toward efforts to promote thrift. On one hand, trade union-
ists suspected that the ruling classes encouraged workers to save in order

Figure 21. Following the defeat of Germany in May 1945, Britain's "Keep on Saving" campaign proclaimed the twin goals of beating Japan and financing reconstruction and the new welfare state (depicted in the blueprint). Reproduced by permission of TNA, NSC 5/170.

to maintain lower wages and discourage demands for state-provided welfare. On the other hand, most Labour leaders passionately believed in the virtues of working-class thrift and self-reliance. The unions and Labour Party cooperated closely with the National Savings Committee during the two world wars and the years in between. Governing from 1945 to 1951, the Labour Party embraced the cause of savings promotion so fervently that the postwar National Savings Movement and social democracy became indistinguishable to many Britons. The trade unions regarded increased National Savings as a bulwark against the rampant inflation that was eroding wages. They further accepted the logic that greater savings meant more investment in British industry and of course more jobs.[52]

The Labour Party's savings and austerity campaigns formed part of the grand vision advanced by social democrats throughout postwar Western Europe. Supplementing taxation, national savings financed emerging welfare states. In Britain, the coalition government began planning for comprehensive welfare programs during the war itself. Wartime posters urged the nation to "keep on saving" not only for victory, but to fund the postwar needs of education, housing, and health (figure 21). Aneurin Bevan, Labour's postwar health minister and former Welsh coal miner, praised the National Savings Movement for helping finance his government's ambitious social targets. These included care for babies and the elderly, improved housing, and the establishment of Bevan's new National Health Service. "Self-discipline and self-control," not personal spending, would be the key. If the nation were to enjoy these planned social services, argued Bevan, "we have to deny ourselves other things now, in order that we may be able to accomplish them later on." Indeed, many Britons accepted austerity policies as a continuation of the wartime spirit of shared sacrifice and fairness. Conspicuous consumption by the wealthy offended them, while saving appeared to be for the greater good. It was time, proclaimed Labour's Chancellor of the Exchequer Cripps, for the nation to "renounce and to denounce that easy-going get-rich-quick attitude to life that in all levels of society has found its post-war devotees."[53]

This age of austerity did not last forever. Western European economies recovered, and the harsh frugality of the early postwar days subsided. Self-proclaimed "consumer revolutions" broke out by the end of the 1950s. Americans no longer imagined Europeans as austere, even as the major continental nations boasted household saving rates more than twice as high as the United States.[54] Instead, those who worried about the paucity of saving in America looked across the Pacific, where twentieth-century Japan developed the century's most potent model of mobilizing savings.

8

"LUXURY IS THE ENEMY": JAPAN IN PEACE AND WAR

Ever see a Japanese War Bond? . . . Japanese civilians are
buying other bonds like it by the millions. One of those
Japs is your counterpart—and your fanatical enemy. . . . You
have more money than he does. But he can live on a lot
less than you do. He eats only a few ounces of rice a day.
He wears wooden sandals and patched clothes. He's patient,
patriotic, disciplined by years of "thought control." . . . Can
you match *your* Jap's self-denial?
                    —Advertisement for U.S. War Bonds, 1945[1]

There *was* something "fanatical" about Japanese savings campaigns
in World War II. The Japanese declared war on extravagance more
than a year before attacking Pearl Harbor. In July 1940 the government
issued "Regulations Restricting the Manufacture and Sale of Luxury
Goods." For the next five years, the slogan "Luxury is the Enemy" appeared everywhere, in magazines and newspapers and on red cloth banners and community signboards.[2] No other belligerent—Axis or Ally—
wrung as much savings out of their people. By 1944 Japanese households
saved an extraordinary 40 percent of disposable income, compared to
roughly 26 and 25 percent, respectively, in the United States and Britain. The Japanese saving rate includes neither an additional 10 percent
in taxes nor skyrocketing communal exactions.[3] Statistics do not begin
to convey the human suffering wrought by the wartime savings campaigns. Households were left with little to spend on the basic necessities

of food, clothing, and shelter—much less on "luxuries." Many a child emerged from the war undersized and malnourished.

Yet there was also something familiar in Japan's drive for war saving. U.S. war bond ads, like the one above, implored Americans to *match* the enemy in "self-denial." By the time the war broke out, the great powers had all become adept at mobilizing the savings of their people. The Japanese state may have mounted the most intrusive campaigns at the dawn of the twentieth century, but Western governments certainly caught up in the Great War of 1914–18. Like Western savings drives, Japanese campaigns in World War II communicated that thrift strengthened not only the nation but individual households. Their brutal success rested on more than top-down "thought control" and unquestioning patriotism. Japanese people internalized the wartime culture of thrift because they themselves played active roles in forming that culture, both before and during the war. They participated in campaigns for reasons that went beyond the state's messages. While the regime harangued the nation to sacrifice and cast aside notions of individualism, the people themselves often understood exhortations to save in more self-interested terms. From women's leaders to local housewives, Japanese commonly drew on government campaigns to empower themselves vis-à-vis others. Moreover, state officials were frequently compelled to negotiate with the people. Just as in democratic Britain and the United States, drives in authoritarian Japan employed state-of-the-art methods of persuasion.

Most Japanese prefer to remember the war years in a very different way—as the "dark valley" between the vibrant, urbanizing 1920s and the democratic postwar era. In 1999 the national museum of wartime and early postwar life opened in Tokyo. The Shōwa Memorial Museum dedicates itself to communicating to "future generations the everyday hardships of the Japanese people."[4] Older Japanese, observe two oral historians, tend to look back on World War II as "some natural cataclysm," something that "had 'happened' to them, not in any way been 'done' by them."[5] In most scholarly accounts, too, Japan under militarism—with its rhetoric of austerity and sacrifice—stopped the burgeoning consumer culture of the 1920s in its tracks.[6]

Unquestionably the Japanese suffered acute deprivations in World War II, but the story of the wartime campaigns also reveals the growth of middle-class norms about saving and consumption that continued during the conflict itself. Many individuals strove to modernize daily habits and advance their consumer lives, even as they saved for the state. Ironically, much that we associate with *postwar* Japan's middle-class culture—the stereotypical "housewife" and her scrupulous management of family finances—was shaped by developments occurring during the nation's darkest times.

"For My Own Good and the Good of the Nation": The Interwar Years

The Japanese campaigns of World War II in turn owed a great deal to the new generation of savings drives that the state mounted between the two world wars. Interwar campaigns introduced modern techniques of propaganda and organization in line with contemporary savings promotion in the West. Earlier efforts at the time of the Russo-Japanese War had targeted the rural populace; they encouraged villagers to save in large measure by discouraging consumption, particularly traditional spending on alcohol or ceremonial occasions. By the 1920s Japanese officials confronted a rapidly urbanizing society that would not so readily subscribe to blandishments to economize.

World War I was the turning point. The conflict was not simply twentieth-century Japan's "Good War." It had been a *Great* War, militarily and economically. Having vanquished overseas German forces in a mere two months, Japan sacrificed little in blood and treasure while experiencing a remarkable economic boom for the rest of the war. Japanese manufacturers swept into Asian, East African, and Middle Eastern markets abandoned by the warring Europeans. Emblematic were the nouveau riche businessmen known as *narikin* and famously caricatured for lighting ¥100 bills just to find their way out of geisha houses.[7] The surging economy benefited less affluent Japanese, too, as large numbers entered the ranks of the industrial working class. Others became white-collar "salarymen" working in large companies and government offices. Young women also moved into new occupations as typists, telephone operators, teachers, nurses, and bus girls. Enjoying rising incomes, city people sampled a dazzling array of commodities. Stylish department stores appealed to the broader middle classes, and entertainments like the cinema and baseball games became affordable. Scholars often pinpoint the 1920s as the advent of Japan's "mass consumption society."[8]

Tanizaki Junichirō captured the new age in *Naomi*, his much read novel serialized in 1924–25. When we first encounter the narrator Jōji, he is the model of diligence and thrift. Born in the countryside, this sober young man studied engineering in Tokyo and labored six days a week for an electrical firm. He carefully budgeted and, little by little, saved "quite a bit." Yet Jōji's frugality would not long survive his infatuation with Naomi, a café waitress and ultimate "modern girl" in the parlance of the time. How Jōji dissipates his wealth reads like a guide to the emerging urban lifestyle. The couple spends lavishly in ways unimaginable before World War I. They frequent restaurants, vacation at the beach, go ballroom dancing, and live in a Western-style "culture home." Cinema, especially Hollywood, appears at the core of their existence. Jōji can't stop talking about Naomi as his Mary Pickford, the leading star of the silent movies.[9]

For the Japanese state, the challenge was to persuade the urban populace to avoid the snares of Naomism and continue saving. Initial attempts were clumsy, to say the least. In 1922 the Home Ministry kicked off a savings campaign for "economy in consumption" (*shōhi setsuyaku*). Although Japan emerged from World War I victorious and prosperous, officials warned of the coming "peacetime economic war" in international trade. The nation's competitive position was being eroded by rising prices, sharply declining savings, increasing foreign debt, and insufficient investment capital. The authorities left no doubt as to the culprit. Having adopted "habits of luxury and self-indulgence" during the wartime boom, "the people keep consuming at a furious pace." Popular spending, notably on imported luxury goods, contributed mightily to Japan's growing trade deficit from 1919, claimed the bureaucrats.[10] Complain as they might, officials lacked the means of stopping city people from spending. So the state fell back on earlier methods of ha-

ranguing and micromanaging the countryside. To encourage economizing, the Home Ministry required district chiefs to submit detailed
village-by-village surveys of the time and money spent on weddings
and funerals. Headmen fastidiously recorded the types of wedding ceremonies, who attended, and even what was served at banquets.[11] No
wonder progressive Japanese ridiculed these hortatory campaigns as
anachronistic efforts to extract savings from those with the smallest
margins to economize.[12]

To appeal to the newly affluent middle classes, the authorities soon
recognized they would have to market thrift just as advertisers sold
toothpaste. From 1924 to 1926, the government mounted a different
sort of campaign that became the prototype for savings drives in both
World War II and the postwar years. Quaintly titled the Campaign to
Encourage Diligence and Thrift (Kinken Shōrei Undō), it nonetheless
made unprecedented use of modern media including advertisements,
motion pictures, essay contests, and radio (the latter inaugurated in
1925). The government conducted seven "Diligence and Thrift Weeks"
to encourage people to open savings accounts and purchase bonds and
life insurance. Most eye-catching were the 2.3 million colorful posters
that blanketed trains, temples, post offices, and other public buildings.
Over the next twenty years, the regime employed some of the nation's
finest graphic artists to produce scores of different savings posters (see
plate 8).[13]

If Japanese savings campaigns of the 1920s and 1930s resembled
contemporary Western efforts, this was no coincidence. Since the late
nineteenth century, Japan had been a major player in the global marketplace of ideas and institutions associated with strengthening the
nation-state. Initially Japanese adopted European postal and school
savings. The British subsequently applied lessons of Japanese war saving in 1904–1905 to the National War Savings Movement of World
War I. When in turn interwar Japanese planners decided to update their
own programs, they investigated the national savings campaigns introduced by Western belligerents in World War I. Japanese officials surveyed the U.S. war savings campaign, impressed by its political success
in inculcating "a sense of the nation" among Americans. Sales of Thrift
Stamps not only taught schoolchildren patriotism, they reported, but

also "contributed to the campaign to assimilate the many Americans born in other countries."[14]

Nevertheless, Japanese interest in U.S. policies paled by comparison with enthusiasm for the British model. Among countries outside the British Empire, Italy and Japan most closely investigated the National Savings Movement, recalled one member of the National Savings Committee.[15] Britain had after all been Japan's closest ally, and its savings-promotion apparatus was indisputably the world's leading model. At the height of World War I, the Japanese government dispatched teams of bureaucrats to London, where they thoroughly surveyed programs of home-front mobilization including war savings campaigns. After the war, observed Japanese officials, the British government continued to promote saving, unlike the United States. In 1924 the Ministry of Finance's resident officer in London sent his superiors an influential report on the merits of the National Savings Movement. Later that year the ministry resolved to "emulate the British system."[16]

Just as the British Treasury inaugurated the National Savings Committee to coordinate the network of local savings committees, the Japanese government created the Central Council to Encourage Diligence and Thrift. The council worked with the bureaucracy to establish a nationwide hierarchy of campaign committees at the prefectural, city, town, and village levels. Inspired by the National Savings Movement, the Japanese drive also enlisted the cooperation of teachers, urban social work organizations, women's organizations, and various religious associations including Christian groups. The circular nature of transnational emulation may best be grasped in the case of savings associations. Prior to 1914 the Japanese state had impressed British observers by systematically organizing the rural populace into savings associations that required members to make regular deposits. In the course of World War I, Japanese authorities in turn observed how the British organized more than forty thousand War Savings Associations to sell War Savings Certificates. Under the Campaign to Encourage Diligence and Thrift, officials went beyond the traditional focus on the countryside to establish large numbers of savings associations in urban neighborhoods and in workplaces among workers and white-collar employees.[17]

The Japanese moreover avidly participated in the international networks that spread new techniques of mass persuasion, most vividly in the case of posters. Japan's Foreign Ministry methodically collected hundreds of mobilization posters from its allies in World War I. Several inspired Japanese posters in the 1920s.[18] Japanese bureaucrats further monitored Western publicity efforts by taking part in the international thrift movement. They were in fact present at its creation. In 1924 the Ministry of Communications dispatched a postal savings official to attend the First International Thrift Congress in Milan. Although organizers had invited representatives of savings institutions from China, India, Java, and Siam, Fujiwara Yasuaki was the lone Asian in attendance. Thus began a close relationship between the Japanese postal savings system and the International Thrift Institute and its successors. The Japanese government routinely sent representatives to the thrift congresses. Also, the postal savings system and private savings banks annually commemorated World Thrift Day on October 31—though growing nationalist sentiment prompted the state in 1936 to establish the alternative "Diligence, Thrift, and Savings Day" on March 10, the date of the Meiji emperor's rescript on thrift of 1879.

Right up to the outbreak of World War II in 1939, the postal savings bureau regularly exchanged posters and other promotional materials with the International Thrift Institute's affiliated savings and postal savings banks around the world. While Japanese officials and artists kept up to date on the newest savings propaganda in Europe and North America, their Western counterparts studied Japanese poster art. International Thrift Institute staff repeatedly praised the Japanese postal savings bank for pursuing a "systematic programme of Thrift Publicity, utilizing the most up-to-date media" including films. They commented appreciatively on the distinctive combination of "Japanese painting" and modern poster art. Japanese savings posters reduced motifs to "a few essential elements," distinguished by "the fundamental care taken in order to make a decorative composition of the subject, to which a fanciful wording lends harmony and artistic worth."[19]

The interwar savings campaigns were intensely nationalistic in their appeals. Echoing Western propaganda of 1914–18, they urged Japanese to save and economize as a vital national duty—the difference being

Figure 22. Savings as Japan's ultimate weapon, 1924. Quoted are Akiyama Saneyuki's famous words, "The fate of our Empire depends on this one action," uttered before the Japanese navy smashed the Russian fleet in 1905. In this poster, smoke from the menacing fleet bears the words "higher prices, luxuries, and an excess of imports." The defending Japanese ship (unseen) flies the ensigns of "diligence, frugality, and saving." [Naimushō] Shakaikyoku, *Kinken kyōchō gaikyō* [Report on savings promotion] (Tokyo: Shakaikyoku, 1925), 30.

that the Japanese drives occurred *after* World War I. In this as in other mobilization efforts, the Japanese state—even in peacetime—behaved much as a nation at war.[20] Savings posters could be downright militaristic. One in 1924 depicted an enemy fleet bearing down on Japan, armed with luxury imports. Japanese were urged to fire back by spending less on luxuries, saving their money, and producing more domestic goods (figure 22).

Other posters exhorted the populace to save more so the nation could catch up with Western nations. To a remarkable degree, Japanese savings campaigns relied on statistics in their visual appeals. Bar graphs conveyed that the country ranked dead last in national wealth vis-à-vis the other powers (figure 23). "Countrymen!!! Look at These Figures," screamed one 1929 poster crammed with tables quantifying Japan's trade deficits, soaring national debt, and lowest per capita wealth among the powers.[21]

Interwar savings campaigns also adopted softer messages more attuned to urban life and middle-class values. Increasingly the Japanese state coupled patriotism with appeals to self-interest. Proclaimed one of the most compelling posters of the age: "Diligence and Thrift: It's for My Own Good and the Good of the Nation" (see plate 9).

Rationalizing Consumption and Daily Life

There was something democratic about the interwar savings campaigns' appeals to the cities. Like British and U.S. campaigns in World War I, Japanese drives broadened the social bases of campaign workers. By the mid-1920s, savings-promotion officials found common ground with some unlikely allies: urban progressives who advocated improved consumption for the Japanese people, or what they called "cultured living" (*bunka seikatsu*). These were liberal intellectuals, academic specialists, and leaders of the burgeoning women's groups. What brought progressives and bureaucrats together was the recognition that most Japanese lacked the margin to increase consumption significantly. Households, they agreed, could improve living standards primarily by "rationalizing" consumption. By keeping household accounts and eliminating "wasteful

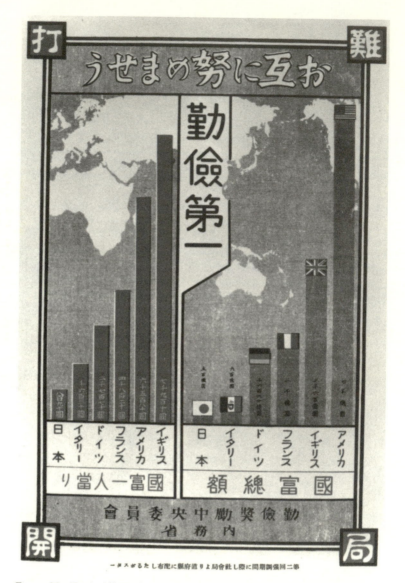

Figure 23. "Let's All Work Together: Diligence and Thrift Is Number One!" Only by working harder and saving more, suggests this 1925 poster, will Japanese rival the Western powers. Measuring aggregate national wealth, the bar graph on the right ranks the United States first, followed by Britain, France, and Germany. Japan scrapes the bottom, just below Italy. Naimushō Shakaikyoku, *Kinken shōrei undō gaikyō*.

Plate 1. Ca. 1890. One of several woodblock prints commissioned by Japan's Ministry of Education to illustrate the didactic stories in Samuel Smiles's *Self-Help*. In this print, France's Bernard Palissy (1510–1590) was so intent on improving the quality of his country's earthenware that after many experiments he ended up burning the family's shelves and chairs to fire the kiln. His wife and children feared he had gone mad, but finally the enamel melted, "and he prevailed." Commentary by Sinead Kehoe. Artist unknown. Reproduced by permission from the Princeton University Art Museum. Gift of Mr. and Mrs. Jerome Straka.

Plate 2. "Step by Step, Fuji is Attained; *Rin* by *Rin*, Wealth is Gained," Japan, 1925. In this avings campaign poster, Aesop's ant saves for himself and the nation (symbolized by Mt. Fuji). A ɔ was worth only one-thousandth of a yen. Naimushō Shakaikyoku, *Kinken shōrei undō gaikyō*.

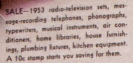

THE WO

Will it be a glittering new world plastics and television and unratio
Yes, of course—but we must m more. We must make it a world human being of every race and no to eat and to wear, a snug place t to get an education, and an oppor freedom from insecurity and pove speech and worship.
We must make it a world in things of life are there for the which every human being has the his share.

SALE—1953 radio-television sets, message-recording telephones, phonographs, typewriters, musical instruments, air conditioners, home libraries, house furnishings, plumbing fixtures, kitchen equipment. A 10c stamp starts you saving for them.

TRIPS WITH THE GANG . . . $18.75 put into a bond now will probably buy a post-war bicycle—perhaps one made of magnesium or pressed wood—strong as steel and half as heavy—easier to pedal. Or start saving for an inexpensive midget auto, power bike, fold boat, sailboat, outboard, glider, clubhouse, diving raft, etc. Remember—stamps don't increase in value, bonds do. Fill up a stampbook and trade it for a bond as often as you can.

WAR BONDS FOR EDUCATION . . . Whether it's to be Liberal Arts, Agriculture, Science, Business School, or graduate work in Law, Medicine, Teaching, etc.—War Bonds will help see you through and set you up in business afterward.

SPARE-TIME HOBBIES . . . Will row's workshop (tool chest, workbe grinder, etc.)? Photographic labora larger, print dryer, projector)? Ch Microscope? Telescope? Sewing one-third in value. Prices are ex

Page 10

Plate 5. While savers in other nations in World War II dreamed of simple consumer pleasures after the war, this Treasury Department newsletter encouraged American

1953 . . .

VACATION IN Madagascar, Alaska,
Hawaii, Venezuela. Week end in Mexico
City, Newfoundland . . . This isn't a dream.
If you could ride with the air freight, you
could do it today. Your War Bonds will
help make it possible tomorrow.

"IF YOU DON'T NEED IT, DON'T BUY IT"—A good wartime motto, and especially true of sporting goods. But it's not
too early to start staking out your claim to our post-war production. What will it be: Ski equipment? Shotgun? Field
glasses? Horse? Camping equipment? Skates? Tennis
racket? Golf clubs? Put business ahead of pleasure—put
the money into War Stamps and Bonds and let it work for
Victory today, for prosperity tomorrow.

[...] of 1953. More than 80 miles
[...] miles to the gallon—safe even
[...] earth). Or would you rather
[...] refrigerator—or house? Easy
[sta]mps or Bonds.

THE CLOTHES OF TOMORROW—Water-
repellant, wrinkle-free, color-fast, moth-proof,
inexpensive. "It's War Stamps and patches
for the duration," as one Junior Miss puts it,
"but just watch my plumage when it's over!"

schoolchildren to save up for a dazzling set of purchases, including one's own private
air car. "The World of 1953," *Schools at War* ([April] 1943): 10–11.

Plates 3 and 4 follow plate 5.

Plate 3. "Buy Your 'Victory' Bonds," 1917. Although this French-Canadian poster appears to copy James Montgomery Flagg's famous "I [Uncle Sam] Want You" placard, both the Canadian and American posters were in fact based on the 1914 recruiting poster "Britons, [Lord Kitchener] Wants You." Poster, "Souscrivez à L'Emprunt de la 'Victoire,'" CWM 19920166-186. © Canadian War Museum.

Plate 4. "For the Flag! For Victory! Buy National Bonds," France, 1917. Posters in World War I commonly juxtaposed male soldiers and women savers. In this variant, Marianne—the personification of France—evokes the importance of women on the home front. Poster by Georges Bretin Scott. Library of Congress.

Plate 6. In 1944 this evocative poster kicked off Britain's "Keep on Saving" campaign—aimed at mobilizing savings for final victory and postwar reconstruction. The fiery cross was traditionally used by Scottish clans to rally members to the common defense. Reproduced by permission of TNA, NSC 5/141.

Plate 7. British campaigns employed racial caricatures of the Japanese enemy to motivate citizens to keep on saving, 1945. Reproduced by permission of TNA, NSC 5/628.

一銭ヲ笑フ者ハ
一銭ニ泣ク

百万ノ富モ
一銭カラ

内務省勤儉奨励中央委員會

Plate 8. "He Who Laughs at One *Sen* will Cry over One *Sen* [when he no longer has it] . . . The Wealth of the Millionaire Comes from One *Sen*," Japan, 1926. This savings campaign poster is striking in the combination of modernist graphic art and traditional themes. Visually it appeals to many faiths. Who is the wise man? Is he the Buddha, Confucius, or a Christian saint? The text, too, suggests an ancient East Asian saying, but would also have reminded Japanese of Benjamin Franklin's "A penny saved is a penny earned." Naimushō Shakaikyoku, *Kinken shōrei undō gaikyō.*

Plate 9. A schoolboy writes: "Diligence and Thrift: It's for My Own Good and the Good of the Nation," Japan, 1925. Unlike earlier austerity drives, interwar Japanese campaigns communicated that saving would also improve people's lives. Naimushō Shakaikyoku, *Kinken shōrei undō gaikyō*.

Plate 10. "Savings Build the New East Asia," Japan, 1939. As Japanese forces bogged down in China, the Ministry of Finance commissioned this poster for the Economic Warfare Campaign at home. The Western-inspired print portrays Korea (bottom right) and China (bottom left) as traditional societies in need of modernization from Japan, represented by the industrial worker and crane hoisting the national savings target of ¥10 billion. Courtesy of the Communications Museum, Japan, XD-E13.

expenditures," one might both save more and spend wisely on those goods that improved daily life.

Consumer-centered ideas penetrated the state itself. In alliance with home economists, educators, and other specialists, the Ministry of Education in 1920 launched the first of several "daily life improvement campaigns" (seikatsu kaizen undō). The global modernity of the message was unmistakable. Campaigns sought to improve the nation's hygiene, housing, and clothing. The Daily Life Improvement League recruited members in Tokyo neighborhoods by offering silver badges bearing the Western letters "BL" for "Better Life."[22] The improvement campaigns appealed to urban residents because they offered practical instruction in how to economize while recognizing the benefits of the new consumer culture. The Ministry of Education—in cooperation with women's groups—sponsored a series of well-attended public lectures and exhibitions. There one could learn about simplifying weddings or how to conserve rice by mixing in cheaper, yet nutritious, grains and beans. The Home Ministry, too, soon shifted to promoting saving in the name of daily life improvement. In 1925 the ministry's Social Bureau sponsored lectures on such topics as "rational, budgeted living and saving," the "rational consumption" of nutritious foods, and "scientific diligence and thrift."[23]

Europeans would have readily identified with Japanese practices of rationalized consumption, for the discourse was truly transnational. Influenced by U.S. and European specialists, Japanese reformers had been promoting better nutrition and more hygienic use of domestic space since the late nineteenth century. Following World War I, Frederick Winslow Taylor's concept of scientific management in the United States kicked off a new international movement to apply methods of industrial efficiency to management of the home. American ideas of housekeeping offered the prospect of higher living standards and acquisition of labor-saving appliances. By contrast, Europeans—like Japanese—concluded that households' best chance of realizing modest improvements lay in becoming more efficient with what they had. During the early 1920s, German home economists and feminists popularized the terms "rational household management" and "rationalization of consumption." They soon became buzzwords in Japan as well. Symbolic of the age was the Frankfurt kitchen. Its space-saving design and standardized parts were intended to minimize wasteful motions and save families money. The city of Frankfurt installed ten thousand of these kitchens in public housing for working families in the late 1920s. In promotional films, the housewife was a study in efficiency. She whirled from task to task often on a specially designed stool with castors.[24] In Japan, too, housewives' magazines and home economists popularized model kitchens and cost-saving techniques. Few Japanese actually built such kitchens before World War II, but most heard messages of rationalized consumption repeatedly and nearly always in tandem with calls to save money.[25]

The movement for household rationalization helped propel Japanese women to central roles in the interwar savings campaigns. Although middle-class women in England and the United States had been keeping household account books since Victorian times, Japanese married women did not become commonly associated with household saving and consumption until the 1920s. Earlier savings drives rarely targeted wives because the patriarch or sometimes the mother-in-law retained control over finances in the typical three-generation family. Following World War I, the state's attitudes toward women changed dramatically. In investigations of wartime Europe and North America, Japanese bureaucrats highlighted the contributions of women's groups to the war efforts. The vital roles of Western women in savings and economizing drives did not escape their notice. To mobilize Japanese women, the Home Ministry in 1920 began organizing women's associations (*fujinkai*) in villages and neighborhoods throughout the nation. These residential associations, essentially compulsory in membership, emerged as key intermediaries in subsequent savings campaigns.[26]

The perceived lessons of World War I convinced Japanese bureaucrats and political leaders also to involve nongovernmental women's groups, even those politicized groups that demanded women's suffrage and other rights. Indeed, the interwar cabinets that mounted the most vigorous savings campaigns were those headed by the era's most democratic leaders representing the Kenseikai party (later reorganized as the Minseitō). In the Campaign to Encourage Diligence and Thrift in 1926, Prime Minister Wakatsuji Reijirō and Finance Minister Hamaguchi Osachi hosted more than one hundred representatives of women's organizations, proclaiming that the nation's women "are in charge of the consumer economy." Aiming to deflate the economy to expand exports and return to the gold standard in 1929–30, the incoming Hamaguchi cabinet mounted a new campaign to reduce consumption and boost savings. The government called upon women's organizations to bring about "economy in the kitchen of every home." Excepting some socialist associations, independent women's groups enthusiastically assisted the campaign.[27]

Behind the growing prominence of women in savings campaigns lay a major reconceptualization of gender roles. Increasingly the state and society defined women as "housewives"—those responsible for household finances and consumption. We see this in campaign posters. Lagging behind Western propaganda in World War I, Japanese savings posters did not feature a woman until 1926. Yet by the mid-1930s, campaign images abounded of the woman as housewife, mother, and saver (figure 24). Mass-circulation housewives' magazines did the most to popularize the identity of the household manager. The pioneer in this effort was Hani Motoko, a Protestant reformer and editor of *Fujin no tomo* (Woman's Companion, est. 1908). Influenced by Anglo-American norms of housewifery, Hani strove to cultivate "middle-class" consciousness among Japanese women. Her magazine passionately encouraged readers to record income, expenditures, and savings in household account books called *kakeibo*. In 1904 Hani herself authored one of the era's most popular account books. The more commercial *Shufu no tomo* (Housewife's Companion) first appeared in 1917. It remains today the most widely read housewives' magazine. The annual issue, which featured the account book for the new year, was a major source of *Shufu no tomo*'s popularity. Prized for tips on how to economize in the home, housewives' magazines gradually normalized the image of woman as the family's resourceful saver.[28]

Household rationalization initially appealed primarily to urban middle-class women and men, but the movement spread to the countryside in the course of the 1930s. Hit hard by the Great Depression, rural communities became the object of state policies that mixed relief measures with programs to reinvigorate village solidarity and self-help.

Figure 24. "Reflections of Love in Savings Bright," Japan, ca. 1935. This postal savings poster targeted the emerging middle-class mother and housewife. Note the woman's modern hairstyle. Yūsei Kenkyūjo, *Modanizumu no jidai*, 11. Courtesy of the Communications Museum, Japan.

Central officials ordered the establishment of village "economic revitalization committees" to reduce household debt, boost savings, and improve hygiene. Comprised of local notables and farmers, the committees did not simply invoke traditional values of frugality, but also imposed urban middle-class virtues. They required villagers to spend less on "old customs" like lavish weddings and funerals, while closely supervising household account-keeping. Rural women joined their big-city sisters in reading magazines offering advice on how to keep accounts and raise healthy children. The semiofficial monthly, *Ie no hikari* (Light of the Home), reached one million farm households by 1935.[29]

Thus as Japan became embroiled in total war after 1937, it could draw upon an elaborate set of *peacetime* mechanisms for promoting saving. Not all Japanese would eagerly respond to wartime savings campaigns. But a goodly number of activists—as well as ordinary people—continued to encourage saving among compatriots, convinced that the drives advanced modernity and daily life improvement.

"Blow the Anglo-Americans Away with Your Savings"

For Americans, World War II began with the Japanese attack on Pearl Harbor on December 7, 1941. Yet the Japanese had been at war for much of the previous decade after the army took over Manchuria in 1931–32. The conflict entered its middle phase in summer 1937 when Japan embarked on full-scale war with China. The Japanese ventured into new territory in more ways than one. The imperial state faced the daunting prospect of financing the military occupation of the world's most populous country. Japan could no longer turn to the financiers of London and New York as it had during the Russo-Japanese War. This time, remarked a veteran official, the Anglo-American powers supported China, and "they won't lend Japan a penny."[30] By 1938 government planners anguished over the precarious state of war finance. Although China's major cities had fallen, Japanese troops could neither control the countryside nor prevent Chinese Nationalist forces from fleeing to the interior. Japanese leaders talked openly of a "protracted war" that would sorely tax the resources of the nation.

On April 19 the cabinet approved an ambitious plan to raise the level of national savings by ¥8 billion that fiscal year. From a financial perspective, Japan would end up fighting the last war. After dusting off previous surveys of Allied savings campaigns in World War I, officials again chose Britain's National War Savings model.[31] The Japanese government created a powerful agency whose sole purpose was to direct the war savings campaign. The Ministry of Finance established the National Savings Promotion Bureau, together with an advisory National Savings Promotion Council. Like Western counterparts, Japanese experts professed to have learned from the economic mistakes of World War I, particularly the need to check inflation. Stepped-up national saving would finance war production, underwrite the expanding supply of war bonds, and soak up rising purchasing power. To reach the populace, the National Savings Promotion Bureau mobilized the vast apparatus of the Japanese state, working closely with the ministries of Home Affairs, Education, Agriculture and Forestry, Welfare, and Colonies. The newly created National Spiritual Mobilization Central League provided many campaign workers by deputizing affiliated organizations of religions, moral reformers, businesses, veterans, women, and youth throughout the nation.[32]

Like other belligerents, the regime mobilized the growing mass media. Newspapers and magazines urged national saving, in tandem with posters, pamphlets, records, radio, motion pictures, exhibitions, and sometimes advertising balloons. The national savings drive also hired popular artists, including several cartoonists.[33] Best known was Yokoyama Ryūichi, whose comic strip about a boy named Fuku-chan delighted wartime and postwar readers alike. During the Pacific War (1941–45) against the United States and Britain, Fuku-chan served valiantly (figure 25). This cartoon character, adorable to be sure, spent the war telling Japanese to "Blow the Anglo-Americans away with your savings."[34]

Indeed, the Japanese government drew on savings to finance World War II to a far greater extent than Britain and the United States. Although the regime increased income and corporate taxes significantly from 1937 to 1945, taxation never provided more than one-fourth of Japanese war finance. The remainder came from government bonds.

Figure 25. Fuku-chan and family join in the "all-out savings offensive," 1943.
Unsigned, but apparently drawn by the popular cartoonist Yokoyama Ryūichi.
Nakamura Yukio, *Chochiku sōshingun* (Tokyo: Musubi Shobō, 1943).

In both Britain and the United States, by contrast, taxation funded
roughly 50 percent of government spending. Japan most resembled its
ally Nazi Germany, where taxation similarly financed only one-quarter
of war expenditures in 1943.

In Japan, too, the people's savings indirectly financed war loans
in large part. Unlike Americans, Japanese rarely owned war bonds, although the public could buy them at post offices. Instead the Bank of
Japan underwrote more than half of total government debt. The Bank
of Japan then sold the bonds to financial institutions, which purchased
the issues with money on deposit. The Ministry of Finance's Deposit
Bureau nearly matched the Bank of Japan's network in buying government bonds. Drawing most of its funds from postal savings, the Deposit
Bureau alone purchased a further 35 percent of government debt during the last two years of the war.[35] The postal savings system emerged
as one of the few Japanese winners in World War II. Already in 1936
Japanese postal savings had become the largest such system in the world

with some 48 million accounts, rivaling Britain's Post Office Savings Bank in total savings. Postal savings in wartime grew at a torrid pace. Recognizing that nearly every yen saved at the post office directly financed the war effort, the authorities pressed small depositors to shift to postal savings, postal life insurance, and postal annuities. Postal deposits of these three types rose more than twice as fast as total national savings between 1938 and 1943, dwarfing any other type of saving.[36]

Why did Japanese policymakers finance the war through savings, rather than substantial tax hikes? In Germany Hitler and other top Nazis feared that higher direct taxes would provoke popular resistance. Japanese officials likewise worried about the political costs of raising taxes. Ujiie Takeshi, chief of the National Savings Promotion Bureau, admitted as much in public. Although taxes were only one-third as large as national savings, he granted, the public found them onerous enough. Were the government to rely solely on taxes, "the people would scream."[37] Japanese appeared more willing to fund the war effort through savings, which unlike taxes remained in their possession. Having ruled out major tax increases, some bureaucrats and experts proposed that the people be legally compelled to save. Their recommendations preceded John Maynard Keynes's compulsory savings proposal by more than a year. Compulsory savings schemes would fare no better in Japan than in Britain. Japanese leaders rejected overt compulsion as unenforceable and counterproductive. Mused Vice Minister Ishiwata: "Let's say we compel saving by law. Are we going to fine people who don't save? Are we going to send them to jail? There's no way that's going to happen."[38]

In fact, "voluntary" saving increasingly resembled taxation. As the costs of war mounted, the regime issued larger numbers of bonds and printed more money much as Germany did in both world wars. Prices soared. Rampant inflation essentially taxed the Japanese people, who were pressured into making low-interest loans to the state while the real value of their savings plummeted. The China War dragged on. With no end in sight in 1941, Japanese leaders overreached spectacularly. Launching a new war against the United States and its Allies, they strained national finances to the extreme. Convinced that ever-greater savings could be wrung out of the people, the regime raised annual national savings targets at a punishing pace in the course of the Pacific War. Individual quotas were allocated to prefectures and financial institutions. In 1940 the state extended quotas to cities, towns, villages, and individual savings associations. The authorities pressed each entity to achieve its quota. In most years, they were ruthlessly effective in reaching or exceeding national savings targets. In mid-1944 with the Americans advancing to within bombing range of the home islands, the cabinet revised the annual target from ¥36 billion to a theretofore unthinkable ¥41 billion. Such an increase, officials privately admitted, would "truly not be easy to achieve by year's end in light of the present living conditions of the people."[39] But they surpassed it, as they would the next year's incredible target of ¥60 billion. By the time the war ended, the state had raised the national savings target to eight times what it had been in 1938.[40]

Japanese encountered exhortations to save nearly everywhere, it seemed. Even when they went out on the town, individuals discovered they must also buy special certificates in proportion to their spending. These could only be deposited in savings institutions. New oxymorons appeared: "shopping savings," "restaurant savings," and "theater savings." Financial institutions further pressed households to open accounts on the occasion of birthdays and weddings. It became common for homes to possess five to ten savings passbooks.[41]

Save, or "We Won't Give You Rations"

Nor could the spendthrift hide at home. There he or she encountered the ubiquitous savings association. When the government launched the war savings campaign in 1938, officials proclaimed savings associations to be the "front line in effecting saving." So these groups remained until the end of the war. Although campaign organizers ruled out legal compulsion, they warmly endorsed the "semi-compulsory" nature of the savings association.[42] For the masses below the middle class, explained postal savings bureaucrats, "the most effective way of getting them to practice thrift and saving is to organize an association, establish regulations, and introduce group compulsion over members."[43] Savings associations regularly collected residents' savings, depositing them in post offices and other financial institutions.

What distinguished wartime savings drives from earlier campaigns was the state's determination to organize the entire populace into savings associations. Make sure "absolutely no one evades participating in a savings association," prefectural promotion officers were instructed.[44] Savings associations formed in government offices, companies, schools, and among trade associations, youth groups, women's organizations, and religious associations. The great majority of savings associations were residential, based on hamlet associations (*burakukai*) in the villages and block associations (*chōnaikai*) in cities and towns. Subunits of the savings associations coincided with "neighborhood associations" (*tonarigumi*), the lowest rung in the wartime regime's formidable mechanisms of mobilization and micromanagement. Officials organized roughly every ten households into a neighborhood association. The total number of savings associations grew steadily during the China and Pacific wars. By the end of 1944, they enrolled fifty-nine million members. Considering that family members also engaged in group saving at schools and work, nearly every household belonged to at least one savings association—and many to two, three, or even four.[45]

To reach greater numbers of savers, the government sponsored the National Savings Association Law in 1941. All savings associations became legal entities known as "national savings associations." The law empowered the authorities to establish savings associations, which individuals were compelled to join. Unquestionably the measure spurred the formation of savings associations. The law also offered a new incentive to save, granting tax-exemption for interest on deposits made via savings associations.[46]

Officials regarded workplace associations as the greatest challenge—particularly those in the so-called boom industries (see figure 26). These were the war-related factories where profits and wages had soared since the outbreak of hostilities. Workers' income, if freely spent, would have serious inflationary consequences. Finance Minister Kaya Okinori castigated boom-industry employees for daring to think of their windfall earnings as "their money and theirs to spend." This smacked of the "old individualism," considering those wages resulted from "the blood, sweat,

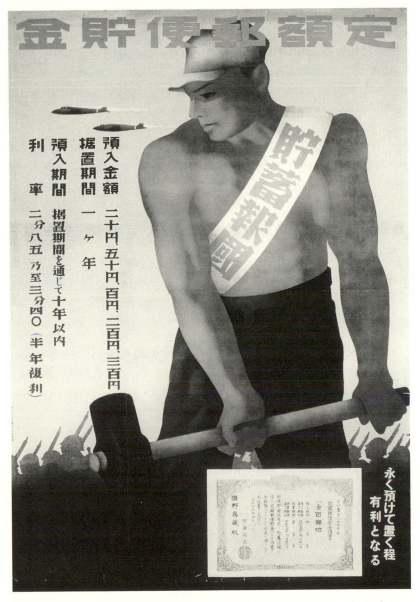

Figure 26. "Savings Patriotism," Japan, 1941. The manly, often bare-chested worker appeared in the savings posters of all the belligerents in World War II. Courtesy of the Communications Museum, Japan, XD-B62.

and tears of the Japanese people."[47] While the British and U.S. governments also encouraged saving on the shop floor, Japanese bureaucrats in 1938 went further to devise regulations that *mandated* how much savings associations should extract from each employee according to pay, marital status, and other factors. A young male worker with no dependents whose income had increased since the outbreak of the China War would have seen at least 30 percent of his wages deducted for savings, and possibly 60 to 80 percent on monthly earnings of more than ¥50. Employees could withdraw their savings only with the approval of the association head—usually their manager—and then only in the case of an accident or calamity.[48]

Whereas workplace savings associations collected savings according to formulae, residential savings associations functioned more arbitrarily. The state engineered a system in which the most visible compulsion was exercised by neighbor upon neighbor. Once individual savings associations were allocated savings quotas in 1940, local leaders confronted ever-increasing demands from above. To meet quotas, residential associations found themselves making crucial decisions about which households should tender more in savings, and which less. These decisions might reduce a family to basic subsistence and even malnutrition. By 1943 savings associations were under strict orders to extract savings based on thorough investigations of neighbors' lives.[49]

To make people save, residential savings associations employed an array of draconian sanctions. What happened to those families who could not save at the assessed levels? Well, "we just tell them: 'Then, we won't give you rations,'" replied one block association head in Nara prefecture. This was no idle bluff. The most effective forms of local compulsion involved the hamlet and block associations' powers to distribute rationed goods. The regime rationed nearly all essential commodities from rice to fuel and clothing. At the height of the Pacific War, the government ordered savings associations to extract no less than nine types of special savings besides the usual monthly deposit. These included savings to commemorate birthdays, school entrance, and feats of bravery in the war. Particularly onerous were "Momotarō and Hanako-san savings." The birth of a child required the neighborhood association to make a commemorative deposit in the family's savings account—¥5 for a boy and ¥3 for a girl. If the family's passbook did not record such a deposit, the town office refused to register the child for any rations whatsoever.[50]

How effective were the savings associations in promoting saving? By one measure, the savings associations' quota amounted to only 11 percent of the national savings target in 1942. Benefiting from windfall profits, corporations and the wealthy generated the bulk of war savings. However, savings associations accounted for a growing proportion of national savings in the last years of the war. The number of associations mushroomed during these years, and the weight of privately held bonds declined. Savings associations channeled huge sums of money to financial institutions that the regime would have had difficulty extracting by other means. Above all, savings associations enabled state campaigns to reach all classes and all locales. As in the U.S. and European cases, a generation of Japanese emerged from World War II acculturated to saving on a regular basis—often in view of neighbors, coworkers, and fellow pupils.[51]

Resistance and Negotiation

Wartime savings campaigns were far from flawless. Heavy-handed interventions into people's daily lives provoked resentment. Sometimes Japanese refused to comply. Yet rarely did popular irritation impair the regime's ability to mobilize savings. How do we explain the generally high levels of compliance? Patriotic fervor and vigilant policing were important factors, but we must also consider less obvious explanations. First, the Japanese state responded more nimbly to noncompliance than we might have expected. Savings-promotion officials frequently rethought unsuccessful methods, devising new incentives to save. In addition, many Japanese came to attach rather positive meanings to household saving that went well beyond the imperative to sacrifice for the nation.

To be sure, people often grumbled about being forced to save and economize while others continued to lead comfortable lives. In one government survey of thirty-eight towns and villages in late 1937, several local leaders reported that lower-income residents saved more for the war than the rich. In Kagawa prefecture the notables of Wada village sounded almost Marxist: "it's the poorer people who put up the money and bought them. The big capitalists didn't purchase the [war] bonds." Others ridiculed the campaign to encourage economizing on consumption, arguing it did more harm than good: "If the farm villages cut back on consumption any more than they're now doing, people's health and physiques will decline. There's no margin to economize." Sometimes campaign officials displayed little understanding of just how poor many villages were. The Aichi prefectural government distributed an austere "sample menu" as part of "Minimal Living Day." In at least one community, villagers greeted the model menu with derision because the featured "foods are costlier than our most lavish banquets."[52]

By 1940, after three additional years of fighting, ordinary Japanese continued to grumble about making sacrifices unlike the "class that has prospered under the emergency." Some took official pan-Asianist rhetoric seriously enough to believe they sacrificed for fellow Asians as well. This was no doubt the result of propaganda urging Japanese to "Build the New East Asia" by achieving the national savings target of ¥10 billion (see plate 10). Protested one self-styled "patriot" from Nagano prefecture: "We deposit more than ¥10 billion in the national treasury, and the people are made to suffer shortages in materials. What do we have to show for this? We seize no territory; we impose no indemnity; we don't take over the Chinese economy; we don't infringe on the sovereignty of China ... In the final analysis, our all-out fighting has produced results close to nil."[53]

As the war drew to its disastrous conclusion, campaign organizers spoke openly of the public wrath that their aggressive methods provoked. In 1943 even the state-sponsored Greater Japan Women's Federation reported numerous complaints of "unfairness" voiced by people forced to save "again and again"—in women's associations, neighborhood associations, schools, and at work.[54] Hayashi Kimio, a Waseda University economist, criticized the unfairness of the entire system. Block and neighborhood associations assigned savings quotas to each household on an arbitrary basis, he reported to the press. One Tokyo ward assessed some families ¥1 per month and others ¥10.[55] In a remarkably candid analysis, the chief of the Postal Savings Bureau agreed that unfair allocations and the "bureaucratic cast" of savings-promotion activities were turning people against saving.[56]

We do not think of militaristic Japan as a place where market research played much role in official policies. In actuality, the regime employed leading advertisers not only to craft propaganda but also to gauge its impact on the public. In this respect, Japan's authoritarian leaders behaved not so differently from their democratic enemies. The British relied on Mass-Observation, and the U.S. government on Likert surveys and Gallup polls. In August 1944 the Ministry of Finance released to the press a survey of the "people's savings psychology" and popular reactions to national savings propaganda. The ministry had commissioned the Japan Advertising Council, a state-organized body of admen, to survey neighborhoods primarily in the industrial areas of metropolitan Tokyo.[57] The findings proved sobering to officials. When asked whether they experienced "unpleasant aspects" of savings promotion, 37 percent of the sample cited the "promotion officers" who went door to door, and 21 percent mentioned the intrusive neighborhood associations. Respondents also expressed irritation with savings-related performances, lecture meetings, and the seemingly endless circulating notices (kairanban) used by neighborhood associations.

Nonetheless, other responses in the survey of savings psychology surely cheered the authorities. Of the various savings instruments, postal savings won the popularity contest. Fully 77 percent claimed to actively save through the state-run postal savings system. Respondents praised the friendliness of postal employees, and many cited the ease of withdrawing funds. The survey offered further evidence of the regime's success in raising public consciousness about national saving. When asked the precise amount of the 1944 national savings target, an impressive 64 percent answered correctly. Finally propagandists were keen to assess people's motivations. In reply to the question of why one should save (in addition to winning the war), some 57 percent answered "for untimely needs," 34 percent "for the children," and 23 percent "for old age."

The bureaucracy occasionally drew on such surveys to revise counterproductive policies. One issue concerned the tough restrictions placed on withdrawals by savings associations and institutions. By mid-1943 many Japanese reportedly feared Allied bombing would incinerate the local post office or bank, and they sharply cut back on making deposits. To dissuade people from hoarding money, the authorities moved quickly to assure the public of the safety of deposits. Government agencies placed ads in all the newspapers announcing absolutely no restrictions on withdrawals. Even if one's post office or bank were destroyed, one could withdraw savings in installments from financial institutions elsewhere.[58]

Recognizing the limits of compulsion, the campaigns also introduced several incentives that survived into peacetime. Tax exemption for savings association members was one of the most attractive. The post offices moreover expanded the prewar practice of "collection savings." Postal workers would visit homes and collect monthly installment deposits.[59] "Individualism" may have been out of fashion, but wartime propaganda continued to communicate the interwar message that households could simultaneously save for themselves and save for the nation. As Germans kept responding to appeals to "Save in Wartime— Build Later," so, too, did many Japanese financially plan for the future even as the regime exhorted civilians to make ready for the ominous "decisive battle." Even as the Allies closed in on Japan in 1944, the government was still successfully selling postal annuities with glossy ads that outlined the virtues of preparing for "living expenses in old age, or for your children's educational expenses."[60]

Making Saving Appealing

The savings campaigns could not have succeeded without the active assistance of the populace. The Japanese people went well beyond the state's admonitions to invest the act of saving with meanings that empowered them and promised to improve their lives. This was particularly true for women. With most men mobilized, millions of women assumed new roles as managers of the household and leaders of communal life. Women became both the objects of the savings campaigns and their local agents. We may divide them into two groups, although the distinctions often blurred in fact. There were middle-class urban women who had long participated in suffrage and "daily life improvement" movements and who read housewives' magazines. Far more numerous were local leaders and members of the huge semiofficial women's associations.

For veterans of the interwar middle-class women's groups, the China and Pacific wars opened up unprecedented opportunities to participate in public life.[61] State agencies eagerly sought the cooperation of women's groups in campaigns to urge austerity and saving at the grass roots. In 1938 Hani Motoko, the well-known editor of *Fujin no tomo*, began serving on the National Savings Promotion Council, and officials appointed eleven women's leaders to the Emergency National Lifestyle Improvement Council. One was Ichikawa Fusae, Japan's best-known suffragist. The following year the National Savings Promotion Bureau employed thirty-one women as "savings lecturers." They toured the cities and countryside in an effort to promote saving among ordinary women. Government-appointed lecturers ranged from the conservative educators Yoshioka Yayoi and Inoue Hideko to several members of Ichikawa's Women's Suffrage League and the left-leaning reformer Oku Mumeo.[62]

When the regime proclaimed "Luxury is the Enemy" in 1940, many former suffragists and other middle-class women took to the streets on its behalf. They officiously issued warning cards to passersby who sported permanent waves, carried expensive handbags, or wore ostentatious high heels and makeup. Often the vigilantes did the state one better. Whereas the ordinance of July banned only the manufacture and sale of luxury goods, women's "volunteer squads" sought to eliminate total use of these items.[63]

Middle-class women promoted saving in ways that differed significantly from the state's emphasis on popular sacrifice. Their various understandings endured long after the war. For home economists like Hani Motoko, cooperating with wartime savings campaigns advanced the prewar cause of improving daily life. Assisting her was a veritable army of housewives who loyally read her magazine *Fujin no tomo* and formed "friends' societies" (*tomo no kai*). Hani distanced herself from the regime's calls for self-denial and diminished living standards. The war savings drive should instead serve as an opportunity to bring "science" and "rationality" to people's lives.[64]

Invariably Hani advanced the state's agenda of imposing austerity, albeit with a middle-class lilt. If only housewives would eschew wasteful expenditures and become "resourceful," she wrote, families could save more while leading satisfying consumer lives. In nationwide lectures sponsored by the National Savings Promotion Bureau, Hani encouraged audiences to adopt a "simple life." The simple life would not be an "impoverished life" but a "truly comfortable life in terms of the human spirit and one's body." Who would lead "the masses" to this promised life? None other than "our sound middle class," she cheerfully admitted. To Hani, those most in need of instruction were factory workers' families. Their women mismanaged the home and were surprisingly wasteful, she complained, not because of "laziness," but out of a "pitiful lack of education."[65] In September 1938 Hani organized "housewives' life-guidance squads." Middle-class women taught workers' wives how to keep household account books and prepare nutritious foods. Central ministries and prefectural offices were only too happy to subsidize Hani's movement. Many companies soon adopted the squads' training courses.[66]

Remarkably, women's leaders like Hani continued to identify saving with the sound, rationalized life amid the stark deprivations of the Pacific War after 1941. Even as living standards deteriorated, Hani repeated the mantra that families could generate war savings if they "eliminate waste, live wisely, and plan well." To increase household income, her magazine advised women and children to work in war production; to rationalize expenditures, mothers should arrange cooperative child care and neighbors should cook together.[67] Hani was still at it in 1943, haranguing readers to achieve the daunting national savings target of ¥23 billion by cutting unnecessary expenditures on weddings.[68]

While middle-class reformers harped on squeezing out waste, *Shufu no tomo* offered a more upbeat approach. Japan's most popular housewives' magazine trumpeted national saving as the surest path to enriching one's family. By 1935 *Shufu no tomo* boasted a circulation of 850,000. The war, of course, influenced its tone. Exhortations to save and sacrifice filled its pages. Yet to a surprising degree the commercially savvy

Shufu no tomo continued to appeal to the self-interests of housewives as it had before the conflict.[69]

During the war years of the late 1930s, nearly every issue of *Shufu no tomo* instructed housewives on how to "make money" through saving and clever investments. "Are you capable of becoming rich?" asked a leading businessman in one column. To become wealthy, he explained, one must not only save, but aggressively seek the highest rate of return. At a time when the government called on all Japanese to save at the post office, he dismissed postal savings as the "primary school of saving." Readers should instead seek out the private banks, or risk having the "goddess of Good Fortune walk two steps behind you."[70] Another columnist likewise counseled an employee-turned-housewife to keep her money in her former company's savings plan, rather than buy war bonds offering lower rates of return.[71]

Then there was the column Lessons in Saving and Spending Money, which ran from 1938 to early 1940. In each issue, the jovial banker Wada Kenji recommended methods of saving, budgeting, and "life planning." One should buy war bonds, he advised, but a shrewd family might also invest in less patriotic ventures. Why not buy an old house and rent it out, or purchase land and wait for the price to rise? In September 1939, even as Japanese forces bogged down in China, Wada devoted one column to "Failure-Free Ways of Making Money on Stocks." There was nothing "immoral" about making money, he maintained: "If you're going to be prim and proper about these things, you can't make money."[72]

While tips on buying stocks or speculating in land may have appealed to the upper crust of readers, *Shufu no tomo* offered less affluent readers stories of resourceful housewives who succeeded in saving 30 or 40 percent of household income. In the starring roles were wives of lower-echelon civil servants, teachers, factory foremen, and agricultural technologists. Featuring photographs of the smiling wife, husband, and children, they told triumphal tales of cutting wasteful expenditures. Nonetheless by 1942, it became impossible to meet national savings targets through "resourcefulness" alone. *Shufu no tomo* shifted to a different type of success story, profiling housewives who *increased* household income by taking on side jobs such as sewing uniforms.[73]

Shufu no tomo in wartime thus popularized attractive images of the middle-class housewife/saver that would become the norm in postwar Japan. Playful illustrations showed housewives seizing husbands' monthly salaries and doling out small amounts of "pocket money" in exchange. Advice columns urged the wife to save nearly all of her salaryman's semiannual bonuses. Columnists encouraged housewives to save, first and foremost, to finance secondary and higher education. In letters to the editor, mothers—including those with minimal schooling—told of how they saved and sacrificed for the paramount goal of advancing their children's education.[74]

For many progressives, savings drives also offered opportunities to control behavior they deemed extravagant and antisocial. Influential Japanese Protestants embraced "savings patriotism" with fervor. The Salvation Army and the Japan Women's Christian Temperance Union had long campaigned to abolish licensed prostitution and outlaw the practice of keeping mistresses among wealthy men. The key to saving, declared the Salvation Army's venerable Yamamuro Gunpei, lay in households ceasing to spend huge sums on alcohol, tobacco, and "dissipation." Morality mixed with economics. Protestant and women's groups allied with the authorities to close or restrict dance halls, cafés, and geisha houses. In their campaigns against "luxury," many social democratic women—Christian and non-Christian alike—aimed at forcing the "wealthy class" to abandon ostentatious consumption and save for the good of society. Later in postwar Japan, Kōra Tomiko became known for her pacifism and political visits to the Soviet Union and Communist China. Yet in 1938 as a member of the Emergency National Lifestyle Improvement Council, Kōra called for public campaigns against women of leisure who bought camel-hair and all-cotton coats in defiance of restrictions on imported luxuries.[75]

Much more so than Britons and Americans, Japanese women seized on the antiluxury drives to rein in philandering husbands. *Shufu no tomo*'s columns warned housewives about husbands who squandered family income on sex and drink. In one cartoon, a hostess waves farewell to a salaryman who floats to heaven having emptied his pockets at the "Café Poverty." Women's leaders highlighted the adverse impact of male infidelity on national saving. It was not enough to prohibit luxury goods; the state must also ban "extravagant behavior," by which they meant consorting with geisha or mistresses. As official savings lecturers, Ichikawa Fusae and other women labored to stamp out these "inappropriate habits of consumption." With unconcealed delight they personally investigated Tokyo's *machiai*, the high-class houses of assignation frequented by businessmen and politicians.[76]

As the war wore on, local women activists and the wartime women's associations joined middle-class women to champion war saving as in the interests of the household. In 1943 the vice president of the nearly twenty-million-member Greater Japan Women's Federation publicly criticized the Ministry of Finance for using the savings associations to single-mindedly extract savings. Her organization coached members to save not simply out of patriotism but—equally important—to stabilize their own lives.[77] With men away at work or at the front, even humble women now identified themselves as "housewives" responsible for family finances. Many read articles about home economics in housewives' magazines or the agricultural cooperatives' *Ie no hikari*. Quite a few, like the leader of a village women's association in Ishikawa prefecture, kept *Shufu no tomo*'s annual household account book, and they energetically instructed other women in its use. Women commonly headed the savings associations and neighborhood associations.[78]

Savings drives offered local women unprecedented opportunities to elevate their status vis-à-vis the state, men, and fellow women (figure 27). Women on the home front were lauded as "women warriors." As one savings association leader put it, "women may be called weak, but in their service to the nation, they possess substantial reserves of strength." Her own women's unit in a Tokyo ward relentlessly pressed neighbors to save at the assessed levels, cajoling them "to cut back on living expenses" and "reconstruct their lives." Once a month her lieutenants visited each home. In a mere two hours they would gather the hefty sum of ¥82,000. The energy these women put into collecting was "downright ferocious" (*osoroshii*). She said this tongue-in-cheek. But "ferocious" may best describe how financially bled neighbors regarded such displays of power by thousands of intrusive women throughout Japan.[79]

Figure 27. "Cut Waste, Buy Government Bonds … China Incident Bonds Sold at the Post Office," 1939. Dressed in her white-apron uniform, the leader of a government-sponsored women's association exhorts neighbors to save. She holds a European-inspired savings box shaped like a raindrop. Refer to figure 2. Courtesy of the Communications Museum, Japan, XD-F2.

Consequences

Can you ever be too rich? Too thin? Or save too much? No one would dare ask the first question of the war-ravaged Japanese in 1945. As for the latter two propositions, the answers would sadly have been "yes." Even before U.S. bombing devastated Japanese cities in 1945, wartime mobilization of wealth and resources—exacerbated by the Allies' naval blockade—left millions badly clothed and dangerously malnourished. Experts calculated that a human being must consume a minimum of roughly 2,165 calories per day. Yet Japanese consumption fell to an estimated 1,900 calories in 1944 and plummeted to 1,680 calories during 1945. Had the war continued, judged economist Jerome Cohen, "there would have been starvation in the urban centers of Japan during the winter of 1945–46."[80] That the regime would wring more and more savings out of the emaciated populace in the war's final years is remarkable, even criminal. Clearly one could save too much.

The political consequences of the savings campaigns were no less tragic. The very success in extracting savings enabled Japanese leaders to prolong a war they lacked the resources to sustain.[81] Arisawa Hiromi, the influential economist and consultant to the government, recalled the following. In 1936 he would be asked to specify the point at which military spending could increase no further. Replied Arisawa: "But I used to say that an economy has a lot of flexibility, and that, for example, a 10 percent cut in the national living standard could squeeze out about ¥1.5 billion for military expenditures, so the limits could not be drawn so strictly. The real question was whether the people could endure the lowered living standard."[82] As it turned out, the Japanese people would endure enormous deprivations with little overt resistance. The regime postponed the inevitability of defeat at a tremendous human cost. Economists never did determine the breaking point. U.S. bombing and Soviet intervention ended the war first.

As in Europe, the wartime messages of saving and austerity did not perish in the flames of Japan's bombed cities. A quarter-century later the government began surveying the "savings behavior and savings consciousness" of Japanese households. Respondents were asked to judge a number of statements. Surely the oddest phrase was "Luxury is the

Enemy." In the first survey in 1977, fully 42 percent "somewhat agreed" or "strongly agreed" with the slogan that so many had encountered in wartime. Subsequent surveys confirmed considerable sympathy, with the level of agreement declining only gradually to 28 percent as recently as 1997.[83] Moral qualms about extravagance are hardly unique to Japan. But to call luxury the "enemy" after decades of peace? Unquestionably the Japanese people experienced wartime exhortations to save in ways that went well beyond the war effort itself. Postwar Japanese would keep on saving, for themselves and often for the nation.

9

POSTWAR JAPAN'S NATIONAL SALVATION

In wartime, we promoted saving with the slogans, "Wage
War until We Win" and "All for Victory." But in the
coming savings campaign, "Economic Recovery" and
"Revival of the Realm" will be our watchwords as we
remind everyone, too, of the importance of saving to the
savers themselves.
       —Ministry of Finance, secret memo, 1946[1]

Japan waged one of history's most total wars. Its defeat in August
1945 was no less total. Some sixty-six cities lay in ruins, the targets
of wave upon wave of B-29 bombers. This proud nation—which had so
successfully maintained its independence against nineteenth-century
Western imperialism—suffered immediate military occupation by the
Allied forces. Over the next six and a half years the Japanese government took orders from the Supreme Commander of the Allied Powers
(SCAP) in the person of General Douglas MacArthur and briefly General Matthew Ridgeway. Though nominally an Allied operation, the
Americans dominated the occupation from start to finish. For a great
many Japanese, the stunning defeat gave rise to profound disillusion-
ment with the elites who had led the nation into ruinous war. An
assertive labor movement organized more than half of the industrial
workforce, and Communist and Socialist parties threatened the hold of
the conservative establishment.[2]

    This would seem an inauspicious time for the government to call
upon the people to make further sacrifices. Committed to democratiz-
ing Japan, the American occupiers sharply criticized the "virtually

compulsory" features of the wartime savings campaigns.[3] Nor was the populace capable of saving much. Rampant inflation eviscerated the savings so dutifully put aside in wartime. Families withdrew remaining funds to buy food at exorbitant prices on the black market. Japanese uncharacteristically engaged in *dissaving*. Household saving rates plunged into negative territory. Depositors in the supposedly state-guaranteed postal savings system suffered additional losses. Bombing and fires destroyed the records of nearly fifty-two million accounts held in postal facilities. For many depositors it took years to restore their original accounts (only 62 percent of which had been successfully reclaimed by the end of 1957). Moreover, the Ministry of Finance's Deposit Bureau had invested a large chunk of the people's savings in Japan's colonies and occupied territories. We speak today about American banks holding "toxic assets." Imagine what happens when your bank—the postal savings system—makes huge loans throughout the empire, and then the empire itself disappears following Japanese surrender in 1945? More than ¥6 billion in overseas investments vaporized, and postal depositors were compelled to indemnify the state for a portion of the losses. If that were not enough to blast public trust in financial institutions, the government partially froze all other savings deposits in March 1946 in an effort to reduce the money supply and convert Bank of Japan notes into "new yen."[4]

Saving Japan

Under the circumstances, we would hardly expect a defeated and occupied nation to revive the punishing savings campaigns of wartime. Yet that was precisely the course taken by the government of the New Japan, as it was rebranded once again. In November 1946 the Bank of Japan and Ministry of Finance launched the first of nine National Salvation Savings Campaigns. They ran until the end of 1949.[5] Not even in war had officials so explicitly linked saving to "national salvation." By this they meant the survival of Japan as an independent, significant nation. Economic bureaucrats conducted the postwar campaigns with the remarkable self-confidence that the grand campaigns of yesteryear could be revived with little popular resistance, and much cooperation. In a 1947 radio address, Finance Minister Yano Shōtarō urged the nation to "reduce your daily living standards as much as you can, economize, and above all save your unspent money." No detail escaped the minister, as he implored people to use fewer tissues when blowing their noses.[6]

The National Salvation Savings Campaigns aimed to restore the discipline of the bunker, albeit for peaceful ends. The succeeding finance minister, Kurusu Takeo, pined for the good old days when everyone recognized luxury as the enemy. The wartime savings drives had after all imposed "healthy discipline" on consumers, helped finance national debt, and subdued inflationary pressures. Given the needs of postwar economic recovery, "the importance of accumulating capital has not in the least changed from wartime to the present." Yet Japanese consumers were proving less cooperative, the finance minister complained. Following the war, the people experienced "psychological liberation" from pressures to save, and their "sense of thrift hit rock bottom." Worse, "*their desire to consume*, which had been suppressed during the war, burst forth and added fuel to the fire of inflation."[7] This was an extraordinary statement, considering how many Japanese at the time were struggling to survive.

Ministry of Finance officials grudged they could no longer compel people to save, nor would wartime appeals still persuade. However, rather than alter the campaign machinery fundamentally, they opted for new slogans. As part of the makeover, the ministry pledged that the National Salvation Savings Campaign would be a "truly democratic people's campaign." Not that the bureaucrats had suddenly embraced popular initiative. A democratic people's campaign would be one where the state *made* the "people understand the absolute necessity of saving for the revival of the realm and building the economy of the New Japan."[8]

Officials relentlessly communicated how small savings would fuel economic growth based on exports. No one did this as poignantly as Vice Minister of Finance Ikeda Hayato in a savings-promotion speech to the citizens of Hiroshima in 1947. A native of that unfortunate city, Ikeda alluded to the recent atomic bombing and praised residents for extraordinary efforts at rebuilding. Yet without wasting more words on the human toll, he explained that recovery would come about only if every Japanese engaged in "diligence and vigorous efforts" and submitted to "lives of austerity." The key to achieving a higher standard of living in the future lay in increasing exports of manufactured goods. To spur exports, Ikeda elaborated, people must save all of their unspent income, which the government and banks would then invest in industry. Standing in Hiroshima, a city that had endured more than its share of suffering from the last bout of mobilization, the vice minister veered toward the melodramatic. Only by continued austerity, he warned, "will our country exist in the future."[9] Ikeda has gone down in history for his later role as the prime minister whose Income Doubling Plan of 1960 would stimulate household spending. But back in 1947, he was no champion of consumption as the engine of Japanese recovery.

For that matter, neither were the Americans. Although officials of the Occupation (or SCAP) disliked the undemocratic aspects of Japanese savings campaigns, they supported the National Salvation campaigns with surprising enthusiasm. One SCAP staffer reported on the drive's "marked degree of success" in increasing savings to check inflation and provide the vitally needed credit for the rehabilitation and expansion of the Japanese economy. It was "a most commendable program in all its aspects deserving the full support of the Japanese people."[10] Indeed, the Americans rarely missed the opportunity to tout the importance of saving over consumption for postwar Japan. This is ironic, for SCAP did its utmost to convey images of U.S. abundance to the Japanese people. In 1947 Japanese national radio began broadcasting "News from America" (Amerika tayori) showcasing American affluence and homes filled with electrical appliances. Millions of Japanese further learned of American consumer life from the comic strip *Blondie*, introduced by the daily *Asahi shinbun* in 1949.[11]

Yet the Americans were more intent on demonstrating the occupiers' unsurpassed power and wealth than on exporting their model of mass consumption to East Asia. The Japanese themselves were in no position to embrace the model. The gulf between postwar Japan and the United States was enormous. Not until 1952 would Japan's per capita levels of consumption recover to the prewar high of 1934–36. In 1946 food accounted for fully 68 percent of household expenditure, and households still devoted 49 percent of their consumption to food as late as 1955. Few Japanese could afford the vacuum cleaners or toasters depicted in *Blondie*—much less many of the basic necessities. Prior to 1950 they bought so little cloth and clothing that the nation's once vital textile industry came to a virtual halt.[12]

Far from encouraging domestic spending, Washington expected Japanese to pull themselves up by the bootstraps—that is, by saving and sacrifice. Americans commonly overestimate our generosity toward occupied Japan. In 2003 during the early months of the U.S.-led occupation of Iraq, Senator Lamar Alexander (R-Tenn.) remarked: "After World War II we built schools and roads and hospitals in Japan and in Germany when we did not have those things in Tennessee."[13] Stirring words, but not exactly true. In Western Europe, yes, the United States financed the Marshall Plan in the late 1940s and 1950s. The plan aimed in part to create mass consumer markets based on the postwar American formula of consumer-driven growth.[14] However much Americans would like to believe otherwise, the United States never offered the Marshall Plan to Japan. Washington pushed the Japanese to tighten their belts not only to finance recovery and fight inflation, but also to pay the huge costs of housing and supplying occupation forces. Although the Americans provided emergency food relief, U.S. aid totaled less than half of what the Japanese government was compelled to pay to maintain the occupation.[15] The Japanese people, according to Under Secretary of the Army William Draper in 1948, "will have to work hard and long, with comparatively little recompense for many years to come." Joseph Dodge, the banker whose U.S. mission in 1949 forced the adoption of harsh austerity measures, called upon the Japanese government to hold the standard of living to levels prevailing *before* the early 1930s.[16] The American taxpayer, Dodge insisted, would not maintain the Japanese people; they must themselves "accumulate capital by producing more cheaply and by saving and economizing."[17]

Reinforcing the Japanese state's penchant for savings campaigns were trends in the rest of the postwar world. While the American model of mass consumption struck both the occupiers and occupied as inappropriate, Japanese officials voraciously studied contemporary European programs that promoted saving and restrained consumption. Japan was hardly alone, they observed, in adopting austerity measures to recover from the war. Nearly all the former belligerents were doing so, noted Finance Minister Yano in 1947. In the new Five-Year Plan, the Soviet people were "resigning themselves to austere living" and making "spirited efforts at recovery." The French and Belgians, he rightly observed, had mounted nationwide drives to reduce prices, and the Dutch launched a savings campaign under the no-nonsense slogan "Work Hard, Save Much."[18] Eager to keep abreast of the latest in global savings-promotion techniques, Japan's postal savings bureau in 1951 rejoined the International Thrift Institute, which had relocated to Amsterdam after the war. Throughout the 1950s and early 1960s, Japanese officials regularly reported on vibrant savings campaigns in Western Europe.[19]

Once again, Japanese bureaucrats expressed their greatest admiration for postwar Britain's National Savings Movement. Let us return to Vice Minister Ikeda's memorable speech in Hiroshima in 1947. The British won the war, he informed the audience, yet they "have not chosen the easy path." In the postwar era,

> they have rationed even bread, which had been freely sold in *wartime*. The British people ... have persevered, wearing extremely old and shabby clothes, and eating small meals. Why must the victorious British maintain harsh lives of austerity? The answer, without a doubt, is that the money and material saved by lives of austerity can be applied, in full, to economic recovery. ... In the near future, free trade will be re-established in the world. These people are in a hurry to establish a favorable position that allows them to strut upon the stage of global economic competition.[20]

Like the Japanese, the British strove to revive exports by boosting savings while severely constraining domestic consumption. Japanese bureaucrats were in awe of Britain's success in securing the emergency loan of $3,750,000,000 from the United States in 1946. The British could borrow at this extraordinary level, judged the Bank of Japan, only because their citizens, "who have little to spare," saved money while "living in destitution and austerity."[21]

And like the British government, the postwar Japanese state maintained many of the wartime policies that encouraged saving. As before, officials announced an annual savings target and allocated targets to each prefecture.[22] Another carryover was the wartime innovation of "model savings districts." Officials worked with civic groups and financial institutions in designated communities with an eye toward making these districts exemplary cases for "those locales that save erratically and those classes that lack an understanding of saving."[23] The government also retained the wartime incentive of tax exemption on interest earned on deposits made through the national savings associations.

The postwar campaigns continued to rely on the national savings associations, though phrased in the oxymorons of the New Japan. Increasing savings was "not simply a matter of voluntary saving by the individual," explained the Ministry of Finance, but "fundamentally requires cultivation within *democratic* savings associations based on mutual, collective encouragement."[24] Although Japanese could no longer be compelled to join savings associations as of 1947, prefectural officials were nonetheless ordered to organize or revive savings associations rapidly, for the Ministry of Finance desired "total participation by the entire nation."[25] By 1949 there were eighty thousand national savings associations enrolling ten million members.

Achieving "Economic Independence"

For three years the National Salvation Savings Campaigns harangued the Japanese. Results were nonetheless mixed. In one survey taken in September 1948, more than half of the respondents replied they were unable to put anything aside.[26] Household savings rates remained negative from 1947 to 1949, as families drew down their reserves to survive. Even the Ministry of Finance acknowledged that the campaigns failed to enlist the cooperation of many citizens below the middle classes.[27]

By other measures, however, the National Salvation campaigns were a success. The rapid growth in total savings on deposit exceeded the expectations of planners. Increases in total deposits in fiscal 1948 and the first half of 1949 ran at roughly four times what they had been during the first five months of the campaign. Japanese managed to increase savings at a time when most were still struggling to make ends meet. Economizing in everyday life played a crucial role in checking inflation, the worst of which passed by the end of 1949. Domestic savings proved crucial to financing postwar Japan's recovery and growth, for neither the U.S. government nor private foreign investors were inclined to extend loans at favorable rates to their devastated former foe.[28]

Just as important, the campaigns did much to restore popular confidence in the nation's financial institutions. In 1947 the government announced an end to the freeze on deposits enabling funds to be freely withdrawn. The authorities moreover introduced or reintroduced incentives to encourage saving. Interest rates rose steadily—for example, to 4.7 percent on one-year deposits in autumn 1949. Tax exemption on interest was granted not only to those who made regular contractual deposits through the national savings associations, but also to all postal savings depositors. To boost savings, officials went so far as to encourage tax *evasion*. The saver was permitted to open time (fixed-term) deposits without registering his or her true name. This practice effectively exempted all time deposits from taxation. Time deposits became wildly popular over the course of the National Salvation Campaigns, accounting for the greatest number of new accounts.

Although SCAP officials generally supported the National Salvation drives, the campaigns faced their first American challenge in September 1949. A U.S. mission headed by Professor Carl Shoup advised the Japanese government to check inflation primarily by tax collection, rather than voluntary saving. Concerned about widespread tax evasion, the Shoup report recommended abolition of unregistered deposits. Savings-promotion officials look back upon this period as their darkest hour. U.S. pressure closed down the National Salvation campaigns in late 1949.

In retrospect, the bureaucrats needn't have worried. SCAP authorities had neither the knowledge nor inclination to stamp out Japan's infrastructure of savings promotion. In 1950 the Ministry of Finance directed that the savings campaign continue at the local level as an "independent" movement. Within the next few months, according to the leading official history, savings promotion committees were "autonomously" organized in nearly every prefecture. The Ministry of Finance

and Bank of Japan in fact cosponsored several nationwide drives between 1950 and early 1952. These included the "Special Campaigns to
Hasten Economic Independence." The populace was told to save, this
time, to generate the capital necessary for Japan to take its place as
an "independent nation" once the occupation ended. In September
1951 Japan and its former enemies concluded the San Francisco Peace
Treaty. The Allies agreed to terminate the occupation on April 1 of the
following year. No sooner had Japan signed the treaty than economic
bureaucrats busily prepared to overturn what remained of the American restrictions on centralized savings promotion.[29]

On April 15, 1952, just days after the occupation ended, officials
unveiled the Central Council for Savings Promotion. This would be
a permanent organization on the order of Britain's National Savings
Committee. Although the Central Council's name (chochiku zōkyō) was
officially translated as "Savings Promotion," most Japanese would have
rendered it as the Central Council to Increase Savings. According to its
charter, the Central Council served "as the nucleus of nongovernmental savings promotion," working to "enlighten public opinion on behalf
of increasing savings."[30] Despite some changes in mission, the renamed
organization is still active today.

Japan's savings promoters lost no time signaling that the Allied
occupation was over. New posters resurrected the nationalist symbols
of the prewar savings campaigns. Fearing the revival of ultranational-
ism, SCAP censors had banned images of Mt. Fuji in films and other
media.[31] Yet with the end of the occupation in sight, Mt. Fuji re-
appeared in postal savings posters. Superimposed on Japan's majestic
mount was a dove with a halo (figure 28). Another previously taboo
symbol, the rising-sun flag, resurfaced in Central Council posters over
the next half-decade. Japanese were now exhorted to save to build
an economically prosperous nation, not a militarized great power. But
as before, they were to do so for the sake of the nation. The ends had
changed since wartime, while the means—the intrusive savings campaigns—survived defeat and occupation with barely a scratch.

The Central Council for Savings Promotion plunged into the work
of encouraging people to save more. The 1952 national budget for savings promotion increased twentyfold to ¥100 million. Bureaucrats did

Figure 28. "Your Savings Build the New Japan," 1951. Mt. Fuji, featured in prewar and wartime propaganda, returns in this postal savings poster as the symbol of national purpose, now focused on peace and prosperity. Courtesy of the Communications Museum, Japan, XD-B42.

all they could to exempt interest on most savings from taxation. Re-versing U.S. efforts to clamp down on tax evasion, they once again permitted savers to hold multiple time deposits without registering their true names. With great fanfare the state completely eliminated taxation of interest on savings deposits from 1955 to 1957. In 1963 new legisla-tion permanently exempted interest on small savings accounts of any type. The government kept raising the ceiling on savings exempted from taxes, eventually to ¥3 million per person in 1974.

For all the authorities' insistence on the "private" status of the Central Council, this was a heavily bureaucratized venture. Council members represented financial institutions, business associations, media, the academic community, popular organizations, and state agencies. Nonetheless, Bank of Japan officials have performed all day-to-day op-erations to the present. The civil servants coordinated a vast network of prefectural savings-promotion committees, banks, local governments, schools, and national and grassroots groups. Armed with substantial media budgets, they churned out posters and banners while securing the cooperation of newspapers, magazines, and radio stations. By the mid-1960s most Japanese families owned a television set. Central Council officials worked closely with popular weekly television pro-grams, notably *Okusama no hiroba* (Madame Housewife's Forum), to raise housewives' consciousness of the need to save more.[32]

Although officials emphasized the benefits of saving to families, strident appeals to economic nationalism persisted long after Japan re-gained political independence in 1952. Asserting that the Japanese economy required greater amounts of domestic capital to achieve *true* independence, campaigns still urged citizens to save "to hasten inde-pendence." Like Britain's National Savings Movement in the early postwar years, the Japanese government related saving to a do-or-die struggle to finance export industries and restrain consumption of im-ports. Not until the latter half of the 1960s would Japan enjoy sustained international trade surpluses. In 1957 an acute balance of payments deficit prompted the state to launch savings drives to "Promote Ex-ports and Conserve Foreign Exchange." Such campaigns, year after year, helped shape an enduring popular consciousness of national crisis and vulnerability. As late as 1987, when U.S. leaders were vocally criticizing

Japan for its skyrocketing trade surpluses, fully 30 percent of Japanese respondents in one poll believed their nation still suffered trade *deficits* vis-à-vis America.[33]

Among the institutions mobilized to promote saving, the state continued to rely on two prewar stalwarts to mold postwar Japan's culture of thrift. In the aftermath of World War II, officials reorganized school savings programs into "children's banks" (*kodomo no ginkō*). At their highpoint in the 1950s, more than thirty thousand schools and eight million schoolchildren participated. The Central Council annually hosted ceremonies to commend some two hundred "superior children's banks." Social studies curricula, too, cultivated the "spirit of saving." Millions of Japanese children regularly deposited their yen at school over the next several decades, long after most American schools had abandoned school savings programs.[34]

Then there's the post office. Postal savings loomed even larger in postwar savings promotion than before 1945. As a share of household deposits, postal savings rose steadily in the postwar era peaking at 34 percent in 1999.[35] The Japanese postal savings system is today the world's largest financial institution. The system exploited its incomparable access to the populace. Whereas commercial banks possessed relatively few branches concentrated in urban areas, more than fifteen thousand post offices offered depository services throughout the country in the 1950s. Some twenty-four thousand do so today.

Postal savings officials went from innovation to innovation in the quest to lure customers from the banks. Improving on prewar practices, they inaugurated a highly popular service whereby postmen collected savings. The postwar post office's most attractive financial product has been the *teigaku* deposit, which accounted for half of the total value of postal deposits by 1960 and an astounding 91 percent in 1988. These are ten-year, fixed-rate time deposits that permit withdrawal, penalty free, any time after six months. At times of rising interest rates, many customers happily shifted funds out of *teigaku* accounts into higher-yielding deposits. Most commercial banks could not compete, unwilling to incur the interest-rate risk inherent in *teigaku* deposits. Postal savings thus enjoyed a significant interest-rate advantage over the banks. The post office further encouraged saving by selling life insurance on very favorable terms to policyholders, waiving for instance the requirement of thorough medical examinations. Postal life insurance grew to account for 30 percent of all life insurance by 1999.

Besides convenience and higher interest, the postal savings system marketed other selling points. One was safety. All postal deposits remained government guaranteed, whereas small savings accounts in other financial institutions received no such protection until the introduction of the Deposit Insurance Corporation in 1971. The security of postal savings persisted in the public imagination, particularly at times of financial volatility. Postal deposits surged during Japan's 1990s downturn amid reports of weak and failing banks. Second, postal savings received preferential tax treatment. Although interest on all small savings accounts became tax exempt from 1963 to 1988, postal depositors benefited disproportionately. Few paid taxes, no matter how large their savings. That was because postal employees systematically encouraged customers to open multiple accounts at different post offices—each up to the tax-exempt limit.

The postal savings system operated more like a well-oiled political machine than a financial institution. Clerks tenaciously urged customers to open accounts, receiving bonuses for each new account. The most ardent champions of postal savings have been the thousands of "commissioned postmasters," local notables who run smaller post offices and exert considerable influence in their communities. When central bureaucrats revived nationwide savings campaigns in 1952, they immediately organized the commissioned postmasters into a "Promotion League" to advance the drives at the grass roots. This was another repudiation of the U.S. occupiers who had previously dissolved the old postmasters' association as an undemocratic relic of Imperial Japan. Recognizing the postmasters' ability to mobilize voters, the Liberal Democratic Party allied closely with the postmasters and significantly expanded postal savings. In power with one short break from 1955 to 2009, LDP governments created thousands of new "special post offices" headed by commissioned postmasters. The postal savings lobby rallied the public itself. In 1970 the government established the first of several Postal Savings Halls to promote "a better understanding of Postal Savings" and enhance its image. Any postal depositor might use the low-cost facilities, which included hotel rooms, swimming pools, and even wedding halls and planetariums. The Postal Savings Halls became a huge hit, boasting fifty million guests from 1972 to 1983 and plenty of new cheerleaders.[36]

Postal savings' self-promoting efforts are only half of the story. The Japanese state as a whole retained a direct stake in boosting postal savings because of its importance to public finance. The Ministry of Finance's Deposit Bureau had managed the vast pool of postal savings since 1885. Despite U.S. attempts to weaken the bureaucracy's control, the Ministry of Finance emerged from the occupation with expanded powers over the investment of postal savings. Postal deposits remained at the core of the ministry's Trust Fund Bureau, successor to the Deposit Bureau. Along with postal life insurance funds, the Trust Fund monies in turn flowed into the new Fiscal Investment and Loan Plan established in 1952.

As postal savings soared, the bureaucracy found itself with ever-increasing amounts of capital that it invested without parliamentary approval. Often called the "second budget," FILP funds amounted to one-third to one-half of the regular budget from 1953. Relying on those funds, the Japan Development Bank and other government banks loaned large portions of the people's savings to heavy and export industries during the 1950s and 1960s. FILP "became the single most important financial instrument for Japan's economic development," judges Chalmers Johnson.[37] Since the 1970s, with Japanese industry enjoying ready access to private sources of capital, finance officials have redirected FILP money increasingly to local governments and the improvement of living standards. At the end of the twentieth century, the FILP-funded Government Housing Loan Corporation provided more than one-third of home loans. Postal saving thus acquired enormous legitimacy in postwar Japan. As the nation's largest women's federation explained to members in 1955, "your [postal] savings make your family, town, or village a paradise."[38]

Democratizing Thrift

Japanese household saving rates took off after 1950, cresting to 23 percent in the mid-1970s. Only the Italians saved as much. Most economists doubt that the Japanese government's savings-promotion programs contributed significantly to the high level of saving. Yet that may have more to do with the economics profession's difficulties in measuring the impact of moral suasion. For example, many economists used to relate Japan's high saving rates to firms' routine payment of bonuses to ordinary employees. These might total 60 percent of one's annual salary, and households commonly saved large portions of the semi-annual bonuses. We should not, however, ignore the role of policy and persuasion in normalizing this practice. Beginning in the 1950s, housewives' magazines, savings-promotion officials, the postal savings system, and commercial banks mounted public relations offensives to convince people to save their bonuses.[39] The Japanese might have increased saving rates even in the absence of state promotion. The early postwar decades witnessed exceptionally rapid growth. From 1950 to 1973 the Japanese economy grew at more than 10 percent per annum. Typically households in fast-growing economies tend to save at higher rates as consumption lags behind rising incomes.[40]

Still, would the Japanese have saved as much? The wealth of qualitative evidence suggests that savings-promotion efforts reached deeply into society to continue shaping Japan's culture of thrift. When they proclaimed the postwar campaigns would be "democratic," the bureaucrats were right about one thing. Across the ideological spectrum, the cause of increasing savings enjoyed remarkably high levels of support from political parties, popular organizations, and ordinary Japanese. As in contemporary Europe, much of the Left vocally backed the twin missions of restraining consumption and augmenting national savings. In October 1946 Japan's Socialist Party joined four centrist and conservative parties to call upon the government to mount postwar savings campaigns to stabilize the yen and fight inflation. Significantly, several Socialist leaders had been prewar Protestant reformers who worked with the imperial state to inculcate habits of thrift in the populace.[41] In the postwar years, too, the government subsidized Christian organizations to assist in the campaigns. The Ministry of Finance employed the famous Christian socialist reformer Kagawa Toyohiko to lecture savings-promotion officers.[42]

Upon becoming Japan's first Socialist prime minister in 1947, Katayama Tetsu, another Christian, launched a new set of National Salvation Savings Campaigns. To finance exports and rebuild the national economy, the prime minister pledged to cultivate the "beautiful customs of diligence, thrift, and saving—long part of our national character."[43] His government also revived the interwar daily life improvement movement under the postwar name of "New Life Campaigns." These drives taught households how to save in their quest to rationalize and "bring science" to daily life by cutting waste and "luxuries." In 1955, when a conservative cabinet institutionalized these drives under the New Life Campaign Association, Katayama, Kagawa, and other Socialist leaders proudly served as directors.[44]

Along with much of the labor movement, the Socialist Party embraced austerity and national saving as beneficial to the working class and the Japanese people as a whole. No less than the economic bureaucrats, Socialists were shocked by the nation's early postwar hyperinflation, and they favored soaking up purchasing power. While labor unions in contemporary America favored mass consumption as good for employment, the Japanese Left—like European counterparts—regarded saving as the best means of generating jobs; the people's surplus would be channeled into investment in production. Although they criticized conservative governments on other issues, several prominent Marxian economists cooperated with the bureaucracy to promote saving.[45] Minobe Ryōkichi, the progressive economist and future governor of Tokyo, wrote Ministry of Education–approved textbooks that instructed students in the importance of saving. Household savings not only benefited one's family, but also "becomes the capital for industry and the public good, and they function as the driving force in the national economy and the development of social life." Though a socialist, Minobe subscribed to a strikingly middle-class view of the housewife's duty to "rationalize consumption." In "our families," he noted, "the mother or older sister keeps a household account book.... Those who do this well have relatively *rich consumer lives* even if their income is relatively low."[46]

Within large companies, workers' wives eagerly took part in employer-sponsored New Life movements from the 1950s to the 1970s. There, sometimes to the consternation of trade unionist husbands, they learned methods of household budget-keeping and cutting "waste in daily life." Rather than envision increased demand as the key to a vibrant economy, many working-class families continued to believe that improvements in daily life would result from limiting consumption and boosting savings.[47]

Building on wartime developments, Japanese women became even more central to encouraging saving and rationalizing consumption. Postwar officials relied on local women's associations to run the national savings associations—so much so that savings associations became known as "mothers' banks." Savings associations also formed around the women's auxiliary of agricultural cooperatives. Found in most villages and urban neighborhoods, women's associations in the 1950s worked hard to shape the savings habits of the community. Take the case of the award-winning "women's association/egg savings association" in one rural town in Miyagi prefecture. Every Saturday the group's lieutenants fanned out to visit members' homes and gather eggs. On Sunday a wholesaler bought the eggs, and on Monday the association head deposited a share of the proceeds in each member's savings account.[48] In 1952 local women's organizations, with support from the state, coalesced into the National Federation of Regional Women's Organizations (Zen Chifuren). Claiming some 7.8 million members at its peak in the early 1960s, the federation provided the foot soldiers in the savings campaigns of the next several decades.[49]

Getting women to keep household account books has been at the core of postwar Japanese savings promotion. Victorian Britain and America also popularized such practices, and housewives' federations in contemporary West Germany and elsewhere cooperated with governments and banks to teach women techniques of "family budgeting." Nonetheless, the methodical housewife-saver became a cultural icon in postwar Japan as perhaps nowhere in the West (figure 29). During the 1950s more and more wives recorded the details of family finances in standardized account books issued by housewives' magazines and government agencies. By 1965 half of all surveyed households reported they kept account books (41 percent of them regularly). They would continue to do so at those levels for the next twenty-five years. Keeping a typical Japanese account book was not for the languid. Each day, one recorded income and then itemized expenditures into ten or more categories including taxes, food, housing, utilities, clothing, health,

Figure 29. "I'll Keep Planning Our Household Finances," 1955. The idealized Japanese housewife of the early postwar decades. Her modernity lay in rationalizing consumption and increasing savings. Courtesy of the Communications Museum, Japan, XD-C50.

education, self-cultivation and entertainment, transportation and tele-phone, socially obligatory expenses, and one-time special costs. Food expenditures were further divided into the subcategories of rice, side dishes, eating out, and "treats." At the end of the day, literally, the diligent housewife calculated the cash balance as well as outstanding debts and amounts deposited in savings. Account books from the 1990s further instructed users to record all credit card purchases. By contrast, among free-spending Americans at the time, the whole point of using plastic was to *delay* thinking about whether one could afford the purchase.[50]

The excruciating demands of the account books prompted some women to refuse to keep them. Yet the bigger surprise is how many Japanese women utilized the ledgers more or less as designed. Accord-ing to official surveys from 1973 to 1984, roughly half of those surveyed who kept accounts replied that they recorded income and expenditures *every day*. Another one-fifth claimed they itemized expenses daily but calculated balances monthly. The remaining one-quarter budgeted on a monthly basis.[51] Economists have yet to model the impact of house-hold account keeping on saving and economizing. However, if a large proportion of the households systematically monitor spending by means of account books in Society A (Japan) and very few keep such budgets in Society B (say, the United States), wouldn't we expect to see sub-stantial differences in saving rates—all other things being equal?

Widespread account-keeping challenges economic thinking in an-other way. American economists tend to view saving as the product purely of individual decision-making. Yet setting aside money in post-war Japan could be an intensely public act subject to collective pres-sures. Residential women's associations did not simply collect monthly savings from members. In what were called "group activities focused on household account books," activist women coached neighboring wives in techniques of monitoring family finances and maximizing savings. Often they pried into the intimate details of other families' spending habits. A married woman's status within the community became defined to a significant extent by how well she kept the account book. A great many Japanese wives felt the need to "keep up with the Joneses" not in spending, but in economizing. This anxiety was captured in a 1959 cartoon. "Mrs. O sure gave up keeping her account book in a hurry," snicker three housewives behind the back of one embarrassed working woman.[52]

Pressure on women to keep household account books came from many quarters. The increasingly popular housewives' magazines, notably *Shufu no tomo* and *Fujin no tomo*, continued their prewar drive to encourage financial management, publishing annual account books. Just as important were coordinated efforts by the state and various women's organizations. As she had done before and during the war, *Fujin no tomo*'s Hani Motoko frequently assisted the postwar savings campaigns. Comprised of loyal readers at the grass roots, her "friends' societies" received generous state subsidies to spread the use of account books among other women.[53] Government agencies began publishing their own household account books in 1947, and the Central Council for Savings Promotion and its successors issued countless copies of their "Household Account Book for the Bright Life" from 1952 to 2001. The mammoth National Federation of Regional Women's Organizations and other women's groups helped distribute the official account books. Calling it the organization's "best seller," the Central Council annually issued two million free account books by the mid-1990s, while women's magazines and other commercial publishers sold an additional seven million ledgers.[54]

State campaigns benefited from a profound change in gender relations within the family during the 1950s and 1960s. As the Japanese economy surged, husbands secured good-paying jobs that made it possible for women to stay at home without paid employment. For the first time, large numbers of Japanese women envisioned themselves as "housewives." It also became the norm for husbands to tender monthly earnings to prudent wives, who took charge of spending and saving. Wives thereby gained a potent means of controlling husbands who frequented the ubiquitous hostess bars and consorted with prostitutes (figure 30). Women's leaders gleefully advised housewives to dole out only small amounts of "drinking money" to their men while saving the rest.[55] The wife's control of the purse strings fast emerged as a symbol of modernity. Women's groups would denigrate "feudalistic" villages where patriarchy

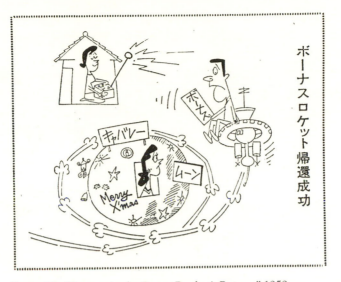

Figure 30. "Success in the Bonus Rocket's Return," 1959 cartoon. Using a remote control to capture her husband's bonus, the clever housewife boosts household savings and stops him from squandering the family's money on hostesses and drink at the "Cabaret Moon." *Chochiku* (Central Council for Savings Promotion), no. 27 (1959): 1.

still reigned—that is, where housewives had not yet emerged as the primary keepers of the household account book.[56]

During the 1950s the nation's largest women's federations threw themselves into encouraging saving in formal alliance with the state. One of the most enthusiastic organizations was the Housewives Association (Shufuren), usually portrayed as a fiercely independent proponent of consumer protection. Led by Oku Mumeo, a prewar feminist with socialist leanings, the Housewives Association nonetheless paralleled official efforts in its own campaigns to persuade every housewife to keep an account book and join the "housewives' savings movement."[57] In 1954 the Housewives Association became a permanent member of the Central Council for Savings Promotion—along with the more conservative National Federation of Regional Women's Organizations and the woman's auxiliary council of the Agricultural Cooperatives.

The three women's federations and others joined with the Central Council to convene the National Women's Meeting for "New Life and Saving" in 1959. Over the next four decades this annual meeting brought together officials and women's delegates to devise strategies for rationalizing household finances. Oku, too, championed the rationalization of spending as good for the housewife and good for the nation. In place of consumption, she urged members to "strive for a life with imagination and resourcefulness," for "unless the clever housewife maintains her household, this country will not rise."[58] Echoed by women's leaders and officials alike, this deep-seated ambivalence toward consumption reinforced Japan's savings ethic even as material life rapidly improved.

Striking a "Balance" between Consumption and Saving

Consumerism arrived officially in 1959. In its annual *Whitepaper on National Life*, the Economic Planning Agency declared Japan to be in the throes of a "consumer revolution." This was one revolution that would be televised, as millions watched on recently purchased televisions. After years of austerity, families acquired a set of consumer durables heretofore unimaginable. Not so long ago Japanese had died to defend the imperial household's "three sacred treasures": the mirror, jewel, and sword. The 1950s generation whimsically recycled the term to refer to the television, washing machine, and refrigerator. A mere 5 percent of Japanese households owned black-and-white television sets in 1957. By the mid-1960s the television would be found in nearly every home, alongside the two other treasures.[59]

From these material changes followed a cultural transformation of sorts. After decades of devaluing consumption, state agencies began encouraging spending on consumer durables.[60] In 1960 the government of Ikeda Hayato—the former finance bureaucrat who once urged the citizens of Hiroshima to save all they could—announced a plan to double national and per capita income by the end of the decade. Gone, it seemed, were the traditional values of diligence and thrift. Now "consumption is *the* virtue," proclaimed the media. Inspired by the successful creation of consumer demand in the United States, some Japanese business leaders during the 1950s envisioned the production of an "American-style middle-class society" as crucial to the nation's prosperity, writes Simon Partner. Even more than exports, the steady expansion of domestic consumption drove Japan's high economic growth from 1955 to the mid-1970s.[61]

By many measures, Japan took on the trappings of a mass-consumption society. Per capita income did not double by 1970; it quadrupled. Real per capita consumption increased at a frenetic 7.5 percent per year from 1955 to 1973. Food's share of household budgets steadily declined from 50 to 20 percent (1955 to 1988), enabling consumers to afford a greater array of goods and services.[62] Moreover, the rapid rise of installment buying and other forms of credit permitted less affluent Japanese to purchase the new mass commodities. An enormous advertising industry emerged to market consumption as the basis of the "bright life." Consumers moved beyond the "three sacred treasures" to acquire the "three C's": the car, color TV, and cooler (air conditioner). Thanks to substantial increases in housing loans, homeownership became the norm during the 1970s.[63] Ever since, foreign visitors have been mesmerized by images of Tokyoites spending, spending. Attired in expensive clothes and hooked up to the latest gadgets, Japanese seemingly worshipped at the shrine of mass consumption.

Appearances can be deceptive. The unmistakable rise in Japanese consumption levels was not matched by the advent of an American-style *consumer culture* that privileged spending over restraint. Inculcated habits of thrift did not diminish noticeably, but rather coexisted with the new consumption. As incomes grew, households became capable of increasing *both* saving and spending. Household saving rates soared from 14 percent in 1959 to an extraordinary 23 percent in 1976. Far from spending lavishly, consumers often afforded costly durables only by severely cutting back on other expenditures, including housing.[64]

Japan's new consumption resembled "consumer revolutions" in Western Europe at the time. In none of these cases do we see Europeans or Japanese catching up to Americans in levels and patterns of consumption. In 1960 Japanese households still devoted 38 percent of consumption to food and only 10 percent to housing and home-related expenditures. Similarly in West Germany and France, respectively, food accounted for fully 43 percent and 46 percent, and housing for merely 18 percent and 11 percent. In contrast, Americans spent only 32 percent on food and an incomparable 29 percent on housing, including furniture and household goods.[65] For most Japanese and Europeans, consumption continued to be something that had to be "rationalized" within limited budgets.

Assisted by the major women's organizations, the well-funded Central Council for Savings Promotion maintained nationwide savings campaigns through the prosperous 1960s and beyond. Proponents of thrift found themselves adapting their messages to the sensibilities of the new age. While acknowledging the benefits of improved consumption, government spokesmen and women's magazines advised the Japanese people to strike a *balance* between consumption and other vital needs of the household and nation—including saving, investment, social welfare, and the environment. Similar thinking pervaded contemporary European societies (see figures 31 and 32). The French of the 1950s became famous for critiques of Americans' seemingly limitless consumption. The American model, observes one historian, appeared to threaten French conceptions of a "balanced economy and traditional ways of production, selling, saving, and spending."[66]

In Japan during the 1960s, many economists warned of the perils of "*un*balanced" consumption. The catchphrase "consumption is the virtue" should by no means be taken as a repudiation of the importance of saving, argued Koizumi Akira; Japan's high growth could only be sustained by the new investment generated by greater saving. To Usami Jun, governor of the Bank of Japan, "The difference between a civilized country and a backward country is whether it accumulates capital in large or small amounts." Rather than spend freely, the people "should endeavor to live rationally and save to increase the wealth of Japan as a whole."[67]

The recently announced Income Doubling Plan did not promise immediate improvements in consumption, explained Okazaki Kaheita, chairman of the Central Council for Savings Promotion. To develop the economy and raise living standards, the plan required "high-level saving," which remained essential to bring "balance to Japanese life."

Figure 31 (left). "Keep a Balance in Life," Japan, 1955. An early version of the Japanese government's message to balance consumer desires against the needs of accumulating sufficient savings. Courtesy of the Communications Museum, Japan, XD-C52.
Figure 32 (right). The British poster, 1950, that inspired the Japanese poster. Reproduced by permission of TNA, NSC 5/652a.

Such judgments were influenced by contemporary American critiques of mass consumption, notably Vance Packard's *The Hidden Persuaders* (1957) and *The Waste Makers* (1960). According to Okazaki, *The Waste Makers* revealed how American industry chronically overproduced for the consumer economy with Packard urging Americans to restore the balance among factors in the economy. Packard's diagnosis might fit Japan better than the United States, Okazaki ventured, considering how much Japanese squandered on restaurants, clothes, and expensive skis they used only once or twice a year.[68] Women's leaders also echoed Packard. Oku Mumeo of the Housewives Association condemned the advertising industry for persuading Japanese to buy anything marketed as a "new brand." Led by Oku, the consumer movement instructed

Japanese to become "wise consumers" (*kashikoi shōhisha*) who would "rationalize how we buy and use things."[69]

Too much spending might exacerbate another imbalance. Anxious about Japan's recurrent deficits in the balance of international payments, the government sent mixed messages to the consumer. To support domestic industries, officials and manufacturers encouraged the consumption of "national products," especially electrical goods. Spending on imports was another matter. Even at the height of the "consumer revolution" in the early 1960s, savings campaigns harangued the nation to economize overall and on imports in particular. As conveyed by numerous pamphlets, one's patriotic duty still lay in boosting the nation's savings. These would finance the industrial production necessary to expand exports and pay for imported raw materials (figure 33). Speaking to women's groups around the country, Bank of Japan officials blamed consumers for the worsening trade imbalance. After all, hadn't they "unwittingly bought surprisingly large quantities of imported items like instant coffee and raisins"?[70]

In the course of the 1970s, feelings of ambivalence gave way to widespread criticisms of mass consumption itself. Although several developments fueled these discontents, the precipitant was unquestionably the "Oil Shock" of 1973—74. That was when Arab members of OPEC (Organization of the Petroleum Exporting Countries) embargoed oil. Energy-dependent Japan experienced galloping inflation, major shortages, and the first decline in GNP since the early postwar years. Among conservatives as well as progressives, the Oil Shock served as the backdrop for a national morality play about the evils of affluence and the opportunity for spiritual rebalancing. National leaders were uncommonly philosophical. Having succumbed to "material affluence" and "mass consumption" during the high-growth era, Japanese were said to have discovered "a new form of affluence" as they cut back spending.[71] The media, too, reported on consumers' return to saving and stinginess, blaming Japan's current economic woes on recent high living. "It's undeniable," wrote a weekly magazine, "that one of the main causes of rising inflation has been that motto, 'Consumption is the virtue.'"[72]

Japanese opinion reflected global trends of ecological awareness. In Europe and to a lesser extent in the United States, environmental

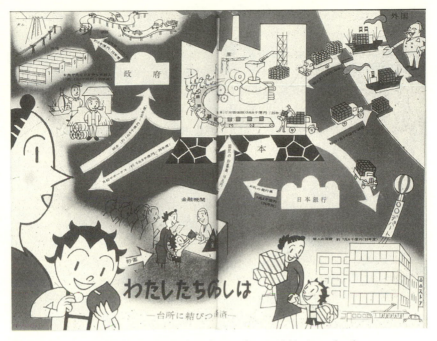

Figure 33. "The Economy as Linked to the Kitchen," 1962. Aimed at housewives, this cartoon communicates that savings benefit the nation by financing industrial production (center). Although some production results in individual consumption (lower right), a huge portion is shipped abroad to remedy Japan's trade deficit. The sinister Western tycoon (upper right) personifies "foreign countries," which send ¥2 trillion in goods to Japan whereas Japanese exports total only ¥1.5 trillion. *Yasashi keizai no hanashi* [Economics made easy] (Tokyo: Chochiku Zōkyō Chūō Iinkai, 1962), Ministry of Finance, Japan.

movements arose to demand energy conservation and sustainable development. Established in 1979, West Germany's Green Party became mainstream enough to enter the governing coalition two decades later. In his polemic *Small Is Beautiful* (1973), British economist E. F. Schumacher articulated the new agenda of seeking the "maximum amount of well-being with the minimum of consumption." Although European environmentalists did not espouse older notions of thrift, their conservationism and condemnation of "overconsumption" reinforced propensities to save. In practice, stringent recycling laws in Europe and Japan curbed the previous "throwaway" ethos while discouraging consumers from buying new products on the American scale.[73]

Whereas the relation between thrift and environmentalism remained implicit in Europe, the Japanese state successfully fused the causes of saving, economizing, and conservation in the public mind. In 1974 savings-promotion officials played a central role in fashioning the People's Campaign to Value Resources and Energy. More than one hundred organizations took part representing consumers, women, educators, the media, business, and local governments. Myriad local campaigns harangued the populace to save and economize on goods and energy. Casting their involvement in socially progressive terms, women's and consumer advocates denounced the recent consumer boom as out of balance with society's needs for a more generous welfare state and a cleaner environment. The social critic Higuchi Keiko seized upon the Oil Shock as an opportunity for consumers to move from material affluence to a "truly affluent society"—one that neither destroyed the natural environment nor discarded the weak.[74] Injunctions to economize filled the pages of housewives' magazines. The language of "balance" appeared everywhere, illustrated in one cartoon as a scale that balanced "spiritual affluence" against a heap of consumer goods. And a new catchphrase was heard o'er the land: "*economizing* is the virtue."[75]

The American Other

Japan quickly recovered from the Oil Shock and resumed its rise as the world's second largest economy. Leaders felt more convinced than ever of the virtues of Japan's energetic promotion of saving. The 1980s were a time when Japanese savings behavior took center stage as an international issue as well. The nation's savings-promotion program evolved from an exemplar for developing countries into a model for the world's largest economy. It was a giddy moment in Tokyo. High savings had tamped down inflation and provided the cheap capital for industrial expansion, Japanese officials boasted. Meanwhile in the United States, "sluggish savings and investment" constrained productivity increases and accelerated inflation. America's troubles left Japanese "convinced that maintaining a steady savings attitude in our household economy" would surely contribute to price stability, improved productivity, and higher living standards.[76]

Plenty of Americans also took note of Japan's high household saving rate of about 20 percent. Revised data now calculates the U.S. saving rate at nearly 9 percent in 1979, although Americans at the time believed it to be around 4 percent. Malaise about perceived decline at home prompted the publication of a slew of books on the "Japanese Model," notably *Japan as Number One: Lessons for America*. Americans, noted the world-famous economist Paul Samuelson, "envy the Japanese for their ingenuity, drive, cleverness and thrift." Lawrence R. Klein, winner of the 1980 Nobel Prize in Economics and a leading Keynesian, nonetheless urged the United States to go from "being a high-consumption economy to being a high-saving economy if we are to reindustrialize and improve our standard of living."[77] In a speech to the Japanese parliament in 1983, President Ronald Reagan lavishly praised Japanese for achieving the highest saving rates among industrialized nations. This, he argued, was because Japanese tax policies incentivized saving by exempting most interest on deposits and keeping tax burdens low.[78]

Newly confident, Japanese came to regard thrift as a key marker of their unique "national character" and a source of superiority vis-à-vis the West. This was a big change from the early postwar years, when officials indentified with European savings-promotion efforts and sometimes cast Americans as more prudent than Japanese. Journalists and politicians now spoke disparagingly of the "English disease," in which welfare dependency led to a "diminished will to work," and the "American disease" marked by wastefulness and laziness.[79] In 1987 Toyama Shigeru, chairman of the Central Council for Savings Promotion, wrote a best seller extolling the enduring Japanese spirit of hard work and thrift. As for the United States, he scoffed, the Puritan ethic of thrift had collapsed. Americans' rampant use of credit cards resulted in "excessive consumption," and "millions of households live in debt."[80]

As Japan amassed ever-increasing trade surpluses in the 1980s, the issue of savings became a flashpoint in U.S.-Japanese relations. Western governments heatedly accused the Japanese of "excessive *saving*" and underconsumption. It was all relative of course. Compared to Americans, Europeans lived in small homes and were great savers. But in a report leaked to the press in 1979, the European Economic Commission blasted Japan as a country of "workaholics" who live in "what westerners would regard as little more than rabbit hutches."[81] Bowing to foreign pressure, the Japanese government in 1986 released the Maekawa Report, which promised to expand domestic consumption while curtailing programs that actively promoted saving. Two years later the Central Council for Savings Promotion tactfully renamed itself the Central Council for Savings Information. The state would no longer "promote" or "increase" savings, but merely provide information on how to save. More consequential was the elimination in 1988 of tax exemption on savings interest for nearly all Japanese, excepting the elderly and a few other categories. Henceforth interest on savings would be taxed at a flat rate of 20 percent.[82]

However, Japanese leaders remained unpersuaded of the virtues of a consumption-driven economy. In publications intended for the home audience, officials and economists warned that the Maekawa Report should not alter the commitment to promoting high saving—lest Japanese lose the values that made them so successful. Before authoring the report that bore his name, Bank of Japan governor Maekawa Haruo ardently defended savings-promotion policies. High household saving enabled Japan to subdue inflation, he observed, while Americans amid double-digit inflation turned from saving money to buying more and more.[83] Nor did the Japanese people come forward to thank the Americans for trying to improve their consumer lives. Women's and consumer groups furiously opposed the government's decision to abolish tax exemption for savings. One protest rally in Hibiya Park drew six thousand people.[84]

For the first time, Japanese officials took to lecturing the *Americans* on the need to promote saving and investment so as to restore the "balance" between those factors and out-of-control consumption. When U.S. negotiators in 1990 attempted to remove Japan's structural impediments to imports and foreign investment, the Japanese side shot back with its own prescriptions for reducing America's glaring fiscal deficits. The U.S. government should curb Americans' "excessive consumption" by restricting credit cards and introducing Japanese-style tax preferences for saving.[85] This cockiness rested on Japan's new status as the world's greatest creditor nation while the United States was now the biggest debtor. The Japanese had become, far and away, the largest holders of Treasury bonds and bills. Then as now, the vast savings of East Asians enabled the U.S. government and American people to live beyond their means.

"From Saving to Investment"

Japanese self-assurance was not to last much longer. The nation's abundant savings contributed to soaring stock and real estate prices. In 1990–91, the bubble burst after the Bank of Japan raised interest rates. For the next eleven years the Japanese economy would be mired in a state of slow growth or no growth. Japan and the United States again traded places. The U.S. economic boom of the 1990s convinced American policymakers and economists of the brilliance of financial deregulation, consumer-driven growth, and the massive expansion of credit. Predictably, Washington pressed Japanese to stop saving so much and instead consume their way out of recession.

By the late 1990s, many Japanese acknowledged the anachronistic nature of savings-promotion mechanisms designed for a different age when saving had indeed been Japan's "national salvation." This past decade has witnessed some important changes. The most politically contentious has been the reform of the postal savings system. As the nation's "lost decade" wore on, Japanese and Western critics questioned why Japan required a colossal government savings bank in an age of financial liberalization. Equally problematic, the Ministry of Finance through the Fiscal Investment and Loan Plan retained control over investing the world's largest pool of savings. Incredibly little had changed since 1885. Tied up in local projects and a great many nonperforming loans, the nation's capital—charged critics—could be more productively invested to advance growth. Effected in 2001, the first reforms transferred responsibility for investing deposits from the Ministry of Finance to postal authorities. Nonetheless, investments largely flowed to the FILP as before. Other changes would probably never have oc-curred had it not been for a maverick politician known for his Elvis impersonations. Koizumi Jun'ichirō took over the doddering Liberal Democratic Party and became prime minister in 2001. He chose to make privatization of postal savings the central issue in the 2005 gen-eral election, successfully running reformers against his own party's en-trenched postal savings lobby. The new parliament enacted legislation mandating gradual privatization, beginning in 2007 and ending in 2017.

What privatization means for the depositor is far from clear. Fully guaranteed by the government, postal savings reached the height of its popularity amid widespread bank failures in the 1990s. However, reform measures from 2002 eliminated many of postal savings' historical ad-vantages. As of 2007 the state no longer guarantees postal deposits. They are now covered by American-style deposit insurance up to ¥10 million (about $105,000), the same as for bank deposits. A decade of near-zero interest rates further diminished the allure of the ten-year *teigaku* time deposit. Japanese steadily moved money out of postal savings into the banks. From 2000 to 2007, postal savings' share of total deposits sunk from one-third to one-quarter.

On the other hand, postal savings' dynamic role in encouraging saving may well persist. The newly "privatized" Japan Post Bank dwarfs the next largest bank. With more than twenty-four thousand branches, it reaches small savers as no other bank. Moreover, the postal savings system remains an aggressive marketer aiming to become a "one-stop financial shop." For instance, post offices recently began selling invest-ment trusts (mutual funds). Postal savings may never emerge as a truly private bank. Koizumi retired in 2006. Other leaders in the two major parties are less passionate about privatization. Some 75 to 80 percent of postal savings remains invested in government bonds. At the end of the ten-year privatization process, the Japan Post Bank will likely still function as a highly accessible postal savings system that makes it easy to save.[86]

In a second development, the government retreated from running nationwide savings campaigns. According to stated policy in 1997, the Central Council for Savings Information no longer asked people to increase savings. They were encouraged instead to plan their lives so as to strike that proverbial "balance between saving and consumption."[87] I must confess, I did not fully appreciate the nuances on my visits at the time to the busy work floor of the Central Council's secretariat inside the Bank of Japan. It sure looked like savings promotion. Officials were working closely with local women's groups to encourage account-keeping in the nearly five hundred model Life Planning and Savings Districts. They also kept conducting the annual contest for the best essays on "household account book-keeping and life planning," with 63,500 entrants in the year 2000. The short films sent to schools, though slick as anime, likewise conveyed the wisdom of an earlier time. *The Greedy Princess* featured Princess Catherine, a spoiled brat, who gets all the luxuries she wants until her fairy godmother places her with a poor family where she learns "thrift and habits of healthy living." In *Children Captured by the UFO*, three tykes spend wastefully. They buy a cake, throw away the insides, and just eat the frosting. The eco-aliens who nab them worry that if such children multiply, the earth's nature and resources will be destroyed. The kids come to understand the consequences of wastefulness and return to earth with a proper respect for goods and money.[88]

By the year 2000, the old methods of savings promotion were wearing thin. Children's banks had all but disappeared. Married women, who increasingly worked outside the home, could no longer be relied upon to serve as Japan's version of savings commandos. Influenced by America's success and anxious about Japan's rapidly aging society, policymakers began urging savers to accept more risk and seek higher rates of return. Near-zero interest in bank and postal deposits would not build retirement savings. Finance officials advised the nation to shift "from saving to investment."

In 2001 the government unveiled a new approach. The Central Council for Savings Information became the Central Council for Financial Services Information. This time, it was more than a change in name. The organization no longer explicitly encourages Japanese to save. The revamped Central Council provides consumers with helpful information on an array of financial instruments. These include not only savings deposits, but also stocks, credit cards, even derivatives. As the government cut back on pledges to guarantee savings deposits in full, the Central Council worked to persuade the public to take "personal responsibility" for judging the risks of their investment choices. Much of the information appears on its website, which soon averaged one million hits per month. Five hundred volunteers serve as local Financial Services Information Advisors. Most are financial planners and other professionals, in contrast to the leaders of women's groups who volunteered as savings advisors under the old system. The Central Council's other top priority has been to institute financial education in model schools and eventually nationwide.[89]

Whether these transformations will alter twentieth-century Japan's culture of thrift remains to be seen. Pressed by the Americans, the Japanese government in 1998 mounted a halfhearted campaign to get the nation to spend its way out of recession.[90] However, in none of the recent policy debates—whether postal savings privatization or introducing an investment consciousness—have the Japanese protagonists called on people to consume more. It's all about shifting savings into more productive investments. In several respects, the Central Council for Financial Services reinforces old-fashioned habits of saving. An already risk-averse populace is being educated about the many risks involved in equities, as well as the dangers of overindebtedness lurking in consumer credit. The Central Council no longer issues household account books, but that's in part because housewives' magazines continue to publish these ledgers in the millions. The organization remains committed to encouraging Japanese to engage in financial "life planning." It offers online diagnostic tools, free downloads of account-keeping software, and tips on how to stay with your household account book even when you hate it. The financial education program teaches children the importance of saving, ecological living, and avoiding *toraburu* (trouble) brought on by credit cards and internet shopping.[91] Oh, and schools can still borrow *The Greedy Princess* and *Children Captured by the UFO*.

Nor is it clear that the Japanese will decisively shift "from saving to investment." Stocks did in fact rise as a percentage of household financial assets after 2004. The share in equities has since retreated in the wake of the 2008 stock market crash. In comparative terms, the persistence of small saving in Japan is striking. In 2006 half of Japanese households' financial assets were in savings deposits and merely 16 percent in stocks, private investments, and investment trusts. Even the cautious Germans invested only one-third of their financial assets in bank and postal accounts. At the other extreme, Americans placed a minuscule 13 percent in savings deposits, but nearly half in stocks and mutual funds.[92]

This brings us to the most puzzling development of the past decade. Once the highest in the world, Japan's household saving rate slowly declined during the 1990s before going into free fall after 1999. In 2008 it stood at a mere 2.3 percent, among the lowest of OECD nations. Japanese households, declared *The Economist*, had "lost their appetite for thrift."[93] Such conclusions are off the mark. The saving rate has not declined because Japanese joined the ranks of America's shopaholics. Far from it. Consumer spending per household has essentially been flat since 1993, and in many years has fallen in real terms. The 1990s and early 2000s, it is true, were a time of economic sluggishness in Japan, yet stagnation in consumption continued amid the sustained recovery of 2002–2007. By contrast, American consumer spending until the recent financial meltdown increased every *quarter* since 1991, despite recession (2001) and slow income growth thereafter.[94] Neither can we blame the erosion of Japanese saving on a growing addiction to credit. Although Japanese assumed fairly high levels of housing and consumer debt during the 1990s, debt as a percentage of household financial assets has steadily dropped over the past decade.[95] Even credit cards failed to beguile most consumers. In 1992 the government finally permitted banks to issue cards with a revolving credit feature, yet Japanese responded in a most un-American fashion. Twelve years later, more than two-thirds of Japanese card users were paying monthly credit card bills on time and in full, while in the United States nearly two-thirds borrowed against their cards.[96]

If not greater consumption or credit-bingeing, what does account for the current phenomenon of Japanese saving so little? One plausible explanation draws from the well-known "life-cycle" hypothesis. Japan's population is aging faster than any other. As a greater proportion of the nation enters into retirement, the elderly necessarily spend down wealth.[97] Nevertheless, the life-cycle thesis does not explain why rapidly aging populations in Germany and several other European countries have not experienced appreciable declines in their high saving rates.

The most compelling explanation is at once the most depressing. The Japanese are saving less, first and foremost, because a great many households have suffered punishing drops in income since the late 1990s. No other major economy experienced anything like eleven years of stagnation, followed in 2002 by a recovery unaccompanied by perceptible increases in household income. Japanese companies have slashed hours and salaries, besides cutting back on hiring young people as regular employees. As families struggle to maintain relatively modest levels of consumption, they have less margin to save.[98]

For better or worse, decades of savings promotion have left their mark on the Japanese people. Over the past twenty years we have seen little of the profound cultural embrace of consumption that occurred in the United States. Japanese households cope with stagnant incomes by continuing to "rationalize" consumption. To make ends meet, they spend more on some things while cutting back on others. The postwar housewives' culture of monitoring spending has proved remarkably resilient. Women's magazines are still filled with stories of resourceful housewives who deal with a bad economy by adopting "economizing lifestyles."[99] Although the media trumpets the decline of thrift among youth, recent surveys reveal that nearly half of married women in their twenties and 43 percent of those in their thirties keep household account books. We would also err in assuming that most households no longer have savings. In 2008, Japan led the OECD countries in net household financial assets (383 percent of nominal disposal income). In net wealth (financial, real, and other assets minus liabilities), it ranked fourth behind Italy, the United Kingdom, and France, but well ahead of the United States. If the risk-averse Japanese—unlike Americans and Britons—did not partake in rising housing and equity prices since the mid-1990s, neither did their assets collapse in the real estate and financial meltdown of 2008. The dearth of consumer spending undoubtedly constrains the Japanese economy, yet the abundance of home-grown savings permits the government to finance extraordinarily high levels of national debt at low rates and independent of foreign interference in ways that Americans today might envy.[100]

Or they might not. When dealing with Japan, Anglo-American economists tend to be prescriptive. Supremely confident of their own model, they have been quick to tell the Japanese what to do: stimulate consumption, unleash the forces of consumer credit, push savers to accept more risk. Despite the household debt crisis presently afflicting the United States and Britain, *The Economist* still complains that Japanese consumers "rarely shift credit-card debts from one card to another."[101] We might do better to understand the historical forces that shaped how Japanese actually behave, and how the Japanese model of savings promotion—in its prime—became crucial to the rise of Asia's other dynamic economies.

10

EXPORTING THRIFT, OR
THE MYTH OF "ASIAN VALUES"

> More than 2,000 years ago there emerged in China
> Confucianism represented by Confucius and Mencius. . . .
> From Confucius to Dr. Sun Yat-sen, the traditional Chinese
> culture presents many precious ideas and qualities . . .
> [including] the traditional virtues taught from generation
> to generation: long suffering and hard working, diligence
> and frugality in household management, and respecting
> teachers and valuing education.
> —Chinese Premier Wen Jiabao, at Harvard University, 2003[1]

Thanks to a surging U.S. economy in the 1990s, Americans re-
gained confidence in mass consumption as the key to prosperity.
This vision has proved intoxicating, and few Americans imagine that
other nations might approach consumption differently. Predicted the
Council on Foreign Relations' Walter Russell Mead, "to keep their
economies growing, Asian societies must develop the consumer mentality of the West. If history is any guide, Asian governments will encourage the mass retreat from thrift, just as Washington did. . . . There's
no getting around it; Asia's little emperors [the young] are going to
have to get charge cards, just like their decadent, spendthrift, individu-
alistic counterparts in the West."[2]

Perhaps Mead is right, and consumer culture will inevitably triumph in Asia as it did in the United States. But to do so, the "history"
that is his guide must overpower alternative histories in the fast-growing
economies of East and Southeast Asia. As in the rest of the world,

Asian states and publics understand "consumption" in complex ways that go far beyond the simple act of spending money. On the one hand, regimes have encouraged greater consumption to improve living standards and bolster their legitimacy. On the other, most Asian nations remain openly ambivalent about unfettered consumption for a variety of economic, social, political, and moral reasons.[3] In Japan, we'll recall, postwar officials and women's publications continually urged households to strike a "balance" between consumption and saving. As their economies took off, other Asians similarly spoke of the need to "rationalize" consumption, refrain from wasting money on luxuries, and avoid "excessive consumption." Moreover, Asians frequently engaged in what Laura Nelson calls "consumer nationalism." The very act of spending tested one's patriotism. Campaigns exhorted citizens to buy "national products" and conversely shun fancy imported goods.[4] Conspicuous consumption has also been widely represented as a threat to social stability. In Malaysia, where officials strive to maintain a delicate balance among ethnic groups, the state has worked hard to inculcate thrift and "positive spending habits" in the majority Malays to raise their living standards to those of wealthier minority groups.[5]

It comes as no surprise that states in East and Southeast Asia coupled drives to restrain spending with intrusive campaigns to boost household savings. Noted the World Bank in 1993, every successful economy in the region boasted high household saving rates. Massive pools of savings provided ready sources of low-cost capital for industrial investment and the "East Asian Miracle."[6]

Why do Asians save so much? Ask Asian leaders, and they'll tell you thrift is a cultural trait deeply embedded in their traditions. As Asia's preeminent military and then economic power for the past century, Japanese long touted "diligence and thrift" as a uniquely Japanese custom. Other Asians are more likely to relate high saving to a common regional heritage. By the early 1980s, "Confucianism" emerged as the magic bullet that would explain why South Korea, Taiwan, Singapore, Hong Kong, and later China were following in Japan's footsteps of rapid economic development. Together with overseas Chinese scholars, Western observers highlighted the role of Confucianism in what two American political scientists termed "the Eastasian urge to save."

Confucian philosophy, they elaborated, "hailed prudence and frugality, demanded sacrifice for future employment, and condemned parents who failed to provide for their offspring."[7]

South Koreans and ethnic Chinese were soon trumpeting the role of Confucianism in creating East Asian–style capitalism. The government of Singapore embarked on the vigorous promotion of "Confucian Ethics" in schools and society. Even China's Communist regime—in Chairman Mao Zedong's time, no friend of the allegedly reactionary ancient philosopher Confucius—has jumped on the bandwagon. To promote Chinese language and culture, it today runs more than three hundred "Confucius Institutes" around the world. Economic growth in the predominantly non-Chinese nations of Malaysia, Indonesia, and Thailand subsequently gave rise in the early 1990s to the new discourse of "Asian values." As formulated by Singapore's former prime minister Lee Kuan Yew and Malaysia's then prime minister Mahathir bin Mohamad, "thrift" figures prominently among the cardinal Asian virtues. It takes its place alongside "hard work," the "deferment of present enjoyment for future gain," and the subordination of the individual to the family.[8]

To be sure, many East and Southeast Asian societies appear culturally disposed toward thrift. But I question the timelessness and uniqueness of so-called Asian values regarding saving and consumption. We've learned that the world's cultures of thrift did not spring forth spontaneously. They were historically formed and re-formed by ideas and institutions. In Asia, too, states and various groups energetically worked to inculcate habits of saving. They employed government-run savings institutions, launched savings campaigns, and mobilized schools, communities, and the media to encourage thrift. Nor should we overlook the crucial role of transnational knowledge in the evolution of Asian developmental strategies. As heretical as it may sound, the widespread "urge to save" in Asian economies has less to do with their shared "Asianness," and may be more related to their common adoption of savings-promotion practices from other countries. Although European colonial powers introduced some of the methods, the primary catalyst has been Japan and its historic efforts to increase national savings. Before 1945, Japanese imposed the "Japanese model" on their colonies and occupied territories. More recently, Asian nations consciously emulated the policies underlying postwar Japan's economic miracle.

Japanese themselves devoted considerable resources to exporting savings promotion to the rest of Asia. Following World War II, international organizations and economists advised developing nations to "mobilize domestic savings" to finance growth.[9] By the 1960s, Japan emerged as the poster child in this international campaign. Led by the influential planner Ōkita Saburō and his Japan Economic Research Center, Japanese economists touted high saving rates and low consumption to explain the nation's rapid growth—and "its implications for developing countries."[10] After the yen sharply appreciated against the U.S. dollar in 1985–87, Japanese officials became outright missionaries for the cause. As Japanese businesses heavily invested in Southeast Asian production, representatives of the government confidently counseled Southeast Asian states to mobilize household savings. Japan's Postal Savings Bureau played a leading role, funding yearly meetings of Asian government savings bank officials. Japanese bureaucrats would lecture counterparts on the virtues of the nation's postal savings system, citing its historical success in establishing the "idea of saving in the minds of the people." The state's promotion of saving, they asserted, had proved invaluable to curbing inflation, accumulating capital, and stabilizing society at large.[11] Similarly the Bank of Japan sponsored working seminars on "Savings Promotion," which brought together central bank officials from Asia and the Pacific.[12] These meetings marked one more chapter in the little-known story of learning from the Japanese experience among emerging Asian economies—including South Korea, Singapore, Malaysia, and China.

South Korea

Within Asia, the Republic of Korea most closely emulated Japanese programs for encouraging saving. This is both surprising and unsurprising. Anti-Japanese sentiment runs deep among South Koreans. Yet we must also recognize the profound institutional legacies of Japan's colonial rule of Korea from 1910 to 1945. The Japanese trained most of those who would later staff the Republic of Korea's bureaucracy, schools, businesses, and military. Japanese-trained officers dominated the South Korean military until 1980. Even after independence, despite official anti-Japanism, Korean elites continued to study Japanese policies. They read and spoke Japanese better than any other foreign language, and many admired postwar Japan's impressive economic growth.[13]

The South Korea regime inherited the infrastructure of savings promotion from the Japanese. Japan's postal savings system sank deep roots in colonial Korea. By the end of 1944, Korea boasted more than thirteen million postal savings accounts—five times the number in colonial Taiwan.[14] Large numbers of Koreans had become accustomed to saving at the post office. After 1945 the new South Korean regime quickly moved to indigenize postal savings. Korean officials also continued the colonial state's practice of organizing the people into national savings associations and other semiofficial associations. Many of these associations dated back to the 1930s. Under the Rural Revitalization Campaign, colonial authorities and local elites formed village-level bodies to encourage Koreans to plan their finances, reduce debts, and increase saving.[15]

Ironically the outbreak of the Korean War prompted South Korea leaders to revive the harsh war savings campaigns their people had recently experienced under Japanese rule. Desperate to finance rebuilding after the devastation of the war's first months, the government in 1951 mounted "The Campaign to Save for Certain Victory." Organizers redeployed the old Japanese slogans nearly verbatim. They, too, set a national savings target.[16] And just as their colonial masters had earlier established the wartime National Savings Promotion Council, the South Korean state instituted its own National Savings Promotion Council in 1952. The council worked closely with the Bank of Korea's new Savings Section, sitting atop a hierarchy of organizations reaching down to village and town savings-promotion committees. True to the wartime Japanese model, Korean officials concentrated on increasing the numbers of national savings associations in locales and workplaces (see figure 34).[17]

Although the campaigns of the 1950s expanded the grassroots organization of savings promotion, they did little to increase household

Figure 34. "How to Develop the National Savings Campaign," South Korea, 1955. Handbill by Kim Yong-hwan. We see the striking legacy of Japanese colonial practices in the Korean campaign's use of lectures and discussions with residents, touring squads that enlighten the villages, blaring sound trucks, oratorical contests, children's banks, stronger savings associations, and commendations for good savers. Hanguk Ŭnhaeng, *Chigŭm ŭn jŏchuk*, 8.

savings. Most Koreans were too poor to put much aside. High levels of inflation further discouraged saving. Moreover, unlike early postwar Japan, where low-cost foreign capital was scarce, the South Korean government and economy relied on massive U.S. aid and loans.[18]

The cause of savings promotion took on new vigor under the authoritarian rule of President Park Chung-hee. Park came to power in a military coup in 1961. He governed until his assassination in 1979. The president had earned his spurs in the Japanese-led Manchurian Army in World War II. Park openly admired not only Japan's postwar model of economic development, but also the prewar regime's success in molding a people willing to sacrifice for the nation-state. He promptly established the Japanese-style National Reconstruction Movement to mobilize youth groups, women's associations, and other semiofficial organizations. The movement's nationwide network promoted "self-help spirit," the "elimination of empty courtesies and rituals," "rice saving," and the "rationalization of living." Park described these activities as part of a "New Life system." Undoubtedly he referred to postwar Japan's "New Life movement," which similarly aimed at persuading people to improve daily lives by rationalizing consumption and saving money.[19]

Soon after taking power, President Park declared his leading models to be Japan's "Meiji Reform" and West Germany's "Miracle on the Rhine." To achieve the comparable "'miracle' on the Han River," Koreans would need to adopt "an austere living atmosphere" in which "spending should be checked in favor of savings." In his first Five-Year Plan for Economic Development, Park pledged to boost domestic savings to finance high growth, export-led development, and "an independent economy" that would be less reliant on foreign capital. The president singled out the West Germans for their frugality. At the time, they must have appeared more appealing than the unpopular Japanese. Park's Germans all saved, and were "sparing in eating, clothing and spending." No one bested German financiers as patriotic consumers. They "rode in German cars while traveling, ate German bread, used German film and German waste paper." Traveling to Italy and Switzerland, they "left nothing but waste paper and excrements."[20]

Yet the Japanese soon replaced Germans as Park's favorite role models. Within the South Korean bureaucracy, emulation of Japanese economic policies became standard operating procedure following the normalization of Japanese-Korean relations in 1965. Four years later President Park created the Central Council of Savings Promotion within the Bank of Korea. The similarity in name with the Bank of Japan's own Central Council for Savings Promotion was hardly a coincidence. Savings-promotion officials in the two central banks actively shared information in the inauguration and subsequent operation of Korea's Central Council.[21] Like its Japanese namesake, the Central Council of Savings Promotion sought to promote a "voluntary savings movement" and the people's "enlightenment in the spirit of thrift."[22] The Korean council, too, sponsored nationwide activities to encourage saving in the schools, model savings districts, companies, and Saemaŭl (New Community) organizations. Household saving rates steadily rose during the heyday of the Central Council's campaigns—from 9 percent in 1975 to 17.6 percent in 1989. These increases reflected rising real incomes, but Korean economists and officials also cite the contributions of the government's moral suasion drives and introduction of attractive savings instruments.[23]

Women's groups provided the foot soldiers in the savings campaigns, much as they did in Japan. Officials formed the Women's Central Council for Savings Life in 1967, incorporating some twenty women's associations. The women's council became a core part of the Central Council of Savings Promotion. Convergence between Korean and Japanese practices extended to everyday gender relations. Korean officials and women's organizations similarly represented the "housewife" as the household's primary saver and financial manager. The Korean savings campaigns moreover normalized the practice in which housewives keep highly detailed household account books.[24] Called *kakeibo* in Japanese and *kagaebu* in Korean, the government-issued account books were nearly identical, revealing the large degree of Korean emulation. In both nations, household account books powerfully motivated housewives to economize and save.

Korea's Central Council of Savings Promotion in fact went further than the Japanese council to discourage consumption itself. The state mounted a series of nationalistic "frugality campaigns" from the 1970s to the 1990s. Citizens were harangued not simply to eliminate "excessive consumption" (*kwasobi*) and wasteful ceremonial expenses. Only by buying domestic products and rejecting foreign "luxuries" would the nation's trade balance improve, they were told. Popular economizing would also increase the stock of national savings that could be invested in Korean production. In a typical poster in 1988, the Central Council of Savings Promotion warned shoppers to "Give End-of-the-Year and New Year's Presents Only According to Your Standing" (which we might translate as "forget about the Joneses"). Another in 1996 cautioned the nation not to abandon saving and start thinking of "consumption as a virtue," now that Korea had nearly caught up to the advanced countries.[25]

The government's moral suasion efforts could not curb the growing consumer desires of Koreans. Yet as levels of consumption rose in the 1980s, the drives reinforced popular anxieties. Many feared the burgeoning consumer culture was widening the gap between the nouveaux riches and the poor while eroding Korean's national identity. The relentless campaigns played an important role in persuading South Koreans to work long hours and make consumer choices based on a calculus of what would be good for the nation.[26]

The frugality campaigns have an interesting history that interweaves indigenous and foreign influences. Organizers commonly traced the origins to neo-Confucian ideals of the Chosŏn era (1392–1910), when Korea's *yangban* (scholar-officials) extolled the virtues of simplicity and frugality. In their resistance to imported goods, the campaigns further modeled themselves on colonial-era Korean nationalist movements that urged countrymen to boycott Japanese goods and buy Korean manufactures. This is ironic because the Japanese imprint on the frugality campaigns is also unmistakable. Korean anti-import messages replicated those of Japan's own "buy national products" campaigns of the interwar era and 1950s. Likewise, imperatives to "rationalize" consumption and reduce the costs of weddings and funerals owed much to prewar Japanese daily life improvement campaigns and the postwar New Life movement. Even the Korean campaigns' term for "frugality" derives from the twentieth-century Japanese word for "economizing" (*setsuyaku*), rather than older East Asian terms for "frugality."

Christianity, a Western import, provided the final ingredient in Korean consumer nationalism. Korean Protestants played central roles in the historical development of frugality campaigns. Cho Man-sik, the Presbyterian secretary-general of the Pyongyang YMCA, spearheaded the 1920s movement to buy Korean products. As in prewar Japan, Christians melded Confucian and Protestant ideals of austerity and thrift, and they often served as leading spokesmen in the regime's savings campaigns. While Christians never accounted for more than 1 percent of the Japanese, Christianity in Korea would grow to embrace roughly one-fourth of the South Korean population today. The Seoul YMCA worked closely with the government in the frugality campaigns of the late twentieth century. In 1986 the Seoul YMCA sponsored the "Social Forum for the Cultivation of the Consciousness of a Wholesome Consumer Lifestyle." Bemoaning Korean society's "extravagance (*sach'i*) and an all-out dedication to pleasure," speakers advocated "ascetism" and saving to solve the nation's problems.[27] When the U.S. special trade representative in 1990 attacked the current frugality campaign for obstructing American imports, a Korean Presbyterian minister rebuked her for maligning Koreans' dedication to hard work, providence, and frugality.[28]

The South Korean state was still promoting saving and discouraging excessive consumption in 1996–97, the time of the most recent frugality campaign. Western manufacturers and governments denounced that drive as nothing less than an officially sponsored anti-import campaign. The Korean government denied any involvement, insisting disingenuously that the "frugality campaign is a voluntary movement by civic groups with a view to encouraging rational and reasonable consumption."[29] Yet beyond the Western gaze, Korean officials not only encouraged saving, but also lauded the Japanese model. In its savings-promotion measures, reported one government-sponsored study at the time, contemporary Korea "resembles Japan of the old days." Korea had "followed" the Japanese model in many respects, acknowledged the report, and it would likely do so in the future. Even as foreigners complained about Japan's growing balance of payments surpluses in the 1980s, noted the Korean researchers, Japanese campaigns continued to urge people to save—no longer to accumulate capital—but for the needs of a rapidly aging society. "There is much for us to study here," the investigators concluded.[30]

To the surprise of many, a dramatic turn of events soon shattered the Republic of Korea's commitment to savings and economizing campaigns. South Korea was hit hard by the Asian financial crisis of late 1997. The government accepted a massive emergency loan from the International Monetary Fund, and in its wake came unprecedented outside scrutiny of economic policy. For a variety of reasons including fears of Western protests, the Bank of Korea quietly disbanded the twenty-eight-year-old Central Council of Savings Promotion at the end of the year. This development coincided with the growing influence of American-trained officials and economists who advocated a more consumption-driven economy.

In the years following the Asian financial crisis, South Korean officials carried out the most sweeping transformation of policies toward saving and consumption of any advanced economy in recent times. The state and banks did a volte-face by providing large amounts of consumer credit to the public. The government pointedly encouraged citizens to use credit cards, granting tax benefits every time they charged. While the Japanese economy of thrifty consumers remained mired in stagnation, the South Korean economy reignited, in part because of expanding consumer spending in 2001–2002. The transition to a credit-based economy has since occurred in fits and starts. A backlash ensued in 2003 when Korean credit-card and other household debt skyrocketed to American levels. Economic growth ground to a near halt.[31] The Korean media was abuzz with stories of the "credit card problem," reporting on the sharp rise of indebtedness among millions of consumers.[32] Nevertheless, the economy revived, and with it trends toward greater borrowing and lower saving. Household saving rates dropped from some of the highest in the world to 2.9 percent in 2008. A highly intrusive presence in everyday life not very long ago, Korean savings and frugality campaigns now seem a distant memory.

Singapore

Like the Republic of Korea until 1997, the government of Singapore has been impassioned about promoting saving in recent decades. It remains so. Singapore developed a unique approach that combines Japanese-style encouragement of voluntary saving with an elaborate system of *compulsory* saving. The linchpin in the regime's efforts is the Central Provident Fund. The CPF dates back to 1955 when Singapore was still under British colonial rule. It began life as an old-age pension fund that obligated both the employee and employer to deposit a small fixed proportion of the employee's salary. Beginning in 1968, members received permission to withdraw funds from individual CPF accounts for the purposes of purchasing public-housing flats and paying monthly mortgage installments. Thereafter mandatory contribution rates spiked upward, peaking in the 1980s at 25 percent each from employee and employer. In 2010 mandatory contribution rates for those younger than fifty stood at 20 percent from the employee and 15 percent from the employer. Besides financing housing and retirement, CPF funds may be withdrawn—with restrictions—to pay for medical and educational expenses.[33]

As the state expanded the compulsory savings program during the 1970s and 1980s, it also actively encouraged voluntary saving in banks and especially the Post Office Savings Bank (POSB; later the POSBank). Singaporean households managed to save high percentages of income even after making hefty contributions to their CPF accounts. By 1988 voluntary saving reached 11 percent of gross income. The postal savings system lured customers by means of school savings programs, attractive "POSBank Girl" tellers, and other types of marketing schemes seen in Japan and elsewhere.[34]

The mobilization of savings stands at the center of governance in Singapore as nowhere else. In the absence of generous state-funded programs, CPF and voluntary savings accounts function as self-financed systems of social security. Ideologically, the ruling People's Action Party (PAP) hypes these institutions as Singapore's self-help alternative to degenerate Western welfare states. Politically, leaders envisioned the CPF and the encouragement of home ownership as giving the people "a deep and abiding stake in the country," echoing British language of the nineteenth century.[35] Economically, the Singaporean state has exercised total control over the massive funds of both the CPF and postal savings. The success of Singapore's industrial and social development policies owes much to governmental investment of the people's deposits. For the purposes of macroeconomic stabilization, the regime often manipulated CPF contribution rates to improve Singapore's competitive position in world markets. Confronted by recession in 1986, the government sharply reduced labor costs by cutting only the *employer's* contribution rate from 25 to 10 percent.[36] Similarly the authorities halved the employer's rate in the wake of the 1997 financial crisis.

The origins of Singapore's encouragement of savings are by no means obvious. Were we to consult former prime minister Lee Kuan Yew (now the retired "Minister Mentor"), he would invariably speak of "Confucian values" of thrift prevailing among the Chinese majority. In the 1990s the government began promoting the more inclusive idea of "Shared Values" to appeal to all three of Singapore's major ethnicities—Chinese, Malays, and Indians. The Ministry of Education's Civics and Moral Education curriculum teaches the value of thrift by highlighting traditional sayings and folktales from each of the three cultures.[37]

Others, however, are skeptical of explanations based on Confucian or Asian values. A historical examination of Singaporean savings promotion bears them out. As in most countries, the modern encouragement of thrift in Singapore developed from the interplay of external and indigenous influences. We begin with the colonial legacy. It was after all the British who introduced the Post Office Savings Bank to Singapore in 1877.[38] With the National Savings Movement in full swing back home, colonial authorities also founded the Central Provident Fund in 1955. British attitudes profoundly shaped Lee Kuan Yew and several other English-educated leaders of the future People's Action Party. Called "Harry" until his thirties, Lee imbibed the paternalism of his former colonial masters in seeking to civilize the tropical inhabitants of the city-state. He disdained the Chinese business community as venal and backward during the 1960s. Not until the late 1970s would he discover the virtues of Confucianism.[39] As for Chinese culture's putative thriftiness, Lee placed little faith in Singaporean workers as late as the 1970s. They "spend freely and save less," he complained, "so it is necessary that we should *enforce* savings through CPF contributions."[40]

In addition, the Japanese model of savings promotion significantly shaped Singapore's programs at several junctures. During World War II, Japan occupied Singapore for three and a half years. The Japanese mounted war savings campaigns, and they expanded the colonial postal savings system throughout Malaya. Despite heavy-handed tactics, the Japanese occupation's reliance on popular mobilization impressed those who would later lead Singapore. Postwar Japanese businesses invested significantly in Singapore from the late 1950s, and Lee Kuan Yew eagerly sought Japanese governmental assistance in industrializing the new nation. Singaporean planners studied the lessons of the Japanese developmental state, for its history suggested that resource and capital limitations could be overcome by mobilizing domestic savings.[41]

The Japanese postal savings system undoubtedly inspired Singaporean officials, who redesigned both the CPF and Post Office Saving Bank to similarly channel popular savings to developmental projects. The influential finance minister Goh Keng Swee frequently referred to the Japanese state's penchant for investing in industrial expansion. In

1967 Goh set about to transform the moribund Post Office Savings Bank into an effective instrument for mobilizing national savings. Together with the CPF, the POSB would soak up the people's purchasing power and "provide the Government with a non-inflationary source of funds for the development of the infrastructure." The Ministry of Finance assumed responsibility not only for investing POSB funds, but for running the bank itself.[42]

Goh opted for a path of development that imaginatively combined Japanese experience and Victorian virtues. He advised developing countries to throw away books about economic growth and instead "read the essays of Samuel Smiles—his exhortations to thrift, industry, ambition, honesty, perseverance, etc."[43] Looking back on how his "small island nation with no natural resources" achieved growth rates comparable only to Japan and South Korea, Goh singled out the unheralded role of domestic savings.[44] In the realm of education, too, Singaporean schoolchildren recently studied "The Story of Japan's Industrial Development," from which they were expected to learn "about the qualities of the Japanese such as a thrifty people and positive work attitude."[45]

Lastly, Singapore's systematic encouragement of saving reflects the dynamic, autocratic style of the People's Action Party. The PAP's founding fathers not only mediated transnational influences from Britain, Japan, and other nations, they also innovated as they transformed the CPF. Leaders drew on a string of successes to cultivate among the public an aura of themselves as infallible visionaries.[46] Goh Keng Swee likened PAP leaders to Moses leading the Israelites to the Promised Land. They, too, had, "to exhort the faithful, encourage the faint-hearted and censure the ungodly." Or as Lee Kuan Yew put it, "I am often accused of interfering in the private lives of citizens. Yet, if I did not, had I not done that, we wouldn't be here today.... We decide what is right. Never mind what the people think."[47]

Like Japanese and South Korean officials, Singaporean rulers have been wary of excessive consumption. Lee warned early on that the nation was "caught in the meshes of the consumer society." Advertisements, he lamented, urged people to "buy what they do not really need, as finance companies and other mechanisms encourage people to buy now and pay later."[48] Concerned about rising consumer credit especially

Figure 35. As part of Singapore's National School Savings Campaign in the mid-1970s, Post Office Savings Bank (POSB) staff regularly visited the schools to inculcate the "savings habit" at any early age. Post Office Savings Bank, *First Hundred Years of the Post Office Savings Bank of Singapore*, 35. Reproduced by permission from the POSB/DBS Bank. Today, POSB continues to promote savings in schools with its Schools Outreach Program, reaching out to more than 90,000 primary school students in 80 schools annually.

among the young, the government today strictly controls the issuance of personal loans and credit cards. Borrowers must demonstrate substantial income to qualify. The Ministry of Education recently redoubled its efforts at thrift education because, as one official explained, "now, more than ever, we must arrest consumerism."[49]

Nonetheless, to restrain consumption, the Singaporean state relies less on moral suasion than in South Korea and Japan. With a population of less than five million, the city-state thrives on free trade depending on both exports and entrepôt trade. Mounting a series of "buy national products" drives would have been suicidal economically. Moreover, the one-party regime long ago identified sustained improvements in consumption as key to its political survival. Leaders need not permit genuine democratic participation, but they are compelled to provide the goods. In this "air-conditioned nation," observes Cherian George, the government initially provided basic public housing, but had then to satisfy growing consumer appetites for, among other items, air-conditioning.[50] Not that the state *encourages* unrestrained consumption. Singapore's ruling elites simply have less need to dissuade the people from extravagance. By adjusting contribution rates and other features of the CPF, they retain the capacity to drain purchasing power while directing much of the family's consumption toward housing.

Malaysia

Malaysia's emulation of Japanese-style campaigns has a more recent history. This Southeast Asian nation was Japan's most enthusiastic student at the beginning of the twentieth-first century. Like neighboring Singapore, the former British colony inherited a compulsory savings program called the Employees Provident Fund (EPF). Unlike Singapore's Central Provident Fund, the EPF permits only limited withdrawals to finance home buying, education, and medical expenses. Contribution rates have remained below those of the CPF (in 2010, only 8 percent from employees and 12 percent from employers). The EPF's accumulations nonetheless grew to become the government's major source of financing developmental expenditures by the 1990s.[51]

The Malaysian state also devoted substantial resources to stimulating voluntary savings. In 1974 the government transformed the sleepy colonial-era Post Office Savings Bank into the National Savings Bank (Bank Simpanan Nasional), the leading force in mobilizing small savings. As in Japan and Singapore, National Savings Bank funds have directly financed national economic development.[52] Indeed, bank officials expanded operations in conscious emulation of postal savings institutions in the successful Asian developmental states. Information-sharing among the region's economic bureaucracies occurred in a number of forums, including ASEAN (Association of Southeast Asian Nations).

The National Savings Bank derived the most useful transnational knowledge from the Geneva-based International Savings Banks Institute, successor to the old International Thrift Institute organized in 1924. The Institute's leading members represented European postal savings systems and savings banks associations, plus Japan's gargantuan postal savings bank. As new theories of economic development privileged the mobilization of domestic savings, the ISBI supported the expansion of savings promotion in Southeast Asia. In 1973 the Institute founded its Asia and Pacific regional office in Bangkok, Thailand. A decade later, representatives of Asia's government savings institutions were meeting annually to exchange information and personnel in ISBI-sponsored forums. The fast-growing economies of Malaysia, Singapore, Thailand, and Indonesia assumed leadership of the regional office, financially assisted by Japan's Postal Savings Bureau.[53]

Savings promotion took center stage in Malaysia during the early 1990s. Officials worried that savings were insufficient to sustain investment in the surging economy. Stepping up its commitment to the "promotion of savings and the savings habit," the central bank (Bank Negara Malaysia) exhorted consumers to check inflation by reducing spending on "luxuries and unnecessaries."[54] National leaders noted the strong correlation between high national savings and high economic performance among the booming Asian economies. Concerned about declining saving rates, Finance Minister Anwar Ibrahim demanded Malaysian society become "more disciplined" and avoid "conspicuous consumption."[55]

Ideology loomed large in Malaysia's national savings policies. Mahathir bin Mohamad, the charismatic prime minister who ruled from 1981 to 2003, championed pan-Asian unity as a counterweight to Western hegemony. He warned repeatedly of the political dangers to a country like Malaysia if it depended too much on foreign capital: "As can be seen from the world economy recently, the sentiments of foreign investors can change according to developments that have nothing to do with domestic economic developments. Although we will continue to welcome foreign investments into Malaysia, we need to be prepared to have our own capabilities that we determine ourselves."[56] In 1996 the government established a Cabinet Committee on the Promotion of Savings and proceeded to launch the National Savings Campaign. In the face of the Asian financial crisis the following year, Malaysia alone eschewed IMF assistance. Mahathir imposed currency controls to shield his economy from the vicissitudes of international finance. The National Savings Campaign openly advanced his agenda of a more self-sufficient Malaysian economy. Besides promoting thrift, the campaign instructed the nation to avoid imported goods and "buy locally made products."[57]

Savings campaigns also formed an integral part of Mahathir's efforts to help ethnic Malays (Bumiputra) catch up to the more prosperous Chinese and Indian minorities. Roughly 58 percent of the population was Malay, 24 percent Chinese, and 8 percent Indian. The program was as much social policy as political patronage. In the wake of murderous communal violence in 1968, leaders of all ethnic groups embraced the goal of closing the economic gap between Malays and Chinese. Officials commonly describe the Bumiputra as held back by traditional spendthrift ways. Since the late 1970s, the government has worked to build up the assets of Malays through special banks and unit trusts (mutual funds) that provide attractive, above-market rates of returns. In this predominantly Muslim nation, the state moreover manages "Islamic banking." Encouraging thrift within Islamic strictures, the program for instance promotes saving to enable Malays to make the pilgrimage (Hajj) to Mecca.[58]

Malaysian leaders freely acknowledged the importance of the Japanese model in the savings campaigns. Mahathir emerged as Asia's outspoken admirer of Japan. In 1981 he announced Malaysia's "Look East" policy, aimed at introducing the Japanese work ethic and managerial approaches. Japanese businessmen returned the affection with large-scale direct investment in Malaysia.[59] In tones that recall the wartime Greater East Asia Co-prosperity Sphere, Mahathir cast Japan in a world-historical role. Japan would act as the leader and teacher of Asia, standing up to a degenerate West plagued by family breakdown and "hedonistic values."[60]

At the operational level, too, bureaucrats in the Bank Negara Malaysia developed a fascination for Japanese savings promotion. The Japanese state had created an extensive grassroots network, they noted, achieving high saving rates in the absence of abundant natural resources.[61] Following the establishment of their own Cabinet Committee on the Promotion of Savings, Bank Negara officials visited the Bank of Japan's Central Council for Savings Information in 1997. They returned with a trove of savings campaign materials. One year later the Malaysian central bank set up a Japanese-style Savings Promotion Secretariat to coordinate the campaigns. At Japanese-sponsored conferences on savings promotion for Asian central bank officials, the Malaysians were reportedly the most enthusiastic.

Having chosen the Japanese model, the Bank Negara staff *literally* translated the documents and objectives of Japanese savings campaigns. Malaysian campaigns likewise targeted women, students, and workers. The Savings Promotion Secretariat distributed household account books to women. Schoolchildren received "pocket money books" designed to inculcate the "savings habit." As in Japan, officials sponsored national training programs in "household financial management" for leaders of women's organizations. Inspired campaign organizers assured Malaysians that it should be possible both to save and to spend if they consumed "efficiently." The key, as it had been in Japan, was to recognize the need to "balance consumption and savings."[62]

Malaysian savings-promotion officials face the challenge, as one phrased it, of "tropicalizing" Japanese campaign techniques.[63] Many of the problems of adapting the Japanese model to Malaysia lie in differences in social structures, notably in gender relations. Malaysian society generally lacks the Japanese or South Korean norm of the full-time "housewife" who takes control of her husband's salary and manages household finances. Accordingly, the Bank Negara–issued household account books often failed to stimulate saving. In an effort to persuade Malaysian women to keep regular accounts, the Bank Negara produced a leaner, less intimidating version of the Japanese account book. Even then, Malaysian women and their organizations have not been as enthusiastic about the savings campaigns as organizers would have liked. In 2001, I visited two high-ranking officials at the ministry charged with rallying the nation's women's organizations behind the Bank Negara's savings campaign. When the conversation turned to the distribution of household account books, one of the officials—a woman—shrugged: "Oh, I tried keeping one of those account books myself, but it's so much work. I gave up after three months."

China

Fears of excessive saving by an Asian giant are nothing new. Two and a half decades ago, Japan's high saving rates and alleged underconsumption became a flashpoint in international relations. American commentators worried about the loss of national sovereignty as Japanese savings flowed into huge purchases of U.S. Treasury bonds and bills. At a certain point the media lost interest in the story, even though the Japanese government remained the number one foreign investor in Treasury securities until recently. Today, of course, U.S. complaints single out the Chinese for oversaving. A spate of recent books sounds the alarm about Americans' reliance on Chinese savings to finance their addiction to consumer and mortgage credit.[64] No one can say for sure how much the Chinese people save. Data based on national income is incomplete, nor does it accord with international standards. The most credible estimate places China's household saving rate for 2007 at nearly 26 percent.[65] This is extraordinarily high, although in line with rates in Japan, South Korea, and Italy in previous decades.

Common explanations of why Chinese save have been less than satisfying. Most popular are invocations of "culture"—just as we've seen elsewhere in Asia. More often than not, Chinese leaders today trace the nation's thriftiness back to Confucian values. Compared to Americans who became accustomed to overspending, observed the official *China Daily*, the Chinese people have developed a "tradition of savings since ancient times." Zhou Xiaohuan, governor of China's central bank, recently defended his country's high saving rate as in large part the product of Confucianism, which values thrift, self-discipline, moderation, and an aversion to extravagance.[66] There is something rather forced about these claims. Back in the 1960s, Chairman Mao Zedong denounced Confucius as a "stinking corpse." Only in the last twenty years has the Chinese Community Party conveniently rediscovered the sage's age-old influence on popular behavior. Ironically the inspiration came primarily from abroad, from Confucian revivalists in Singapore and Taiwan and from Westerners who write about the development of "Confucian capitalism" in Japan and the rest of East Asia.[67]

Cultural explanations are all the more dubious when we consider the following. Not so long ago the Chinese people were terrible savers. Under Maoism from 1952 to 1978, household saving rates did not exceed 2 or 3 percent and often sunk to less than 1 percent.[68] If Chinese saved at impressive rates thereafter, surely other factors rank higher than Confucianism.

Another explanation favored by American economists and journalists is that Chinese save excessively in the absence of adequate welfare programs. It is an argument sustained by constant repetition, and little evidence. This analysis comes complete with its own policy recommendation. In the words of the influential economist Stephen Roach, China should build an institutionalized safety net necessary to temper the "fear-driven precautionary saving that inhibits the development of a more dynamic consumer culture."[69] Uncertainty, it is true, may motivate people to save, but so do many other factors. The correlation between high saving and inadequate social benefits is a weak one, globally. Scores of poor nations provide little in the way of social welfare, yet their saving rates are minuscule.[70] Among advanced economies, high-saving nations in continental Europe all *provide* comprehensive welfare benefits. Americans, who aside from the elderly lack sturdy safety nets, conversely saved little in recent decades. Even if China were immediately to institute thoroughgoing social policies that would protect its 1.3 billion people—a rather fantastical proposition— that alone would not necessarily bring down the saving rate.

There are, however, better explanations that conform to the historical and global findings of this book. In China, household saving rates have risen in tandem with rapid economic growth. We have observed this pattern in Asia's other success stories, as well as in Western Europe after World War II. Following Mao's death and the advent of Deng Xiaoping in 1978, the party-state fundamentally transformed the

Communist economy into one based on global trade, foreign investment, and the partial embrace of market principles. The Chinese economy leaped into high growth, the GDP surging 10 percent annually from 1980 to the present. As elsewhere, household savings rose as consumption lagged behind increases in incomes.

Second, Chinese save more because of poor access to credit. As we will learn in the final chapters, saving tends to be inversely related to borrowing. American journalists glory in the story of Chinese conspicuous consumption and the spread of credit cards. Most of these "credit cards" are in fact debit cards tied to bank accounts. Only a small fraction offer revolving credit. The heavily regulated banks have been miserly in extending consumer credit, and they generally require stiff down payments before lending money to homebuyers. This is in sharp contrast to the United States, but not so different from several Asian and European countries where consumer and housing credit is subject to significant regulation. In a fast growing economy like China's, people want to buy cars and other durables, but in lieu of easy credit they need to save in order to consume.[71]

Curiously, few observers consider the possibility that the Chinese party-state might have had a hand in directly encouraging popular saving. Indeed, China represents one of the most compelling cases of the efficacy of aggressive savings promotion. Under Maoist rule, Chinese households saved almost nothing. They had little money, it is true, but they also lacked safe, convenient banking facilities. In the three years following the Communist Revolution of 1949, the regime eliminated all public and private banks, transferring their assets to the central People's Bank of China. The dissolved banks included the Republic of China's fledgling postal savings bank, established in 1919.[72] Although families under Maoism may have saved by hoarding goods and a little cash, they had little incentive to save in lieu of accessible institutions for small savings.

All this changed in the wake of the regime's decision to reform and open the Chinese economy in 1978. Leaders recognized the pressing need to mobilize domestic savings to remedy capital shortages. One year later the state established the Agricultural Bank of China, the Bank of China, and the People's Construction Bank of China. The creation of the Industrial and Commercial Bank of China in 1983 completed the formation of what today constitute the four big state-owned commercial banks. The year 1986 ushered in the next phase, the relentless pursuit of small savers nationwide. The Agricultural Bank and the Industrial and Commercial Bank set up a total of nearly thirty thousand new branches that year. The Agricultural Bank alone doubled the number of its branches, reaching villagers who likely had never before had a savings account. Institutions bear heavily on savings behavior. In 1986 savings deposits increased at a faster clip than at any time since the founding of the People's Republic of China.[73] It was not simply that branches opened and customers streamed in. Bank employees ran nationally coordinated campaigns to persuade the locals to entrust their savings to the new institutions. Including its joint savings projects with the authorities, associations, and cooperatives, the Industrial and Commercial Bank in 1991 claimed one million staff members engaged in "savings mobilization."[74]

Joining the big banks in 1986 was the new—or rather improved—Chinese postal savings system. For all the recent insistence on Chinese exceptionalism, officials methodically emulated the savings-promotion policies of Japan and other thriving Asian economies. Once the regime committed itself to reviving postal savings, Chinese bureaucrats visited Japan's Postal Savings Bureau and Central Council for Savings Promotion in the early 1980s. Their mission was to survey how the Japanese successfully encouraged saving. Cooperative relationships between savings officials of the two nations developed. During the 1990s, Japan's Ministry of Posts and Telecommunications assisted the Chinese in computerizing the postal savings system. Officials from the People's Bank of China moreover actively participated in the Bank of Japan's meetings for Asian central bankers, reporting on Chinese programs to boost savings deposits.[75]

Postal savings became immensely popular among Chinese, for much the same reasons we have seen elsewhere. In many rural and remote areas of China, it is one of the few institutions that serves small savers. The number of branches mushroomed from less than 2,500 in 1986 to 37,000 in 2009. Its popularity also rested on more than two decades of promotional campaigns by postal employees and the local authorities.

As a market share of total deposits, postal savings appears small compared to the four big state-owned commercial banks—only 8.1 percent in 2002. But of course we're talking about the world's largest country. The number of *households* with postal accounts that year came to a mind-boggling 104 million.[76]

Chinese leaders today speak less openly about their efforts to promote saving. Instead officials increasingly pledge to stimulate consumption as a vital prop of the Chinese economy. As in Singapore, the party-state recognizes that its continued legitimacy depends on improvements in the people's material lives. In view of decreased demand from sluggish Western economies, the planners are also aware that domestic consumers may need to buy more if the Chinese economy is to continue high growth. However, the Communist Party's pronouncements on consumption have their tactical side. They aim to reassure American observers, many of whom take any pledge as evidence that China will soon embrace an American-style consumer society.[77]

Unquestionably consumption is rising in China, yet the Asian giant will likely remain a high-saving society for many years to come. The consumption levels enjoyed by Westerners, Japanese, Koreans, and Singaporeans are well beyond the reach of hundreds of millions of Chinese. Consumption as a share of GDP stands at 35–36 percent, half that of the United States. Contrary to many media stories, China's high growth relies overwhelmingly on investment, exports, and government consumption—and relatively little on domestic consumption.[78] Finally, the regime has a powerful stake in promoting household saving for the foreseeable future. Chinese authorities learned a great deal from the Japanese and Singaporean models, in which the state manages and invests large pools of small savings. The Chinese government similarly captures the people's savings at low cost from the state-owned banks and postal savings system. This capital finances companies and infrastructure at home. It also flows into the Singaporean-style sovereign wealth fund that China invests strategically in such things as U.S. Treasury securities and the exploitation of African minerals.[79]

China, the newest savings superpower, now enjoys influence in international relations it could scarcely imagine three decades ago. When Treasury Secretary Henry Paulson recently blamed the China's "superabundant savings" for causing a global credit bubble, the Chinese turned the tables just as the Japanese had done twenty years earlier.[80] Wen Jia-bao issued a scold of his own at the World Economic Forum in Davos, Switzerland. The United States, declared the premier, should be held most accountable for the global economic crisis. America had pursued an "unsustainable model of development characterized by prolonged low savings and high consumption," the "blind pursuit of profit," and "the failure of financial supervision."[81] Make no mistake about it. Chinese leaders have few plans to jettison the policies of savings promotion that have served them so well.

11

"THERE IS MONEY. SPEND IT":
AMERICA SINCE 1945

"There IS money. Spend it, spend it; spend more."
—Ford in Shakespeare's *Merry Wives of Windsor*, Act II,
Scene 2

Q. Mr. President, I would like to ask you a question about
what people should do to make the recession recede.
THE PRESIDENT: Buy.
Q. Buy what?
THE PRESIDENT: Anything.
—President Eisenhower's News Conference, April 9, 1958[1]

Japanese and Chinese leaders were not the only ones to lecture Americans about their lack of thrift. Some Americans too warned of the dire consequences of low saving rates in the United States. Those jeremiads fell on deaf ears. Until recently, that is. In the financial crisis that began in 2007, millions of Americans discovered they lacked the savings to weather the storm. They lost their jobs. They lost their homes. Suddenly Samuel Smiles's Victorian-era injunction resonated in a different time and place. If working Americans, too, failed to accumulate "a store of frugal savings in prosperous times," they would be driven into "bad bargains with their masters," whether employers or mortgage companies.

How did Americans come to be such miserable savers? When I describe the current American predicament to European and East Asian audiences, few have doubts about what went wrong. Americans are profligate. They waste. They're addicted to credit. They lack "our traditions." But such explanations are caricatures ignoring a more variegated historical record. When we last left the Americans at the end of World War II, they *were* good savers. Most had gained access to institutions that made small saving attractive.

However, in the years following 1945, Americans once again diverged from the rest of the world—slowly at first, but with a gallop in recent decades. To explain the low level of American saving, we must consider an array of historical developments that distinguished the U.S. case from economies in Europe and East Asia.

The Decline of "Thrift"

Americans would never again save as they did in World War II. Following victory over Japan in August 1945, Americans spent down savings at a faster clip than at any other time. Personal saving rates plummeted. From 26 percent (1944) they sank to 9.6 percent (1946) and merely 4.2 percent in 1947. Aggregate personal savings fell from nearly $30 billion in 1945 to less than $10 billion in 1947.[2]

There is nothing all that shocking about declining U.S. saving rates after 1945. We'd have been more surprised if Americans kept on saving as fiercely as Europeans and Japanese. Americans saved less because they could. The nation emerged from the war extraordinarily rich when other major belligerents lay stricken. The United States held half of the world's manufacturing capacity and half of its monetary reserves.[3] It had little need to demand austerity from citizens. No bombs had destroyed its cities requiring national savings campaigns to finance reconstruction. America abounded in capital. While postwar Japan and Germany suffered hyperinflation at war's end, the U.S. economy enjoyed impressive price stability. The United States simply did not experience the conditions that compelled postwar savings campaigns elsewhere.

Victorious Americans sat down to a well-deserved feast of consumer spending that others could only envy. Pent-up demand was enormous. Between 1941 and 1944, mean family income shot up more than 25 percent adjusted for inflation. The war effort commandeered most durable goods leaving households with large stores of savings. Manufacturers happily prepared war savers for the postwar splurge. At the height of hostilities, a Royal typewriter advertisement offered an interesting take on why the country fought. The war was about securing the right to "once more walk into any store in the land and buy anything you want."[4] With the return of peace, factories quickly retooled to produce goods for the new mass-consumption society.

What distinguished postwar American consumption patterns was the shift to widespread ownership of consumer durables. These trends first appeared in the 1920s. In the past, noted one Federal Reserve study, businesses owned durable assets and consumers purchased their services. Increasingly families bought those assets outright. It became normal for Americans to own homes rather than rent; purchase automobiles rather than take public transportation; buy washing machines instead of paying for laundry services. The ownership of mechanical refrigerators leaped from 44 to 80 percent of households between 1940 and 1950. Sales of new cars quadrupled from 1946 to 1955. By the late 1950s, three-quarters of households owned at least one automobile.[5]

The postwar drop in saving rates coincided with the decline of promotional activities. Efforts to sell savings bonds at the grass roots became a pale imitation of what they had once been. In 1950 Harold Mackintosh, chairman of Britain's National Savings Committee, visited his counterpart in the U.S. Savings Bond Division. Lord Mackintosh noted the modest scale of the Treasury Department's postwar operations compared to his vibrant National Savings Movement. America lacked anything comparable to Britain's neighborhood "Street" Savings Groups. U.S. officials, he reported, expressed admiration for the army of British volunteers who went door to door encouraging neighbors to purchase National Savings Certificates. It didn't help matters that the federal government had cut the staff of the Savings Bond Division to one-fourth of its wartime size by 1947.[6]

The end of the war brought sharp reductions in those institutions that had promoted systematic saving among the greatest numbers. The Treasury Department's wartime School Savings Program enrolled some

200,000 schools and sold $2 billion in savings stamps and bonds, but many schools dropped the program after the war. The government discontinued sales of savings stamps in 1970. The revival of school savings banks partially filled the void. Pupils regularly made small deposits that were then placed in special savings accounts at the banks. The number of children with such accounts grew during the 1950s. As in the prewar era, however, school savings banks failed to reach most young Americans. School banks claimed only 6.3 million depositors in the early 1960s—not much more than the 4.6 million depositors in 1929 despite substantial population growth. Aside from the geographically limited mutual savings banks, few banks were willing to handle the unprofitable small savings of schoolchildren. Only one bank in the entire state of Illinois reportedly ran a school savings program in 1963. Other banks abandoned student savings, citing large numbers of inactive accounts. By the late 1960s, school savings banks had all but disappeared.[7]

Of more immediate consequence was the precipitous drop in saving at the workplace. As many as twenty-seven million employees had purchased war bonds, week after week. Following the war, participation in payroll savings plans sank to just five million in 1950. Patriotic and peer pressure had eased. The banks might have taken over the payroll savings plans as they did in Japan and elsewhere. In fact few American banks did so. The abrupt decline of payroll savings undoubtedly lowered saving rates among ordinary Americans. Experiments today by behavioral economists confirm the positive impact on saving of automatically enrolling employees in 401(k) retirement plans. When payroll savings plans no longer enrolled large numbers, working people likely did not save at comparable rates in the banks.[8]

As Americans savored the fruits of mass consumption, thrift fast lost its cultural cachet. In 1956 the journalist William Whyte complained that "thrift now is un-American." No longer identifying saving with morality, people "save little because they do not really believe in saving."[9] The word "thrift" itself had become quaint—as likely to invite ridicule as admiration. The New York Times mocked the American Bankers Association's Thrift Week in 1954 by trotting out its own set of antithrift homilies. "Thrift is a wonderful virtue," declared the daily, "especially in an ancestor."[10]

Nor were the children spared in the culture industry's assault on thrift. Generations of young Americans have been raised on the Disney film *Mary Poppins*. Although the story is set in Edwardian England, the movie reflected the emerging consumerist values of postwar America. In the original British novel about the magical nanny, the father (a banker) had been a minor character. In the Hollywood version of 1964, Mr. Banks hogs the stage as the embodiment of all that's wrong with old-fashioned prudence.[11] Joined by a cast of musty bankers, he encourages his children to experience the joys of saving. For as he sings,

> If you invest your tuppence
> Wisely in the bank
> Safe and sound
> Soon that tuppence,
> Safely invested in the bank,
> Will compound.

Michael and Jane will have none of it. Creatures of the new age, the children spend that tuppence. They buy bread to feed the birds—their act of consumption sweetened by generosity. But no longer would the word "thrift" roll off the tongues of Americans, nor would dedications to Prudence or Temperance adorn banks and city squares.

Saving without Sacrifice

This is not to say that Americans stopped saving. One of the nation's best kept secrets is that people saved greater portions of income during the postwar decades than at any time other than World War II. Ironically, at the very moment America developed into a mass-consumption society, saving became widespread. Household saving rates recovered from early postwar lows. From 1950 to 1990, according to the latest measure, rates ranged between 7 and 11 percent. Continental Europeans and Japanese saved at considerably higher rates.[12] Still, it is remarkable that Americans continued to engage in small saving in banks, bonds, and insurance—on top of assuming mortgages and buying consumer durables.

How do we explain this? First off, high economic growth in the postwar decades enabled Americans both to consume and to save comfortably. Thanks to nearly full employment and high rates of unionization, prosperity was distributed more evenly than at any other time. From 1947 to 1973, real median family income doubled, while incomes of the lowest three-fifths rose at a much faster rate than those of the top fifth.[13] The high level of income equality contributed to *mass saving*. Already in the late 1940s, two-thirds of surveyed households were saving.[14] Americans resembled postwar Japanese or West Germans in achieving higher saving rates as real incomes rose, but they differed in one important respect. Unlike, say, Japanese families who typically afforded a television in 1960 by cutting back on vital expenditures such as housing, most Americans could have their cake and save some too.

Just as important, ordinary Americans gained unprecedented access to safe institutions that facilitated small saving. Postwar saving built upon the New Deal's federal deposit-insurance system and the wartime savings bonds program. These innovations smoothed out prewar unevenness in saving based on region, race, gender, and class. America's Golden Age of Saving occurred neither in Franklin's time nor in the Victorian era. It materialized a mere two or three generations ago, beginning in World War II and ending in the 1980s.

U.S. savings bonds in fact persisted. Small-denomination bonds were how most Americans saved in wartime. In 1945 the $42.9 billion in savings bonds exceeded totals in any other type of savings—life insurance, commercial banks, mutual savings banks, or savings and loan associations.[15] Postwar Americans remained fond of savings bonds, particularly E bonds and the new H bond. While institutional and corporate investors abandoned savings bonds for higher-yielding investments, individuals maintained or even increased their bond holdings in the fifteen years following World War II. The bulk of E bonds purchased in wartime were held not only to the ten-year maturity, but beyond.[16]

The populace also saved at banks as never before. The majority of American families entered the postwar era without a bank account. In 1946, 61 percent of surveyed households lacked a basic savings account, and 66 percent possessed no checking account. Historically commercial banks had not been friendly to small savers. Financial institutions were often inconveniently located, and bank failures in the 1930s had done little to inspire popular trust. Big changes followed the end of the war. Between 1946 and 1960, the proportion of households with savings accounts rose from 39 to 53 percent. It peaked in 1977 at 77 percent. Conversely, ownership of savings bonds declined from 63 percent to 30 percent in 1960. Savings accounts offered certain advantages over savings bonds. Some paid higher interest. Money could be withdrawn from the bank anytime, whereas savings-bond holders received less interest if they cashed out before maturity.[17]

Savings and loan associations emerged as the fastest growing segment of the savings market. Individual savings in S&Ls doubled from 1945 to 1953. Successors to the building and loan associations, the S&Ls specialized in accepting deposits and making mortgage loans. A series of federal interventions supported their expansion. Hit hard in the Great Depression, savings and loan associations gained a new lease on life in 1932. Legislation set up Federal Home Loan Banks, which advanced low-interest loans to the associations to stimulate home ownership. In the postwar years, small savers flocked to the more than six thousand S&Ls. Many of these banks had moved to more convenient locations, and some opened branches. Aggressively advertising, managements engaged in what they called "thrift promotion." Besides offering school savings accounts, the associations expanded Christmas clubs and vacation clubs whereby depositors saved for short-term goals.

Postwar changes to the federal deposit-insurance system further convinced savers to shift to the S&Ls. Savings and loan accounts were not insured by the Federal Deposit Insurance Corporation. Established in 1934, the Federal Savings and Loan Insurance Corporation provided weaker protections to S&L customers. In 1950–51 Congress strengthened provisions for paying depositors in case of defaults, increasing public confidence in the S&Ls.[18] Few suspected that their accounts were not in fact guaranteed by the "full faith and credit of the United States," unlike those covered by the FDIC. Still, the FSLIC protected S&L customers for the next three decades. Until it didn't. But that's another story.

Moreover, discourses of thrift held their own against the champions of consumption during the 1950s. Make it a "Thrifty '50," advertised

Minneapolis's Farmers and Mechanics Savings Bank.[19] The Treasury Department revitalized savings bonds campaigns to "encourage thrift" and "regular, systematic savings habits." Such efforts resulted in increased participation in payroll savings plans. In 1954, ads for savings bonds appeared monthly in 800 magazines and 50 farm journals, and on 90,000 street cars and buses; 3,100 radio stations regularly broadcast spots for bonds. Supporting the sales efforts were national tours made by "Mrs. U.S. Savings Bond," the lucky contestant chosen annually from finalists at the Mrs. America pageant.[20]

School savings programs may not have achieved the nationwide coverage we saw in many other societies. Yet where they existed, baby boomers learned habits that stayed with them long after the word "thrift" became passé. In 1951 an estimated six million students attended schools that ran weekly Savings Stamp Days; a total of fifteen million went to schools offering training in "thrift." School savings banks did best in cities where school systems cooperated with savings banks and other banks. Metropolitan school districts commonly employed directors of thrift education. New York City accounted for one-third of the national total of pupils with savings accounts in 1947. New York State boasted 1.2 million school depositors in 2,203 schools in 1958. Maintaining its dynamic prewar program for Minneapolis pupils, Farmers and Mechanics Savings Bank ranked a close third in total school savings behind two New York savings banks. With its incomparable 845 branches throughout California, the Bank of America worked closely with nearly five thousand schools, achieving 1.6 million student accounts by 1963.[21] Decades later one encounters Minnesotans and New Yorkers who insist that school programs started them on a lifetime of saving.

If the passion for "thrift" declined after 1960, the widespread commitment to saving did not. George Katona, long-time surveyor of consumer behavior, was emphatic on this point. Writing in 1965, he dismissed arguments that the nation had lost the will to save because of easy credit or the spread of pension plans. In the minds of "very many Americans, the accepted or desired standard of living consists not only of the possession of consumer goods," but also of the accumulation of ample reserve funds. Americans, he concluded, were "security-minded" as well as "thing-minded."[22]

"Buy Anything": The Political Economy of Abundance

Americans might have saved at rates of 7 to 10 percent indefinitely. But beginning in the 1980s, something snapped. No one factor explains the collapse of household saving in this country. Several long-term developments combined with more recent changes to produce a perfect American storm.

These developments were in large part related to the emergence of consumer spending as the mainstay of both economic policy and popular culture in the United States. In the course of the twentieth century, the U.S. government increasingly promoted consumption, not saving, as the engine of growth. The origins of such thinking are diffuse. Some labor leaders and theorists began arguing for the socioeconomic benefits of consumption as early as the 1880s and 1890s. A better-paid workforce, they reasoned, would consume more, leading to increased production and still higher wages.[23] The business community, for its part, had long insisted that a wealthy economy rested on consumers indulging their desires and circulating money rapidly. At the height of World War I, manufacturers and retailers resisted the U.S. government's war savings campaign more forcefully than elsewhere. Advertisers in the 1920s discovered ingenious methods to stoke consumer demand, contributing to widespread purchases of home appliances and automobiles.[24]

In the ensuing Great Depression, the most forceful proponents of mass consumption were progressives associated with Keynesianism.

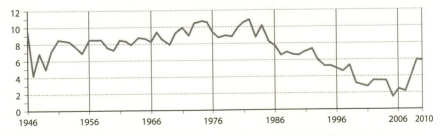

Figure 36. U.S. Personal (Household) Saving Rates, 1946–2010 (Percent of Disposable Personal Income). Source: U.S. Department of Commerce, Bureau of Economic Analysis.

This was, to be precise, Keynesianism spoken with an American accent. Back in England, John Maynard Keynes challenged the conventional wisdom that saving was always a good thing. In an oft-quoted radio address in 1931, Keynes informed listeners that it would be "harmful and misguided" to save more than usual amid the present downturn. For, "whenever you save five shillings, you put a man out of work for a day." Therefore, "O patriotic housewives, sally out tomorrow early into the streets and go to the wonderful sales," armed with the "added joy that you are increasing employment, adding to the wealth of the country." Nonetheless, Keynes would never be a champion of increased consumer spending per se. It was "quite right," he also told his audience, to save more when the economy was not in recession.[25] Above all, Keynes advocated countercyclical policies focused on government spending. In times of deep recession, governments should spend at extraordinary levels to stimulate production, employment, and ultimately consumer demand. Yet in boom times, and especially wartime as we have seen, Keynes favored programs to encourage, even compel greater saving.

American Keynesians, on the other hand, approached saving and spending with exceptional optimism. Although some echoed the master in emphasizing countercyclical policies, many others sought to create a high-growth economy that would be *permanently* sustained by mass consumption. The words they chose are telling. Visions of "abundance" abounded. These were deeply rooted in images of an America blessed by ample land and bountiful harvests. By the late nineteenth century, many became persuaded that industrialization would solve the age-old problem of scarcity and produce consumer goods for the entire society. The Great Depression did not dash this optimism, but stoked it. The problem was not overproduction, they concluded, but "underconsumption." And the solution would be to increase "mass purchasing power." Proclaimed the liberal columnist George Soule in 1932, "everyone ought to have a large enough income to buy what he needs."[26]

Such thinking gained influence among economists and officials in the Roosevelt Administration. Chaired by Secretary of Interior Harold L. Ickes, the National Resources Committee released the first survey of consumer spending in 1939. The rationale is noteworthy. Because of the country's "rich abundance of natural resources and an undreamt-of capacity to convert this natural wealth into useful goods and services," the economy would prosper once "the consumers of the Nation are able to buy the output of goods and services which industry can produce." Mass production must be matched with "mass consumption" befitting an "'American' standard of living."[27]

Keynesian New Dealers could not achieve the desired levels of mass consumption by peacetime policies. The country's entry into World War II enabled Keynesians to imagine a postwar economy in which consumer spending fueled growth on a permanent basis. Suddenly American industry was producing on a scale heretofore inconceivable. In 1944 Robert Nathan, a liberal economist in the government, published the remarkable book *Mobilizing for Abundance*. He laid out many of the arguments that would underpin policies toward consumption and saving in postwar America. To achieve "*continuous* high levels" of production, employment, and income after the war, the nation "must increase consumption and reduce savings." His key to growth could be summarized in five words: "Spending Creates Jobs and Prosperity." Nathan dismissed ethical attempts to distinguish some types of spending as wise or good for employment and others as extravagant. "All spending for goods and services is important," he retorted. The economist presented consumption as an entitlement and quintessentially American. Anyone who criticized consumer spending "is thereby critical of the economic system under which we operate." Under "our economic way of life," people worked to produce goods and services, and their earnings gave them the "right" to buy those goods and services.[28]

At the same time, Nathan and others ridiculed the virtues of saving. It was as if Bernard Mandeville's *Fable of the Bees* had come to life after two centuries of slumber. During the 1910s, the influential economist Simon Patten proposed that extravagance be considered more socially beneficial than abstinence, observing the "non-saver is now a higher type of man than the saver."[29] Nathan, for his part, blamed excessive saving for the onset of the Depression. He also worried about the current extraordinary levels of saving in wartime. If Americans could not reduce overall savings by one-third to one-half, the postwar economy could not maintain full employment. Thrift, he sneered, "may be good for the soul, but ..." Nathan endorsed only one mode of saving, that which created assets such as homes and consumer durables.

Nathan's case rested on a politically progressive understanding of who saved. The affluent tended to save at much higher rates than lower-income households, observed the Keynesians. Accordingly, there were obvious limits to how much the wealthy would consume. If one wanted to induce greater spending to stimulate the economy, the surest way would be to raise the incomes and therefore the purchasing power of lower-income people who constitute the bulk of the populace. This could be done most effectively, the Keynesians argued, by government policy. The government should spend mightily to promote full employment while taxing incomes at highly progressive rates. The new Social Security Act of 1935 would also persuade people to consume, economists believed, by relieving them of anxieties about saving so much for old age. [30]

The Keynesian faith in large-scale government spending would not fare well after World War II. In the battle to enact the Employment Act of 1946, Congressional conservatives—supported by employers— eliminated the key liberal provision stipulating that government intervene to ensure full employment.[31] Yet one part of American Keynesianism survived and thrived. An impressively diverse coalition of groups and ideologies came to believe in the centrality of consumption in postwar economic growth. Manufacturers, merchants, and marketers had no problem recognizing the benefits of mass consumption. Together with sympathetic government agencies and the media, they promoted consumer spending as essential to sustaining the country's ever-surging production. The U.S. Department of Commerce installed a giant population clock in the lobby during the 1950s. Flashing each time a baby was born, the display proclaimed: "More People Mean More Markets." U.S. News and World Report likewise ran the story, "A Bonanza for Industry—Babies. Sixty Million More U.S. Consumers in Next Nineteen Years."[32]

More surprising was organized labor's unequivocal embrace of mass consumption. In postwar Europe and Japan, labor and socialist leaders were conversely supporting savings and austerity campaigns. They regarded increased saving as indispensable to curbing inflation, financing production, and creating jobs. To many on the Left in these nations, the promotion of consumption would only widen the gap between rich and poor while encouraging the purchase of foreign-made goods. American labor officials saw things differently. They were obsessed, notes Lizabeth Cohen, with expanding workers' capacity to spend. Rather than demand more involvement in company decision-making or generous social benefits from the government, postwar unions focused on maximizing wages. Walter Ruether, famed head of the United Auto Workers, cast labor's fight in terms of not only securing better wages to help Joe Smith provide for his family, but also to give the millions of Joneses and Smiths "greater purchasing power because the nation needs this greater purchasing power" to increase production.[33] For American labor to argue that more spending meant more jobs was hardly illogical during the early postwar years. With European and Japanese industries crippled by the war, U.S. manufacturers made nearly everything Americans consumed. "Buy, buy, buy," in the words of one 1958 advertisement, "it's your patriotic duty."[34]

The prospect of a consumer-driven economy achieved bipartisan consensus. Keynesian-minded Democratic administrations strove to increase the purchasing power of ordinary Americans. So did the Republican Eisenhower Administration. In the years following World War II, the federal government introduced or expanded a series of policies that single-mindedly promoted consumption. The tax-deductibility of interest on home mortgages may be the best known. Another was the tax cut. When Keynes wrote in the 1930s, the U.S. government possessed no mechanism to stimulate consumer demand directly. Most people paid no income tax until World War II. The number of American income taxpayers leaped from seven million in 1940 to more than forty-two million in 1946. In 1954 President Eisenhower reduced taxes explicitly to help households "increase their purchasing power." In addition, Congress revised tax legislation in the late 1940s so as to incentivize consumer credit. Interest on loans, including installment buying and personal loans, became tax-deductible. When it came to saving, however, the U.S. tax code was remarkably stingy. Although interest on savings bonds was exempt from state taxes, the federal government taxed interest on savings accounts and savings bonds in full.[35] The postwar U.S. case later struck many as the mirror image of high-saving Japan, where the tax code exempted earnings on most savings accounts while granting no breaks to borrowers.

Nonetheless, there remained considerable ambivalence about encouraging consumption to the detriment of saving. President Eisenhower was personally uneasy about the proconsumption positions of some economic advisors. After advising Americans to buy "anything" at the 1958 press conference, he was reminded that his secretary of treasury had just launched a savings bond campaign asking citizens to be thrifty. Eisenhower quickly recovered. Warning the public against buying "carelessly," the president lashed out against manufacturers who "chucked" items down the people's throats rather than giving them "the things we want."[36]

Intellectual critics of mass consumption went further in a number of best sellers. In *The Affluent Society* (1958), John Kenneth Galbraith, a prominent Keynesian economist, nonetheless denounced the consumer economy as unsustainable. Booms would be followed by busts. Advertisers engaged in "want creation" to convince Americans to buy more and incur greater consumer debt. Overly indebted consumers would then cut back spending, leading to higher unemployment. Ultimately households would be worse off. The Board of Governors of the Federal Reserve, complained Galbraith, was doing little to prevent this scenario, because "nothing in our economic policy is so deeply ingrained, and so little reckoned with by economists, as our tendency to wait and see if things do not improve by themselves." The harshest critic was no doubt Vance Packard, whose blockbuster *The Hidden Persuaders* (1957) excoriated the advertising industry. In *The Waste Makers* (1960), Packard linked excessive consumption to environmental degradation. Manufacturers and marketers deliberately encouraged waste and "thriftlessness" to persuade people to throw away the old and buy the newest products. But "if you decide to save, pay off your debts," as he quoted one syndicated columnist on family finance, "you help slow down business."[37]

The ambivalence about consumption soon receded to the margins of American public discourse inhabited by environmentalists and advocates of simple living. By the 1980s and 1990s, the salience of consumer spending over saving had become the common sense of journalism and policymaking. Keynesian economics declined under President Ronald Reagan and with it the belief in *government* spending to stimulate demand. Consumers, however, were expected to keep on spending to sustain the growing production ostensibly unleashed by Reagan's much lower rates of taxation.[38] What also changed was the relation between spending and domestic production. It no longer mattered *where* goods were made. In 1950 when U.S. firms dominated global manufacturing, labor leaders could plausibly argue that consumer spending created American jobs and prosperity. Yet as European and Japanese manufacturers recovered and other exporting powerhouses arose in Asia, Americans bought more and more from abroad. Exhortations to "buy anything" yielded less payoff to the highly paid, unionized American workers who had been a fixture of the early postwar economy but were fast dwindling.

Over the past thirty years the media has been obsessed with measuring the health of the nation's economy at year's end. Journalists might have reported on levels of income equality, rates of high school completion, or infant mortality. But no. The big story has been whether Americans will flock to the malls at Christmastime in numbers sufficient to sustain economic growth. In 1991 President George H. W. Bush visited a J. C. Penny store accompanied by several television crews. The Consumer in Chief bought four pairs of white socks and a child's sweat suit to "promote the holiday shopping spirit."[39]

U.S. administrations also stepped up efforts to persuade the world of the genius of the consumer-driven economy. In 1993 President Bill Clinton traveled to Tokyo to lecture Japanese students on the need to stop their government from promoting production over consumption and exports over domestic sales. Japanese must buy more to help not just American manufacturers but themselves. For the Japanese people, stated the president, are *"entitled* to no less."[40] In the most recent replay, U.S. officials and economists harangue the Chinese to cease saving excessively and start consuming what they make (see chapter 10).

America's fixation on consumption reached new heights following the terrorist attacks of September 11, 2001. George W. Bush became the first modern president who did *not* propose higher taxes and greater saving to finance the wars in Afghanistan and Iraq. When the House of Representatives passed legislation giving the Treasury Department the authority to issue "Patriot Bonds," the Bush administration did its best to neuter the program. It was more important, spokesmen insisted, to encourage consumers to *spend* to "fight global terrorism." Best remembered was President Bush's advice just two weeks after 9/11. Americans should respond to the terrorists by getting "down to Disney World ... and enjoy life, the way we want it to be enjoyed."[41] Advertising campaigns that autumn urged Americans to shop to demonstrate their patriotism. Don't "let the terrorists get you down," trumpeted car manufacturers offering free credit.[42] At Christmastime 2006, even as several prominent economists predicted the imminent bursting of the housing bubble, Mr. Bush fell back on the familiar: "I encourage you all to go shopping more."[43]

Though ridiculed for his choice of words, the president reflected a deep-seated cultural shift. Among economists and policymakers, Republicans and Democrats, mass consumption had become the prescription for whatever ailed the economy. Gone were the days when presidents urged Americans to buy savings bonds and spend prudently. The growing faith in a consumer-driven economy resulted in policy after policy that encouraged Americans not simply to abandon habits of saving, but to live beyond their means.

Credit and the "American Standard of Living"

The decline of saving in recent decades rests, above all, on the extraordinary expansion of credit in the United States. We may divide household borrowing into consumer credit and housing credit, although the line has often blurred. Both have long histories that distinguish America from the high-saving societies of Europe and East Asia.

Large numbers of Americans became accustomed to consumer credit during the 1920s. The installment plan, its most popular form, dated further back to the latter half of the nineteenth century. As Americans were paid increasingly in wages and salaries, dealers in furniture and pianos offered customers the option of purchasing goods with a down payment and the balance to be repaid in regular monthly installments. By folding the interest charges into the price of the commodity, these practices circumvented English common law on usury. No firm did as much to standardize and globalize the installment plan as Singer Sewing Machine Company. The sewing machine was undoubtedly the world's first mass-produced consumer durable. To make machines affordable to emerging middle-class housewives, Singer pioneered the installment plan at midcentury. The company sold sewing machines all over the world, including Japan where Singer introduced its installment plan in 1907.[44]

Following World War I, consumer finance companies exploded on the scene to finance the installment purchases of durable goods. According to economist Edwin Seligman at the time, installment sales in 1926 amounted to nearly 12 percent of total retail sales. The installment plan enabled Americans of modest means to buy the newest and costliest durable, the automobile. Already in 1925, installment sales accounted for 59 percent of the value of new cars sold. Established as the finance wing of General Motors in 1919, General Motors Acceptance Corporation joined other large finance companies to make automobile credit an integral part of American life. By 1930, installment purchases also comprised well over half of the sales volume for several household goods including washing machines, phonographs, radios, vacuum cleaners, and furniture.[45]

Permitting customers to buy goods without saving up in full, the installment plan enabled Americans to consume at levels far above Europeans. Thanks to the International Labor Office, we are afforded a fascinating snapshot of consumption and savings patterns on both sides of the Atlantic. In 1929 the London subsidiary of Ford Motor asked the ILO to assess relative costs of living in several European cities so as to calculate "how much a European worker would need to expend if his general standard of living were to be approximately equivalent to that of his Detroit counterpart." To no one's surprise, the "American standard of living" was shown to be in a league of its own. Workers in the fourteen surveyed European cities lacked the amenities commonly enjoyed by Ford workers and families in Detroit. European workers rarely lived in detached houses as did a majority of their Detroit counterparts.

Nor were their homes equipped with central heating, electricity, or gas. Bathrooms scarcely existed. Among employees in Ford's factory in Antwerp, Belgium, "no working-class dwelling is equipped to permit of washing oneself properly."

By contrast, the ILO survey found that the families of even the lowest-paid, full-time Detroit workers possessed an array of "modern conveniences." Of the hundred such families surveyed, forty-seven owned cars and eighty had sewing machines. In addition, fifty-one possessed washing machines, forty-five owned phonographs, thirty-six radios, and twenty-one vacuum cleaners. Credit was at the core of Detroit's household spending. A majority of families bought at least one durable on installment that year, and a quarter purchased two or more. The investigators, in large part Europeans, voiced amazement at Detroit workers' savings habits or lack thereof. Although he suffered little or no unemployment in 1929, the typical Detroit worker saved nothing apart from a relatively small portion of income devoted to insurance premiums. Only thirty-seven families in the sample reported savings, whereas nineteen spent all they earned, and an astounding forty-four families lived beyond their means.[46] Installment buying was becoming America's accepted alternative to saving.

Transatlantic differences in consumer credit and saving were accentuated by contrasting government policies. Prior to World War II, the American political system demonstrated little interest in regulating consumer credit to prevent overindebtedness. Joined by bankers and labor unions, middle-class magazines had come to embrace installment buying as good for the economy during the 1920s. Despite reformers' efforts at the state level, legislation to protect consumers from installment lenders' abusive practices never saw the light of day.[47] Europeans, on the other hand, actively restrained the growth of installment credit. Powerful German and French savings banks associations lobbied for stringent regulations during the 1930s.[48] Frenchmen commonly criticized installment buying for undermining the nation's famed prudence. The system, according to one specialist in 1934, created unsustainable desires in consumers to live off future income; they became accustomed to an "artificially high standard of living." Moreover, French law on movable property gave title to the possessor, impeding the seller from repossession in the case of default. Or take the case of Italy, where stigma of consumer credit remains to this day. While the U.S. automobile and home appliance industries surged during the 1920s on the basis of installment sales, public disapproval squelched the formation of Italian consumer finance companies until the 1950s. Not surprising, in 1952, the United States boasted one passenger auto registered for every four persons, in contrast to twenty-six in France, and ninety in Italy.[49]

Within Europe, the installment plan advanced furthest in Britain where it was called "hire purchase." Yet Britons too exhibited greater political discomfort with consumer credit than Americans. In 1938 Parliament enacted the Hire-Purchase Act. While recognizing the legitimacy of hire purchase, the legislation aimed to protect consumers from being duped into assuming crushing levels of debt. The law required that customers be clearly apprised of the extra costs of buying on credit. Most important, the act restricted the seller's right to repossess an item. Once the buyer paid one-third of the purchase price, he could not be deprived of the good until a court or other mediation process judged the merits of the case. Britain's political parties were strikingly unified on the need to regulate installment sales. Although the act began as the private bill of a left-wing Labour Party member, it soon won the approval of the business-friendly Conservative government. Politicians echoed public outrage at the installment sellers called "tallymen" and the violent "bruisers" they employed to repossess items. The archetypal tallyman in media stories preyed on housewives who in turn could not "resist his wiles." In a heart-wrenching case recounted in Parliament, one wife who couldn't say no to the tallymen was reduced to pawning each good as soon as it arrived. One day her husband returned from work to find her dead in a gas-filled room. Holding up a bundle of hire-purchase contracts at the inquest, he cried out: "These are what killed my wife."[50]

Americans never approached Europeans in the latter's ambivalence about installment sales. Nonetheless in World War II, the U.S. government, like other belligerents, discouraged consumer credit to shrink civilian consumption and promote saving. Under Regulation W, the Federal Reserve stringently regulated installment sales, mandating higher down payments and shorter repayment periods. With peace, however, the government abandoned meaningful efforts to control consumer credit. Only in the Korean War did the Federal Reserve briefly re-impose Regulation W.[51] By 1953 installment sales accounted for 30 percent of retail sales in the United States, contrasted with only 15 percent in West Germany. Approximately 45 percent of U.S. house-holds reported using installment debt, compared to 20 percent in the United Kingdom. While most European governments subsequently *tightened* regulations over installment sales in the mid-1950s to contain inflation and increase savings, American consumers found it easier and easier to buy goods on time. Down payments declined, and repayment periods lengthened.[52]

Some commentators voiced alarm at the rise of installment credit and the exposure of millions to the "repossession man." John Kenneth Galbraith famously remarked: "Can the bill collector be the central figure in the good society?" Yet mainstream opinion was ecstatic. As businessmen and economists looked at the rest of the world, the bril-liance of installment sales appeared all too clear. Many, like economist Clyde William Phelps, extolled the installment plan as the linchpin of the vaunted "American standard of living." Visiting trade groups from Britain and France returned home in the early 1950s, he reported, convinced that consumer credit enabled the American worker to live better and produce more. Sneering at "intellectuals" who admonished the masses to save before purchasing, Phelps offered the following doomsday scenario. What would happen if consumers could secure du-rable goods only on a cash basis? He shuddered to think, but when the government had merely restricted installment credit in wartime, hadn't that resulted in declining sales, bloated inventories, and rising com-plaints by consumers?[53]

Defenders and critics debated whether cascading installment sales diminished Americans' propensity to save. The installment plan ac-tually stimulated saving, maintained the defenders. As far back as the 1920s, Professor Seligman theorized that buying on time tended to spur both the borrower's desire to work and his capacity to save to make the payments. Postwar officials and business writers agreed, arguing that that regular, fixed repayments imposed financial "discipline" on families.[54] Even William Whyte, who bemoaned thrift was now "un-American," grudged that middle-class suburbanites had become habituated to a new way of living *within* their means. Each month families found themselves curbing discretionary spending enough to repay their installment debts.[55] Economists increasingly regarded installment buying not as consumption or debt, but as a form of saving. When one borrowed to purchase a durable good like a car or washing machine, they reasoned, the consumer accumulated assets whose services could be used for years.[56] By the 1950s economic statisticians included automobiles and other durables as assets under the category of household saving.[57]

Americans' lavish use of installment credit did not obliterate saving, but defenders exaggerated its salutary effects on thrift. Household ownership of assets, acknowledged the Federal Reserve, was seldom the most cost-effective way for either consumers or the economy to utilize resources. The family vehicle or washing machine stood idle much more than if taxi companies or laundry services had employed those assets.[58] Americans would fill homes and driveways with a growing volume of goods that diminished the assets' utility and their capacity to save. Purchase of the first television might substitute for spending on sports events and movies. But the fourth one? Americans became so accustomed to buying durables on credit that most forgot that consumption could be financed in other ways. Namely they might save now and buy later.

International comparisons are enlightening. Although Western European and Japanese economies experienced "consumer revolutions" during the 1950s and 1960s, they depended far less on credit and more on savings to pay for household goods. In France, when TV sets were flying off the shelves in 1962, only 35 percent of all electronic goods and major appliances were bought on credit—in contrast to roughly 70 percent in the United States.[59] In West Germany, it remained the norm—indeed a mark of middle-class respectability—to save methodically for major purchases including homes and autos. Germans did not lack for words to describe this practice. There was *Absparen* (saving in advance), *Vorsparen* (pre-saving), and notably *Konsumsparen* (saving for consumption). Would-be home owners typically opened special savings accounts at building associations (*Bausparkassen*), patiently depositing until they accumulated a significant portion of the purchase price and then they borrowed the rest. The pollster George Katona discerned stark differences in German and American attitudes. When asked why they saved in 1966, Americans mentioned, above all, "rainy days" (46 percent), followed by retirement (31 percent) and children's needs/education (22 percent). A mere 7 percent said they saved to buy durable goods. By contrast, according to a West German survey the following year, saving for large purchases topped the list at 59 percent as the most popular reason. German respondents recorded high rates of public disapproval of installment buying throughout the 1950s and 1960s.[60]

The growing reliance on installment credit apparently did little to erode the U.S. saving rate, which exceeded 9 percent in 1970. This may have been due in part to the disciplinary effect of the installment plan. A more compelling explanation, however, has been offered by Louis Hyman. Americans incurred debt comfortably during the 1950s and 1960s because of rapidly rising real wages among all income groups. On an annual basis, the nation paid back nearly all installment credit that had been extended.[61] But what would happen when the unparalleled prosperity of the postwar decades came to a close? By then an article of faith among politicians and ordinary people, consumer credit not only continued to surge, it assumed less sustainable forms.

Saving through Housing

Just as consumer credit became recognized as an alternative form of saving, the home mortgage took its place in the postwar United States as the primary, virtually unquestioned means of building household wealth. Housing credit trumped consumer credit in several respects. Interest charges on mortgages were well below those on consumer debt. Unlike durable goods, houses rarely depreciated. On the contrary, inflation-adjusted housing prices *appreciated* modestly at 0.7 percent on an annual basis nationwide from 1940 to 2004.[62] By repaying their loans month after month, millions of homeowners accumulated equity and sizable nest eggs. They also enjoyed years of living in their homes. In booming housing markets, investment in one's home might return gains far above those on savings in banks or bonds. Paying down the mortgage superseded conventional saving for the vast majority of American families. The U.S. rate of home ownership, which stood at 44 percent of American families in 1940, soared to 62 percent by 1960. It reached 68 percent by 2004.

For all its benefits, easy housing credit in postwar America tended to depress overall saving by stimulating consumption and consumer credit. Homeowners, observed the Federal Reserve, were more likely than renters to install washing machines, dryers, and freezers. Moreover, the skyrocketing construction of detached single-family houses in the suburbs during the 1950s required greater numbers of cars and increasing gasoline consumption.[63] Attractive home financing encouraged the building of larger homes. Owners found themselves spending and borrowing more to furnish, renovate, heat, and cool the additional space. The average size of a new single-family home in the United States more than doubled after the early postwar years—from a cramped 983 square feet in 1950 to 2,349 sq. ft. in 2004. A majority of these homes lacked a garage or car port in 1950, whereas by the end of the period, 64 percent included two-car garages and another 19 percent came with garages big enough for three cars. Economists do not commonly relate house size to savings behavior. It's worth considering, though, that the high-saving peoples of Europe and East Asia tend to live in much smaller houses, and larger percentages occupy apartments than Americans. Recently the average size of a Japanese dwelling was only 1021 sq. ft, while newly constructed dwellings averaged 1,226 sq. ft in Germany, 1,212 sq. ft in France, and merely 877 sq. ft in Italy.[64] All things being equal, less space means less stuff and more savings.

Home ownership and mortgages came to define the American way of life in large part because of public policy. For nearly eighty years the federal government has promoted home ownership and housing credit. These policies first appeared as emergency responses to the Great Depression. Established in 1933, the New Deal's Home Owners Loan Corporation (HOLC) helped refinance more than one million mortgages to protect desperate homeowners from foreclosure. One year later legislation created the Federal Housing Administration (FHA), first and foremost, as a jobs policy. Workers in the building trades accounted for roughly one-third of the nation's unemployed. The twin goals of increasing home ownership and supporting homebuilders as a linchpin of the economy continued into the postwar era. They go a long way toward explaining why the federal government so tenaciously promotes easy housing credit to this day.

The FHA was revolutionary. The government agency insured mortgages offered by private lenders. Together with the HOLC, the FHA introduced and standardized the long-term amortized mortgage. Prior to the New Deal era, most mortgages required down payments of at least 30 percent and had to be repaid in full at the end of five or ten years. In practice, homeowners refinanced outstanding debt at the end of each cycle, but many faced foreclosure when incomes and credit collapsed in the Depression. FHA-insured mortgages reduced down payments to 10 percent or less and required monthly payments to be spread over twenty-five to thirty years, making repayment more manageable. Thanks to government guarantees, interest rates on mortgages dropped two to three points. Suddenly homeownership became possible for Americans of moderate means.[65]

Homeownership received its greatest official support following World War II. One in four homes in 1960 had been constructed in the 1950s. Enactment of the GI Bill in 1944 laid the basis for the vast expansion of government-secured mortgages. Millions of veterans took advantage of not only FHA mortgages, but the new Veterans Administration's willingness to provide $2,000 in insurance for the loan. Serving as collateral, this sum enabled veterans to buy a home with no down payments. Congress in the early postwar years enthusiastically appropriated billions of dollars to support FHA and VA loans. As Kathleen Frydl observes, what began as a government benefit soon evolved into the individual's "right" to own a home. Equally enduring has been tax deductibility of home-mortgage interest and property taxes. Although these provisions date back to the federal income tax rules of 1913, the extension of the income tax to most Americans in wartime powerfully encouraged postwar home ownership. This federal subsidy, wrote Kenneth Jackson, already totaled $53 billion annually by 1984 and was four to five times greater than Congress's direct spending on housing.[66]

The U.S. government's promotion of affordable home mortgages had far-reaching consequences for how Americans saved. Postwar politicians evinced little enthusiasm for policies that would encourage rentals for middle-class families, much less lower-income people. Unlike "social housing" in Europe, "public housing" programs in the United States aimed only at the poorest families and then as the last resort. During the late 1940s, the National Association of Home Builders and allies in Congress attacked even modest public-housing legislation as "socialistic" and "communistic," singling out allegedly disastrous results in contemporary Britain. Granting cheap mortgages and tax breaks to homeowners, federal policies in effect punished renters. Renting became so stigmatized culturally that large numbers of apartment dwellers struggled to buy the vaunted single-family house and realize the "American Dream." The incentive structure drove households to plow the lion's share of their wealth into houses rather than diversify savings and retain liquid funds for consumption and emergencies.[67] Nonetheless, the American way of saving worked fairly well in the 1960s and 1970s. Inflation reduced the real burden of housing debt. Most home owners moreover enjoyed fixed-rate mortgages, secure jobs, and cost-of-living wage increases.[68] As with consumer credit, what would happen when the music stopped?

Keep on Borrowing

The last thirty years have witnessed not so much the collapse of thrift in America as the growing imbalance between the institutional encouragement of saving on one hand and consumption and credit on the other. If this had been a baseball game between policies promoting the rival behaviors, the final score would have been something like Debt 15 and Savings 1 or 2. As the innings wore on, the pro-credit gang belted out run after run. The Savings team rarely made it to first base.

Early on, the Savings gang came out swinging. In the late 1970s, conservatives and liberals alike worried about the nation's apparently declining household saving rates. The government's recalibrated statistics now show that Americans achieved some of their highest postwar saving rates in that era. At the time, policymakers and economists were convinced that the saving rate had fallen to 3 percent. U.S. industries struggled to compete with those in high-saving West Germany and Japan. Politicians focused first on promoting saving for retirement. In 1978 Congress established 401(k) retirement accounts at the workplace. Three years later tax legislation laid the basis for Individual Retirement Accounts. In both types of accounts, one put aside money tax-deferred until withdrawal. IRAs remain capped at fairly low annual contributions; 401(k) accounts have higher limits, often supplemented by employers' contributions. Retirement accounts became a popular form of saving. Participants in 401(k)-type plans grew steadily from some ten million in 1985 to nearly fifty-five million in 2005.[69]

If the goal were to spur saving throughout society, however, retirement accounts have fallen short. Even as participation in retirement plans rose, the nation's household saving rates plummeted. For the most part, these plans reward people who are already good savers. Also, rather than increase savings overall, they incentivize households to *shift* assets to retirement accounts from more liquid savings, which do not enjoy tax-deductibility. Like most other tax-advantaged measures in postwar America—notably the home-mortgage deduction—retirement savings plans reinforce income inequality. Lower- and middle-income workers gain little federal tax benefit from owning a 401(k) account or IRA. The majority of American taxpayers—currently in the 10, 15, or 25 percent bracket—might reduce their taxes by no more than that percentage and usually less. Better-paid employees, whose marginal tax rates range from 28 to 35 percent, choose to participate in 401(k) plans at much higher rates than low-wage counterparts when offered the opportunity to do so by employers. Moreover, lower-income workers are less likely to work for an employer who offers a 401(k)-type plan.[70]

Retirement savings schemes in the United States thus represent a sort of reverse Robin Hood. Globally savings-promotion efforts over the past two centuries aimed at inducing not the affluent, but those of modest means, to save. Including 401(k)-type plans and IRAs, retirement savings plans have failed to enroll a majority of working Americans. In 2007 only 40.6 percent of families had a participant in retirement plans through a current job (including those with traditional company-provided pensions). Nor have those who do participate in defined-contribution plans—primarily 401(k)s—adequately saved for retirement. The median balance of such plans stood at merely $31,800 in 2007. That was *before* the financial meltdown eroded the market value of retirement savings. Three years later 54 percent of surveyed workers report their households' total savings and investments (not including their home and any traditional pensions) to be less than $25,000. Incredibly, 27 percent claim less than $1,000 in savings.[71] If things weren't bad enough, the government's promotion of 401(k) plans has encouraged many companies to abandon the more costly defined-benefit plan that guaranteed millions of postwar workers a pension in old age.[72]

The second great effort to promote saving emerged from growing sentiment for financial deregulation in the 1970s and early 1980s. This may seem strange. We now look back on this era as the start of policies that unleashed the consumer finance industry at the expense of saving. Yet at the time, champions of deregulation were equally concerned about the adverse impact of bank regulations on small savers. Interest rates on savings accounts used to be capped by Regulation Q, which covered banks and savings and loan associations. Because of their central role in financing home mortgages, S&Ls were permitted to pay depositors interest rates slightly higher than commercial banks. The S&Ls profited from regulation until the late 1970s, when several years of double-digit inflation threatened their existence while eroding the value of their customers' savings. Depositors transferred billions of dollars from savings and loan accounts to money market funds—nonbank institutions that barely existed five years earlier. Loosely regulated, money market funds offered yields as much as 10 or 11 percent above the S&Ls. A bipartisan consensus developed to eliminate the seemingly outmoded, inefficient aspects of regulation. President Jimmy Carter, a Democrat, worked with Congress to pass the first Depository Institutions Deregulation Act in 1980. By prohibiting banks and S&Ls from paying market rates on deposits, White House officials reasoned, Regulation Q "discourages savings and encourages consumption." Carter celebrated the bill's passage as a big victory for "small savers" who would henceforth receive rates of return similar to those enjoyed by "rich investors."[73]

Deregulation turned out to be a mixed blessing for the small saver. The 1980 legislation did not in fact eliminate Regulation Q, but the Garn-St. Germain Act of 1982—signed by Republican president Ronald Reagan—effectively ended interest rate caps. S&Ls could now offer market rates on deposits while gaining the freedom to make loans beyond home mortgages. Many S&Ls plunged into risky investments to pay depositors higher interest rates and often line their own pockets. Bad investments in commercial real estate between 1983 and 1985 resulted in the failure of more than one thousand S&Ls. The Federal Savings and Loan Insurance Corporation lacked adequate reserves to protect depositors. Taxpayers eventually footed the bill for the largest cleanup of savings institutions since the Great Depression. The surviving savings and loan associations no longer dominated either the small savings or home mortgage market.[74]

Contrary to conventional wisdom, the Great Inflation and S&L debacle did not necessarily diminish Americans' desire to save. Households appear to have been scared thrifty. A great many strove to save more to keep up with inflation. Saving rates rose to the 9–11 percent range during the first half of the 1980s and remained above 7 percent until 1993. At the same time, these developments led to fundamental changes in *how* Americans saved. By the end of the 1980s, writes Joseph Nocera, millions regarded themselves no longer as savers but as "investors." Depositors who had previously saved for years at the same bank began moving their money in and out of money market funds and bank certificates of deposit in the hot pursuit of higher returns.

With the advent of the bull market of 1982–87, many Americans advanced to the next stage of buying stocks or mutual funds made up of stocks. Led by *Money* magazine, the media harangued the nation to buy equities. Stockholding soared during the 1990s, when the inflation-adjusted Standard & Poor index more than doubled. By 2001, 52 percent of households participated in the stock market. Many owned corporate shares directly, but many more bought mutual funds or invested in stock portfolios within their retirement savings plans. No other nation came close. Comparable stock market participation rates in the late 1990s stood at 34 percent in the United Kingdom, 25 percent in Japan, and 19 percent each in Germany and Italy. The U.S.'s middle class, wrote Nocera, had joined the "money class."[75] Americans, enthused economists, need not save as much as Japanese and Europeans who clung to low-return savings accounts; households could build their assets more efficiently by investing in stocks and housing. Hadn't U.S. stock markets substantially outperformed other forms of saving in the long term?

But had middle-class Americans become successful investors? Or did commentators just think they had? In 2004 less than half of the nation's households held any stocks, directly or indirectly; only 35 percent had stock holdings exceeding $6,000. The stock market, concludes the Economic Policy Institute, has been of "little or no direct financial importance to the large majority of U.S. households."[76] For the minority who do hold sizable equity positions, the stock market's booms and busts since 2000 render it an uncertain vehicle for amassing savings—long term or short term. The mania for "investment" led millions of Americans to embrace high levels of risk while abandoning the slow and steady habits that mark small saving.

Bear in mind that retirement savings plans and deregulation of savings institutions have been the two major initiatives aimed at promoting saving. Keeping with the baseball metaphor, it's not clear either crossed the plate. Nearly every other innovation since 1980 has *discouraged* prudence. It started with credit cards. Charge cards for gas stations and department stores became popular following World War II. During the 1950s, these cards commonly offered revolving credit. Rather than repay charges in full at the end of the monthly billing cycle, consumers could choose to repay the debt over time subject to interest charges. Led by the Bank of America, large banks in the late 1950s began issuing universal credit cards that would be honored by a broad array of merchants. These operations coalesced into the two networks we know today as Visa and MasterCard. Bank cards targeted relatively affluent consumers who could be expected to repay in a timely fashion. The banks' credit card operations were not very profitable, particularly amid the inflation of the late 1970s. Usury laws in each state prevented banks from charging rates of interest higher than 18 percent on average, even as the cost of capital soared.

Come the revolution. The same deregulatory fever that eliminated interest rate caps on deposits transformed the credit card industry. In the Marquette decision of 1978, the Supreme Court ruled a bank may charge out-of-state customers the highest interest rate permitted in that bank's home state. Emboldened, New York's Citibank moved its entire credit card division to South Dakota in 1981 after persuading the governor and legislature to eliminate the state's usury laws. Other states joined in the mad dash to lure credit card operations.[77] Bank cards became truly national and increasingly unregulated. Card companies could set interest rates as high as they pleased. The banks' credit card divisions leaped from loss-leaders to cash cows. Innovations in credit-scoring further permitted banks to vastly expand their customer base on the basis of seemingly more accurate risk assessment. In 1970 a mere 16 percent of households possessed a bank credit card. That figure rose to 73 percent by 2001.[78] Few Americans now leave home without one (or two, three, or four).

The explosion of credit cards profoundly affected how Americans save and consume. The nation's love affair with the installment plan cooled after the 1950s. Credit cards emerged as the dominant means of purchasing on credit, excepting car sales on installment. Credit cards eroded habits of saving as the installment plan had not. Behavioral economists confirm that people are likely to spend more and pay higher prices when they use credit cards. Plastic liberated the consumer from the discipline of the installment plan. Gone were those regular monthly payments bounded by one- to three-year terms. With a universal credit card, the amount of each monthly bill varies considerably, and the consumer repays at the time of his or her choosing. Remarkably, nearly half of bank cardholders surveyed over the past three decades admit they "hardly ever" pay off balances.[79] The impersonal nature of bank card purchases moreover removed previous inhibitions against bingeing on installment or charge cards. No longer does the customer deal with a credit manager to beg for more credit or conclude an installment contract. No longer is consumer debt attached to a specific good. And no longer does the defaulter risk humiliation in front of neighbors when the "repo man" comes to reclaim the fridge.

The banks were not ones to merely watch Americans spend beyond their means. To maximize profits, the consumer finance industry devised new practices that actively encouraged households to assume greater debt. By the early 1990s, card companies determined they earned little from those who paid in full each month. Although so-called convenience users accounted for nearly half of cardholders at the time, the industry ironically disparaged their most reliable customers as "deadbeats." The real money would be made on "revolvers," the remaining half to three-fifths of cardholders. The banks vigorously targeted the "subprime" market—poorer households that, according to mathematical models, had not previously qualified for credit cards but appeared capable of taking on more debt. Between 1989 and 2004, very-low-income families (under $10,000) possessing credit cards grew from 23 to 35 percent, far faster than among other income groups. Card companies also lowered the minimum monthly payment to only 2 percent, while substantially raising limits on the money customers could borrow. A cardholder who simply makes the minimum payment each month— and millions do—would repay the original balance in some 35 years.

In 1996 Citibank won a Supreme Court ruling that effectively eliminated the remaining state regulations on fees and maximum interest charges. This cleared the way for practices we know today as predatory lending. Even if one's payment were just hours late, banks began charging not only an exorbitant late fee but a new "default rate" on existing debt. This often raises interest charges from 12 percent to 30 percent or more. Card companies also introduced "universal default," whereby any change in one's overall credit score (say, from a missed payment to *another* lender) triggers the default rate. Few consumers understood the consequences of revolving credit in part because the industry buried the details in pages and pages of fine print.[80]

The credit card's impact on saving varies by income and age. Median household income (in 2008 dollars) has hovered around $50,000 over the last decade. For many families near that level or below, credit card debt depletes savings and makes it difficult to start saving again.

Investigations by Demos and the Center for Responsible Lending reveal the everyday hardships. Their 2005 survey of low- and middle-income households with credit card debt measured median card debt at $5,000, while one-third reported card debt over $10,000.[81] A majority that used credit cards to pay for basic necessities such as rent or groceries had less than $1,000 in nonretirement savings. Nearly half of card-indebted households with incomes under $10,000 and roughly one-quarter of those between $10,000 and $50,000 spent more than two-fifth of their incomes to service those debts in 2004.[82]

Households enjoying upper-middle and higher incomes are better able to handle credit card debt, yet rising balances have also left many with less to save. A majority of bank-cardholding families with incomes of $50,000–99,999 have carried balances in every survey since the early 1980s. Worse, those suffering "debt hardship"—devoting more than two-fifths of income to service card debts—rose to 12 percent in this cohort in 2004. Even among high-income households ($100,000 or more), some 7 percent experienced card debt hardship.[83]

Most troubling for the future of saving are the credit habits of college students. A 2008 survey by Sallie Mae concluded that many students "use credit cards to live beyond their means." Eighty-four percent of undergraduates had credit cards—half of them possessing *four or more*. One-fifth of them carried balances of $3,000 to $7,000. Only 17 percent paid their bill in full each month. Over the past two decades the industry has bombarded undergraduates with solicitations, assisted by colleges that permitted on-campus vendors often in exchange for kickbacks.[84] Students were an easy mark. Prior to 2010, they could sign up for credit cards without parental permission upon turning eighteen. Where once American schools ran savings programs to encourage thrift, credit card companies now cultivate an entire generation addicted to consumer debt.

Dissaving through Housing

Critics have railed against the corrosive effects of credit cards since the 1980s. In those same years a quieter transformation ultimately eviscerated the savings of far greater numbers of Americans. In 1986 Congress passed the sweeping Tax Reform Bill. Contained within the legislation was a provision that fundamentally changed the postwar tax advantages of consumer credit. Home mortgages remained deductible, but the law phased out the deductibility of interest on installment purchases, credit cards, personal loans, and student loans. The only major exception would be home equity loans, sometimes called second mortgages. These involve using one's accrued home equity as collateral. Just as a Supreme Court ruling unleashed the credit card, the Tax Reform Act elevated the home equity loan—a minor product before the mid-1980s—to the American homeowner's favorite form of consumer credit.

What was Congress thinking? The measure sailed through with little debate over the long-term implications of promoting home equity loans. Members appeared more intent on eliminating expensive tax deductions on credit cards and other consumer loans. Some like Senator Christopher Dodd (D-Conn.) thought they were *discouraging* consumer debt and encouraging saving. Home equity borrowers were frequently depicted as "better educated" and more responsible than credit card debtors. Another influential senator, William Roth (R-Del.), attempted to limit tax-deductibility to home equity loans used for home improvements, education, and medical expenses.[85]

It didn't take long for policymakers to question what Congress had wrought. Within months, financial institutions introduced an array of loans secured by home equity (HELs as they were called). Oblivious to congressional concerns, banks touted the attractions of tapping equity to pay for vacations, cars, and weddings. "If you're looking for your cheapest source of money," advertised Chemical Bank, "check your house." New hearings were held in 1987. Experts joined members of Congress to warn of the looming dangers of home equity loans. HELs were variously described as land mines and time bombs. They could do "more damage to American homes than termites," in the words of Rep. Frank Annunzio (D-Ill.).[86] HELs carried even greater risks than credit cards. If one failed to repay, the family might lose its very home. Borrowers should not bet on rising home prices, for as real estate guru John T. Reed observed presciently, "real estate values do not always go up."[87] Above all, HELs threatened to undermine the American way of saving by draining accumulated home equity. It is chilling today to read testimony by the Consumer Federation of America spokesman: "Where will we be twenty years from now when the baby boomers hit retirement age and have no savings to draw on?"[88]

Too late. American homeowners were hooked. By the 1990s the candle of debt was burning at both ends. Lower- and lower-middle-income households struggled to repay credit cards and payday loans. But many middle-income to affluent families, too, effectively stopped saving; home equity loans had become their "giant credit cards."[89] Like bank cards, HELs offer open lines of credit that customers access by simply writing a check or using a linked credit card. Home equity loans in fact proved more attractive to homeowners than credit cards. Secured by property, these loans halved the interest rate charges of credit cards. As housing prices skyrocketed, an owner might borrow tens of thousands of dollars against the home's fattened equity. Incredibly the borrower faced little pressure to repay these unamortized loans. Typically the principal was not due until the end of the fifteen-year term; thereafter one could easily refinance. By 2004 one-quarter of all home-owners carried home equity loans or their equivalent. While the household saving rate dropped to nearly zero, home equity loans jumped from 5 to 11 percent of disposable income between 1990 and 2007.

Why save when you can buy things with easy money? According to surveys of the 1990s and early 2000s, only one-third of the proceeds of home equity loans financed home improvements. One-fourth was spent on consumption, which included educational and medical expenses but also cars, weddings, and vacations. Most eye-opening, the remaining one-third repaid nonmortgage debt, notably credit cards. For the past two decades Americans have been robbing Peter to pay Paul. No longer can we neatly distinguish housing credit and consumer credit—or "good debt" and "bad debt." Housing debt itself fueled the nation's spectacular consumption boom. But at a tremendous cost. HELs led millions to plunder the wealth in their homes. Equity comprised 67 to 70 percent of aggregate home value until the late 1980s.[90] Thereafter homeowners borrowed so heavily that the share of equity steadily declined and went into free fall from 2001. This is extraordinary. Home values soared yet people held less equity in their homes.

HELs had indeed become termites chomping away at the assets of the American people.

First mortgages, too, leaped the banks that had channeled them into the nation's favorite form of saving. Housing prices shot up from the mid-1990s. From 2002 to 2005 they grew at double-digit or near-double-digit rates annually. Americans bought houses at a torrid pace, some to profit and others to jump into the housing market before prices rose further. In this mania many assumed mortgages they could scarcely afford, lured by small or zero down payments and teaser rates. Most vulnerable were holders of the now-infamous subprime mortgages. Taking a cue from the credit card industry, lenders targeted lower-income families considered credit risks. Borrowers were disproportionately African American and Hispanic. Subprime mortgages reached a quarter of all new mortgages from 2004 to 2006. Home ownership soared to 69 percent. Home equity loans and mortgages—subprime and prime—indebted Americans more than any other form of credit. Debt as a share of household disposable income rose from 86 to an incredible 141 percent (1989–2007). Most of the increase can be attributed to the near doubling of housing debt to 103 percent.[91]

How do we explain the many recent developments that suppressed saving? Let's begin with the globalization of the finance industry. During the 1990s and 2000s, foreign capital gushed into the United States. In 2005 soon-to-be Federal Reserve chairman Ben Bernanke singled out a "global saving glut" for creating artificially low interest rates. The Chinese in particular saved too much, he charged, investing their mounting surpluses in the United States. Awash in money, the financial industry lent freely and American consumers borrowed recklessly.[92] Although Bernanke rightly identified the importance of foreign capital, he ignored what was happening stateside. After all, China did not force American financial firms to engage in predatory lending, nor did it compel them to invest so heavily in housing and consumer credit to the neglect of production and infrastructure.

This brings us to the lack of financial regulation. The political system might have restrained the growth of excessive lending, but it chose instead to liberate the financial industry. The push for deregulation culminated in the 1999 repeal of the Glass-Steagall Act, which for seven decades had separated the heavily regulated commercial banks from the risk-taking investment banking sector. Concurrently there emerged a vast network of mortgage companies, hedge funds, and payday lenders. Such nonbanks required no deregulation because they had never really been regulated.

These changes diminished Americans' propensity to save. Unchecked by federal and state governments, predatory lending practices lured millions to assume unsustainable levels of debt. Congressional efforts to protect consumers were beaten back by the wealthiest lobby this country has ever seen. Financial firms have contributed more than $1.7 billion to congressional candidates since 2000, much of it to committee members who oversee the industry's operations. The growing securitization of mortgage and card debt further emboldened banks to extend credit to higher-risk customers. Banks no longer held many of their mortgages, selling the loans to other firms that sliced them into exotic securities. It mattered little whether the borrower repaid the principal; bankers amassed huge profits in various fees, interest charges, and refinancing.[93] The new business model severed the traditional link between savings deposits and loans. Banks had few reasons to attract small savers anymore. Nor did the government see much need to encourage Americans to save when foreign savings and financial innovations provided money like manna from heaven.

Although the financial industry and political allies bore the greatest responsibility for excessive lending, left-of-center groups played a supporting role. Progressives had long championed what became known as the "democratization of credit." Postwar labor unions and the Democratic Party promoted the extension of housing and consumer credit to working-class families. By the late 1960s, access to credit emerged as a key issue in the struggle for civil rights and equality. The National Organization of Women (NOW) and other feminist groups agitated for the end of lenders' policies that denied credit to single and divorced women as well as wives who lacked their husbands' authorization. The Equal Credit Opportunity Act (1974) prohibited discrimination in lending on the basis of sex and marital status. The law was soon revised to ban discrimination against African Americans and other minorities.[94] The Community Reinvestment Act of 1977 has encouraged banks and savings and loan associations to expand lending, particularly to those in lower-income neighborhoods. The legislation sought to remedy past discriminatory practices in the mortgage market while promoting home ownership in the inner cities. In the wake of the 2008 financial crisis, a host of politicians and economists blamed liberal credit policies for causing the subprime mortgage debacle. The Community Reinvestment Act and congressional supporters, they charged, pressured banks—with the financial backing of government-sponsored Fannie Mae and Freddie Mac—to extend mortgages to people who could ill afford them.[95] Federal officials contested the charge, noting the bulk of subprime mortgages had been initiated by financial firms not covered by the Community Reinvestment Act.[96] Politics aside, this much is clear. Many progressives had no sympathy for predatory lending practices. But in their quest to democratize credit, congressional liberals did little to regulate a financial industry that claimed to be improving the lives of lower-income Americans.

The final ingredient in the savings debacle has been the decline in household income. Marked by unusually equal income distribution, postwar prosperity enabled most Americans to save as well as borrow. Beginning in the 1970s, the growth in family incomes slowed for lower- to middle-income households. After a burst in earnings during the 1990s, the so-called jobless recovery set in. For those not in the top one-tenth, incomes stagnated or declined after 2000. Median real family incomes fell from $52,500 to $50,535 in 2005; they recovered somewhat during the next three years before plunging a further 3.6 percent in the 2008 recession.[97] The century's first decade witnessed the most sustained erosion of wages and salaries since the Great Depression. Tragically Americans assumed record levels of debt at the moment they were least able to repay. Overindebtedness often was the effect, not the cause, of drops in income. Struggling to keep afloat, many relied on credit cards as their "plastic safety net" while resorting to usurious payday loans from stores that dotted inner cities and small towns alike.[98]

The collapse of household saving has been stunning. From an internationally respectable rate of 7 percent in the early 1990s, the saving rate sank like a stone. Revised statistics show it falling to less than 1.4 percent in 2005. Saving rates of course do not tell the full story.

Many Americans in the middle- and upper-income brackets possess significant financial assets—retirement accounts, stocks, mutual funds, savings and checking accounts, and money market funds. In 2007 those in the upper-middle quintile (60–79.9 percent) had median financial assets around $58,000. Alternatively we might measure "savings" by net worth, which calculates the market value of all financial and housing assets minus liabilities. Due to soaring home prices, the majority of Americans saw their net worth soar. Between 1998 and 2007, median net worth climbed 31.8 percent to $120,300.[99]

Nonetheless, the 2007 Survey of Consumer Finances also reveals the depths of the savings problem in this country. From the dawn of popular saving, the principal motivation has been to accumulate enough money to deal with life's uncertainties. So it is troubling that a majority of American households lack adequate liquid savings in the form of savings, checking, or money market accounts. The bottom quintile had median savings in these transaction accounts of only $800; the next lowest merely $1,600. Most surprising, the middle one-fifth of households claimed median transaction-account savings of only $3,300. The total median financial assets of these Middle Americans came to less than $19,000. Much of that was tied up in retirement accounts, which generally cannot be tapped in a pinch without paying substantial penalties and taxes. A large portion of the populace thus lives without the reserves to cope with health emergencies, unemployment, or unanticipated car repairs. Rising net worth has had little impact on the lower two-fifths of families. They are less likely to own homes and have almost no exposure to stocks. Median net worth of those families dramatically *declined* from 2001 to 2007. As for Americans who appeared to benefit when housing prices surged, many recently discovered that one's net worth on paper is not the same as money in the bank.

An implosion of household finances of this magnitude would have alarmed U.S. policymakers a few decades earlier. Some did worry. Wrote former Federal Reserve Chairman Paul Volcker in 2005: baby boomers are "spending like there's no tomorrow.... [P]ersonal savings in the United States have practically disappeared." However, most influential economists remained upbeat. Wouldn't rising home prices and net worth more than compensate for low levels of saving?[100] Despite the "negligible" household saving rate and inadequate retirement savings, testified Federal Reserve chairman Alan Greenspan that same year, the U.S. economy "seems to be on a reasonably firm footing."[101] By March 2007, 8 percent of subprime mortgages were already in foreclosure or in arrears. Still, prominent economists continued to disparage regulatory efforts that might impede subprime borrowing. Harvey Rosen, former chair of President George W. Bush's Council of Economic Advisers, posed the public policy choices in the starkest of terms. It came down to "whether to make it harder for people to get these loans, and just shut people out, or let people make the choice and know that sometimes they will make mistakes."[102]

And as we Americans like to say, mistakes were made. Many now blame consumers and homeowners for making those mistakes and getting themselves hopelessly into debt. This story would benefit, though, from a more historical view. Institutional and political developments combined to reshape the nation's economic culture in the decades following 1945. It became harder and harder to save, for that would mean resisting messages to borrow and spend that seemingly came from everywhere: from advertisers, bankers, business writers, economists, national leaders, and of course the neighbors. By the turn of the twenty-first century, the decision to live beyond one's means appeared not reckless, but the mark of a good American.

12

KEEP ON SAVING? QUESTIONS FOR
THE TWENTY-FIRST CENTURY

Now there's a parable at the end of the Sermon on the
Mount that tells the story of two men. The first built his
house on a pile of sand, and it was soon destroyed when a
storm hit. But the second is known as the wise man, for
when "the rain descended, and the floods came, and the
winds blew, and beat upon that house, it fell not, for it was
founded upon a rock." We cannot rebuild this economy
on the same pile of sand. We must build our house upon
a rock. We must lay a new foundation for growth and
prosperity, a foundation that will move us from an era of
borrow and spend to one where we save and invest, where
we consume less at home and send more exports abroad.
                —Speech by President Barack Obama, 2009[1]

In the years after World War II, Japanese and Europeans came to
think of consumer spending as a good thing, but one that must be
balanced against the imperatives of saving, investment, social stability,
and the environment. The need to establish such a balance made little
sense to most Americans. That no longer may be true. The current
economic crisis burst more than the housing bubble. Sharp drops in
housing and equity prices have shaken Americans' confidence that the
Way to Wealth lies in buying assets rather than old-fashioned saving
from income. Net worth sank an estimated 17 percent from 2007 to
October 2008. Since then the stock market has recovered significantly,
but housing prices—upon which most Americans rely for net worth—

remain at the end of 2010 some 30 percent below their peak in 2006.[2] Big gains in asset prices for the vast majority of households are unlikely in the foreseeable future given high unemployment and forecasts of millions of additional foreclosures. Consumer and housing credit remain tight. Gone, too, is the "wealth effect." Believing themselves wealthy because of the market value of homes and portfolios, families had spent entire incomes and then borrowed more. Households now struggle to rebuild wealth in an environment where heady rates of return are no longer attainable.

Lo and behold, Americans have begun saving again. The household saving rate, which had been 2.1 percent two years earlier, rose to 5.9 percent in 2009. Reporters rushed to write stories about the nation's "new frugality."[3] The rate declined to 5 percent in the first five months of 2011. Saving is now at the highest levels since 1993, although well below postwar U.S. averages and those in many contemporary countries. Will Americans keep on saving? Is saving itself desirable? If so, what steps might the nation take to encourage saving?

Long off the table, these questions now preoccupy leadership at the highest levels. In his very own Sermon on the Mount, President Obama envisioned a future where "prosperity is fueled not by excessive debt or reckless speculation," but where Americans go back to "saving their pennies to buy their dream house." For the first time in postwar U.S. history, an administration consciously seeks to strike a balance between consumption and saving. Announced in 2009, the new agenda calls for "rebalancing" the U.S. and global economies—a theme *The Economist* echoes in its recent report, "Time to Rebalance." This is a daunting challenge. If Americans spend less and save more, who will purchase our products? U.S. leaders look to the consumers of Asia particularly the Chinese to pick up the slack. It's worth remembering, though, that for the past three decades Washington harangued Germans and Japanese to save less and buy more, with little effect. Consumption in Germany and Japan barely grew between 1992 and 2007, failing to exceed 60 percent of GDP. What's more, personal consumption in China as a share of GDP has sharply *declined* in recent years to less than 36 percent in 2009.[4] We face an unpleasant reality. In the coming years no one in the world will consume the way Americans did, not even Americans.

Any effort to promote saving within the United States will also encounter fierce political and cultural resistance. Policymakers and journalists are enthralled by the "paradox of thrift." Like many of Keynes's formulations, the concept has been Americanized to extol consumption pure and simple. Everyone's heard the argument. Saving may be good for the individual, but bad for the country especially now when the economy is sluggish. In a nation where consumption makes up 70 percent of the GDP, it's said, if people are encouraged to save, they would spend less, and weaken the overall economy. One confronts this notion less in other countries, and for good reason. As genuinely Keynesian economists are quick to note, the most effective way to stimulate an economy in a recession is for *governments* to spend, not financially embattled households.[5] As in everything, there are also balances to consider. If a large segment of the population does not save or pay down debts, we as a society must foot the bill for those who cannot cope with medical expenses, unemployment, loss of homes, and years of retirement. Families with savings, it should be obvious, are better positioned to help spend the economy out of recession than insolvent households.

Accordingly, some experts argue that the time has come for federal and state governments to devise policies that encourage lower- and middle-income Americans to save. It's worth considering the long history of savings promotion around the world. What has worked? What hasn't?

During the 1980s Americans looked to the high-saving Japanese for models. Today the solutions are less likely to come from Asia. The Chinese are currently the world's greatest savers, but China offers few lessons to a democratic, mature economy like the United States. Most popular savings are captured by the four gargantuan state-owned banks plus the postal savings system. China's high rates of saving may further be explained by the well-known phenomenon of consumption lagging behind rapidly rising incomes—something we saw in Japan, other Asian economies, and West Germany. More viable institutional models may be the compulsory, state-managed "provident funds," notably in Singapore, but also Malaysia, Hong Kong, and China itself. Ironically, Japan and South Korea, the two East Asian nations that most vigorously promoted voluntary saving not so long ago, currently record some of the lowest household saving rates among the OECD countries. In 2008 they stood at 2.3 and 2.9 percent, respectively, although the Japanese rate rose to 5.0 percent the following year amid the global financial crisis. The South Korean state abandoned its intrusive savings campaigns a decade ago, encouraging instead the greater use of consumer and housing credit. The Japanese experienced less of a cultural shift away from thrift. Instead declining incomes and the fast-aging population steadily chipped away at savings. Still, there are things to be learned from Japan. The renamed Central Council for Financial Services Information retains the centralized structure of the old savings-promotion body while embracing the up-to-date mission of advancing financial education among adults and the nation's schools.

Reconsidering the Cultures of Thrift, or How I Spent My European Vacations

Casting our gaze across the Atlantic, we detect a major divide between the British Isles and the continent. For a century and a half, Britain had been the transnational pace-setter in establishing norms of thrift and the institutions that supported them. By the 1960s, support for the National Savings Movement was wearing thin. Many local savings committees no longer functioned, and membership in the neighborhood Savings Groups steadily declined.[6] Along with economists, Conservative and Labour governments questioned the efficacy of the National Savings structure—comprised of the Post Office Savings Bank, Trustee Savings Banks, National Savings securities, and local volunteers.

In 1973 the government-appointed Page Committee recommended "winding up" the venerable National Savings Movement. The final report was a scathing repudiation of nearly every historical rationale for savings promotion. National Savings institutions, observed the panel, had "accrued" over 163 years "with little rationalisation." State encouragement of saving had done little to dampen demand or curb inflationary pressures. Nor did National Savings efficiently finance government debt, which the marketplace might do at lower cost. National Savings institutions moreover served depositors poorly by capturing savings at below-market rates. Most damning, the committee doubted whether promotional activities had any direct effect on the saving rate. Many witnesses argued "the Government could not turn personal savings on and off like a tap." The government subsequently eliminated National Savings Stamps, a mainstay of the Savings Groups. It also began transforming the nineteenth-century Trustee Savings Banks into full-service banks free to invest as they chose, rather than send deposited funds to the National Debt Commissioners. In 1978 the curtain came down on the National Savings Movement itself. The sixty-two-year-old National Savings Committee ceased operations in England and Wales as did its counterpart in Scotland. Organizers bade a tearful farewell to the tens of thousands of volunteers, feeling something terribly "British" had been lost.[7]

The passing of the National Savings Movement was part of a larger cultural shift. The British went on to embrace the American model of consumer-driven economics more fully than any other nation in the world. In 1986 the Conservative government of Margaret Thatcher engineered the Big Bang, setting in motion the massive deregulation of the finance industry. Under Tony Blair's New Labour during the 1990s, the City of London joined New York as one of the two centers of global finance. In a few short years, Britons abandoned austere lifestyles for the brave new world of credit-card debt, adjustable-rate mortgages, and home equity loans. The credit revolution fueled a frenzy of home-buying. From 1973 to 2004, British home ownership leaped from 52 to 69 percent (while U.S. rates rose more gradually from 62 to 68 percent).[8] As in the United States, the advent of easy credit coincided with a precipitous drop in British saving rates during the 1990s and into the 2000s. In recent years they have approached zero and occasionally have been *negative*. Britain's experience reminds us that not all nations with long histories of savings promotion continue to save. Cultures may change, sometimes fundamentally.

Just a few miles across the English Channel, things look very different. For most American economists and policymakers, the rest of Europe remains terra incognita. Yet the continent may well be the place to seek solutions for rebuilding savings in the United States. While Britons and Americans binged on credit, several Western European nations maintained high saving rates (see appendix). Rates in the two largest continental economies, Germany and France, have averaged above 10 percent since 1995. Germans remain great savers despite the absorption of East Germany. Belgium and Austria, historically aggressive in savings promotion, continue to boast strong saving rates. Rather than wholeheartedly embrace the vision of a credit-driven economy, Europeans quietly went their own way. While consuming more, they could not or would not keep up with shopaholic Americans. In 2003 French and German consumption levels stood respectively at merely 73 and 69 percent of U.S. levels—about where they had been in 1970. No other nation remotely approached the Americans except for the highly leveraged British; they increased spending to 86 percent of that in the United States.[9]

Why do Europeans keep on saving? There are particular economic factors in each case, but we should not ignore the weight of a shared history, institutionally and culturally. Today's thrifty societies retain the accessible, inclusive public institutions that have promoted small saving for more than a century—or two. In France the institutions have changed remarkably little. The 17,000-branch postal savings bank has fended off all attempts at privatization. To this day the state legally charges the local savings banks (caisses d'épargne) and postal savings bank with encouraging saving. The primary instrument for small saving is a veritable blast from the past. Originating in 1818, the Livret A account survived wars, occupations, and globalization. Capped currently at 15,300 euros, these savings accounts are tax-free. They require no maintenance fees and very small minimum deposits. Nearly every Frenchman possesses a Livret A, including children whose parents routinely open an account in the child's name at birth. Joining it are other tax-exempt accounts with colorful names: Livret Bleu, Livret Jaune for youth, and Livret d'Épargne Populaire for lower-income savers. These regulated small-saver accounts totaled 22 percent of all liquid financial assets held by French households in 2007. For years the European Commission and commercial banks pressed the French government to eliminate the exclusive right of the postal savings bank and savings banks to offer the Livret A (as well as the Crédit Mutuel's monopoly over the Livret Bleu). Finally in 2009 other banks were permitted to offer the Livret A. If anything, this ostensible liberalization has made the iconic Livret A more popular. Paying 1.75 percent interest in mid-2010, the state-guaranteed account represents a safe haven in the wake of the global financial meltdown. More than ten million Livret A were opened in 2009 alone, resulting in a total of sixty million Livret A and Livret Bleu today.[10]

If small saving in France appears more a patriotic act than an individual financial decision, this is no accident. The state casts saving as vital to building a cohesive society. As it has since the nineteenth century, the government arbitrarily sets the interest rate on Livret A accounts with an eye toward encouraging saving. When one prime minister refused to bring the interest rate down to market levels, he declared there might be economic reasons to do so, but that would be "a bad thing to do socially."[11] What's more, funds from the Livret A and other small-saver accounts are still deposited in the state's Caisse des Dépôts et Consignations (Bank for Deposits and Consignations). The government touts this arrangement to remind citizens that the Livret A provides a "social mode of saving." That's because the CDC draws on those deposits to finance the construction of nearly all social housing (public housing) in France. In recent years policymakers have campaigned for the financial inclusion of the entire populace. The Law against Exclusion (1998) equates access to banking services with the rights to work, housing, and health care. Such legislation commits the state and savings banks to eliminate *exclusion bancaire* by offering basic banking services to low-income households at a low price. Thanks to public policies, an incredible 99 percent of all French households possess a bank account, as do 92 percent of households receiving welfare benefits.[12]

Germany employs a different mix of institutions for small savers, but with similar results. Established in 1939 the postal savings bank (now Deutsche Postbank) boasts fourteen million customers who take advantage of accessible post offices and other retail outlets. Many also save in the cooperative *Volksbanken* and Raiffaisen banks that date back to the mid-nineteenth century. Most popular are the 200-year-old local savings banks (*Sparkassen*). Saving banks are seemingly everywhere, historically located at the center of German cities and towns. In 2007 the 446 savings banks operated 16,000 branches. Savings in those banks and their partners amounted to 39 percent of total customer deposits in Germany and more than half of all savings deposits. By contrast, the big private banks have shown little interest in the savings of ordinary Germans until recently. The *Sparkassen*, it will be recalled, are public institutions. Most have been "owned" by municipalities or regional governments for a century and a half. Much like France's central government, individual German states mandate that savings banks encourage a savings mentality (*Sparsinn*) among the people. The *Sparkassen*, too, constantly remind depositors that their savings contribute to the public good. Most of these not-for-profit savings banks are specifically charged with financing local governments' borrowing, investing in the region's small and medium enterprises, and donating surpluses to social welfare and cultural programs. "*Gut für Deutschland*," advertises the German Savings Banks Association. "*Gut für Bremen*," proclaims that city's venerable *Sparkasse*.[13]

Germany promotes the saving mentality with strong doses of moral suasion and material incentives. Established by the German Savings Banks Association in 1958, the well-funded advisory service on "Money and Housekeeping" seeks to hone the "financial management skills" of Germans. Housewives remain the core constituency, although the organization targets all adults. One key goal is to help families "prevent excessive debt and private insolvencies." For those who cannot master their expenses, the organization operates a debt-advisory service. Besides distributing huge quantities of informational brochures and budget-keeping software, the advisory service sponsors financial literacy lectures in cooperation with adult education centers and welfare institutions.[14]

Encouraging savings habits among young people remains one of the highest priorities. German banks of all types spend roughly a quarter of their marketing budget on appeals to children and teenagers. An extraordinary 85 percent of young people aged fourteen to twenty-four held a savings account in 2003. The vast majority of younger children, too, have their own *Sparbuch* (savings book). Savings banks in particular offer children and students special no-fee accounts that often pay above-market interest. The banks' thinking reflects the long history of youth savings programs. They are prepared to swallow the transaction costs of tiny deposits while cultivating the thrifty, loyal customers of tomorrow. In the Bremen Sparkasse, every branch employs a clerk responsible for dealing with children and teenagers. To teach financial planning, the employee routinely asks the parents of a seven- or eight-year-old to begin depositing pocket money in an account from which the child may freely withdraw (with the parent's prior approval).

In addition, German savings banks continue to run school savings programs at the national and local level. Some thirty years ago, at a time when school savings banks were in decline elsewhere, the German Savings Banks Association revitalized its School Service. Savings bank employees routinely visit schools to talk about money and saving, especially around October 31 each year. That's World Savings Day (Weltspartag), created by the International Thrift Congress in 1924. The School Service also provides instructional materials and events for teachers and students. The Service sponsors a widely adopted course in stock-market training, aimed at educating students about the opportunities and risks in investment. At the same time, the School Service reinforces long-standing injunctions to save in banks, life insurance, and building society funds. Teaching materials mention how high saving was "very important in Germany" in financing postwar recovery and growth. Most eye-catching has been the bimonthly comic magazine *KNAX*, published since 1974 by the German Savings Banks Association. Avoiding overt exhortations to save, *KNAX* creates a cuddly image of the savings banks among preteens (figure 37). It claims a circulation of 1.4 million, the largest of any comic magazine in Europe. *KNAX* is also distributed in Austria, Denmark, Norway, and Luxemburg.[15]

The German government plays an equally vigorous role in supporting small saving. It does so by granting subsidies and tax incentives. Initially the goal was to boost overall saving to accumulate capital to rebuild the West German economy after World War II. Gradually policy shifted to incentivizing saving by low- and middle-income households. During the 1990s, reunification revived older impulses to encourage saving for the purpose of financing new infrastructure and home construction in the former East Germany. Worried about looming gaps in the public pension system, the authorities have moved in the past

Figure 37. In this trademark cartoon from Germany's popular *KNAX* comic magazine, children bring their piggybanks to the friendly local savings bank. Courtesy of the Deutsche Sparkassenverlag.

decade to subsidize retirement plans that invest in stocks and mutual funds. Moreover, the Wealth Formation Law (Vermögensbildungsgesetz), enacted in 1961 and periodically revised, grants public supplements to employers' contributions to workplace savings plans. What's distinctive about the German government's approach is the focus on fostering contractual saving, whereby one is obligated to make regular deposits in a savings plan, life insurance policy, or building society contract. This is in fact how most Germans save, and helps explain *why* Germans save so much.[16]

The thrifty nations of Europe do not simply promote saving, they often restrain credit in ways that seem almost un-American. And in a sense they are. Europeans commonly remark upon the U.S. economy's "excessive" reliance on household debt to drive economic growth. The public frequently rallies behind policies that regulate credit as a conscious repudiation of the American Other, or what the French like to call the "Anglo-Saxon" model. Visiting German consumer experts in the 1950s disapprovingly noted the "tremendous willingness of Americans to improve their standard of living at all times, even if that mean[t] heavy borrowing against future income."[17] This is not to say that postwar Europeans shunned consumer credit. French consumer finance companies enthusiastically adopted the practices of their American counterparts during the 1950s. One of them, Cetelem, became the largest consumer lender in Europe. In West Germany, too, consumers in the 1950s availed themselves of installment loans provided by special banks (*Teilzahlungsbanken*). The thrift-obsessed savings banks initially took a dim view of consumer credit. Gradually from the late 1960s the *Sparkassen* introduced overdrafts on checking accounts and a broad range of consumer loans.[18]

Nonetheless, ambivalence about household debt persists in much of Western Europe to this day. The major continental economies never experienced the revolution in consumer credit that occurred in the United States after 1980. By 2004, consumer debt as a share of household disposable income soared to 25 percent in the United States and 24 percent in Britain, yet Germany recorded only 16 percent, France 12 percent, and Italy merely 6 percent.[19] The French appeared headed toward American-style deregulation in the mid-1980s. Banks plunged into consumer lending, competing with the consumer finance companies to offer cards with revolving credit. History, however, does not always run in one direction. French policymakers on both the Left and Right protested that easy credit led households to reduce saving and assume unsustainable levels of debt. In one consumer survey, half called credit cards a "trap from which one never escapes." By the end of the 1980s, observes Gunnar Trumbull, the French state moved to *reregulate* and restrict consumer credit. Quite unlike the American experience, a powerful agency of the French state prevented the creation of a credit scoring system accessible to all lenders. Instead the Bank of France inaugurated an official "black list" of borrowers who fell behind in their payments, and it required all consumer leaders to check applicants against the list. While consumer finance companies continued to offer credit cards, French banks largely abandoned the consumer lending business—another glaring contrast to developments in the United States.[20]

But don't we see an explosion of credit cards in Europe? There is considerable confusion on this point. I had dinner recently with a visiting German historian. When we put our cards down at the meal's end, I couldn't resist asking what he called his card. "Why, it's a credit card," he replied. "Must you pay the balance in full each month?" I inquired. "Of course," said he. I had him. "Well, here's my American card. I can charge up to $45,000 and at the end of the month all I have to pay is the 2-percent minimum. Now, *that's* a credit card," I declared in a burst of American triumphalism.

The fact is that in Germany, Europe's largest economy, few people possess a genuine credit card with revolving credit—that is, a card against which one might borrow. Most "credit cards" in Germany, as in the Netherlands and other European countries, are actually delayed debit cards. Issued by banks, delayed debit cards permit the holder to charge up to an authorized limit, but the balance must be paid in full at the end of each monthly period. In Belgium, *all* of the major "credit cards" (for example, Visa or Eurocard) are delayed debit cards.[21] For Americans used to applying for credit cards online, the process of obtaining a delayed debit card at a German savings bank is shockingly personal, even paternalistic. To minimize the chances of default, the *Sparkasse* requires that card balances be repaid from one's account at the bank. A clerk individually assigns the customer a limit on charges. He bases this on an interview and the bank's knowledge of the customer's long-standing savings habits. The clerk may authorize a 5,000-euro credit limit (about US$6,500) for an applicant who has an adequate, steady income, while setting the limit at only 500 or 1,000 euros for an individual deemed to lack the means to repay easily. Or the clerk may refuse to issue a delayed debit card at all. What happens if a cardholder charges more than the balance in his or her current account? In that case, replied one savings banker, "we suggest maybe it's time to give the card back."[22]

Although Americans have long predicted that consumers will flock to credit cards the world over, European societies remain wary.

Europeans generally prefer debit cards to credit cards. As revealed by a recent MasterCard survey of debit cardholders in Germany, Belgium, Britain, Italy, Spain, and Poland, 70 percent believe debit cards protect them from overspending.[23] In one telling moment in 1995, Citibank decided that Germans were ready to accept the credit card. The American bank teamed up with the German Railroad Company (Deutsche Bahn) to offer a Visa credit card. Protests by consumer protection groups forced the two companies to offer in addition BahnCards that lacked the credit function. Even though the revolving credit function was free, less than 15 percent of BahnCard customers chose the option, and less than half of that small group ever used the credit card function. A spectacular failure, Citibank withdrew from the arrangement after just four years.[24]

European discomfort with consumer credit stems in large part from fears of "overindebtedness." The term holds little meaning for Americans, appearing rarely in popular discourse or official policy. Whether one becomes hopelessly indebted is considered a matter of personal responsibility in the United States. The debtor may turn to a private debt consolidation service or go through the costly legal process of declaring bankruptcy. The continental European approach is very different. There, overindebtedness has been defined as a *social* problem that should be prevented before it spreads further. Over the past two decades, governments have moved aggressively to protect households from assuming too much debt. Belgium was the pioneer. In 1987 the National Bank of Belgium established the Central Credit Register to monitor and prevent overindebtedness. Lenders are required to report all contracts of credit to this office, including installment plans, credit cards, and home mortgages. The government's current definition of overindebtedness would strike most Americans as shockingly strict. The central office records the names of individuals with "overdue debts"— defined as not having paid three monthly installments or credit card bills in full or in part. To discourage the indebted from borrowing more, Belgian law further requires lenders to consult the Central Credit Register before extending any credit. The classification of overindebtedness commonly triggers the provision of state-provided social services that help individuals restructure payments while dealing with their marital problems, substance abuse, and other underlying issues.[25]

Comprehensive policies against overindebtedness exist in much of Western Europe. The Bank of France, as we have seen, maintains a negative list of those with overdue debts, as does Denmark. French debtors apply in large numbers to structure their repayments in state-organized "Commissions on Overindebtedness," comprised of representatives from the Bank of France, local government, consumer rights groups, and the French association of credit institutions. Variations on these systems also exist in the Netherlands, Germany, Austria, and Sweden. Besides emphasizing prevention, the European programs differ from American policies on debt in two additional ways. Whereas U.S. bankruptcy law offers individuals the chance to write down debts quickly in a so-called fresh start, European governments generally take a tough-love approach. Defaulters are expected to repay all or most of their debts over a lengthy period. In Austria, the process may last seven years. Because overindebtedness is commonly regarded as antisocial behavior, the repayment regime carries with it a strong whiff of rehabilitation. Second, Europeans largely avoid American-style judicial proceedings and for-profit debt counseling, instead employing the public services of their welfare states.[26] European concerns with overindebtedness bear heavily on savings behavior. Households on the continent save at high levels not simply because of greater prudence, but also because states and societies have made it difficult for them to borrow more than they can repay.

Likewise, several European nations indirectly encourage saving by *not* promoting homeownership as assertively as the U.S. government. Household saving rates tend to be lower in nations with high rates of homeownership and where mortgages have been relatively easy to finance. In the 1970s, when U.S. homeownership stood at 62 percent, Australia and Canada achieved similar levels. By contrast, in the major continental European countries—notably high savers like West Germany, Netherlands, and France—only one-third to two-fifths of families owned homes. Even after European homeownership surged during the early 2000s, rates in France, the Netherlands, and Austria remain relatively low at 54, 53, and 56 percent, respectively. A mere 40 percent of Germans own their homes. Low ownership in several European nations may be explained by requirements of high down payments. In

Germany, stringent requirements and tax policies encourage homebuy-ers to save a significant share of the purchase price in special building-association accounts, before the bank lends them the balance. Studies from the late 1960s found that up to a third of Germans with such ac-counts reportedly did not intend to buy a home, believing it simply to be a good way to save. It's also true that the European governments subsidize rental housing not only for the poor but for many middle-income residents. These pro-rental policies have encouraged large por-tions of the population to put their surplus savings into financial assets rather than real estate as in the United States.[27] We must note, too, that home equity loans barely exist in several advanced economies, in-cluding Germany and Japan.

Finally, European experiences suggest a positive relationship be-tween welfare states and high saving. This finding may not sit well with American economists, most of whom are convinced that national pen-sions and other welfare programs strongly discourage saving (see intro-duction). The fact is that the high-saving nations of Europe—among others Germany, France, Belgium, and Austria—all provide generous, comprehensive social benefits. To be sure, the famed welfare states of Scandinavia historically exhibited lower household saving rates. Since 2001, however, even the welfare superpower Sweden has recorded sav-ing rates between 7 and 13 percent.

The link between welfare states and high saving is not as puzzling as economists would have us believe. The lack of sturdy safety nets in the United States makes poor and middle-income households more vulnerable to financial insolvency than their European counterparts. According to an influential study by Elizabeth Warren and others, the overwhelming majority of personal bankruptcies among middle-class families are related to job loss, illness, and injury. In the absence of adequate unemployment benefits and universal health insurance, mil-lions of Americans deplete their savings on crippling medical costs and the sudden loss of income. By comparison, European governments no longer need intrusive policies to promote saving. They achieve fairly high saving rates simply by keeping most of their citizens from falling into destitution. As several cross-national studies have shown recently, generous welfare provision and easy credit appear to be inversely correlated. That is, continental European states tend to respond to life's emergencies by providing social benefits, while the American system offers families more credit.[28] As counterintuitive as it seems, if a society wants households to save, first it may have to stabilize their livelihoods.

Many Americans will no doubt find European policies toward saving and credit distasteful. Efforts to expand the welfare state have long met with resistance in this country. Few would relate kindly to European practices that restrict home loans and credit cards—much less to paternalistic interventions that aim to protect individuals from becoming "overindebted." Still, considering the dire financial circumstances in which so many Americans today find themselves, feelings of distaste are no longer an excuse for ignoring the elements that promote saving and solvency in other advanced economies.

Lessons of History

Although they garner little publicity, there are many excellent proposals circulating that would encourage saving in the United States. Some grow out of innovative programs developed by social welfare specialists benefiting from collaboration with development and behavioral economists. We may broadly divide them into (1) the promotion of saving among the broader populace, (2) programs aimed at increasing "asset-building" among lower-income households, (3) youth savings programs and expansion of financial education, and (4) the regulation of credit and savings products. General savings-promotion proposals focus on broadening participation in employer-provided individual retirement accounts, the 401(k)-type plans. The goal is to require all large and medium employers to offer retirement accounts to every employee. Influenced by behavioral economists, the schemes would automatically enroll employees at a certain default contribution rate (say, 3 percent) unless they opted out.[29]

Programs for lower-income Americans have been more ambitious. The Individual Development Account stands out. Michael Sherraden, a professor of social work, proposed IDAs in the late 1980s with an eye toward universalizing them among Americans. In practice, IDAs have been used in demonstration projects to encourage the poor to save by matching their monthly deposits. Federal and state governments, together with nonprofit organizations, provide the matched funds. The projects also offer financial education to the self-selected participants. The results of the pilot projects have been promising, but the architects themselves acknowledge that IDAs have reached few Americans. Ironically, the IDAs have been more influential transnationally in Britain, Taiwan, Canada, and several developing nations.[30] A related program promotes Child Development Accounts. This has been a ten-year project, in which accounts were opened for some 1,100 lower-income children, aimed at increasing their social and economic opportunities. Overall, these initiatives represent a promising new direction in social policy. They seek to promote comprehensive "asset-building," which includes saving, homeownership, and acquisition of postsecondary education and small-business skills.

In only one area have we seen concrete action by the federal government. Shocked by financial firms' high-risk ventures that culminated in the meltdown of 2008, Congress passed the Dodd-Frank Bill in 2010. This is the most sweeping financial regulation since the Great Depression. Among its many provisions, the legislation created the Consumer Financial Protection Bureau, which will oversee the full array of savings, credit, and other financial products available to the public. The agency has unprecedented powers to protect consumers from predatory lending practices, untransparent credit card agreements, and unreasonable bank fees. Whether it will reduce household overindebtedness remains to be seen.

As proponents of savings promotion readily admit, the United States is not even close to adopting the comprehensive policies that would reestablish a balance among saving, consumption, and credit. It is rare for a historian like myself to offer recommendations for public policy— all the more so, considering I have spent my career mainly studying other countries. But the challenges that America confronts today might well benefit from a fuller consideration of history and practices elsewhere. In an effort to imagine effective solutions, I humbly suggest some lessons from my global history of saving.

1. *Improve small savers' access to the banks.* Historically commercial banks have been unfriendly toward small depositors. In country after country, the mass of the population did not save regularly until the establishment of safe, convenient, and accessible savings institutions. Accessibility remains a problem today in poor urban and rural areas of the United States. The Federal Reserve's latest survey reveals that 7.9 percent of families are "unbanked"—that is, they lack a savings or checking account. That may not seem like much, but the proportion of the unbanked rises to one-quarter of those in the lowest income quintile and one-tenth in the next lowest quintile. When asked why they have no bank account, individuals most commonly reply that they "do not like dealing with banks." Specifically many cite excessive service charges and high minimum balances. The unbanked save considerably less frequently than those at the same income level who have bank accounts. They also deplete savings when cashing paychecks and benefit checks at fee-based cashing services.[31] If we truly wish to encourage saving among lower- and lower-middle-income families, the nation's banks should be persuaded to lower fees on small accounts.

2. *The centrality of the federal government in universalizing access.* Demonstration projects, such as the Individual Development Accounts, cooperate with a handful of sympathetic banks and credit unions. Nonetheless, the histories of Europe, East Asia, and the United States show that it is exceedingly difficult to improve the financial health of households on a grand scale without decisive state intervention. A brief list of innovations would include postal savings, state-supported savings banks, savings bonds, and federal deposit insurance. How might the U.S. government today convince banks to encourage small saving by the working poor and young people? What might be done to stimulate banks to offer attractive small-savings instruments like France's Livret A or Germany's contractual savings plans? Banks will protest that the transaction acts of small accounts are prohibitive. Yet if greater saving by lower- and middle-income Americans is socially desirable, the government will have to think creatively about how to incentivize banks to do the right thing. In other countries, states mandate and often subsidize special small-saver accounts that carry low minimums and higher interest rates.

It is unlikely, however, that most banks in the United States would respond favorably to savings-promotion initiatives. That, too, has been a familiar part of our global story. Accordingly, the federal government should seriously consider the revival of postal savings or an alternative form of a national savings bank. To avoid competition with the banks for larger depositors, postal savings would offer small-saver accounts capped at an amount that would serve young people and families of modest means. This proposal will no doubt strike American readers as outlandish. Yet when we survey current global trends, it is not so crazy. Postal savings, notes one recent report, remains vibrant in many advanced economies. We need only look at France, Germany, and Britain. In Japan, too, the world's largest postal savings system is still very popular, and clearly efforts to privatize it have stalled. Everywhere the global financial crisis prompted savers to return in droves to state-guaranteed postal deposits. Recognizing the decline in mail and package deliveries, several national post offices have discovered that the key to continued profitability lies in postal financial services.[32] The introduction of checking and small savings accounts at U.S. post offices may well generate healthy competition. A century ago when American commercial banks faced the prospect of a government-run postal savings bank, they suddenly opened their doors to small savers.

3. *Revise the tax laws to encourage low-and middle-income people to build assets of various types.* In the history of saving, it has rarely been difficult to persuade the affluent to save. The challenge is to encourage the humbler majority to do so. The U.S. tax code generally reverses these historic priorities. It grants the lion's share of tax benefits to wealthier savers and homebuyers, encourages overinvestment in housing, fosters overindebtedness by privileging home equity loans, and provides paltry incentives to lower- and middle-income people to build assets. Indeed, two-thirds of American wage earners currently do not itemize deductions when paying taxes, and thus benefit in no way from the vaunted mortgage deduction.[33] Politics aside, we could easily redesign the tax code to balance saving and borrowing. A ceiling might be placed on the tax-deductibility of mortgage interest so as to encourage homeownership among middle-income families without subsidizing the purchase of expensive homes. Or, we might convert the mortgage

deduction into a flat credit that would advantage lower- and middle-income homebuyers. At the very least, renters should be granted comparable tax breaks. This is a good time, too, to reduce the deductibility of home equity loans to more modest levels to protect consumers from draining substantial equity from their homes. Similarly, the fairest way of universalizing retirement savings accounts would be to offer a substantial tax credit, rather than a deduction. Retirement savings—as important as they are—are only one form of saving. Families require incentives to save for the short term, as well. We might consider the tax-free treatment of all small savings as in France and Germany, or Japan before 1988. Tax breaks have influenced savings behavior in ways that go well beyond the actual benefit. They send cultural messages about what sorts of behavior a society values. Does society want me to build my assets or buy a house I can't afford?

4. *Youth saving.* School savings programs are making a comeback in places like Japan and Germany. They no longer take the form of bring-in-your-pennies-on-Monday, but instead offer financial education that instructs young people about an array of financial products—savings and checking accounts, stocks, credit cards, and student loans. These programs are expanding in the United States, too, but they remain plagued by lack of coordination and problems of quality control. In Japan and elsewhere, central banks and other agencies play crucial roles in devising and disseminating financial education curricula. There is no reason why the newly created Consumer Financial Protection Bureau could not do the same in this country. More also could be done to encourage banks to offer special youth accounts with no minimum balances and paying interest that students can actually see. Although American banks view such accounts as unprofitable, savings banks in Germany and other countries still find that youth accounts lead to customer loyalty in adulthood. The United States is also behind other nations in permitting teenagers the freedom to manage their bank accounts. While it's a common sight elsewhere to see young teens withdraw money from their postal savings or savings bank accounts, laws in the United States seem determined to produce financially irresponsible young adults by denying children the right to make withdrawals until age seventeen or eighteen.

5. *Promote saving in terms of "financial inclusion."* How we talk about saving affects the prospects of a savings agenda in this country. Proponents of savings promotion will persuade few if they discuss the issue primarily in terms of a welfare policy for the poor. Nor will they be able to stand up to bankers who insist that small savings are too costly. It's worth considering how successful efforts over the last two centuries have linked popular saving to citizenship, or membership in the national community. Nineteenth-century Britons, we'll recall, concluded that working people with money in the bank acquired a "stake in the country." In its latest incarnation, governments in Europe promote the access of all citizens to banking facilities in the name of "financial inclusion."[34] Or as the French would say, the banks' *exclusion* of some is tantamount to denying people their civil rights. We saw the link between financial exclusion and the denial of citizenship graphically in the treatment of African Americans in the South in the decades following the Civil War. For the past sixty years, Americans have fixated on the democratization of homeownership and credit. In the midst of record foreclosures and crippling debt, we should do more to *democratize saving* as one means of bringing about a more equitable society.

None of the proposals above would rob Americans of the boons of consumption and credit. People who save also spend, and they borrow to buy homes and finance education. The key, as Japanese and Europeans have long argued, is the need for balance. From a global perspective, the United States dangerously departed from that balance over the past two to three decades. As the economic downturn continues, Americans find themselves in more agreement with the rest of the world than they might think. It has become apparent that a good society rests on the financial solvency of its households. Will we keep on saving, or return to the late-twentieth-century culture of debt? Americans pay little attention to how other nations promoted small saving and protected their citizens from overindebtedness. This may be the time to start.

_____ ACKNOWLEDGMENTS _____

This project has taken me across the globe. I would like to thank the following institutions for their cooperation, beginning with the Bank of Japan's Public Relations Department, whose staff graciously shared materials related to savings-promotion operations. I am particularly grateful to Okazaki Ryōko and Masunaga Rei, as well as Ohta Takashi, former vice-governor of the Bank of Japan. Inoue Keiko of the Communications Museum in Tokyo tirelessly assisted me in locating and reproducing the stunning Japanese posters that appear in this volume. The Institute of Fiscal and Monetary Policy facilitated my work in the archives of Japan's Ministry of Finance. I am also indebted to the Postal Savings Bureau within the former Ministry of Posts and Telecommunications. Nancy Lockkamper of the World Savings Banks Institute (Brussels) introduced me to the Institute's incomparable archives, and she and Anne-Françoise Lefevre arranged my subsequent visits to France's National Federation of Savings Banks, the Association of Italian Foundations and Savings Banks, and Senegal's Postefinances. Thorsten Wehber of the German Savings Banks Association energetically supported my research on the institutional encouragement of saving in Germany. I further benefited from meetings with Susanne Wranik of the Association of German Independent Public Savings Banks (Bremen) and Wolfgang Blümel of the Hamburg Savings Bank. Hasbullah bin Abdullah of the Bank Negara Malaysia was extraordinarily informative about savings-promotion programs in Malaysia. While in South Korea, the future prime minister, Chung Un-chan, and my former classmate Kim Yongdeok of Seoul National University—together with the staff of the Bank of Korea—did much to advance my understanding of that nation's savings campaigns. As a historian, I have been afforded the rare opportunity to participate in contemporary policy-related discussions about how to encourage saving and improve financial access in the United States. For this I thank David Blankenhorn and Barbara

Dafoe Whitehead of the Institute for American Values; Ray Boshara, Reid Cramer, and Jamie Zimmerman of the New America Foundation; and Michael Sherraden of Washington University in St. Louis.

This book benefits from the insights of many colleagues. Charles Yuji Horioka first brought Japanese savings-promotion efforts to my attention some twenty years ago, and ever since has graciously answered my myriad questions about the economics of saving. Andrew Gordon has remained unfailing as an intellectually generous colleague for nearly four decades. Another friend and collaborator, Patricia L. Maclachlan, nudged me toward considering consumption, as well as saving, in my analysis. Lawrence Glickman's suggestions improved the manuscript overall and the chapters on the United States in particular. A short list of those who thoughtfully commented on my draft chapters and presentations would include James Bartholomew, Thomas Bender, Amy Borovoy, Miguel Centeno, Lizabeth Cohen, Devin Fergus, Kathleen Frydl, Shinju Fujihira, Marilena Gala, C. Andrew Gerstle, Michael Gordin, Hendrick Hartog, Janet Hunter, Andrew Isenberg, Harold James, Jerome Karabel, Jürgen Kocka, Atul Kohli, Kevin Kruse, Jonathan Levy, Edward Lincoln, Jan Logemann, Christine Marran, Sonya Michel, Jonathan Morduch, Susan Naquin, Laura C. Nelson, Philip Nord, Cormac O'Grada, Akiko Ohta, Okada Kazunobu, Nakamura Masanori, Masao Nakamura, Karsten Paerregaard, Daniel Rodgers, Richard Samuels, Wayne Soon, Frank Trentmann, Utsumi Takashi, Guy Vanthemsche, and Naoyuki Yoshino.

I employed several gifted, imaginative research assistants who frequently suggested new ways of looking at the cases. I am grateful to Andres Blanco, Daniel Bouk, Brooke Fitzgerald, Mark Moll, Sang-ho Ro, Abigail Stewart, Sarah Teasley, Klaus Veigel, Tong Bao Wee, and Janine Yoong.

My research at home and abroad was made possible by the generous support of the Smith Richardson Foundation, Abe Fellowship program, National Endowment for the Humanities, Social Science Research Council and American Council of Learned Societies, Fulbright-Hays Faculty Research Grant, and the Woodrow Wilson International Center for Scholars.

Finally I wish to thank the staff of Princeton University Press—Beth Clevenger, Clara Platter, and Sarah Wolf—for their excellent work in producing this book. Words are insufficient to express my gratitude to Brigitta van Rheinberg, who while serving as editor in chief of the Press, patiently worked with me to craft a book that would engage contemporary debates over saving, consumption, and credit.

APPENDIX

Net Household Saving Rates for Selected OECD Countries, 1985–2009 (Percent of Disposable Household Income)

	1985	1990	1995	2000	2005	2007	2008	2009
Australia	12.1[a]	6.7[a]	6.3	2.6	0.4	0.5	4.5	—
Austria	10.5	10.3	11.8	9.2	9.7	11.6	11.8	11.1
Belgium	11.1[b]	9.5[b]	16.4	12.3	10.2	11.4	11.9	13.5
Canada	16.0[a]	13.3[a]	9.4	4.8	2.2	2.9	3.7	4.7
France	10.2[a]	9.2[a]	12.7	11.8	11.4	11.9	11.6	12.5
Germany	12.1	13.7	11.0	9.2	10.5	10.8	11.7	11.1
Italy	21.5[b]	21.7[a]	17.0	8.4	9.9	8.5	8.2	7.1
Japan	16.5	13.9	11.9[c]	8.8	3.9	2.5	2.3	5.0[e]
Korea	15.4[a]	23.6[a]	18.5	9.3	7.2	2.9	2.9	3.6
Netherlands	5.6	18.2[a]	14.3	6.9	6.4	7.0	5.7	6.8
Spain	7.8[b]	8.6[b]	11.5[bc]	5.9	4.7	3.6	6.6	11.9
Sweden	3.2	3.4	8.3	4.3	5.5	8.8	11.2	12.9
Switzerland	—	9.6	12.7	11.7	10.1	12.7	11.8	—
United Kingdom	6.9[b]	5.6[b]	6.7	0.1	−1.2	−3.2	−2.8	1.2
United States[d]	8.5[a]	6.7[a]	5.7	3.0	1.5	2.1	4.2	6.2

Notes: Unless otherwise indicated, all rates from 1995 to 2009 have been recalibrated according to the 1993 SNA (System of National Accounts).

[a] Pre-1995 rates recalibrated according to 1993 SNA.

[b] Converted from gross saving rate to net saving rate by using a conversion factor of 0.7 (the approximate ratio of the average net household saving rate to the average gross household saving rate for those countries and years). See Horioka, "Are the Japanese Unique?" 117.

[c] Estimates in OECD Economic Outlook, 2007/2.

[d] U.S. rates provided to the OECD may vary slightly from recently recalibrated rates by the U.S. Department of Commerce, Bureau of Economic Analysis.

[e] Economic and Social Research Institute, Cabinet Office, Japan.

Sources: For 1995–2009 rates, see OECD National Accounts Statistics, accessed March 3, 2011; for 1990, OECD Economic Outlook, 2007/2, no. 82 (December 2007), Annex Table 23; for 1985, see 2003/1, no. 73 (June 2003), Annex Table 24.

ABBREVIATIONS

CJ   *Chochiku jihō*
CU   Chochiku Zōkyō Chūō Iinkai, *Chochiku undō*
KCSIG   Kokumin Chochiku Shōreikyoku, *Kokumin Chochiku Shōrei
        Iinkai gijiroku*
NACP   National Archives at College Park, MD
SHZS   Japan, Ministry of Finance, Shōwa zaiseishi shiryō
SZS   Japan, Ministry of Finance, Sengo zaiseishi shiryō
TNA   The National Archives of the United Kingdom: Public
        Record Office

NOTES

Introduction

1. Ben S. Bernanke (Governor, Federal Reserve Board), "The Global Saving Glut and the U.S. Current Account Deficit," March 10, 2005, Richmond, VA, http://www.federalreserve.gov/boarddocs/speeches/2005/200503102/, accessed August 4, 2010.

2. Charles Yuji Horioka, "Why Is Japan's Household Saving Rate So High? A Literature Survey," *Journal of the Japanese and International Economies* 4, no. 1 (March 1990): 49–92; Kent E. Calder, "Linking Welfare and the Developmental State: Postal Savings in Japan," *Journal of Japanese Studies* 16, no. 1 (Winter 1990): 31–59.

3. Alan Greenspan, "The Crisis," April 15, 2010, p. 4, http://www.brookings.edu/~/media/Files/Programs/ES/BPEA/2010_spring_bpea_papers/spring2010_greenspan.pdf, accessed June 19, 2010.

4. Aware of international comparisons, two economists nonetheless wrote the "last few decades have witnessed sharp declines in rates of saving for many developed countries," yet could cite no other example than the United States. B. Douglas Bernheim and Antonio Rangel, "Behavioral Public Economics: Welfare and Policy Analysis with Non-standard Decision-Makers," in Peter Diamond and Hannu Vartiainen, eds., *Behavioral Economics and Its Applications* (Princeton: Princeton University Press, 2007), 20.

5. Victoria de Grazia, *Irresistible Empire: America's Advance through Twentieth-Century Europe* (Cambridge: Belknap Press of Harvard University Press, 2005).

6. Daniel T. Rodgers, *Atlantic Crossings: Social Politics in a Progressive Age* (Cambridge: Belknap Press of Harvard University Press, 1998).

7. See Niall Ferguson, *The Ascent of Money: A Financial History of the World* (New York: Penguin, 2008).

8. Ross Harvey, "Comparison of Household Saving Ratios: Euro Area/United States/Japan," in Asis Kumar Pain and Nirbachita Karmakar, eds., *Household Savings: Perspectives and Country Experiences* (Punjagutta, Hyderabad, India: Icfai University Press, 2007), 95–105.

9. David F. Bradford, "Market Value versus Financial Accounting Measures of National Saving," in B. Douglas Bernheim and John B. Shoven, eds., *National Saving and Economic Performance* (Chicago: University of Chicago Press, 1991), 15–44.

10. On the impact of postal savings accounts in Mexico, see Fernando Aportela, "Effects of Financial Access on Savings by Low-Income People," December 1999, www.lacea.org/meeting2000/FernandoAportela.pdf, accessed August 4, 2010.

11. Axel Börsch-Supan, ed., *Life-Cycle Savings and Public Policy: A Cross-National Study of Six Countries* (Amsterdam: Academic Press, 2003), 1–31, 89, 144.

12. Franco Modigliani with Richard Brumberg, "Utility Analysis and the Consumption Function: An Interpretation of Cross-Section Data," in Kenneth K. Kurihara,

386 NOTES TO CHAPTER 1

ed., *Post-Keynesian Economics* (New Brunswick, NJ: Rutgers University Press, 1954), 388–436; Milton Friedman, *A Theory of the Consumption Function* (Princeton: Princeton University Press, 1957).

13. Martin Feldstein, "Social Security, Induced Retirement and Aggregate Capital Accumulation," *Journal of Political Economy* 82, no. 5 (September–October 1974): 905–26.

14. Börsch-Supan, *Life-Cycle Savings*, 16–21.

15. For a somewhat broader list of motivations, see Martin Browning and Annamaria Lusardi, "Household Saving: Micro Theories and Micro Facts," *Journal of Economic Literature* 34, no. 4 (December 1996): 1797.

16. David Blankenhorn, "There Is No 'Paradox of Thrift,'" *Weekly Standard* 14, no. 37 (June 15, 2009): 23–27; also Thomas J. Stanley and William D. Danko, *The Millionaire Next Door* (Atlanta, GA: Longstreet Press, 1996).

17. Especially Daryl Collins, Jonathan Morduch, Stuart Rutherford, and Orlanda Ruthven, *Portfolios of the Poor: How the World's Poor Live on $2 a Day* (Princeton: Princeton University Press, 2009); also Anne Case, comment, in Diamond and Vartianinen, *Behavioral Economics*, 113–14.

18. Margaret Sherrard Sherraden and Amanda Moore McBride, *Striving to Save: Creating Policies for Financial Security of Low-Income Families* (Ann Arbor: University of Michigan Press, 2010); Mark Schreiner and Michael Sherraden, *Can the Poor Save? Saving and Asset Building in Individual Development Accounts* (New Brunswick, NJ: Transaction, 2007).

19. Peter Tufano and Daniel Schneider, "Using Financial Innovation to Support Savers: From Coercion to Excitement," and Sendhil Mullainathan and Eldar Shafir, "Savings Policy and Decision-Making in Low-Income Households," in Rebecca M. Blank and Michael S. Barr, eds., *Insufficient Funds: Savings, Assets, Credit, and Banking among Low-Income Households* (New York: Russell Sage Foundation Press, 2009), 149–90, 121–45; Richard H. Thaler, "Mental Accounting Matters," *Journal of Behavioral Decision Making* 12, no. 3 (September 1999): 183–206; Bernheim and Rangel, "Behavioral Public Economics," 25.

20. Richard H. Thaler and Cass R. Sunstein, *Nudge: Improving Decisions about Health, Wealth, and Happiness* (New Haven: Yale University Press, 2008), 5.

21. Börsch-Supan, *Life-Cycle Savings*, 8–9.

CHAPTER 1: THE ORIGINS OF SAVING IN THE WESTERN WORLD

1. Thomas James, *Aesop's Fables: A New Version, Chiefly from Original Sources* (London: J. Murray, 1848), 12.

2. *Proverbs*, 6:6–8, King James Bible.

3. See William Cronon, *Changes in the Land: Indians, Colonists, and the Ecology of New England* (New York: Hill and Wang, 1983), 40–41, 53, 55; nature-banking is discussed by Arthur F. McEvoy, *The Fisherman's Problem: Ecology and the Law in the California Fisheries, 1850–1980* (Cambridge: Cambridge University Press, 1986), 213, also 27. I am grateful to Andrew Isenberg.

4. Pierre-Étienne Will and R. Bin Wong, *Nourish the People: The State Civilian Granary System in China, 1650–1850* (Ann Arbor: Center for Chinese Studies, University of Michigan, 1991), 9–10, 14–15, 63, 68.

5. H. Oliver Horne, *A History of Savings Banks* (London: Oxford University Press, 1947), 4–5.

6. Ibid., 2.

7. Daniel Duet, *Les Caisses d'épargne Françaises et leur activité: Tradition ou évolution (1818–1981)*, published doctoral thesis (Paris: Les Éditions de l'épargne, 1983), 107.

8. Ibid., 66–72, 90.

9. Max Weber, *The Protestant Ethic and the Spirit of Capitalism*, trans. Talcott Parsons (New York: Charles Scribner's Sons, 1958), 41, 115; Caisse des Dépôts et Consignations, *Le Livret A—Une histoire de l'épargne populaire* (Paris: La documentation Française, Caisse des Dépôts et Consignations, 1999), 15.

10. Weber, *Protestant Ethic*, 117, 167, 172–74.

11. Robert S. Duplessis, *Transitions to Capitalism in Early Modern Europe* (Cambridge: Cambridge University Press, 1997), 136.

12. Duet, *Caisses d'épargne Françaises*, 66–67.

13. George M. Foster, "Peasant Society and the Image of Limited Good," in Jack M. Potter, May N. Diaz, and George M. Foster, eds., *Peasant Society: A Reader* (Boston: Little, Brown, & Co., 1967), 305, 315, 318.

14. Caisse des Dépôts, *Livret A*, 15; Duet, *Caisses d'épargne Françaises*, 82.

15. Rosa-Maria Gelpi and François Julien-Labruyère, *The History of Consumer Credit: Doctrines and Practice*, trans. Mn Liam Gavin (Houndsmills, Basingstoke, Hampshire: Macmillan, 2000), 48–52; see also Raymond de Roover, "New Interpretations of the History of Banking," in Julius Kirshner, ed., *Business, Banking, and Economic Thought in Late Medieval and Early Modern Europe* (Chicago: Chicago University Press, 1974), 200–38.

16. Horne, *History of Savings Banks*, 8–9; Joseph Wechsberg, *The Merchant Bankers* (New York: Pocket Books, 1966).

17. Gelpi and Julien-Labruyère, *History of Consumer Credit*, 42–44; De Roover, "New Interpretations," 213, 223–25.

18. Duet, *Caisses d'épargne Françaises*, 79, 80; Caisse des Dépôts, *Livret A*, 14.

19. *World Thrift*, 1927, no. 1: 41–42; Leonard W. Labaree, ed., *The Papers of Benjamin Franklin*, vol. 7 (New Haven: Yale University Press, 1963), 327.

20. Werner Sombart, *The Quintessence of Capitalism: A Study of the History and Psychology of the Modern Business Man*, trans. M. Epstein (New York: E. P. Dutton, 1915), 103, 104, 107, 109.

21. Ibid., 105–106.

22. Ibid., 115–16.

23. Italics mine. Daniel Defoe, *The Complete English Tradesman*, 1839 ed. (Gloucester: Alan Sutton, 1987), 4, 6, 73, 83.

24. Ibid., *The Life and Strange Surprizing Adventures of Robinson Crusoe* (1719; rev. ed., Oxford: Oxford University Press, 1999), 6–7, 148, 153–54.

25. Ibid., *The Farther Adventures of Robinson Crusoe* (1719), reprinted in *Robinson Crusoe*, vol. 2 (London: William Clowes, 1974), 193.

26. Sombart, *Quintessence of Capitalism*, 116.

27. Harold A. Larrabee, "Poor Richard in an Age of Plenty," *Harper's Magazine* 212, no. 1268 (January 1956): 64–66.

28. Benjamin Franklin, *The Autobiography of Benjamin Franklin*, comp. D. H. Montgomery (Boston: Ginn and Company, 1927), 103; H. W. Brands, *The First American: The Life and Times of Benjamin Franklin* (New York: Doubleday, 2000), 123–24, 130.

29. "Father Abraham's Speech," in Labaree, *Papers of Benjamin Franklin*, 7:340–42, also 326–27. Franklin's italics throughout.

30. Labaree, *Papers of Benjamin Franklin*, 7:327–29, 333, 336–38; in Japan, see Imai Terako, "Nihon ni okeru Furankurin no juyō—Meiji jidai" [Importance of Franklin in Japan in the Meiji era], *Tsudajuku daigaku kiyō*, no. 4-2 (1982): 22.

31. Labaree, *Papers of Benjamin Franklin*, 7:344–50.

32. Quoted in Duet, *Caisses d'épargne Françaises*, 150; Larrabee, "Poor Richard in an Age of Plenty," 66.

33. Quoted in Duet, *Caisses d'épargne Françaises*, 94, 134.

34. Daniel Defoe, *An Essay upon Projects*, ed. Joyce D. Kennedy et al. (New York: AMS Press, 1999), 65–67, also 57–58, 62.

35. Joachim Faiguet, "Epargne," *Encyclopédie, ou, Dictionnaire raisonné des sciences, des arts et des métiers*, comp. Denis Diderot and Jean Le Rond d'Alembert, vol. 5 (Paris: Briasson, 1755), 748–49.

36. Quoted in Duet, *Caisses d'épargne Françaises*, 110.

37. Jeremy Bentham, *Pauper Management Improved: Particularly by Means of an Application of the Panopticon Principle of Construction* (London: R. Baldwin, 1812), 3, 172–73, 180–85, 193; Horne, *History of Savings Banks*, 28–29.

38. Adam Smith, *An Inquiry into the Nature and Causes of the Wealth of Nations*, ed. Edwin Cannan (Chicago: University of Chicago Press, 1976), 1:359–60, 362–63, 2:179.

39. Bernard Mandeville, "The Grumbling Hive: or, Knaves Turn'd Honest," 1705, and "Remarks," 1714–23, in *The Fable of the Bees*, ed. Irwin Primer (New York: Capricorn Books, 1962), 27–38, 74–75, 122–23.

40. Robert L. Heilbroner, *The Worldly Philosophers: The Lives, Times and Ideas of the Great Economic Thinkers*, 4th ed. (New York: Simon and Schuster, 1972), 98; see also Frank Trentmann, "The Modern Genealogy of the Consumer: Meanings, Identities and Political Synapses," in John Brewer and Frank Trentmann, eds., *Consuming Cultures, Global Perspectives: Historical Trajectories, Transnational Exchanges* (Oxford: Berg, 2006), 24–29.

41. John Stuart Mill, *Principles of Political Economy*, 2nd ed. (London: J. W. Parker, 1849), 1:85, 90.

42. Donald Winch, "Introduction," in T. R. Malthus, *An Essay on the Principle of Population* (Cambridge: Cambridge University Press, 1992), viii–ix, xiii–xiv.

43. Malthus, *Essay*, 308–309, 318–19.

44. Patricia James, *Population Malthus: His Life and Times* (London: Routledge & Kegan Paul, 1979), 222–23.

45. Duet, *Caisses d'épargne Françaises*, 46–47, 71–72, 119–21; Horne, *History of Savings Banks*, 97.

46. Quoted in Horne, *History of Savings Banks*, 21.

47. Caisse des Dépôts, *Livret A*, 123.

48. Italics mine. *Sheffield Mercury*, December 5, 1818, quoted in Horne, *History of Savings Banks*, 13.

49. Daniel Duet, *Les Caisses d'épargne* (Paris: Presses Universitaires de France, 1991), 5.

50. Hans Greisinger, "Mission and Tasks of the Savings Banks in the Modern Economy," *World Thrift*, 1969, no. 4 (July/August): 589, 592.

51. Jürgen Mura, "Germany," and Josef Wysocki, "Introduction," in Jürgen Mura (Wissenschaftsförderung der Sparkassenorganisation), ed., *History of European Savings Banks*, vol. 1 (Stuttgart: Deutscher Sparkassenverlag GmbH, 1996), 12–13, 106–107.

52. Wander Frederik van Leeuwen, "The Netherlands," in Mura, *History of European Savings Banks*, 1:247–48.

53. Italics mine. Greisinger, "Mission and Tasks of the Savings Banks," 587.

54. Frank Trentmann, "Introduction," in his *Paradoxes of Civil Society: New Perspectives on Modern German and British History* (New York: Berghahn Books, 2000), 3–4, 13–14, 21–22.

55. Quoted in Asa Briggs, *The Age of Improvement, 1783–1867* (London: Longman, 1979), 16.

56. Horne, *History of Savings Banks*, 22–27.

57. Paul Johnson, *Saving and Spending: The Working-Class Economy in Britain, 1870–1939* (Oxford: Clarendon Press, 1985), 48–49, 54, 55, 58.

58. Horne, *History of Savings Banks*, 8–9, 16

59. Michael Moss and Iain Russell, *An Invaluable Treasure: A History of the TSB* (London: Weidenfeld and Nicolson, 1994), 23.

60. Horne, *History of Savings Banks*, 43.

61. Moss and Russell, *Invaluable Treasure*, 25–26.

62. Horne, *History of Savings Banks*, 49, also 47–48.

63. Moss and Russell, *Invaluable Treasure*, 33.

64. Peter H.J.H. Gosden, "Great Britain," in Mura, *History of European Savings Banks*, 1:137.

65. Horne, *History of Savings Banks*, 76–77, 82; text of Savings Banks Act appears in Moss and Russell, *Invaluable Treasure*, 32.

66. Gosden, "Great Britain," in Mura, *History of European Savings Banks*, 1:138.

67. Quoted in Horne, *History of Savings Banks*, 99, also 100–102.

68. Briggs, *The Age of Improvement*, 206–11; Moss and Russell, *Invaluable Treasure*, 35–38.

69. Horne, *History of Savings Banks*, 32.

70. John Tidd Pratt, *The History of Savings Banks in England, Wales, and Ireland* (London: C.J.G. & F. Rivington, 1830), xxi.

71. See Christian Dirninger, "Austria," and Ingvar Körberg, "Sweden," in Mura, *History of European Savings Banks*, 2:20–21, 325–29; Wysocki, "Introduction," in ibid.,

1:11–12; for transnational diffusion, see Duet, *Caisses d'épargne*, 7; *Caisses d'épargne Françaises*, 88–90; Horne, *History of Savings Banks*, 87–91.

72. Letter to Editor of the *Annals of Banks for Saving*, October 1817, quoted in Horne, *History of Savings Banks*, 90, also 89.

73. Caisse des Dépôts, *Livret A*, 79–82, 124–25; Antoine Moster and Bernard Vogler, "France," in Mura, *History of European Savings Banks*, 1:76–77, 80.

74. Charles Dickens, *The Life and Adventures of Martin Chuzzlewit* (London: Penguin,1999), 336.

CHAPTER 2: ORGANIZING THRIFT IN THE AGE OF NATION-STATES

1. Samuel Smiles, *Workmen's Earnings, Strikes, and Savings* (London: John Murray, 1861), 94.

2. Advertisement, *The Times* (London), November 12, 1859, p. 12; Samuel Smiles, *The Autobiography of Samuel Smiles, LL.D.*, ed. Thomas Mackay (London: John Murray, 1905), 223, 308, 387, 389, 398, 400–401; Earl H. Kinmonth, *The Self-Made Man in Meiji Japanese Thought: From Samurai to Salary Man* (Berkeley: University of California Press, 1981), 14, 23.

3. William Davis, *Friendly Advice to Industrious and Frugal Persons, Recommending Provident Institutions, or Savings Banks* (London: Binns and Meyler, 1817), 8.

4. Duet, *Caisses d'épargne Françaises*, 134.

5. See statue by Archibald McFarlane Shannon, 1908, in Moss and Russell, *Invaluable Treasure*, 97.

6. Robert Louis Stevenson, *Treasure Island* (New York: American Book Co., 1913), 228–29.

7. Charles Dickens, *The Personal History of David Copperfield* (Harmondsworth, Middlesex, England: Penguin Books, 1966), 231.

8. Moss and Russell, *Invaluable Treasure*, 51, 92.

9. Smiles, *Autobiography*, 229, 398–400.

10. Quoted by Peter W. Sinnema, "Introduction," in Samuel Smiles, *Self-Help, with Illustrations of Character, Conduct, and Perseverance* (Oxford: Oxford University Press, 2002), xi; Adrian Jarvis, *Samuel Smiles and the Construction of Victorian Values* (Thrupp, Gloucestershire: Sutton Publishing, 1997), 31, 33.

11. Italics mine. Smiles, *Self-Help*, 244–45, 254.

12. Ibid., *Workmen's Earnings*,71, 73.

13. Ibid., 43–44, 63, 65–66, 67, 163, 164, also 151.

14. Ibid., *Thrift* (London: John Murray, 1875), 142–43.

15. Ibid., *Workmen's Earnings*, 65–66, 68.

16. Moss and Russell, *Invaluable Treasure*, 83; Victoria de Grazia, ed., *The Sex of Things: Gender and Consumption in Historical Perspective* (Berkeley: University of California Press, 1996), 5.

17. Smiles, *Workmen's Earnings*, 15–30, 46, 52.

18. Moss and Russell, *Invaluable Treasure*, 84.

19. Smiles, *Workmen's Earnings*, 55–57.

20. Ibid., *Thrift*, 346, 367, 383.

21. Mrs. [Isabella Mary] Beeton, *Mrs. Beeton's Book of Household Management*, ed. Nicola Humble (Oxford: Oxford University Press, 2000), 13, see also 8, vii, xx–xxi.

22. Smiles, *Thrift*, 20, 43, 45, 46–47.

23. Michel Foucault, *Discipline and Punish: The Birth of the Prison*, trans. Alan Sheridan (New York: Vintage Books, 1977).

24. Smiles, *Thrift*, 148–49; on school savings, see 163.

25. Ibid., 77, 250–51.

26. Great Britain, Post Office, *The Post Office: An Historical Summary* (London: His Majesty's Stationery Office, 1911), 113.

27. William Lewins, *A History of Banks for Savings in Great Britain and Ireland* (London: S. Low, Son and Marston, 1866), 312.

28. M. J. Daunton, *Royal Mail: The Post Office since 1840* (London: Athlone Press, 1985), 8–9, 43–44.

29. C. R. Perry, *The Victorian Post Office: The Growth of a Bureaucracy* (Woodbridge, Suffolk, UK: Boydell Press, 1992), 3, 11.

30. With W. H. Wills, "Post-Office Money-Orders," March 20, 1852, in Harry Stone, ed., *Charles Dickens' Uncollected Writings from Household Words, 1850–1859*, vol. 2 (Bloomington: Indiana University Press, 1968), 394.

31. W. L. Maberly (Secretary to the Post Office), in Daunton, *Royal Mail*, 82, see also 84–86, 91.

32. Quoted in Horne, *History of Savings Banks*, 175–76.

33. Howard Robinson, *The British Post Office: A History* (Princeton: Princeton University Press, 1948), 404.

34. Lewins, *History of Banks for Savings*, 229–30, 236–39, 295–96, 306.

35. Great Britain and Ireland, Post Office Savings Bank, *Reports, Minutes, and Memoranda from 30th November, 1860, to 13th September 1861* (London: W. P. Griffith, 1862), 32, 60.

36. Lewins, *History of Banks for Savings*, 203, also 183–225.

37. *The Times*, January 17, 1862, p. 8.

38. Lewins, *History of Banks for Savings*, 241–42.

39. Horne, *History of Savings Banks*, 111.

40. Smiles, *Workmen's Earnings*, 91; Lewins, *History of Banks for Savings*, 298.

41. Memo from F. Hill, Assistant Secretary of the Post Office, to Lord Stanley of Alderley, the Postmaster-General, January 19, 1861, in Great Britain and Ireland, Post Office Savings Bank, *Reports*, 32–33.

42. *Hansard's Parliamentary Debates*, 3rd ser., vol. 162, April 8, 1861, pp. 277–78.

43. *The Times*, November 2, 1865, p. 7.

44. Great Britain and Ireland, Post Office Savings Bank, *Report upon the Progress of Post Office Savings Banks* (London: W. P. Griffith, 1862), 5–6, 7; Great Britain, Post Office, *Post Office*, 114–15, 117; Moss and Russell, *Invaluable Treasure*, 83, 90, 83, 92.

45. Daunton, *Royal Mail*, 105.

46. Shaftesbury, in *The Times*, June 22, July 19, 1870, p. 6.

47. Russell Gurney (Member of Parliament), in *The Times*, May 19, 1870, p. 6.

48. Moss and Russell, *Invaluable Treasure*, 83, 90.

49. Henry Fawcett, *The Post Office and Aids to Thrift* (London: G. E. Eyre and W. Spottiswoode, 1881), 3, 5–6; Robinson, *British Post Office*, 4.

50. Smiles, *Thrift*, 175.

51. Johnson, *Saving and Spending*, 49, 55, 58, 88–99.

52. Great Britain and Ireland, Post Office Savings Bank, *Report*, 55–57; 81; Great Britain, Post Office, *Post Office*, 114.

53. Moss and Russell, *Invaluable Treasure*, 97.

54. Daunton, *Royal Mail*, 149–50.

55. Great Britain and Ireland, Post Office Savings Bank, *Report*, 81–82.

56. Post Office Savings Department, Publicity, "History of P.O.S.B. Publicity from 1881," 1935, The National Archives of the United Kingdom: Public Record Office, NSC 26/5.

57. See D. Eleanor Westney, *Imitation and Innovation: The Transfer of Western Organizational Patterns to Meiji Japan* (Cambridge: Harvard University Press, 1987), 11–12; Rodgers, *Atlantic Crossings*, 31; Dietrich Rueschemeyer and Theda Skocpol, eds., *States, Social Knowledge, and the Origins of Modern Social Policies* (Princeton: Princeton University Press, 1996).

58. E. Cummings, "Social Economy at the Paris Exposition," *The Quarterly Journal of Economics* 4, no. 2 (January 1890): 212–15; Rodgers, *Atlantic Crossings*, 8–14.

59. Caisse Générale d'Épargne et de Retraite de Belgique, *Mémorial 1865–1965 de la Caisse Générale d'Épargne et de Retraite de Belgique* (Bruxelles: CGER, 1965), 144.

60. B. Seebohm Rowntree, *Land & Labour: Lessons from Belgium* (London: Macmillan, 1910), 466, 509.

61. Thomas Wilson (U.S. Consul in Ghent), report to Assistant Secretary of State, J. C. Bancroft Davis, April 15, 1882, in *Postal Savings Banks in Foreign Countries*, 55th Cong., 1st sess., 1897, S. Doc. 154, 56.

62. Erik Buyst, Martine Goossens, Leen Van Molle, and Herman Van der Wee, *Cera 1982–1998: The Power of Co-operative Solidarity* (Antwerp: Mercatorfonds, 2002), 23, 25, 60; Guy Vanthemsche, "Belgium," in Mura, *History of European Savings Banks*, 1:30, 32.

63. Henri Dumortier, 1859, in Caisse Générale d'Épargne, *Mémorial*, 78.

64. Quoted in Caisse Générale d'Épargne, *Mémorial*, 64, also 85; Buyst, *Cera*, 23.

65. Buyst, *Cera*, 25, 60–61, 71; Caisse Générale d'Épargne, *Mémorial*, 139, 151.

66. Quoted at the Congress of Catholic Workers, Antwerp, 1902, in Leen Van Molle, "L'épargne et les caisses d'épargne en Belgique 1890–1914," in August van Put et al., eds., *Les Banques d'épargne belges: Histoire, droit, fonction economique et institutions* (Tielt: Lannoo, 1986), 122.

67. Italics mine. Jules Frédéric, "School Saving in Belgium," in International Thrift Institute, *Third International Thrift Congress, Paris, 20th–25th May, 1935* (Milan: International Thrift Institute, 1937), 1136.

68. Smiles, *Thrift*, 132.

69. Quoted in Jean-Pierre Thiolon, *Les Caisses d'épargne* (Paris: Berger-Levrault, 1971), 24; Caisse des Dépôts, *Livret A*, 140–42.

70. See Eugene Weber, *Peasants into Frenchmen: The Modernization of Rural France* (Stanford: Stanford University Press, 1976).

71. Caisse des Dépôts, *Livret A*, 138, 147–48 ; Duet, *Caisses d'épargne Françaises*, 238.

72. Caisse des Dépôts, *Livret A*, 167, also 122–23, 143, 147–48, 168–70; Smiles, *Thrift*, 250–51; on Belgium, see Caisse Générale d'Épargne, *Mémorial*, 204–206.

73. *La Vie Française* [French life]. February 12, 1979, quoted in Duet, *Caisses d'épargne Françaises*, 15, n. 2.

74. Peter Hertner, "Italy," in Mura, *History of European Savings Banks*, 1:194–96, 223; *Postal Savings Depositories*, 47th Cong., 1st sess.,1882, H. Rep. 473, 17–18.

75. Carl E. Schorske, *Fin-de-siècle Vienna: Politics and Culture* (New York: Knopf, 1979), 90–91.

76. Buyst, *Cera*, 52–53, 71.

77. Körberg, "Sweden," in Mura, *History of European Savings Banks*, 2:328, 334; Enrique Rodríguez, "The Traditional Independence of the Swedish Savings Banks," unpublished paper, Swedbank, Stockholm, 2000, pp. 3–5.

78. Mura, "Germany," in Mura, *History of European Savings Banks*,1:107, 124–25; Deutche Postbank AG, "The History of Postbank Savings," http://www.postbank.com/ pbcom_ag_home/pbcom_au_about_us/pbcom_au_history/pbcom_au_history_savings .html, accessed January 26, 2006.

79. Honorary Secretary of the Gloucester Penny Bank, *Penny Banks for Villages and Small Towns* (London: Longman, Green & Co., 1861).

80. Duet, *Caisses d'épargne Françaises*, 144; Caisse des Dépôts, *Livret A*, 124, 147.

81. Caisse Générale d'Épargne, *Mémorial*, 78; Vernon Mallinson, *Power and Politics in Belgian Education, 1815 to 1961* (London: Heinemann, 1963), 68–69, 71–101.

82. Frédéric, "School Savings in Belgium," 1129.

83. Ibid., 1130–31; Caisse Générale d'Épargne, *Mémorial*, 156–57; Cassa di Risparmio delle Provincie Lombarde, *First International Thrift Congress, Milan, 26–31 October 1924* (Milan: Organising Committee of the Congress, 1925), 177; Caisse Générale d'Épargne et de Retraite de Belgique, *La Caisse Générale d'Épargne et de Retraite et ses différent services* (Bruxelles: Vanbuggenhoudt, 1910), 13.

84. Caisse des Dépôts, *Livret A*, 147–48 ; Sara Louisa Oberholtzer, "School Savings Banks," *Annals of the American Academy of Political and Social Science* 3 (July 1892): 15–16.

85. Smiles, *Thrift*, 163–64, 251.

86. Great Britain, Post Office, *Post Office*, 116; Thomas Henderson, "School Savings," in International Thrift Institute, *Third International Thrift Congress*, 1138–41.

87. *World Thrift*, 1938, no. 7: 227–28.

88. Henderson, "School Savings," 1143–44.

89. Niall Ferguson, *The World's Banker: The History of the House of Rothschild* (London: Weidenfeld & Nicolson, 1998), 582–83.

90. Ferguson, *World's Banker*, 941–46.

91. Duet, *Caisses d'épargne Françaises*, 241–45; Rodríguez, "Traditional Independence of the Swedish Savings Banks," 3, 6–7.

92. Moster and Vogler, "France," in Mura, *History of European Savings Banks*, 78.

93. Caisse Générale d'Épargne, *Caisse Générale d'Épargne*, 2–3, 15–16 ; Caisse Générale d'Épargne, *Mémorial*, 96–97.

94. D. E. Schremmer, "Taxation and Public Finance: Britain, France, and Germany," in Peter Mathias and Sidney Pollard, eds., *The Cambridge Economic History of Europe*, vol. 8 (Cambridge: Cambridge University Press, 1989), 376, 397, 399.

95. LeBastard, in Thiolon, *Caisses d'épargne*, 24.

96. "Elections Législatives de 1881" [Legislative elections of 1881], and "L'épargne en France et dans quelques pays étrangers" [Savings in France and other countries], ca. 1907, in Caisse des Dépôts, *Livret A*, 146, 149, 167, also 137–38, 171; Thiolon, *Caisses d'épargne*, 34 ; Moster and Vogler, "France," in Mura, *History of European Savings Banks*, 1:81.

97. Schremmer, "Taxation," 347, 352–54, 400.

98. *The Times*, November 2, 1865, p. 7.

99. For Gladstone in 1859, see Horne, *History of Savings Banks*, 146–47, also 80, 149–50, 225, 276–77, 225; *Postal Savings Depositories*, 47th Cong., 1st sess., 1882, H. Rep. 473, 14.

100. Moster and Vogler, "France," in Mura, *History of European Savings Banks*, 77–78.

101. *The Times*, December 29, 1908, p. 8.

CHAPTER 3: AMERICA THE EXCEPTIONAL

1. *To Establish Postal Savings Depositories*, 60th Cong., 1st sess., 1908, S. Rep. 525, 37.

2. Nan Oppenlander-Eberle, *Good Fairy Thrift* (Swarthmore: Chatauqua Association of Pennsylvania, 1917), quoted in David M. Tucker, *The Decline of Thrift in America: Our Cultural Shift from Saving to Spending* (New York: Praeger, 1991), 89.

3. See Michael Kammen, "The Problem of American Exceptionalism: A Reconsideration, *American Quarterly* 45, no. 1 (March 1993): 1–43; "Review Essays: American Exceptionalism," *American Historical Review* 102, no. 3 (June 1997): 748.

4. Yukichi Fukuzawa, *The Autobiography of Yukichi Fukuzawa*, trans. Eiichi Kiyooka (New York: Columbia University Press, 1966), 115–16.

5. *New York Times*, September 6, 1914, p. 12.

6. Quoted by W. Espey Albig, "The Savings Banks' Part in Thrift Education," in Committee on Thrift Education of the National Education Association and the National Council of Education, *Thrift Education; Being the Report of the National Conference on Thrift Education* (Washington, DC: National Education Association, 1924), 46.

7. T. D. MacGregor, *The Book of Thrift: Why and How to Save and What to Do with Your Savings* (New York: Funk & Wagnalls, 1915), 23–24.

8. Emerson W. Keyes, *A History of Savings Banks in the United States, from Their Inception in 1816 down to 1877*, 2 vols. (New York: Bradford Rhodes, 1876–78), 1:43–44; also Rohit Daniel Wadhwani, "Citizen Savers: The Family Economy, Financial Institutions, and Social Policy in the Northeastern U.S. from the Market Revolution to the Great Depression" (Ph.D. diss., University of Pennsylvania, 2002), 46.

9. *The Christian Disciple*, December 1816, quoted in Keyes, *History of Savings Banks*, 1:39; also Wadhwani, "Citizen Savers," 21–22.

10. Society for the Prevention of Pauperism in the City of New-York, *Documents Relative to Savings Banks, Intemperance, and Lotteries* (New York: E. Conrad, 1819), 3–6.

11. Keyes, *History of Savings Banks*, 1:38; Society for the Prevention of Pauperism in the City of New-York, *The Second Annual Report of the Managers of the Society for the Prevention of Pauperism, in the City of New-York* (New York: E. Conrad, 1820), 41.

12. Quoted in Keyes, *History of Savings Banks*, 1:307, 309.

13. W. David Lewis, *From Newgate to Dannemora: The Rise of the Penitentiary in New York, 1796–1848* (Ithaca: Cornell University Press, 1965), 5; Wadhwani, "Citizen Savers," 24–26, 50–53.

14. James Henry Hamilton, *Savings and Savings Institutions* (New York: Macmillan, 1902), 162–63; Keyes, *History of Savings Banks*, 2:520–22.

15. Hamilton, *Savings and Savings Institutions*, 192, n. 1, 193–94, 196; Wadhwani, "Citizen Savers," 156.

16. George K. Holmes, "The Concentration of Wealth," *Political Science Quarterly* 8, no. 4 (December 1893): 590; Stephan Thernstrom, *Poverty and Progress: Social Mobility in a Nineteenth-Century City* (Cambridge: Harvard University Press, 1964), 128–31; Wadhwani, "Citizen Savers," 167–68; George Alter, Claudia Goldin, and Elyce Rotella, "The Savings of Ordinary Americans: The Philadelphia Saving Fund Society in the Mid-Nineteenth Century," *Journal of Economic History* 54, no. 4. (Dec., 1994): 740–42, 765.

17. Wadhwani, "Citizen Savers," 167–71; Edward L. Robinson, *One Hundred Years of Savings Banking, 1816–1916* ([New York]: Savings Bank Section, American Bankers Association, 1917), 23.

18. Horatio Alger, Jr., *Ragged Dick and Struggling Upward* (East Rutherford, NJ: Viking Penguin, 1985), 70, 92.

19. Quoted in Wadhwani, "Citizen Savers," 186, n. 47; for data on female savers at the PSFS, see ibid., 167–68, 181–86, and Alter, Goldin, and Rotella, "Savings of Ordinary Americans," 738, 744, 747.

20. Lydia Maria Child, *The American Frugal Housewife: Dedicated to Those Who Are Not Ashamed of Economy*, 12th ed. (Boston: Carter, Hendee, 1832), 4.

21. Lendol Calder, *Financing the American Dream: A Cultural History of Consumer Credit* (Princeton: Princeton University Press, 1999), 68–69, 86, 90; Tucker, *Decline of Thrift*, 25–36.

22. Wadhwani, "Citizen Savers," 186–94.

23. Oliver Optic [William Taylor Adams], "The Savings Bank; or How to Buy a House," in Freeman Hunt, *Worth and Wealth: A Collection of Maxims, Morals and Miscellanies for Merchants and Men of Business* (New York: Stringer & Townsend, 1856), 267–77.

24. For statistics on savings and other banks, see United States, Office of the Comptroller of the Currency, *Annual Report of the Comptroller of the Currency, 1910* (Washington, DC: Government Printing Office, 1911), 46, 69–70; George E. Roberts, *Objections to a Postal Savings Bank, Address by Geo. E. Roberts, President of The Commercial National Bank of Chicago, Delivered before the Minnesota State Bankers Association, at Its Annual Meeting held at Lake Minnetonka, June 15th, 1909* (n.p.: [1909]), 11.

25. Susan B. Carter and Richard Sutch, "Myth of the Industrial Scrap Heap: A Revisionist View of Turn-of-the-Century American Retirement," *Journal of Economic History* 56, no. 1 (March 1995): 9; Alter, Goldin, and Rotella, "Savings of Ordinary

Americans," 735, 736; Lance E. Davis and Robert F. Gallman, "Capital Formation in the United States during the Nineteenth Century," in Peter Mathias and M.M. Postan, eds., *The Cambridge Economic History of Europe*, vol. 7, part 2 (Cambridge: Cambridge University Press, 1978), 30–54, 64–65.

26. Alter, Goldin, and Rotella, "Savings of Ordinary Americans," 736.

27. *Annual Report of the Comptroller of the Currency, 1910*, pp. 43–47.

28. On stock savings banks and building and loan associations, see Donald Bruce Schewe, "A History of the Postal Savings System in America, 1910–1970" (PhD diss., Ohio State University, 1971), 7–10; Tucker, *Decline of Thrift*, 50.

29. J. W. Bell (president of the St. Louis Safe Deposit and Savings Bank), in House Committee on the Post Office and Post Roads, *Postal Savings Banks, Hearings on H.R. 3353*, 55th Cong., 2nd sess.,1900, 38; see also Donald Sham, "The Origin and Development of the United States Postal Savings System" (PhD diss., University of California, Berkeley, 1942), 48–49, 53, 57–60, 63–64; Schewe, "History of the Postal Savings System," 19–20.

30. Italics mine. Roberts, *Objections to a Postal Savings Bank*, 5.

31. National Monetary Commission, *Special Report from the Banks of the United States* (Washington, DC: Government Printing Office, 1909), 56–59.

32. Hamilton, *Savings and Savings Institutions*, 195, 197.

33. Wadhwani, "Citizen Savers," 196.

34. Hamilton, *Savings and Savings Institutions*, 133, 137–38, 192.

35. Ibid., 163, 202–206; Keyes, *History of Savings Banks*, 2:430; on the lack of banks in the South, see C. Vann Woodward, *Origins of the New South, 1877–1913* (Baton Rouge: Louisiana State University Press, 1971), 183.

36. See Bruce J. Schulman, *From Cotton Belt to Sunbelt: Federal Policy, Economic Development, and the Transformation of the South, 1938–1980* (New York: Oxford University Press, 1991), 8–12; Peter A. Coclanis, "The Paths before Us/U.S.: Tracking the Economic Divergence of the North and the South," in David L. Carlton and Peter A. Coclanis, eds., *The South, the Nation, and the World: Perspectives on Southern Economic Development* (Charlottesville: University of Virginia Press, 2003), 12–23.

37. Hamilton, *Savings and Savings Institutions*, 200–201.

38. Quoted in Carl R. Osthaus, *Freedmen, Philanthropy, and Fraud: A History of the Freedman's Savings Bank* (Urbana: University of Illinois Press, 1976), 55, 64, also 1–5, 10, 14–15, 49, 64–70, 135.

39. Quoted in Osthaus, *Freedmen, Philanthropy, and Fraud*, 9, also 8, 95, 134–35.

40. State Charities Aid Association, *Postal Savings Banks for the United States of America*, no. 41 (New York: State Charities Aid Association, 1885), 6; Osthaus, *Freedmen, Philanthropy, and Fraud*, chap. 7.

41. Geo(rge) R. Gibson, "The Postal Savings Bank System," *The Banker's Magazine and Statistical Register* 32, no. 6 (December 1877): 470.

42. "The Freedmen's Savings Bank," *The Independent* 26 (December 31, 1874): 28.

43. E.g., "National Savings Banks," *Littell's Living Age*, no. 909 (November 2, 1861): 198.

44. *New York Times*, May 16, 1867, p. 4, also October 3, 1864, p. 4; Sham, "Origin and Development," 22–23.

45. *To Establish Postal Savings Depositories*, 29–35. "Stake in the Country" appears in John Wanamaker, "Postal Savings Banks: An Argument in Their Favor by the Postmaster-General," February 26, 1891, ibid., 8.

46. Sham, "Origin and Development," 138–42.

47. *Postal Savings Depositories*, 11.

48. Wanamaker, "Postal Savings Banks" and "From the Report of the Postmaster-General, 1890," in *To Establish Postal Savings Depositories*, 11–13, 17, 38.

49. See Rodgers, *Atlantic Crossings*.

50. *Postal Savings Depositories*, 13–20; *To Establish Postal Savings Depositories*, 42–43; *Nature and Practical Workings of Postal Telegraphs, Telephones, and Postal Savings Banks of Foreign Countries*, 55th Cong., 2nd sess., 1897, S. Doc. 39; *Postal Savings Banks in Foreign Countries*, 59th Cong., 2nd sess., 1907, H. Doc. 723.

51. James A. Gary, "Postal Savings Depositories," in *To Establish Postal Savings Depositories*, 80; for references to Canada, Germany, and Japan, see 2, 9, 42, 48.

52. Schewe, "History of the Postal Savings System," 21, 50.

53. *To Establish Postal Savings Depositories*, 29.

54. State Charities Aid Association, *Postal Savings Banks*, 3–7.

55. Jane Addams, "Banks Boon to the Poor," *News* (Chicago), December 15, 1906, quoted in Sham, "Origin and Development," 35; Jane Addams, *Twenty Years at Hull-House* (Urbana: University of Illinois Press, 1990), 175; also Florence Kelley, "Postal Savings Bank," *Charities and the Commons* 21 (January 23, 1909): 718–19.

56. Hamilton, *Savings and Savings Institutions*, 3–4, 173, 423–26; see also Rodgers, *Atlantic Crossings*, 11–13, 29–31, chap. 3.

57. House Committee on the Post-Office and Post-Roads, *Postal Savings Bank: Hearings before the Committee on the Post-Office and Post-Roads*, March 1910 (Washington, DC: Government Printing Office, 1910), 181; also David Bennett King, "Organized Aids to Thrift, *The Independent* 38 (June 17, 1886): 6.

58. On Populists and petition drives, see Schewe, "History of the Postal Savings System," 23–25, 36–37; Sham, "Origin and Development," 27.

59. *To Establish Postal Savings Depositories*, 35.

60. *Postal Savings Banks*, 55th Cong., 3rd sess., 1899, S. Rep.1504, in *To Establish Postal Savings Depositories*, 44; also Schewe, "History of the Postal Savings System," 37–38; Sham, "Origin and Development," 24.

61. House Committee on the Post-Office, *Postal Savings Bank*, 4; also Sham, "Origin and Development," 28–29, 183.

62. Gibson, "Postal Savings Bank System," 470–71.

63. E. R. Gurney, "The Imminence of the Postal Savings Bank," *Proceedings of the Wyoming Bankers Convention* (1908), 33–34, quoted in Sham, "Origin and Development," 198.

64. Edward W. Kemmerer, *Postal Savings: A Historical and Critical Study of the Postal Savings Bank System of the United States* (Princeton: Princeton University Press, 1917), 35.

65. See F. D. Wimberly (Farmers' Union), in House Committee on the Post-Office, *Postal Savings Bank*, 175–78; Sham, "Origin and Development," 167–83.

66. William H. Taft, "Postal Savings Banks: State Fair Grounds, Milwaukee, Wisconsin, September 17, 1909," in *The Collected Works of William Howard Taft*, vol. 3:

Presidential Addresses and State Papers, ed. David H. Burton (Athens: Ohio University Press, 2002), 165; also Schewe, "History of the Postal Savings System," 41–56, 66–69.

67. George von L. Meyer, testimony to subcommittee of Senate Committee on Post-Offices and Post-Roads, March 7, 1908, in *To Establish Postal Savings Depositories*, 124–26; Sham, "Origin and Development," 65–68.

68. Italics mine. William R. Creer, in House Committee on the Post-Office, *Postal Savings Bank*, 37, 39.

69. *New York Times*, August 26, 1909, p. 3.

70. John Alden, Esq., in Senate Committee on Post Offices and Post Roads, *Industrial Savings Bill: Hearing before a Subcommittee of the Committee on Post Offices and Post Roads*, 66th Cong., 1st sess., 1919 (Washington, DC: Government Printing Office, 1919), 13.

71. On the postal savings system in operation, see Kemmerer, *Postal Savings*, chaps. 2–6; Schewe, "History of the Postal Savings System," 94–186, 223–25.

72. James Hilton Manning, *Century of American Savings Banks* (New York: B. F. Buck, 1917), 167–68; Sham, "Origin and Development," 39; George F. Zook, "Thrift in the United States," *Annals of the American Academy of Political and Social Science* 87 (Jan. 1920): 207.

73. Oberholtzer, "School Savings Banks"; for statistics on school savings banks, see *Annual Report of the Comptroller of the Currency, 1910*, p. 67, *1929*, p. 148.

74. Hamilton, *Savings and Savings Institutions*, 82, also 71–81.

75. Sham, "Origin and Development," 320–24; Schewe, "History of the Postal Savings System," 148–49.

76. S. W. Straus, *History of the Thrift Movement in America* (Philadelphia: J. B. Lippincott, 1920), 49, 53–54, 68–69, 91.

77. Manning, *Century of American Savings Banks*, 173–75; also American Bankers Association, *School Savings Banking* (New York: Ronald Press, 1923), 72–73.

78. Albig, "Savings Banks' Part," in Committee on Thrift Education, *Thrift Education*, 47.

79. H. R. Daniel, "School Savings-Bank Systems," in Committee on Thrift Education, *Thrift Education*, 40–41.

80. Straus, *History of the Thrift Movement*, 49; Manning, *Century of American Savings Banks*, 315.

CHAPTER 4: JAPANESE TRADITIONS OF DILIGENCE AND THRIFT

1. Masae Fukuzumi, *Sage Ninomiya's Evening Talks—Ninomiya-Ō Yawa*, trans. Isoh Yamagata, in Tadaatsu Ishiguro, ed., *Ninomiya Sontoku: His Life and "Evening Talks"* (Tokyo: Kenkyusha, 1955), 163–65.

2. Chochiku Kōdō to Chochiku Ishiki ni kansuru Chōsa Kenkyūkai, *Dai 6-kai chochiku kōdō to chochiku ishiki ni kansuru chōsa hōkokusho* (Tokyo: Chochiku Kōdō to Chochiku Ishiki ni kansuru Chōsa Kenkyūkai, 1998), 2.

3. Toyama Shigeru, *Nihonjin no kinben-, chochiku-kan* (Tokyo: Tōyō Keizai Shinpōsha, 1987), 4, 5, 7.

4. Charles Yuji Horioka, "Consuming and Saving," in Andrew Gordon, ed., *Postwar Japan as History* (Berkeley: University of California, 1993), 259, 280–84.

5. Quoted in Alfred Stead, ed., *Japan by the Japanese* (London: W. Heinemann, 1904), 410.

6. Tomeoka Kōsuke Nikki Henshū Iinkai, ed., *Tomeoka Kōsuke nikki*, vol. 2 (Tokyo: Kyōsei Kyōkai, 1979), 572.

7. Kobayashi Sakutarō, in *Jitsugyō shōnen* [Business youth] 2, no. 3 (September 1, 1908): 9, quoted in Andrew Gordon, *The Evolution of Labor Relations in Japan: Heavy Industry, 1853–1955* (Cambridge: Council on East Asian Studies, Harvard University, 1985), 83.

8. Yahagi Eizō, "Wagakuni o fukyō narashimuru michi" [Road to enriching and strengthening our country], *Shimin* 8, no. 3 (June 7, 1913): 25, 27.

9. Herman Ooms, *Tokugawa Village Practice: Class, Status, Power, Law* (Berkeley: University of California Press, 1996), 53, 199; Donald H. Shively, "Sumptuary Regulation and Status in Early Tokugawa Japan," *Harvard Journal of Asiatic Studies* 25 (1964–65): 153.

10. Shively, "Sumptuary Regulation," 150–52.

11. Herman Ooms, *Charismatic Bureaucrat: A Political Biography of Matsudaira Sadanobu, 1758–1829* (Chicago: University of Chicago Press, 1975), 34, 50–54, 60.

12. See David L. Howell, *Geographies of Identity in Nineteenth-Century Japan* (Berkeley: University of California Press, 2005).

13. Ooms, *Tokugawa Village Practice*, 369.

14. Shively, "Sumptuary Regulation," 126–27, 129, 135, 154–55.

15. Mandeville, *The Fable of the Bees*, 37.

16. Saikaku Ihara, *The Japanese Family Storehouse, Or the Millionaire's Gospel Modernised*, trans. G. W. Sargent (Cambridge: Cambridge University Press, 1959), 26.

17. See Gene A. Brucker, *The Society of Renaissance Florence: A Documentary Study* (New York: Harper and Row, 1971); Diane Owen Hughes, "Distinguishing Signs: Ear-Rings, Jews and Franciscan Rhetoric in the Italian Renaissance City," *Past and Present*, no. 112 (August 1986): 3–59. On the Lutheran and Calvinist cases, see Robert Kingdon, "The Control of Morals in Calvin's Geneva," in Kyle C. Sessions and Phillip N. Bebb, eds., *Pietas et Societas: New Trends in Reformation Social History: Essays in Memory of Harold J. Grimm* (Kirksville, MO: Sixteenth Century Journal Publishers, 1985); Lyndal Roper, *The Holy Household: Women and Morals in Reformation Augsburg* (Oxford: Oxford University Press, 1989).

18. Ooms, *Tokugawa Village Practice*, 132, 200–202.

19. Shively, "Sumptuary Regulation," 134.

20. Herman Ooms, *Tokugawa Ideology: Early Constructs, 1570–1680* (Princeton: Princeton University Press, 1985), 144.

21. Yūseishō, *Yūsei hyakunenshi* (Tokyo: Yūseishō, 1971), 155.

22. Shunsaku Nishikawa, "The Economy of Chōshū on the Eve of Industrialization," *Economic Studies Quarterly* (Japan Association of Economics and Econometrics) 38, no. 4 (December 1987): 335; E. S. Crawcour, "The Development of a Credit System in Seventeenth-Century Japan," *Journal of Economic History* 21, no. 3 (Sept. 1961): 348–49, 354–56; Ronald P. Toby, "From Village Moneylender to Rural Banker: Changing

Credit in Protoindustrial Japan," in Gareth Austin and Kaoru Sugihara, eds., *Local Suppliers of Credit in the Third World, 1750–1960* (New York: St. Martin's Press, 1993), 55–58, 77.

23. See Miyamoto Matao and Takashima Masaaki, *Shōmin no ayunda kin'yūshi* [Financial history trod by the common folk] (Osaka: Purodakushon F, 1991), 100–104, 131–32, 154; Tetsuo Najita, *Ordinary Economies in Japan: A Historical Perspective, 1750–1950* (Berkeley: University of California Press, 2009), chaps. 3, 6; for granaries, see Ikeda Yoshimasa, *Nihon shakai fukushishi* (Kyoto: Hōritsu Bunkasha, 1986), 115–17.

24. Mary Elizabeth Berry, *Japan in Print: Information and Nation in the Early Modern Period* (Berkeley: University of California Press, 2006), 27–32.

25. Translated in Ihara, *Japanese Family Storehouse*, 240, also xxx.

26. Defoe, *Complete English Tradesman*.

27. Tetsuo Najita, *Visions of Virtue in Tokugawa Japan: The Kaitokudō, Merchant Academy of Osaka* (Chicago: University of Chicago Press, 1987), 20–21.

28. Ihara, *Japanese Family Storehouse*, 35–39, 59–63, 71, 137, 144, 146.

29. Robert N. Bellah, *Tokugawa Religion: The Values of Pre-Industrial Japan* (Glencoe, IL: Free Press, 1957), 161, also 2–3, 133, 157; Najita, *Visions of Virtue*, 77–78, 95–96.

30. *Ken'yaku seika*, quoted in Toyama, *Nihonjin no kinben*, 38–42.

31. Kaigo Tokiomi, *Nihon kyōkasho taikei: Kindaihen*, vol. 3 (Tokyo: Kōdansha, 1962), 17–18, 68, 144–46, 250–52, 400–401.

32. Fukuzumi Masae, comp., *Ninomiya-Ō yawa* [Sage Ninomiya's evening talks], 1885, in Ninomiya Sontoku-Ō Zenshū Kankōkai, ed., *Ninomiya Sontoku-Ō zenshū*, vol. 1 (Tokyo: Ninomiya Sontoku-Ō Zenshū Kankōkai, 1937), 453.

33. Nagasawa Minao, "Gaikokujin kara mita Sontoku" [Ninomiya Sontoku as seen by foreigners], in Nagasawa Minao, ed., *Ninomiya Sontoku no subete* (Tokyo: Shinjinbutsu Ōraisha, 1993), 153–54.

34. Garrett Droppers, "A Japanese Credit Association and Its Founder," *Transactions of the Asiatic Society of Japan* 22 (1894): 86, also viii.

35. Kanzō Uchimura, *Japan and the Japanese* (Tokyo: Minyūsha, 1894), reprinted in *Uchimura Kanzō Zenshū*, vol. 3 (Tokyo: Iwanami Shoten, 1982), 228–49.

36. For Ninomiya's background and activities, see Eiji Takemura, *The Perception of Work in Tokugawa Japan: A Study of Ishida Baigan and Ninomiya Sontoku* (Lanham, MD: University Press of America, 1997), 109–11; Droppers, "Japanese Credit Association," 69–81.

37. Thomas C. Smith, "Ōkura Nagatsune and the Technologists," in Albert M. Craig and Donald H. Shively, eds., *Personality in Japanese History* (Berkeley: University of California, 1970), 127–54; Helen Hardacre, "Creating State Shintō: The Great Promulgation Campaign and the New Religions," *Journal of Japanese Studies* 12, no. 1 (Winter 1986): 37–38.

38. Bellah, *Tokugawa Religion*, 128.

39. Fukuzumi, *Sage Ninomiya's Evening Talks*, 106, 108.

40. Takemura, *Perception of Work*, 116, also 113–14.

41. Fukuzumi, *Ninomiya-Ō yawa*, 1:500.

42. Ibid., 1:453, 467, 500–501; Toyama, *Nihonjin no kinben*, 62–65.

43. Ibid., *Sage Ninomiya's Evening Talks*, 181–84.

44. Ibid., *Ninomiya-Ō yawa*, 1:475–76; Toyama, *Nihonjin no kinben*, 59–60.

45. Sakamoto Shigeharu, *Nōritsu gishi Ninomiya Sontoku* (1936), quoted in William M. Tsutsui, *Manufacturing Ideology: Scientific Management in Twentieth-Century Japan* (Princeton: Princeton University Press, 1998), 97; Toyama, *Nihonjin no kinben*, 51, 61–62.

46. Droppers, "Japanese Credit Association," 72–73, 85, 87–90, 94; Takemura, *Perception of Work*, 116–17, 138, 146–48.

47. "Imeeji historii—Kinjirō—Kinjirō-zō no rekishi o tadoru" [Image history—tracing the history of Ninomiya Kinjirō statues], *Hōtoku hakubutsukan tomonokai dayori*, no. 23 (October 1991); Toyama, *Nihonjin no kinben*, 49, 52; Takemura, *Perception of Work*, 199–203; Najita, *Ordinary Economies*, 154–63.

48. Droppers, "Japanese Credit Association," 94–95.

CHAPTER 5: SAVING FOR THE NEW JAPAN

1. Namiki Gensuke, *Risshin kiso chokin shōka* (1901), in Chochiku Zōkyō Chūō Iinkai, *Chochiku undō: Chozōi 30 nen no ayumi* (Tokyo: Chochiku Zōkyō Chūō Iinkai, 1983), 6–7.

2. Ichiki Kitokurō, "Kokuun no hatten to kinken kyōdō no seishin" [Development of national prosperity and the spirit of diligence, thrift, and cooperation], *Shimin* 4, no. 7 (August 7, 1909): 8, 10.

3. See chapter 2; in Japanese translation in Rōdo Rōzuberii, "Ijin to taikoku wa kinken no seika desu" [Great men and empires arise from thrift], *Shimin* 4, no. 1 (April 7, 1909): 9.

4. Ichiki, "Kokuun no hatten," 10–11.

5. Hazel J. Jones, *Live Machines: Hired Foreigners and Meiji Japan* (Vancouver: University of British Columbia Press, 1980), 6–7.

6. See Mark Ravina, "Japanese State-Making in Global Context: World Culture and Meiji Japan," in Richard Boyd and Tak-Wing Ngo, eds., *State Making in Asia* (New York: Routledge. 2006), 35–52; Angus Lockyer, "Japan at the Exhibition, 1867–1877," in Tadao Umesao et al., eds., *Japanese Civilization in the Modern World: Collection and Exhibition* (Osaka: National Museum of Ethnology, Senri Ethnological Studies, no. 54, 2001).

7. Shimomura Hiroshi, *Tomi to chochiku* [Wealth and saving] (Tokyo: Dōbunkan, 1911), 8–10.

8. Westney, *Imitation and Innovation*, 5–6, 20–22, 25.

9. Kume Kunitake, *The Iwakura Embassy, 1871–73: A True Account of the Ambassador Extraordinary & Plenipotentiary's Journey of Observation through the United States of America and Europe*, ed. Graham Healey and Chushichi Tsuzuki (Chiba, Japan: The Japan Documents, 2002), 2:88–89.

10. Kume, *Iwakura Embassy*, 2:103; for education, see 2:27–28, 3:22, 277, 4:184–86; on postal services and other communications, 2:99–103, 3:14, 219.

11. Iwase Tadanari, cited by Maejima Hisoka, *Kōsōkon* [Autobiography] (1914), in Saeki Shōichi and Kano Masanao, eds., *Nihonjin no jiden*, vol. 1 (Tokyo: Heibonsha, 1981), 353, also 352, 430.

12. Maejima Hisoka, *Yūbin sōgyōdan* [On founding the post] (Hayama-machi, Kanagawa-ken: Maejima Hisoka Denki Kankōkai, 1956), 22; Maejima, *Kōsōkon*, 396–97.

13. Norio Tamaki, *Japanese Banking: A History, 1859–1959* (Cambridge: Cambridge University Press, 1995), 25–39.

14. Quoted in Yūseishō Chokinkyoku, *Yūbin kawase chokin jigyō 80 nenshi* (Tokyo: Yūcho Kenkyūkai, 1957), 7–8.

15. Maejima Hisoka, *Kōsōkon*, 406–407; Yūseishō, *Yūsei hyakunenshi*, 158–60, 164, 170, 173–74, appendix, 30.

16. Edwin P. Ruebens, "Foreign Capital and Domestic Development in Japan," in Simon Kuznets et al., eds., *Economic Growth: Brazil, India, Japan* (Durham, NC: Duke University Press, 1955), 179–240.

17. John Russell Young, *Around the World with General Grant*, vol. 2 (New York: American News Co., 1879), 545.

18. Ian Buruma, *Inventing Japan, 1853–1964* (New York: Modern Library, 2003); Katalin Ferber, "'Run the State Like a Business': The Origin of the Deposit Fund in Meiji Japan," *Japanese Studies* 22, no. 2 (2002): 131–51.

19. Matsukata Masayoshi, "Ōkurashō-chū chokinkyoku setchi narabi chokin kisoku goseitei no gi jōshin," May 26, 1884, in Meiji Zaiseishi Hensankai, *Meiji zaiseishi*, vol. 10 (Tokyo: Maruzen Kabushiki Gaisha, 1905), 44–46.

20. Hugh T. Patrick, "Japan, 1868–1914," in Rondo Cameron et al., ed., *Banking in the Early Stages of Industrialization* (New York: Oxford University Press, 1967), 268–70; Juro Teranishi, "Availability of Safe Assets and the Process of Bank Concentration in Japan," *Economic Development and Cultural Change* 25, no. 3 (April 1977): 451–54, 466–67.

21. Mukai Yurio, "Ōkurashō yokinbu seido no seiritsu to tenkai" [Establishment and development of the Ministry of Finance's Deposit Bureau system], in Shibuya Ryūichi, ed., *Meiji-ki Nihon tokushu kin'yū rippō shi* (Tokyo: Waseda Daigaku Shuppanbu, 1977), 535, also 518, 545; *Nihon kin-gendaishi jiten*, s.v. "Nishihara shakkan" [Nishihara loans].

22. Yūseishō, *Yūsei hyakunenshi*, 170–72; Kyōwa Ginkō, *Honpō chochiku ginkōshi* [History of Japanese savings banks] (Tokyo: Kyōwa Ginkō, 1969), 9–11, 19–27, 41–42, 188; Meiji Zaiseishi Hensankai, *Meiji zaiseishi*, 12:861–62; Mukai, "Ōkurashō yokinbu," 508–11.

23. Smiles, *Autobiography*, 230.

24. Kinmonth, *Self-Made Man in Meiji Japanese Thought*, chap. 1.

25. *Saikoku risshi hen*, quoted in Takahashi Masao, *Nakamura Keiu* (Tokyo: Yoshikawa Kōbunkan, 1988), 82–84; for thrift in the translation of *Character*, see 190–91.

26. Sidney Devere Brown, "Ōkubo Toshimichi: His Political and Economic Policies in Early Meiji Japan," *Journal of Asian Studies* 21, no. 2. (February 1962): 190.

27. Kume, *Iwakura Embassy*, 2:25, 157, 159, 214.

28. Nakamura Masanao, "Changing the Character of the People," February 1875, in William R. Braisted, trans., *Meiroku zasshi: Journal of the Japanese Enlightenment* (Cambridge: Harvard University Press, 1976), 372–74; Kume, *Iwakura Embassy*, 4:185–86.

29. Aesopus, *Isoppu monogatari*, trans. Amenotani Kan'ichi (Tokyo: Yoshikawa Kōbunkan, 1907), 13; Watanabe On, trans., *Tsūzoku Isoppu monogatari* [More Aesop's fables] (1873), in Kaigo, *Nihon kyōkasho taikei: Kindaihen* 1:251, 599, on *Self-Help* as a

text, see 5, 596; Jesuit translation appears in Asakura Kamezō, ed., *Bunmei genryū sōsho* [Sources of civilization series], vol. 1 (Tokyo: Kokusho Kankōkai, 1913), 116, preface, 3–4; cf. Sukehiro Hirakawa, *Japan's Love-Hate Relationship with the West* (Folkestone, Kent, UK: Global Oriental, 2005), 369–70.

30. Samuel Smiles, *Sekkenron* [Thrift], trans. Ekiteikyoku Torishirabe-ka, 2 vols. (Tokyo: Nōshomushō Ekiteikyoku, 1885–86); *Kinkenron* [Thrift], trans. Wakatsuki Yasuji and Takemura Osamu (Tokyo: Naigai Shuppan Kyōkai, 1905).

31. P[aul] Mayet, *Agricultural Insurance, in Organic Connection with Savings-Banks, Land-Credit, and the Commutation of Debts*, trans. Arthur Lloyd (London: S. Sonnenschein, 1893), viii.

32. Kawamura Takeji, *Gakkō chokin shinkōron* [Promoting school saving] (Tokyo, Keigansha, 1906), 17, 12–14, 20–29, 38–39, 135–39.

33. Teishinshō [Ministry of Communications], *Teishin jigyōshi* [History of communications activities], vol. 5 (Tokyo: Teishin Kyōkai, 1940), 45–47.

34. "Jogaku sekai shūki zōkan: shakai hyaku seikatsu" [*Jogaku sekai*'s autumn special: One hundred walks of life], *Jogaku sekai* 4, no. 12 (September 15, 1904): 144; on the Meiji middle classes, see Jordan Sand, *House and Home in Modern Japan: Architecture, Domestic Space, and Bourgeois Culture, 1880–1930* (Cambridge: Harvard University Asian Center, 2003), 9–12, 21–28; David R. Ambaras, "Social Knowledge, Cultural Capital, and the New Middle Class in Japan, 1895–1912," *Journal of Japanese Studies* 24, no. 1 (Winter 1998): 1–33; Sheldon Garon, *Molding Japanese Minds: The State in Everyday Life* (Princeton: Princeton University Press, 1997), 18–19.

35. Fusataro Takano, "The War and Labor in Japan," *Social Economist* 9 (July 1895), and Yokoyama Gennosuke, quoted in Eiji Yutani, "*Nihon no Kaso Shakai* of Gennosuke Yokoyama, Translated and with an Introduction" (PhD diss., University of California, Berkeley, 1985), 82–84.

36. Takahashi Masashi, "Miyagawa Tsuneteru to Kanamori Michitomo," in Dōshisha Daigaku Jinbun Kagaku Kenkyūjo, ed., *Kumamoto Bando kenkyū* (Tokyo: Misuzu Shobō, 1965), 326–27, 330.

37. Quoted in Toyama, *Nihonjin no kinben*, 49–50; also R. C. Armstrong, *Just before the Dawn: The Life and Work of Ninomiya Sontoku* (New York: Macmillan, 1912), xv, 69–70; on Franklin in ethics textbooks, see Karasawa Tomitarō, *Zusetsu Meiji hyakunen no jidōshi* [Illustrated hundred-year history of children since the Meiji Restoration], vol. 1 (Tokyo: Kōdansha, 1968), 375, 383.

38. Tomeoka Kōsuke, "Hōtokuki wa tōyō no jijoron nari" [*Hōtokuki* is the Orient's *Self-Help*], *Shimin* 3, no. 13 (February 7, 1909): 19.

39. Garon, *Molding Japanese Minds*, 46–48.

40. Tomeoka, *Tomeoka Kōsuke nikki*, 2:572–73; also Ikeda, *Nihon shakai fukushi*, 159–60.

41. Mayet, *Agricultural Insurance*, 71–73, 102–103, 105–107; Okada Kazunobu, *Chochiku shōrei undō no shiteki tenkai* (Tokyo: Dōbunkan, 1996), 6–10, 25–26.

42. Unno Fukuji and Ōshima Mitsuko, *Ie to mura* [Household and village] (Iwanami Shoten, 1989), 478–81, 484–88.

43. Seymour A. Broadbridge, "Aspects of Economic and Social Policy in Japan, 1868–1945," in Mathias and Pollard, *Cambridge Economic History of Europe*, 8:1117;

Mark Metzler, *Lever of Empire: The International Gold Standard and the Crisis of Liberalism in Prewar Japan* (Berkeley: University of California Press, 2006), 32, 45–47; Richard J. Smethurst, *From Foot Soldier to Finance Minister: Takahashi Korekiyo, Japan's Keynes* (Cambridge: Harvard University Asia Center, 2007), chaps. 8–9.

44. Kawamura, *Gakkō chokin*, 16–17; Shumpei Okamoto, *The Japanese Oligarchy and the Russo-Japanese War* (New York: Columbia University Press, 1970), chaps. 7–8.

45. Shimomura, *Tomi*, 13–17.

46. Directive of February 1904, in Okada, *Chochiku shōrei undō*, 34, also 35–36; Inoue Tomoichi, *Kinken shōrei gyōsei oyobi hōsei* (Tokyo: Seibunkan, 1904), 41–42.

47. Translation appears in *The Japan Year Book, 1911* (Tokyo: Japan Year Book Office, 1911), 496.

48. Hirata Tōsuke, "Boshin shōsho to kokuun no hatten" [Boshin Rescript and the development of national prosperity], *Shimin* 3, no. 12 (January 7, 1909): 6; Ōura Kanetake, "Boshin shōsho to shōkō dōtoku" [Boshin Rescript and commercial-industrial morality], ibid., 9.

49. Italics mine. Rinoie Ryūsuke, "Kinken jikyō no yōgi" [The need for diligence, thrift, and individual effort], *Shimin* 4, no. 2 (April 23, 1909): 89; see Kenneth B. Pyle, "The Technology of Japanese Nationalism: The Local Improvement Movement, 1900–1918," *Journal of Asian Studies* 33, no. 1 (November 1973): 51–65.

50. Okada, *Chochiku shōrei undō*, 43.

51. Nakagawa Nozomu, "Boshin shōsho no hankyō taru ni, san jirei" [Examples of the Boshin Rescript's impact], *Shimin* 4, no. 2 (April 23, 1909): 50.

52. Sugiura Seishi, "Nichirō sengo no yūbin chokin no tenkai to chochiku shōreisaku" [Development of postal savings after the Russo-Japanese War and savings-encouragement policy], *Shakai keizai shigaku* 56, no. 1 (April 1990): 48–52.

53. Ushio Shigenosuke, "Teijo Hana to kyōfū chochikukai" [Virtuous woman Hana and the Moral Rectification and Savings Society], *Shimin* 3, no. 5 (July 7, 1908): 72–73; Inoue, *Kinken shōrei gyōsei*, 58.

54. Sugiura, "Nichirō sengo no yūbin chokin," 31–35, 52–54: Okada, *Chochiku shōrei undō*, 37, 44.

55. Inoue Tomoichi, "Kyūsai jigyō ni tsuki kibō sūsoku" [Ambitions and models for relief work], *Jizen* 4, no. 3 (January 1913), 66–68.

56. Rinoie, "Kinken jikyō," 91.

57. G. R. Searle, *The Quest for National Efficiency: A Study in British Politics and British Political Thought, 1899–1914* (Berkeley: University of California Press, 1971), 1–2, 57–59.

58. Alfred Stead, *Great Japan: A Study of National Efficiency* (London: John Lane, 1906), vii–ix, xii, xv–xvii, 29, 38, 50, 135, 161.

59. Henry Dyer, *Dai Nippon: The Britain of the East* (London: Blackie & Son, 1904), 402; H. G. Wells, *A Modern Utopia* (London: Chapman and Hall, 1905), chap. 9; Inazo Nitobe, *Bushido: The Soul of Japan*, 17th ed. (Tokyo: Teibi, 1911), v, 56, 89, 93, 145, 149, 161.

60. *The Times*, May 27, 1905, p. 7; February 12, 1905, cited in Searle, *Quest*, 58.

61. Italics mine. *Silver Bullet*, August 6, 1919, p. 115, in Organisation File, National Savings Committee: Origin, History and Development, 1920–1929, TNA, NSC 7/3.

CHAPTER 6: MOBILIZING FOR THE GREAT WAR

1. National Organizing Committee for War Savings, *How to Save and Why*, 1916, p. 2, Organisation File, National Savings Committee: Origin, History and Development, 1915–1916, The National Archives of the United Kingdom: Public Record Office (TNA), NSC 7/1.

2. *War Savings* 1, no. 11 (July 1917): 102, TNA, NSC 3/1.

3. Jay Winter and Blaine Baggett, *The Great War and the Shaping of the 20th Century* (New York: Penguin Studio, 1996), 59.

4. Ferguson, *World's Banker*, 939.

5. T. Balderston, "War Finance and Inflation in Britain and Germany, 1914–1918," *Economic History Review*, 2nd ser., 42, no. 2 (May 1989): 224, 228; Charles Gilbert, *American Financing of World War I* (Westport, CT: Greenwood, 1970), 222.

6. "Saving to Win the War: Ministers on the New Campaign: The Civilian's Duty," *The Times*, March 2, 1916, Organisation File, TNA, NSC 7/1.

7. *War Savings* 1, no. 1 (September 1916): 5.

8. Walther Rathenau, *Von Kommenden Dingen* [In days to come] (Berlin: Fischer, 1917), 39, 90, 131ff., quoted in Frank Trentmann, "The Evolution of the Consumer: Meanings, Identities, and Political Synapses before the Age of Affluence," in Sheldon Garon and Patricia Maclachlan, eds., *The Ambivalent Consumer: Questioning Consumption in East Asia and the West* (Ithaca: Cornell University Press, 2006), 37.

9. James Aulich, *War Posters: Weapons of Mass Communication* (London: Thames & Hudson, 2007), 8, 47–55.

10. Aulich, *War Posters*, 7; Yoshimi Shun'ya, ed., *Sensō no hyōshi: Tōkyō Daigaku Jōhō Gakkan shozō dai-ichiji sekai taisenki puropaganda postaa korekushon* (Tokyo: Tōkyō Daigaku Shuppankai, 2006), 5, 26.

11. "Foreign Savings Methods and Results" [ca. 1919], Foreign Savings Materials, General Files Relating to Liberty Loans and War Savings Bonds, 1917–25, Records of the War Savings Division, Records of the Bureau of the Public Debt, RG 53, National Archives at College Park, MD (hereafter cited as NACP).

12. Caisse des Dépôts, *Livret A*, 179–80.

13. See Gerald D. Feldman, *The Great Disorder: Politics, Economics, and Society in the German Inflation, 1914–1924* (New York: Oxford University Press, 1993), 40–45, 147, 163, 268; Shinju Fujihira, "Conscripting Money: Total War and Fiscal Revolution in the Twentieth Century" (PhD diss., Princeton University, 2000), 129–30, 147; Balderston, "War Finance," 237–38.

14. A Banker [Robert H. Brand], "The Case for Economy," *The Times*, June 9, 1915, p. 9; "Save and Invest," June 26, 1915, p. 9; *Oxford Dictionary of National Biography* (Oxford: Oxford University Press, 2004), s.v. "Robert Molesworth Kindersley." Kindersley's circle included William Schooling, member of the National War Savings Committee and chairman of the prewar Japanophile Agenda Club. Sir William Schooling, "The Social Influence of National Savings," *The Charity Organisation Review* 49, no. 291 (March 1921): 146–58.

15. "The True Inwardness of Continuous Purchases of State Securities," *War Savings* 2, no. 5 (February 1918): 63.

16. See National War Savings Committee, *Annual Report*, 1917, pp. 4–8, 11, in Great Britain, Parliament, House of Commons, House of Commons Sessional Papers, 1917–18, vol. 18; *Annual Report*, 1919, pp. 1, 5, in House of Commons Sessional Papers, 1919, vol. 30.

17. Reginald McKenna, in *The Times*, March 2, 1916, p. 6. G. N. Barnes critiqued "mere propaganda."

18. Committee on War Loans for the Small Investor, *War Loans for Small Investors* (London: His Majesty's Stationery Office, 1916), 4–5, Organisation File, TNA, NSC 7/1.

19. E. H. Carter, "War Savings Organisation in Warwichshire," *War Savings* 1, no. 4 (December 1916): 29–30; ibid. 2, no. 7 (March–April 1917): 77.

20. Letter from A. Bonar Law, *War Savings* 1, no. 5 (January 1917): 37; National Savings Committee, *Annual Report*, 1921, p. 3.

21. Memorandum by Basil Blackett to Robert Kindersley, September 19, 1916, pp. 1–4, Organisation File, TNA, NSC 7/1.

22. *War Savings* 1, no. 4 (December 1916): 27.

23. "From the Chairman to War Savings Workers," December 1918, p. 2, Organisation File, National Savings Committee: Origin, History and Development, 1917–1919, TNA, NSC 7/2.

24. *War Savings* 1, no. 10 (June 1917), 86; 2, no. 2 (October 1917): 14.

25. "Mr. [Theodore] Chamber's Reports," May 9, 1916, p. 23, in Organisation File, NSC 7/1; Memorandum of February 17, 1916, "Interviews between T. L. Gilmour and Representatives of Friendly Societies, Trade Unions and Religious Bodies regarding the Setting Up of War Savings Committees, February–April 1916," TNA, NSC 36/8.

26. National Organizing Committee for War Savings, *How to Save and Why*, 8; E. H. Carter, "War Savings Organisation in Warwichshire," *War Savings* 1, no. 4 (Dec. 1916): 30.

27. "War Savings in Great Britain: An Address by Basil P. Blackett, C. B., of the British Treasury," September 27, 1917, pp. 15–16, British Savings Materials, General Files Relating to Liberty Loans and War Savings Bonds, 1917–25, Records of the War Savings Division, Records of the Bureau of the Public Debt, RG 53, NACP.

28. Susan Kingsley Kent, *Sex and Suffrage in Britain, 1860–1914* (Princeton: Princeton University Press, 1987), 220; "To the Chairman of the National War Savings Committee," [December 1916], 13–14, Organisation File, TNA, NSC 7/1.

29. "To Our Fellow-Countrywomen," n.d. [1918]; Letter, McKenna to Kindersley, October 3, 1916; "To the Chairman of the National War Savings Committee," 13, Organisation File, TNA, NSC 7/1; "Women's Conference," *War Savings* 1, no. 3 (November 1916): 19.

30. "Speakers Notes," 1947, History of the National Savings Committee: Correspondence, Memoranda and Miscellaneous papers, 1946–73, TNA, NSC 7/470; *Annual Report*, 1919, p. 6; Basil P. Blackett, "England's Effort to Pay for the War out of Savings," *Proceedings of the Academy of Political Science in the City of New York* 7, no. 4 (February 1918): 59–70.

31. "Kindersley Committee: Sub-Committee of the National War Savings Committee on Savings after the War," December 10, 1917, p. 1, TNA, NSC 11/63.

32. S. G. Warner, "The Holding of the National Debt," *War Savings* 1, no. 4 (December 1916): 28; "War Certificates in Other Countries," 2, no. 2 (October 1917): 15.

33. E.g., James J. Kimble, *Mobilizing the Home Front: War Bonds and Domestic Propaganda* (College Station: Texas A&M University Press, 2006); *The War*, DVD, directed by Ken Burns (Hollywood, CA: Paramount Home Entertainment, 2007); *Flags of Our Fathers*, DVD, directed by Clint Eastwood (Universal City, CA: Dreamworks Home Entertainment, 2007).

34. Rodgers, *Atlantic Crossings*, 275–86.

35. "War Savings in Great Britain: An Address by Basil P. Blackett," 12–25, RG 53, NACP; Tucker, *Decline of Thrift*, 84; on taxes, bonds, and war savings, see Gilbert, *American Financing*, 84–91, 163–65.

36. U.S. Department of Treasury, National War Savings Committee, *Report*, Aug. 5, 1918, typescript, 10.

37. "'Get Down to Brass Tacks': If You Are Really Trying to Help Win the War," *The War Saver* (National War Savings Committee, Washington, DC) 1, no. 6 (July 1918): 7.

38. "Address of Mr. Frank A. Vanderlip at the Chamber of Commerce Luncheon at the Baltimore Hotel, Kansas City," December 14, 1917, Pamphlet Books, General Files Relating to Liberty Loans and War Savings Bonds, 1917–25, Records of the War Savings Division, Records of the Bureau of the Public Debt, RG 53, NACP; U.S. Department of Treasury, National War Savings Committee, *How to Win the War* (Washington, DC: Government Printing Office, 1918), 6–7;. "President Wilson's Message to War Savers," *The War Saver* 1, no. 1 (March 1918): 1; "Secretary McAdoo Appeals for Nation Wide Economy," ibid., 2.

39. James R. Mock and Cedric Larson, *Words that Won the War: The Story of the Committee on Public Information, 1917–1919* (Princeton: Princeton University Press, 1939), 4, 96–105, 113, 123–25; U.S. Department of Treasury, National War Savings Committee, *Report*, 10a.

40. U.S. Department of Treasury, National War Savings Committee, *Report*, 4, 6, Appendix II; Labert St. Clair, *The Story of the Liberty Loans* (Washington, DC: James William Bryan Press, 1919), 103–104.

41. Mock and Larson, *Words*, 103.

42. Ibid., 125, 213, 219–21.

43. "Foreign Savings Methods and Results" [1919], RG 53, NACP; Lizabeth Cohen, *Making a New Deal: Industrial Workers in Chicago, 1919–1939* (Cambridge: Cambridge University Press, 1990), 76–79.

44. Gilbert, *American Financing*, 164; "Address of Mr. Frank A. Vanderlip," RG 53, NACP.

45. *The War Saver* 1, no. 4 (June 1918): 5; U.S. Department of the Treasury, War Loan Organization, Savings Division, *War Savings in 1919, Second Federal Reserve District, Preliminary Report of the Director of War Savings*, mimeo [New York, 1919], 21.

46. Margaret H. Schoenfeld and Anne Bezanson, "Trend of Wage Earners' Savings in Philadelphia," *Annals of the American Academy of Political and Social Science* 121, supplement (September 1925): 54.

47. Gilbert, *American Financing*, 141–42, 164.

48. "War Savings in Great Britain," 24–25, RG 53, NACP.

49. U.S. Department of the Treasury, War Savings in 1919, 5–6.

50. The War Saver 1, no.1 (March 1918): 7; Arthur T. Hadley, "How to Help the Nation Meet the Cost of the War," ibid.1, no. 5 (June 1918): 1.

51. Nathaniel R. Whitney, Sale of War Bonds in Iowa (Iowa City: State Historical Society of Iowa, 1923), 126, 128–37, 140; Kimble, Mobilizing the Home Front, 17.

52. "Edison Sees Luxury War-Winning Force," New York Times, June 8, 1918, p. 9.

53. Thomas Nixon Carver, War Thrift, Preliminary Economic Studies of the War, no. 10 (New York: Oxford University Press, 1919), 28, 52–58, 62.

54. U.S. Department of the Treasury, War Savings in 1919, 8, 11–13.

55. Gilbert, American Financing, 166–68; Mock and Larson, Words, ix, 427.

56. William J. Carson, Savings and Employee Savings Plans in Philadelphia (Philadelphia: University of Pennsylvania Press, 1932), 10, 13–17; Wadhwani, "Citizen Savers," 342–48.

57. Caisse Générale d'Épargne, Mémorial, 241–42; Caisse des Dépôts, Livret A, 191–92.

58. Saving 2, no. 3 (March 1927): 10, TNA, NSC 3/5; on investment in housing, see "Kindersley Committee," 1, TNA, NSC 11/63.

59. "The Purpose of the Savings Movement," December 1947, p. 2, History of the National Savings Committee, TNA, NSC 7/470; R.H. Mottram, "A History of the National Savings Movement" [1930s], chap. 6, pp. 19–23, NSC 7/472.

60. Filippo Ravizza, in Cassa di Risparmio delle Provincie Lombarde, First International Thrift Congress, 26–31 October 1924 (Milan: Organising Committee of the Congress, Milan, 1925), 328–29, 354, also 135.

61. International Thrift Institute, The International Thrift Institute (Milan: Archetipografia di Milano [1947]), 11; Saving, no. 93 (June 1924): 374; World Thrift, 1937, no. 2: 64.

CHAPTER 7: SAVE NOW, BUY LATER

1. Irving Berlin, Any Bonds Today? Sheet music, Division of Cultural History, National Museum of American History.

2. Quoted in Harold James, "What Is Keynesian about Deficit Financing? The Case of Interwar Germany," in Peter A. Hall, The Political Power of Economic Ideas: Keynesianism across Nations (Princeton: Princeton University Press, 1989), 248.

3. Fujihira, "Conscripting Money," 154–57, 176, 178, 180–81.

4. Detlev J. K. Peukert, Inside Nazi Germany: Conformity, Opposition, and Racism in Everyday Life, trans. Richard Deveson (New Haven: Yale University Press, 1987), 71.

5. De Grazia, Irresistible Empire, 125.

6. R. J. Overy, War and Economy in the Third Reich (Oxford: Clarendon Press, 1994), 272–74, 311; Adam Tooze, The Wages of Destruction: The Making and Breaking of the Nazi Economy (London: Allen Lane, 2006), 353–55, 643–47.

7. Mass-Observation, A Savings Survey (Working Class), Highly Confidential, December 1941, Papers from the Mass-Observation Archive at the University of Sussex,

microform (Marlborough, England: Adam Matthew Publications, 2000), Part 1, Reel 2, pp. 83, 87.

8. Fujihira, "Conscripting Money," 13, 15–16, 217–26.

9. "Speakers Notes," 1947, p. 1, TNA, NSC 7/470.

10. John Maynard Keynes, The General Theory of Employment, Interest and Money (London: Macmillan, 1936), 373.

11. Heilbroner, Worldly Philosophers, 255–68, 273–74.

12. The Times, November 14, 1939, p. 9, November 15, 1939, p. 9, November 28, 1939, p. 7, March 12, 1940, p. 5, June 14, 1940, p. 9, December 23, 1941, p. 2.

13. See criticism by Robert Kindersley, The Times, April 22, 1940, p. 8.

14. The Times, editorial, April 10, 1940, p. 9.

15. National Savings Committee, 24th Report, 1939–46, "The Second War Savings Campaign," TNA, NSC 2/24.

16. War Savings, v. 1, no. 12 (Jan. 1941): 6, TNA, NSC 3/8.

17. National Savings Committee, July 12, 1944, pp. 3–4, Special Campaigns: War Finance Campaign, 1939–45, Combined Operations (Autumn Campaign) 1944, April 1944–June 1945, TNA, NSC 7/175.

18. The Thrifty Pig, Seven Wise Dwarves, Donald's Decision, and All Together, directed by Ford L. Beebe, in Walt Disney Treasures—On the Front Lines, DVD (Burbank, CA: Buena Vista Home Entertainment, 2003).

19. Mass-Observation, Savings Survey, 10, 83, 88–89.

20. Ibid., 6, 9; on motivations, see 22–25, 121–26; Charles Madge, "The Propensity to Save in Blackburn and Bristol," The Economic Journal 50, no. 200 (December 1940): 417–19.

21. Wadhwani, "Citizen Savers," 350–56, 370–73.

22. Bureau of Agricultural Economics, National Survey of Liquid Asset Holdings, Spending and Saving, part 1 (Washington, DC: U.S. Department of Agriculture, 1946), 6.

23. U.S. National Resources Committee, Consumer Expenditures in the United States: Estimates for 1935–36 (Washington, DC: Government Printing Office, 1939), 19–20.

24. Fred Smith, in John Morton Blum, From the Morgenthau Diaries, 3 vols. (Boston: Houghton Mifflin, 1959–67), 3:17–18.

25. Jarvis M. Morse, Paying for a World War: The United States Financing of World War II (Washington, DC: U.S. Savings Bond Division, 1971), 34; Lawrence R. Samuel, Pledging Allegiance: American Identity and the Bond Drive of World War II (Washington, DC: Smithsonian Institution Press, 1997), 8, 13–14.

26. Morse, Paying, 39–40.

27. Gale F. Johnston, in Field Organization News Letter (Defense Savings Staff, U.S. Treasury Department), no. 1 (May 23, 1941): 1; similarly Morgenthau's radio address of April 30, 1941, in Blum, Morgenthau Diaries, 2:301–2.

28. Morse, Paying, 91, 166, 170.

29. J. R. Dunkerley, in Schools at War (Education Section, War Savings Staff, U.S. Treasury Department) (December 1945): 15; Schools at Work (March 1946): 3, 15.

30. Morse, Paying, 172, 182, 184–85, 192.

31. Samuels, Pledging Allegiance, 58–64.

32. See Department of Commerce, Bureau of Economic Analysis figures on National Income and Product Accounts, http://www.bea.gov accessed February 14, 2011.

33. U.S. Department of Agriculture, *National Survey of Liquid Asset Holdings*, part 1, p. 6; Morse, *Paying*, 285.

34. Samuels, *Pledging Allegiance*, 52, 54; Morse, *Paying*, 262–67.

35. "The World of 1953," *Schools at War* ([April] 1943): 10–11.

36. "Statement of Ted R. Gamble … before the Committee on Ways and Means of the House of Representatives," December 3, 1943, p. 1, in Gamble, T.R., no. 1 folder, Speeches Files, Office of the National Director, Historical and Promotional Records, 1941–60, Records of the Savings Bond Division, War Finance Division, General Records of the Department of the Treasury, RG 56, NACP; Mark H. Leff, "Politics of Sacrifice on the American Home Front in World War II," *Journal of American History* 77, no. 4 (March 1991): 1309–12, 1317.

37. *Life*, April 30, 1945, p. 16.

38. *Anti-Inflation Bulletin* (Institute of Life Insurance), December 20, 1944, Suggestions for War Financing, Subject Files, Office of the National Director, Historical and Promotional Records, 1941–60, Records of the Savings Bond Division, War Finance Division, General Records of the Department of the Treasury, RG 56, NACP; Lizabeth Cohen, *A Consumers' Republic: The Politics of Mass Consumption in Postwar America* (New York: Knopf, 2003), 70.

39. International Thrift Institute, *International Thrift Institute*, 15, 24.

40. Yano Shōtarō, "Ōkura daijin rajio hōsō" [Finance Minister's radio broadcast], June 12, 1947, p. 1, Aichi bunsho, Chochiku: Chochiku zōkyōsaku, vol. 2, doc. 21, Sengo zaiseishi shiryō, Ministry of Finance, Japan; Tony Judt, *Postwar: A History of Europe Since 1945* (New York: Penguin, 2005), 16, 71.

41. Thad Paul Alton, *Polish Postwar Economy* (New York: Columbia University Press, 1955), 291, also 66, 97, 229, 291; Mura, "Germany," in *History of European Savings Banks*, 1:114–15.

42. Christopher S. Allen, "The Underdevelopment of Keynesianism in the Federal Republic of Germany," in Hall, *Political Power of Economic Ideas*, 263–89; Josef Hoffmann, "To-day's Problem of Capital Formation," *World Thrift*, 1951: 3–4; ibid., 1956, no. 2 (March): iii.

43. Caisse des Dépôts, *Livret A*, 217–32; Moster and Vogler, "France," in Mura, *History of European Savings Banks*, 1:82–83.

44. *World Thrift*, 1958, no. 2 (March): 68; 1956, no. 1 (January): 28–29, and no. 2 (March): 51; 1957, no. 3 (May): 325; Moster and Vogler, "France," 85.

45. "National Savings Offensive, Autumn Drive: 'Combined Operations.' We've Got to Keep on Saving," July 1944, p. 2, in Special Campaigns: War Finance Campaign, 1939–45, Combined Operations (Autumn Campaign) 1944, TNA, NSC 7/175.

46. Hugh Dalton, in *National Savings* 6, no. 3 (1947): cover, TNA, NSC 3/13; October 8, 1946, p. 3, Minutes of National Savings Committee Meetings, January 1946–December 1948, NSC 1/15; Susan Cooper, "Snoek Piquante," in Michael Sissons and Philip French, eds., *Age of Austerity* (London: Hodder and Stoughton, 1963), 35–54.

47. National Savings and Investments, http://www.nsandi.com, accessed September 14, 2008; commandos: *National Savings* 6, no. 3 (1947): 4; "Six People in Every Ten

Hold National Savings," September 1948, p. 1, in The Public and National Savings Social Surveys, Ltd, 1948, NSC 18/21; "The National Savings Movement, Prepared for Australia, via Commonwealth Office, May 1950," p. 1, in Miscellaneous Historical Papers, 1946–73, TNA, NSC 7/470.

48. *The Times*, April 3, 1946, p. 2.

49. *National Savings* 7, no. 2 (1949): 14–15, also 6, no. 3 (1947): 2.

50. National Savings Movement, "Restraint in Spending Campaign, 1955–56," in Special Campaigns: Restraint in Spending Campaign, 1955–56, NSC 7/349; also "Invest in Britain Savings Campaign," 1952–53, pamphlet, Special Campaigns: Invest in Britain Campaign, 1951–54, TNA, NSC 7/347.

51. "Lend Strength to Britain: The National Savings Campaign for 1951–1952," pamphlet to Local Committees, 1951, p. 1, and "'Lend Strength to Britain' Campaign: Notes for Speakers," December 1951, p. 2, Special Campaigns: Lend Strength to Britain Campaign, 1950–1952," PRO, NSC 7/183.

52. "Statement by the Trades Union Congress," December 1951, in Special Campaigns: Lend Strength to Britain Campaign, TNA, NSC 7/183.

53. Bevan, in *National Savings* 6, no. 2 (1947): 6; Cripps, in 7, no. 2 (1949): 15; Judt, *Postwar*, 73–75, 163.

54. In 1965 and 1970, respectively, personal savings rates were 15.9 and 15.5 percent in West Germany; 16.7 and 16.8 percent in Italy; 14.8 and 17.1 percent in Belgium; 14.7 and 14.8 percent in Netherlands; 11.1 and 12.7 percent in France; 6.2 and 5.5 percent in the United Kingdom; and 6.1 and 8.7 percent in the U.S. OECD, *National Accounts for Member Countries*, 1960–70, in "Report of the Committee to Review National Savings," Chairman: Sir Harry Page, March 1973, 2:9, TNA, NSC 306/12.

CHAPTER 8: "LUXURY IS THE ENEMY"

1. *Life*, May 28, 1945, p. 43.

2. Nagahata Michiko, *Ran no onna* [Women in a time of turmoil] (Tokyo: Bungei Shunjū, 1992), 123.

3. Noguchi Yukio, *1940 nen taisei* [1940 system] (Tokyo: Tōyō Keizai Shinpō, 1995), 135.

4. http://www.showakan.go.jp, accessed January 8, 2009.

5. Haruko Taya Cook and Theodore F. Cook, *Japan at War: An Oral History* (New Press, 1992), 3.

6. Thomas R. H. Havens, *Valley of Darkness: The Japanese People and World War Two* (New York: Norton, 1978), 197.

7. See Wada Ikuo's cartoon, in Andrew Gordon, *A Modern History of Japan* (New York: Oxford University Press, 2003), 141.

8. Takemura Tamio, *Taishō bunka* [Taishō-era culture] (Tokyo: Kōdansha, 1980), chap. 4.

9. Junichirō Tanizaki, *Naomi* [Chijin no ai], trans. Anthony H. Chambers (New York: Knopf, 1985).

10. Naimushō Shakaikyoku, "Shōhi setsuyaku ni tsuite" [Economy in consumption], *Shakai jigyō* [Social work] 6, no. 7 (October 1922): 1–2.

11. "Shōhi setsuyaku shōrei shisetsu ni kansuru ken: Shakaikyokuchō yori shōkai kaitō" [Programs to encourage economy in consumption: Replies to Social Bureau chief] [October] 1922, document: Taishō, no. 1292-50, Shakai, vol. 2, Saitama-ken gyōsei monjo, Saitama Kenritsu Bunshokan, Urawa.

12. Sheldon Garon, "Fashioning a Culture of Diligence and Thrift: Savings and Frugality Campaigns in Japan, 1900–1931," in Sharon A. Minichiello, *Japan's Competing Modernities* (Honolulu: University of Hawai'i Press, 1998), 322.

13. Naimushō Shakaikyoku, *Kinken shōrei undō gaikyō* (Tokyo: Shakaikyoku Shakaibu, 1927), 1, 17–19; Yūsei Kenkyūjo Fuzoku Shiryōkan (Teishin Sōgō Hakubutsukan), ed., *Modanizumu no jidai to yūsei posutaa* (Tokyo: Yūsei Kenkyūjo Fuzoku Shiryōkan, 1997).

14. Naimushō Shakaikyoku, *Beikoku ni okeru setsuyaku undō* [Thrift campaign in U.S.], pamphlet (Tokyo: Naimushō, 1922).

15. R. D. Kingham, "History of Movement: Notes, etc., to Assist Mr. R.H. Mottram, April 1937, 21st Anniversary, 1936–39, Correspondence—Plans for Writing History of the Movement, TNA, NSC 7/241.

16. Ōkurashō Rizaikyoku, "Chochiku shōrei ni oite" [Savings-promotion], December 26, 1924, Kinken shōrei, doc. 24, Shōwa zaiseishi shiryō (hereafter SHZS), no. 5, Ministry of Finance, Japan; also Ōkurashō Rizaikyoku, "Chū-Ei zaimukan hōkoku: Eikoku chochiku shōrei kikan no gaikyō" [Report of resident finance officer in Britain: Britain's savings-promotion institutions], January 30, 1924, doc. 25, SHZS, no. 5.

17. Okada, *Chochiku shōrei undō*, 70–71.

18. See Yoshimi Shun'ya, *Sensō no hyōshi*.

19. *World Thrift*, 1939, no. 8–9: 255–56; also Cassa di Risparmio delle Provincie Lombarde, *First International Thrift Congress*, 77, 105, 120; Zenkoku Chochiku Ginkō Kyōkai, *Zenkoku Chochiku Ginkō Kyōkai kaishi* [History of Association of Japanese Savings Banks] (Tokyo: Tōkyō Ginkō Shūkaijo, 1944), 289–90.

20. Garon, *Molding Japanese Minds*, 13.

21. "Miyo, kono sūji," poster in Monbushō [Ministry of Education], *Kyōka dōin jisshi gaikyō* [Report on moral suasion mobilization] (Tokyo: Monbushō, 1930).

22. Sand, *House and Home*, 184.

23. Nakajima Kuni, "Taishō-ki ni okeru 'seikatsu kaizen undō'" ["Daily life improvement movement" in the Taishō era], *Shisō* (Nihon Joshi Daigaku Shigaku Kenkyūkai) 15 (October 1974): 59–60, 69–71.

24. Mary Nolan, *Visions of Modernity: American Business and the Modernization of Germany* (New York: Oxford University Press, 1994), chap. 10.

25. Sand, 6, 84–88, 182; Itagaki Kuniko, *Shōwa senzen, senchūki no nōson seikatsu: Zasshi "Ie no hikari" ni miru* [Farm life in Shōwa era, prewar and wartime, as seen in *Ie no hikari*] (Tokyo: Mitsumine Shobō, 1992), 88–93.

26. Garon, *Molding Japanese Minds*, 126–29; Chino Yōichi, *Kindai Nihon fujin kyōikushi* [History of women's education in Japan] (Tokyo: Domesu Shuppan, 1979), 174–75.

27. Garon, "Fashioning a Culture of Diligence and Thrift," 325–29; see also Mark Metzler, "Woman's Place in Japan's Great Depression: Reflections on the Moral Economy of Deflation," *Journal of Japanese Studies* 30, no. 2 (Summer 2004): 315–52.

28. Saitō Michiko, *Hani Motoko* (Tokyo: Domesu shuppan, 1988), 52, 62–68; Sand, *House and Home*, 82–83; also Barbara Hamil Sato, *The New Japanese Woman: Modernity, Media, and Women in Interwar Japan* (Durham, NC: Duke University Press, 2003).

29. Kerry Smith, *A Time of Crisis: Japan, the Great Depression, and Rural Revitalization* (Cambridge: Harvard University Asia Center, 2001), 206–209, 214–19, 226, 265–66; Itagaki, *Shōwa senzen, senchūki no nōson*, ii–iii, 32–36.

30. Shimomura Kainan [Hiroshi], "Chochiku shōrei to menhin no hijō kanri" [Savings promotion and emergency controls on cotton goods], *Shufu no tomo* 22, no. 8 (August 1938): 138.

31. Ōkurashō Daijin Kanbō Zaisei Keizai Chōsaka [Ministry of Finance, Minister's Office of Financial and Economic Survey Section], *Sekai taisen tōji ni okeru kakkoku chochiku shōrei seido* [Savings-promotion systems among World War I belligerents], Senji zaisei keizai sankō shiryō, no. 10 (Tokyo: Ōkurashō, 1938), preface.

32. Nagahama Isao, *Kokumin seishin sōdōin no shisō to kōzō* [Thought and structure of National Spiritual Mobilization] (Tokyo: Akaishi Shobō, 1987), 140–41; Ōkurashō Zaiseishi Hensanshitsu, *Shōwa zaiseishi*, vol. 11 (Tokyo: Tōyō Keizai Shinpōsha, 1957), 173–74.

33. Ōkurashō Zaiseishi Hensanshitsu, *Shōwa zaiseishi*, 11:179–81; Kokumin Chochiku Shōreikyoku, "Dōfuken ni okeru kokumin chochiku shōrei jisshi jikō sōran" [Survey on implementing national savings promotion in prefectures], October 20, 1938, Kin'yū chochiku shōrei, vol. 1, section 6, SHZS, no. 9.

34. Yūseishō Chokinkyoku, *Yūbin kawase chokin jigyō*, 400; on Yokoyama's memories of working for the war, see Cook and Cook, *Japan at War*, 95–99, 471–72.

35. Fujihira, "Conscripting Money," 13, 16, chap. 3, especially 104–108.

36. Yūseishō Chokinkyoku, *Yūbin kawase chokin jigyō*, 396; *Chokinkyoku tayori* (October 1936): 3; (March 1937): 4.

37. "Taidan: Hisshō ketsui to kokumin chochiku" [A conversation: The resolution to win and national saving], *Nihon fujin* 1, no. 8 (June 1943): 8.

38. Kokumin Chochiku Shōreikyoku, *Kokumin Chochiku Shōrei Iinkai gijiroku* (hereafter KCSIG), secret, vol. 1 (Tokyo: Kokumin Chochiku Shōreikyoku, 1938), 2nd special committee session, June 14, 1938, pp. 75–76.

39. "Shōwa 19 nendo kokumin chochiku mokuhyōgaku kaitei ni kansuru ken" [Revised national savings target for 1944], September 15, 1944, Kin'yū: Chochiku shōrei, vol. 2, section 6, SHZS, no. 9.

40. Chochiku Zōkyō Chūō Iinkai, *Chochiku hakusho* (Tokyo: Chochiku Zōkyō Chūō Iinkai, 1963), 222.

41. Ōkurashō Zaiseishi Hensanshitsu, *Shōwa zaiseishi*, 11:187–89.

42. See statements by Takahashi Kamekichi and Ishiwata Sōtarō, in KCSIG, 2nd special committee session, June 14, 1938, 1:74–76; Okada, *Chochiku shōrei undō*, 96.

43. Italics mine. Chokinkyoku [Postal Savings Bureau], *Yūbin kawase chokin gyōmu jōkyō* [Current state of postal money-order and savings activities] (Tokyo: Chokinkyoku, 1939), 110.

44. Ishiwata Sōtarō, "Kokumin chochiku shōrei shumu kachō jimu uchiawasekai kyōgi jikō jisshi no ken" [Implementing decisions of conference of national savings-

promotion section chiefs], November 9, 1938, Kin'yū: Chochiku shōrei, vol. 2, section 5, SHZS, no. 9.

45. Ōkurashō Zaiseishi Hensanshitsu, *Shōwa zaiseishi*, 11:235; Okada, *Chochiku shōrei undō*, 100, 104; Ralph J. D. Braibanti, "Neighborhood Associations in Japan and Their Democratic Potentialities," *Far Eastern Quarterly* 7, no. 2 (February 1948): 10–52.

46. Ōkurashō Zaiseishi Hensanshitsu, *Shōwa zaiseishi*, 11:191–92.

47. Kaya Okinori, "Naze chochiku o shinakereba naranu ka" [Why must we save?], *Nihon fujin* 1, no. 4 (February 1943): 35; Okada, *Chochiku shōrei undō*, 104.

48. Ōkurashō Zaiseishi Hensanshitsu, *Shōwa zaiseishi*, 11:175–78; Okada, *Chochiku shōrei undō*, 100–101, 103.

49. Ōkurashō Zaiseishi Hensanshitsu, *Shōwa zaiseishi* 11:179; Okada, *Chochiku shōrei undō*, 126.

50. "Chochiku suishin taichō no kessen zadankai" [Roundtable of savings-promotion captains on the decisive battle], *Shufu no tomo* 28, no. 5 (May 1944): 14–15.

51. Okada, *Chochiku shōrei undō*, 111–13, 116.

52. Quoted in Yoshimi Yoshiaki, *Kusa no ne no fashizumu* (Tokyo: Tōkyō Daigaku Shuppankai, 1987), 6–7, 9–10.

53. February 1940, quoted in Yoshimi, *Kusa no ne no fashizumu*, 32, also 28.

54. Mizuno Masuko, in "Taidan: Hisshō ketsui," 8.

55. *Yomiuri hōchi shinbun*, September 18, 1944, p. 2.

56. Nakamura Jun'ichi, "Chochiku zakkan" [Perceptions of saving], *Teishin kyōkai zasshi*, no. 429 (June 1944): 3.

57. *Nishi Nihon shinbun*, August 20, 1944, p. 3, in Yūbin chokin kan'i hoken kankei kirinuki-chō, Communications Museum, Japan [Teishin Sōgō Hakubutsukan]; Yamana Ayao, *Taikenteki dezainshi* [A History of design from experiences] (Tokyo: Dabiddosha, 1976), 261–64; Barak Kushner, *The Thought War: Imperial Japanese Propaganda* (Honolulu: University of Hawai'i Press, 2006), chap. 3.

58. *Mainichi shinbun*, July 30, 1943, and *Ōita gōdō shinbun*, March 5, 1944, from Yūbin chokin kan'i hoken kankei kirinuki-chō.

59. Yūseishō chokinkyoku, *Yūbin kawase chokin jigyō*, 395.

60. *Nihon fujin* 2, no. 5 (April 1944): back cover.

61. See Yoshiko Miyake, "Doubling Expectations: Motherhood and Women's Factory Work under State Management in Japan in the 1930s and 1940s," in Gail Lee Bernstein, ed., *Recreating Japanese Women, 1600–1945* (Berkeley: University of California Press, 1991), 267–95; Garon, *Molding Japanese Minds*, 140–44.

62. *Josei tenbō* 12, no. 6 (June 1938): 14; 13, no. 4 (April 1939): 18; 14, no. 7 (July 1940): 27.

63. Fujii Tadatoshi, *Kokubō Fujinkai* [National Defense Women's Association] (Tokyo: Iwanami Shoten, 1985), 178–82, 194.

64. Saitō, *Hani Motoko*, 261–62.

65. Hani Motoko, "Warera no mezasu kan'i seikatsu" [The simple life as we see it], in Kokumin Chochiku Shōreikyoku, *Kokumin chochiku shōrei kōenshū* [National savings promotion speeches] (Tokyo: Kokumin Chochiku Shōreikyoku, 1938), 243, 245–46, 248.

66. Saitō, *Hani Motoko*, 263–64, 267.

67. "Kessenka no chochiku taidan" [Discussion on saving for the decisive battle], *Fujin no tomo* 36, no. 4 (April 1942): 36; also 37, no. 7 (July 1943): inside cover.

68. "'Nihyaku sanjū oku' o mezashite" [Approaching 23 billion yen in national savings], *Fujin no tomo* 37, no. 3 (March 1943): inside cover.

69. Saitō Michiko, "Senjika no josei no seikatsu to ishiki—*Shufu no tomo* ni miru," in Akazawa Shirō and Kitagawa Kenzō, eds., *Bunka to fashizumu: Senjiki Nihon ni okeru bunka no kōbō* (Tokyo: Nihon Keizai Hyōronsha, 1993), 286–88, 295.

70. Fukutoku Dōjin [pseudonym], "Anata wa okanemochi ni naremasu ka" [Are you capable of becoming rich?], *Shufu no tomo* 23, no. 1 (January 1939): 184, 187.

71. Sono Shirō, "Senji no katei rishoku sōdan" [Advice on enriching the family in wartime], *Shufu no tomo* 22, no. 5 (May 1938): 286.

72. Wada Kenji, "Kabushiki no shippai no nai rishokuhō" [Failure-free ways of making money on stocks], *Shufu no tomo* 23, no. 9 (September 1939): 236–39; "Shirōto de mo zettai ni shippai no nai rishoku no te" [Absolutely failure-free ways of making money that any amateur can do], 24, no. 1 (January 1940): 385; also 23, no. 5 (May 1939): 136, 138.

73. E.g., *Shufu no tomo* 22, no. 7 (July 1938): 442–49; 24, no. 2 (February 1940): 322–26; 26, no. 3 (March 1942): 193–97.

74. "Chochiku suishin taichō no kessen zadankai," 12; Fukutoku, "Anata wa okanemochi," 185–87; Wada Kenji, "Sukunai shunyū kara kodomo no kyōiku no umidasuhō" [Ways of delivering your child's education when income's tight], 23, no. 6 (June 1939): 146–50; Saitō, "Senjika no josei no seikatsu," 317, 319, 323.

75. Yamamuro Gunpei, "Chochiku hōkoku" [Savings patriotism], *Kakusei* 28 (September 1938): 14; Suzuki Yūko, *Feminizumu to sensō* [Feminism and war] (Tokyo: Marujusha, 1986), 47, 51; also Garon, *Molding Japanese Minds*, chap. 3.

76. Fukutoku, "Anata wa okanemochi," 184; "Zadankai: Zeitaku seikatsu no haishi" [Roundtable: Abolishing luxurious living], *Josei tenbō* 14, no. 8 (August 1940): 21–22; *Josei tenbō* 13, no. 7 (July 1939): 12.

77. Mizuno Masuko, in "Taidan: Hisshō ketsui," 6–7.

78. Fujii, *Kokubō Fujinkai*, 202–203; "Mohan kakeibo de senji kakei ni seikō shita keiken" [Wartime household finance success stories made possible by keeping model household account books], *Shufu no tomo* 24, no. 12 (December 1940): 261.

79. Takiyama Shizuko, "Kan'i hoken o riyō shite" [Making good use of postal life insurance], *Nihon fujin* 1, no. 8 (June 1943): 62–63.

80. Jerome B. Cohen, *Japan's Economy in War and Reconstruction* (Minneapolis: University of Minnesota Press, 1949), 386.

81. Takafusa Nakamura, *Economic Growth in Prewar Japan*, trans. Robert A. Feldman (New Haven: Yale University Press, 1983), 301.

82. Quoted in Nakamura, *Economic Growth in Prewar Japan*, 301.

83. Chochiku Kōdō to Chochiku Ishiki ni kansuru Chōsa Kenkyūkai, *Dai 6-kai chochiku kōdō to chochiku ishiki ni kansuru chōsa hōkokusho*, 2.

Chapter 9: Postwar Japan's National Salvation

1. "Chochiku zōkyō hōsakuan" [Plan for savings promotion], ca. August–September 1946, Aichi bunsho, Chochiku: Chochiku zōkyōsaku, vol. 1, doc. 4, Sengo zaiseishi shiryō (hereafter SZS), Ministry of Finance, Japan.

2. John W. Dower, Embracing Defeat: Japan in the Wake of World War II (New York: Norton, 1999).

3. U.S. State Department, Interim Research and Intelligence Section, [and] Research and Analysis Branch, "Control of Inflation," Report—R & A no. 2451, October 1, 1945, reprinted in Ōkurashō Zaiseishishitsu, Shōwa zaiseishi: Shūsen kara kōwa made, vol. 20 (Tokyo: Tōyō Keizai Shinpōsha, 1982), 491–92.

4. Yūseishō, Yūsei hyakunenshi, 747, 751; Yamaguchi Osamu, Yūbin chokin no hyakunen (Tokyo: Yūbin Chokin Shinkōkai, 1977), 118–20; Horioka, "Consuming and Saving," 283.

5. Chochiku Zōkyō Chūō Iinkai, Chochiku undōshi (hereafter CU), 15.

6. Yano Shōtarō, "Ōkura daijin rajio hōsō," 5, Aichi bunsho, Chochiku: Chochiku zōkyōsaku, vol. 2, doc. 21, SZS.

7. Italics mine. "Ōkura daijin kōen genkō" [Finance minister's address], September 16, 1947, Aichi bunsho, Chochiku: Chochiku zōkyōsaku, vol. 2, doc. 36, SZS.

8. Ōkurashō [Ginkōkyoku], "Chochiku zōkyō ni kansuru ken" [Savings promotion], ca. June 1946, Aichi bunsho, Chochiku: Chochiku zōkyōsaku, vol. 1, doc. 3, SZS.

9. "Jikan chochiku kōen shiryō" [Vice minister's address], April 5, 1947, Aichi bunsho, Chochiku: Chochiku zōkyōsaku, vol. 2, doc. 1, SZS.

10. J. C. Smith (Chief, Money and Banking Branch, Finance Division, Economic and Scientific Section, SCAP), "Statement for Release in Connection with Savings Campaign," ca. September 1948, Noda bunsho, Chochiku zōkyō taisaku, doc. 42, SZS.

11. Shunya Yoshimi, "Consuming America, Producing Japan," in Garon and Maclachlan, Ambivalent Consumer, 67–68.

12. Minami Hiroshi, Zoku Shōwa bunka: 1945–1989 [Shōwa culture, part 2] (Tokyo: Keisō Shobō, 1990), 13–14.

13. New York Times, September 24, 2003, sec. A, p. 17.

14. Lizabeth Cohen, "The Consumers' Republic: An American Model for the World?" in Garon and Maclachlan, Ambivalent Consumer, 58–59; Sheryl Kroen, "A Political History of the Consumer," Historical Journal 47, no.3 (September 2004): 709–36.

15. Richard. B. Finn, Winners in Peace: MacArthur, Yoshida, and Postwar Japan (Berkeley: University of California Press, 1992), 37, 332, n. 25; Dower, Embracing Defeat, 115.

16. Laura E. Hein, Fueling Growth: The Energy Revolution and Economic Policy in Postwar Japan (Cambridge: Council on East Asian Studies, 1990), 147, 158–59, 356, n. 7.

17. Quoted in Kokumin Seikatsu Sentaa, Sengo shōhisha undōshi [History of postwar consumer movement] (Tokyo: Ōkurashō Insatsukyoku, 1997), 61, n. 4.

18. Yano Shōtarō, "Ōkura daijin rajio hōsō," 2.

19. Nagata Makoto, "Kokusai kinken kyōkai to sekai kinken dee" [International Thrift Institute and World Thrift Day], Chochiku jihō [Savings times; hereafter CJ],

no. 19 (January 1954): 80–86; "Kaigai chochiku posutaa, kyatchi fureezu-shū" [Foreign savings posters and catchphrases], ibid., 67–71; "Berugii, Oranda ryōkoku no chochiku undō" [Belgian and Dutch savings campaigns], *CJ*, no. 43 (March 1960): 56–57.
20. "Jikan chochiku kōen shiryō."
21. Tsūka Antei Taisaku Jimukyoku [Office of Currency Stabilization Policy], *Chochiku to infureeshon* [Saving and inflation], pamphlet (Tokyo: Nihon Ginkō, 1947).
22. E.g., Tōkyō-to Tsūka Antei Suishin Iinkai, "Tōkyō-to [cho]chiku zōkyō hōsaku" [Savings-promotion program in Metropolitan Tokyo], ca. October 1946, doc. 26; Nihon Ginkō Kyōto shiten, "Kyōto-fu kyūkoku chochiku undō kin'yū kikanbetsu mokuhyō narabi tasseigaku" [National Salvation Savings Campaign in Kyoto prefecture: targets and achieved savings by financial institution], ca. January 1947, Aichi bunsho, Chochiku: Chochiku zōkyōsaku, vol. 1, doc. 52, SZS.
23. Ōkurashō, "Chochiku jissen mohan chiku setchi yōryō" [Points for setting up model savings districts], ca. April 1947, Aichi bunsho, Chochiku: Chochiku zōkyōsaku, vol. 2, doc. 7, SZS.
24. Ōkurashō, "Shōwa 22 nendo yobikin shishutsusho" [Preparatory budget outlays for 1947], 10, Aichi bunsho, Chochiku: Chochiku zōkyōsaku, vol. 3, doc. 8, SZS.
25. [Ōkurashō], Ginkōkyoku, Kokumin chochiku-ka, "Shōwa 24 nendo kyūkoku chochiku undō hōsaku yōkōan" [1949 National Salvation Savings Campaign plan], April 5, 1949, p. 3, Aichi bunsho, Chochiku: Chochiku zōkyōsaku, vol. 5, doc. 4, SZS.
26. Tsūka Antei Taisaku Honbu [Currency Stabilization Board], "Yokin ni kansuru seron chōsa" [Opinion poll on savings deposits], November 1949, p. 2, Noda bunsho, Chochiku dōkō, 1947–51, doc. 7, SZS.
27. Ōkurashō, "Chochiku suishin kabu kikō no kongo no un'ei ni tsuite" [Future operations of the savings-promotion substructure], ca. January 1949, p. 1, Aichi bunsho, Chochiku: Chochiku zōkyōsaku, vol. 4, doc. 44, SZS.
28. Tsūka Antei Taisaku Honbu, "Chochiku undō sankanen o kaiko shite" [Recalling three years of the savings campaign], November 1949, pp. 5, 8–10, Noda bunsho, Chochiku dōkō, doc. 6, SZS; Tsūka Antei Taisaku Honbu, "Yokin ni kansuru seron chōsa," 1.
29. CU, 16–17, 22–27; Ōkurashō, Nihon Ginkō, "Kōwa kinen tokubetsu chochiku undō yōkō" [Outline of the Special Savings Campaign to Commemorate the Peace Treaty], ca. August 1951, p. 1, Noda bunsho, Chochiku zōkyō, doc. 56, SZS.
30. CU, 148.
31. Kyoko Hirano, *Mr. Smith Goes to Tokyo: Japanese Cinema under the American Occupation, 1945–1952* (Washington, DC: Smithsonian Institute Press, 1992), 52–53.
32. CU, 47, 74, 87; Chochiku Zōkyō Chūō Iinkai, *Chochiku hakusho*, 241; Central Council for Savings Promotion, *Savings and Savings Promotion Movement in Japan* (Tokyo: Central Council for Savings Promotion, 1981), 41–43.
33. *New York Times*, June 5, 1987, sec. D, p. 1; CU, 42, 44–45, 128–30.
34. CU, 17, 20, 72, 162; Kin'yū Zaisei Jijō Kenkyūkai, *"Kodomo ginkō" no un'ei ni tsuite* [Operations of children's banks] (Tokyo: Kin'yū Zaisei Jijō Kenkyūkai, 1995), 4.
35. For an excellent overview, see Thomas F. Cargill and Naoyuki Yoshino, *Postal Savings and Fiscal Investment in Japan* (Oxford: Oxford University Press, 2003), 9, 12, 42, 51–58, 64–69.

36. *Savings Banks International*, 1983, no. 4 (Winter): 52–53; Yūseishō, *Yūsei hyakunenshi*, 763; Patricia L. Maclachlan, *The People's Post Office: The History and Politics of the Japanese Postal System, 1871-2010* (Cambridge: Harvard University Asia Center, forthcoming, 2011).

37. Chalmers A. Johnson, *MITI and the Japanese Miracle: The Growth of Industrial Policy, 1925–1975* (Stanford: Stanford University Press, 1982), 210, also 207–209.

38. *Fujin jihō* [Women's times], no. 30 (July 1955): 2.

39. E.g., *Yūcho jihō* [Postal savings times], no. 324 (August 1974): 3; *Shufu no tomo* (December 1974): 214–19.

40. See Charles Yuji Horioka, "Why Is Japan's Household Saving Rate So High? A Literature Survey," *Journal of the Japanese and International Economies* 4, no. 1 (March 1990): 64–66, 76–80; David D. Selover, *The Japanese Saving Rate: Another Literature Review*, JDB Discussion Paper Series, no. 9312 (Tokyo: Japan Development Bank, 1994), 50–51.

41. Garon, *Molding Japanese Minds*, 163–66.

42. "Dai 3-kai zenkoku chochiku jimu shokuin kōshūkai" [Third national savings officers training course], September 17, 1947, p. 3, Aichi bunsho, Chochiku: Chochiku zōkyōsaku, vol. 3, doc. 1, SZS.

43. "Kyūkoku chochiku tokubetsu undō ni kansuru Katayama naikaku sōri daijin dan" [Interview with Prime Minister Katayama on the Special National Salvation Savings Campaign], September 1, 1947, p. 1, Aichi bunsho, Chochiku: Chochiku zōkyōsaku, vol. 2, doc. 46, SZS.

44. Garon, *Molding Japanese Minds*, 164, also 163–72.

45. Interview with Tachi Ryūichi (professor of economics, University of Tokyo), November 27, 1996, Tokyo. Suzuki Takeo in Chochiku Zōkyō Chūō Iinkai, *Chochiku hakusho*, 2; for Tsuru Shigeto, see "Dai 3-kai zenkoku chochiku jimu shokuin kōshūkai," 2; Morito Tatsuo in Ōkura Zaimu Kyōkai, *Shakai kaihatsu ni shimeru chochiku no jūyōsei* [Importance of saving in social development] (Tokyo: Ōkura Zaimu Kyōkai, 1965), 80.

46. Italics mine. Minobe Ryōkichi, *Keizai to seiji* [Economics and politics] (Tokyo: Jitugyō no Nihonsha, 1955), 11–12, 199; also Minobe Ryōkichi, Uno Masao, and Ujiie Hisako, *Kakei to seikatsu* [Household finance and daily life] (Tokyo: Dōbun Shoin, 1958), 64–65; cf. Laura Hein, *Reasonable Men, Powerful Words: Political Culture and Expertise in Twentieth-Century Japan* (Berkeley: University of California Press, 2004), 162–75.

47. Andrew Gordon, "Managing the Japanese Household: The New Life Movement in Postwar Japan," *Social Politics* 4, no. 2 (Summer 1997): 245–83.

48. *CJ*, no. 20 (April 1954): 120.

49. See Garon, *Molding Japanese Minds*, chap. 6.

50. See Chochiku Kōhō Chūō Iinkai, *Akarui seikatsu no kakeibo, 1992* [Household account book for the bright life] (Tokyo: Chochiku Kōhō Chūō Iinkai, 1991), 9, 23, 124; Chochiku Kōhō Chūō Iinkai, *Chochiku to shōhi ni kansuru seron chōsa, 1996* (Tokyo: Chochiku Kōhō Chūō Iinkai, 1996), 146.

51. Chochiku Zōkyō Chūō Iinkai, *Chochiku ni kansuru seron chōsa, 1987*, p. 124.

52. *Yucho jihō*, no. 141 (April 1959): 13; "Kakeibo o chūshin to shita guruupu katsudō ni tsuite" [Group activities focused on household account book], *Shin seikatsu*

to chochiku: Dai 1-kai zenkoku fujin no tsudoi kiroku [New life and saving: Record of the first national women's meeting] (Tokyo: Chochiku Zōkyō Chūō Iinkai, 1959), 42–49.

53. Ōkurashō, "Shōwa 22 nendo yobikin shishutsusho."

54. Chochiku Kōhō Chūō Iinkai, "Wagaya no maruhi! Yarikuri" [Confidential to our homes! Make do], memo, doc. '96-1, March 1996, p. 2; Fujin jihō, no. 67 (October 1958): 2; CU, 19, 33.

55. See Ono Yoshisa (chair, Nishi-Tamagawa Women's Council), "Dannasama no osake ni baketa" [Lest it be spent on the husband's drinking], Fujin jihō 21 (September. 1954): 1; see Ezra F. Vogel, Japan's New Middle Class: The Salary Man and His Family in a Tokyo Suburb (Berkeley: University of California Press, 1963), 76–77.

56. Fujin jihō 34 (November 1955): 1.

57. Funada Fumiko, "Kotoshi no mokuhyō: Katei no kagakuka e" [This year's goal: bringing science to the home], Shufuren tayori 10 (January 1950): 2; Oku Mumeo, "Shufu chochiku no undō" [Housewives' savings movement], Shufuren tayori 67 (November 1954): 1.

58. Oku Mumeo, "Shin seikatsu e" [Toward new life], Shufuren tayori 52 (August 1953): 1.

59. Keizai Kikakuchō [Economic Planning Agency], Kokumin seikatsu hakusho, 1959 [Whitepaper on national life] (Tokyo: Ōkurashō Insatsukyoku, 1959), 1, 74–77; Simon Partner, Assembled in Japan: Electrical Goods and the Making of the Japanese Consumer (Berkeley: University of California Press, 1999), 247.

60. Patricia L. Maclachlan, Consumer Politics in Postwar Japan (New York: Columbia University Press, 2002), 94.

61. Partner, Assembled in Japan, 5, also 149–56, 168–70; Johnson, MITI, 16.

62. Horioka, "Consuming and Saving," 261, 265, 268–89.

63. Andrew Gordon, "From Singer to Shinpan: Consumer Credit in Modern Japan," in Garon and Maclachlan, Ambivalent Consumer, 137–62; Sand, House and Home, 374–75; Gordon, Modern History of Japan 249, 267.

64. Partner, Assembled in Japan, 163–65.

65. International Labour Office, Year-book of Labour Statistics, 1960, in CJ, no. 53 (September 1962): inside back cover.

66. Richard F. Kuisel, Seducing the French: The Dilemma of Americanization (Berkeley: University of California Press, 1993), 17, 111.

67. Koizumi Akira, "Keizai no antei seichō o sasaeru mono: Shōhi wa bitoku ka" [Factors supporting stable economic growth: Is consumption the virtue?], CJ, no. 50 (December 1961): 15; Usami Jun, "Seikatsu to chochiku" [Daily life and saving], CJ, no. 86 (July 1966): 6–7.

68. Okazaki Kaheita, in Shin seikatsu to chochiku 3 (1961): 7–10; Vance Packard, The Waste Makers (New York: David McKay, 1960), 274–93; Partner, Assembled in Japan, 130–31, 188–89.

69. Oku Mumeo, in Shin seikatsu to chochiku, 3:12–13.

70. Fujin jihō, no. 107 (February 1962): 1; CU, 60–61.

71. Economic Planning Agency, Whitepaper on National Life, 1975 (Tokyo: Economic Planning Agency, 1975), foreword, 132, 136–37.

72. "Infure ni kachinuku: Shin-chokingaku nyūmon" [Fighting inflation: A primer on the new savings school], Shūkan sankei, December 28, 1974, pp. 156, 158.

73. Charter of the Global Greens, Canberra 2001, 5, 14, http://europeangreens.org/cms/default/dokbin/147/147171.charter_of_the_global_greens_canberra_20@en.pdf, accessed July 23, 2009; E. F. Schumacher, Small Is Beautiful: A Study of Economics as If People Mattered (London: Blond and Briggs, 1973), 52.

74. Keiko Higuchi, "Kore kara no shōhi seikatsu" [Consumer life from now on], Kurashi no chie [Tips on living] 94 (1974): 1.

75. Itō Akiko, "Kakeibo kichō no susume" [Encouragement of keeping household account books], Kurashi no chie 116 (November 1977): 1; 118 (March 1978): 3.

76. Central Council for Savings Promotion, Savings and Savings Promotion Movement, 23–24.

77. Ezra F. Vogel, Japan as Number One (Cambridge: Harvard University Press, 1979); Paul A. Samuelson, "Two Success Stories," Newsweek, March 9, 1981, p. 71; Klein, in Business Week, June 30, 1980, p. 61.

78. Ronald Reagan, "Address before the Japanese Diet," November 11, 1983, Public Papers of the Presidents of the United States, book 2 (1983), 1575–77.

79. Kenneth B. Pyle, The Japanese Question (Washington, DC: AEI Press, 1992), 50–51.

80. Toyama Nihonjin no kinben, 163–64.

81. The Economist, April 7, 1979, p. 61.

82. Yomiuri shinbun, March 31, 1988, p. 7; Horioka, "Why Is Japan's Household Saving Rate So High?" 72.

83. Toyama, Nihonjin no kinben, 215–16; Shimomura Osamu, in Pyle, Japanese Question, 112–13; Maekawa, in Kurashi no chie, special issue (February 1982): 3.

84. Zen Chifuren, no. 123 (November 1986): 3; no. 125 (January 1987): 1, 3.

85. Yomiuri shinbun, October 28, 1990, p. 11; November 22, 1987, p. 7.

86. Yoshino Naoyuki, "Yūbin chokin no shōrei to zaisei tōyūshi" [Future of postal savings and FILP], Toshi mondai 99, no. 11 (November 2008): 56–61.

87. "Chochiku Kōhō Chūō Iinkai Heisei 9 nendo undō hōshin" [Campaign policy of Central Council for Savings Information], mimeo, 1997, p. 1.

88. Chochiku Kōhō Chūō Iinkai, Hoshigari hime no bōken (1990) and UFO ni tsukamatta kodomotachi (1991).

89. See http://www.saveinfo.or.jp, accessed August 11, 2009; interviews with the Central Council for Financial Services' Masunaga Rei (Chairman) and Okazaki Ryōko (Manager), July 2002; also with Okazaki, June 10, 2008.

90. Donald MacIntyre, "Spend Japan Spend," Time (Asia ed.), April 20, 1998, pp. 14–16.

91. Kin'yū Kōhō Chūō Iinkai, Kin'yū kyōiku puroguramu [Financial education program] (Tokyo: Kin'yū Kōhō Chūō Iinkai, 2007), 21–23.

92. Kin'yū Kōhō Chūō Iinkai, Kakei no kin'yū kōdō ni kansuru seron chōsa, 2008 [Survey of household finances], p. 3; ibid., 2007, p. 11; for data on consumer spending, debt, and assets, see Kin'yū Kōhō Chūō Iinkai, Kurashi to kin'yū nandemo deeta [Data on living and finances] (Tokyo: Kin'yū Kōhō Chūō Iinkai, 2007), 8, 21, 37. German figures from 2001.

93. *The Economist*, July 5, 2003, p. 67.

94. Figures from U.S. Department of Commerce, Bureau of Economic Analysis.

95. "Index of Consumption Expenditure Level: Two-or-More-Person Households," 1981–2008 (adjusted for inflation and by distribution of household by number of household members), Statistics Bureau, Ministry of Internal Affairs and Communications, http://www.stat.go.jp/data/kakei/longtime/index.htm#time, accessed August 14, 2009.

96. Gordon, "From Singer to Shinpan," 160–62.

97. Charles Yuji Horioka, Wataru Suzuki, and Tatsuo Hatta "Aging, Saving and Public Pensions," *Asian Economic Policy Review* 2, no. 2 (2007): 303–19.

98. Charles Yuji Horioka, "The Causes of Japan's 'Lost Decade': The Role of Household Consumption," *Japan and the World Economy* 18, no. 4 (December 2006): 378–400.

99. E.g., "Watashitachi no tame-teku & setsuyaku waza" [Our techniques for saving and economizing], *Shufu no tomo* 86, no. 10 (July 2002): 68–85; "Kakeibo de fuan o kaishō [Erasing insecurity with an account book], *Fujin no tomo* 102, no. 11 (November 2008): 122–45.

100. Account-keeping statistics in Chochiku Kōhō Chūō Iinkai, *Seikatsu sekkei no tatekata* [Constructing a life plan] (Tokyo: Chochiku Kōhō Chūō Iinkai, 1999), 34; *OECD Economic Outlook*, no. 86 (November 2009), Annex Table 58.

101. *The Economist*, August 15, 2009, p. 66.

CHAPTER 10: EXPORTING THRIFT, OR THE MYTH OF "ASIAN VALUES"

1. "Remarks of Chinese Premier Wen Jiabao, 'Turning Your Eyes to China,'" December 10, 2003, *Harvard University Gazette*, December 11, 2003.

2. Walter Russell Mead, "The Real Asian Miracle; Asia Devalued," *New York Times Magazine*, May 31, 1998, p. 38.

3. See Beng-Huat Chua, ed., *Consumption in Asia: Lifestyles and Identities* (London: Routledge, 2000), 9–10.

4. Laura C. Nelson, *Measured Excess: Status, Gender, and Consumer Nationalism in South Korea* (New York: Columbia University Press, 2000); also Karl Gerth, *China Made: Consumer Culture and the Creation of the Nation* (Cambridge: Harvard University Asia Center, 2003).

5. "Savings Promotion Campaign," PowerPoint presentation to the author, Financial Management and Savings Secretariat, Bank Negara Malaysia, June 25, 2001.

6. World Bank, *The East Asian Miracle: Economic Growth and Public Policy* (London: Oxford University Press, 1993), 16.

7. Roy Hofheinz, Jr., and Kent E. Calder, *The Eastasia Edge* (New York: Basic Books, 1982), 120–22.

8. Fareed Zakaria, "Culture Is Destiny: A Conversation with Lee Kuan Yew," *Foreign Affairs* 73, no. 2 (March/April 1994): 113–14, 116; Mahathir, in *Straits Times* (Singapore), October 4, 1997, p. 62.

9. "Measures for Mobilizing Domestic Saving for Productive Investment," *Economic Bulletin for Asia and the Far East* (United Nations) 13, no. 3 (December 1962): 1.

10. Saburo Okita, *Causes and Problems of Rapid Growth in Postwar Japan and Their Implications for Newly Developing Economies* (Tokyo: Japan Economic Research Center, 1967), 2, 12–14, 20–29.

11. "Fourth Meeting of the Advisory Committee and Meeting of ISBI Members in the Asia-Pacific Region, Tokyo, Japan, 25–27 May 1989: Minutes," pp. 47, 50, doc. 371, Archives of International Savings Banks Institute, Brussels.

12. E.g., 3rd Bank of Japan/World Bank Joint Seminar for Central Bankers from Asian Countries in Transition: Savings Promotion, 25 February–3 March 1998, Tokyo (attending: Cambodia, China, Kazakhstan, Kyrgyzstan, Laos, Mongolia, Myanmar, Vietnam); also, 19th Bank of Japan Seminar for SEANZA Central Banks: Savings Promotion September 16–23, 1997, Tokyo (attending: Australia, China, Hong Kong, India, Indonesia, Iran, Malaysia, Nepal, New Zealand, Philippines, South Korea, Sri Lanka).

13. Bruce Cumings, "The Legacy of Japanese Colonialism in Korea," in Ramon H. Myers and Mark R. Peattie, eds., *The Japanese Colonial Empire, 1895–1945* (Princeton: Princeton University Press, 1984), 479, 495; John Lie, *Han Unbound: The Political Economy of South Korea* (Stanford: Stanford University Press, 1998), 59–61.

14. Postal Division, "Survey of the Postal Savings Bank System," May 3, 1947, Civil Communications Section, Supreme Commander of the Allied Powers, RG 331, NACP.

15. Gi-Wook Shin and Do-Hyun Han, "Colonial Corporatism: The Rural Revitalization Campaign, 1932–1940," in Gi-Wook Shin and Michael Robinson, eds., *Colonial Modernity in Korea* (Cambridge: Harvard University Asia Center, 1999), 70, 83, 87–88.

16. Hanguk Ŭnhaeng, *Chigŭm ŭn jŏchuk I jolsil I pilyohan tae imnida* (Seoul: Bank of Korea, 1997), 5, trans. by Soyoung Lee.

17. Korea Taehakkyo Kyŭngjae Yonguso [Korea University, Economics Institute] *Kukmin jŏchuk undong banghyang gwa chujin jogik ui palchŏn bangan* [Proposal for development of promotional organizations of national savings campaigns] (Seoul: Korea Taehakkyo Kyŭngjae Yonguso, 1996), 21, 24–26, trans. by Ro Sang-ho.

18. Korea Taehakkyo, *Kukmin jŏchuk*, 21; Alice H. Amsden, *Asia's Next Giant: South Korea and Late Industrialization* (New York: Oxford University Press, 1989), 39.

19. Chung Hee Park, *The Country, the Revolution and I*, 2nd ed. (Seoul: Hollym Corp., 1970), 93, also 111, 120.

20. Park, *The Country, the Revolution*, 176–77, 66–67, 111, 147.

21. CU, 84.

22. Korea Taehakkyo, *Kukmin jŏchuk*, 22–23.

23. Interview with Park Jongkyu, June 4, 2001, Seoul; Jongkyu Park and Jin-Yeong Kim, *Declining Saving Rate: Macroeconomic and Microeconomic Evidences* [in Korean] (Seoul: Korea Institute of Public Finance, 2000), 11; e.g., Bank of Korea, *Annual Report, 1979* (Seoul: Bank of Korea, 1980), 8.

24. Korea Taehakkyo, *Kukmin jŏchuk*, 21–22.

25. Hanguk Ŭnhaeng, *Chigŭm ŭn jŏchuk*, 19, 21.

26. See also Nelson, *Measured Excess*, 2, 18–19, 23–25, 114.

27. Ibid., 115–16, also 107–11.

28. *Los Angeles Times*, November 25, 1991, sec. D, p. 3.

29. Ministry of Finance and Economy, "Korean Government Statement on Frugality Campaign on May 9, 1997," http://www.mofe.go.kr/P_R/ep051301.html, accessed January 30, 2002.

30. Korea Taehakkyo, *Kukmin jŏchuk*, 48.

31. Thomas Byrne, "The Korean Banking System Six Years after the Crisis," *Korea's Economy 2004* (Washington, DC: Korean Economic Institute, 2004), 17.

32. *Korea Times*, October 27, 2004; Laura C. Nelson, "South Korean Consumer Nationalism: Women, Children, Credit, and Other Perils," in Garon and Maclachlan, *Ambivalent Consumer*, 188–207.

33. Linda Low and T. C. Aw, *Housing a Healthy, Educated and Wealthy Nation through the CPF* (Singapore: Times Academic Press, 1997).

34. Richard Lim, *Banking on a Virtue: POSBank, 1972–1997* (Singapore: POSBank, 1997), 21–22, 59, 75; Low and Aw, *Housing a Healthy, Educated and Wealthy Nation*, 95, 99, 119.

35. Labor Minister S. Rajaratnam, in *Straits Times*, June 2, 1973.

36. Low and Aw, *Housing a Healthy, Educated and Wealthy Nation*, 86; "Speech by Dr. Richard Hu, Minister of Finance, at the World Economic Forum Meeting in Geneva," September 8, 1987, Singapore Government Press Releases, National Archives of Singapore.

37. "'Thrift' in Our Idioms, Sayings and Folktales," typescript, ca. June 2001, Civic and Moral Education curriculum, Ministry of Education, Singapore.

38. Post Office Savings Bank, *The First Hundred Years of the Post Office Savings Bank of Singapore* (Singapore: Post Office Savings Bank, 1977), 10–11.

39. Kian Woon Kwok, "How to Be Singaporean, Chinese and Modern All at Once," *Straits Times*, October 25, 1998, p. 37; Zakaria, "Culture is Destiny," 125.

40. Italics mine. *Straits Times*, April 28, 1974, p. 1.

41. Hiroshi Shimizu and Hitoshi Hirakawa, *Japan and Singapore in the World Economy: Japan's Economic Advance into Singapore, 1870–1965* (London: Routledge, 1999), 4, 113, 161, 183–84.

42. Lim, *Banking on a Virtue*, 20–21, 29–30, 34.

43. Keng Swee Goh, *The Economics of Modernization* (1972; Singapore: Federal Publications, 1995), 35, also 220.

44. Keng Swee Goh, *Wealth of East Asian Nations* (Singapore: Federal Publications, 1995), 78.

45. "'Thrift' in Our Syllabuses," typescript, ca. June 2001, Ministry of Education Singapore.

46. Low and Aw, *Housing a Healthy, Educated and Wealthy Nation*, 86.

47. Goh (1972) and Lee (1986), quoted in Low and Aw, *Housing a Healthy, Educated and Wealthy Nation*, 86, 11–12.

48. *Straits Times*, April 28, 1974, p. 1.

49. Interview with Lee Kah Chuen (Deputy Director, Humanities and Aesthetics Branch, Curriculum Planning and Development Division), June 21, 2001, Ministry of Education, Singapore.

50. Cherian George, *Singapore: The Air-Conditioned Nation: Essays on the Politics of Comfort and Control* (Singapore: Landmark Books, 2000), 15–17.

51. Al' Alim Ibrahim, ed., *Generating a National Savings Movement: Proceedings of the First Malaysian National Savings Conference, Kuala Lumpur, July 8–10, 1993* (Kuala Lumpur: ISIS Malaysia, 1994), iii.

52. Bank Negara Malaysia, *The Central Bank and the Financial System in Malaysia—A Decade of Change* (Kuala Lumpur: Bank Negara Malaysia, 1999), 513.

53. "International Savings Banks Institute ISBI Regional Office in Southeast Asia," *Savings Banks International*, 1980, no. 3 (Autumn), 46; "Meeting of the Advisory Committee and Meeting of ISBI Members in the Asia-Pacific Region, Kuala Lumpur, Malaysia, 15–18 January 1991: Minutes," doc. 373, Archives of International Savings Banks Institute.

54. Bank Negara Malaysia, *Annual Report, 1990* (Kuala Lumpur: Bank Negara Malaysia, 1991), 125, 127.

55. Anwar Ibrahim, "Keynote Address" (trans. by Janine Yoong), in Al' Alim Ibrahim ed., *Generating a National Savings Movement*, xi–xii; also "Introduction," i–ii.

56. "Speech of Prime Minister Y.A.B. Dato Seri Mahathir Bin Mohamad at the Launching Ceremony of the National Savings Campaign," December 16, 1996, http://www.bnm.gov.my/feature/sav/spch_PM.htm, accessed April 1, 2004, trans. by Janine Yoong.

57. "People Helping in Economic Recovery—Dr. Mahathir," *Bernama* (Malaysian National News Agency), August 29, 1998; Bank Negara Malaysia, *Annual Report, 1996*, p. 71.

58. Bank Negara Malaysia, *Central Bank and the Financial System*, 243–53, 530–31; interview with Hasbullah bin Abdullah (Manager, Financial Planning and Savings Secretariat), June 25, 2001, Bank Negara Malaysia.

59. Hua Sing Lim, *Japan's Role in Asia*, 3rd ed. (Singapore: Times Academic Press, 2001), 1.

60. Mahathir Mohamad and Shintaro Ishihara, *The Voice of Asia: Two Leaders Discuss the Coming Century* (Tokyo: Kodansha International, 1995), 46–47, 80–81, 130–32.

61. Interview with Vijayaledchumy Veluppillai (Director, Economics Department), June 25, 2001, Bank Negara Malaysia.

62. "Savings Promotion Campaign," PowerPoint, Bank Negara Malaysia.

63. Interview with Hasbullah bin Abdullah.

64. Ferguson, *The Ascent of Money*; Eamonn Fingleton, *In the Jaws of the Dragon: America's Fate in the Coming Era of Chinese Hegemony* (New York: Thomas Dunne Books/St. Martin's Press, 2008); Stephen S. Roach, *Stephen Roach on the Next Asia* (Hoboken, NJ: Wiley, 2010).

65. Shikha Jha, Eswar Prasad, and Akiko Terada-Hagiwara, "Saving in Asia: Issues for Rebalancing Growth," ADB Working Paper Series, no. 162 (Manila: Asian Development Bank, 2009), 15, 28.

66. Xiaochuan Zhou, "On Savings Ratio," remarks to G20 London Summit, March 31, 2009, http://english.people.com.cn/90002/96808/96825/6626546.html, accessed October 10, 2010; *China Daily*, February 2, 2009.

67. Fingleton, *In the Jaws of the Dragon*, 17; Daniel K. Gardner, "The Useful Sage," *Los Angeles Times*, October 1, 2010, part A, p. 21.

68. Industrial and Commercial Bank of China, presentation at the "Meeting of the Advisory Committee and Meeting of ISBI Members in the Asia-Pacific Region, Kuala Lumpur," 1991, p. 31.

69. Roach, Next Asia, 246.

70. Fingleton, In the Jaws of the Dragon, 10.

71. Ibid., 128–32; Jha, Prasad, and Terada-Hagiwara, "Saving in Asia," 23.

72. For banking before and after 1978, see Zhaojin Ji, A History of Modern Shanghai Banking (Armonk, NY: M. E. Sharpe, 2003), 178–79, 239–62.

73. Wen Hui Bao (Shanghai), [March] 28, 1987, trans. BBC Summary of World Broadcasts, April 15, 1987, Society and Environment: Outline of Banking Structure Reform, part 3, Far East, Weekly Economic Report; Economic and Technical, China, FE/W1436/A/3.

74. Industrial and Commercial Bank of China, presentation, 31–32.

75. CU, 119; Liu Shiyu (People's Bank of China), "Brief Introduction on Savings Deposits and Investment in China," to 3rd Bank of Japan/World Bank Joint Seminar for Central Bankers from Asian Countries in Transition; Nikkei Weekly, June 27, 1994, economy sec., p. 2.

76. Min'an Peng, "Developing Postal Savings in China," in Mark J. Scher and Naoyuki Yoshino, eds., Small Savings Mobilization and Asian Economic Development: The Role of Postal Financial Services (Armonk, NY: M. E. Sharpe, 2004), 79–92.

77. E.g., Edward Wong, "China's Export Economy Begins Turning Inward: Leaders Want Citizens to Be Consumers," New York Times, June 25, 2010, sec. A, p. 6.

78. Jha, Prasad, and Terada-Hagiwara, "Saving in Asia," 7–9.

79. James Fallows, "The $1.4 Trillion Question," Atlantic Monthly 301, no. 1 (January/February 2008): 36–48.

80. Financial Times, January 2, 2009, World News, p. 5.

81. New York Times, January 29, 2009, sec. A, p. 12.

CHAPTER 11: "THERE IS MONEY. SPEND IT"

1. "The President's News Conference of April 9, 1958," Public Papers of the Presidents of the United States, Dwight D. Eisenhower, 1958 (Washington, DC: Government Printing Office, 1959), 303.

2. George Hanc, The United States Savings Bond Program in the Postwar Period (New York: National Bureau of Economic Research, 1962), 54.

3. David M. Kennedy, Freedom from Fear: The American People in Depression and War, 1929–1945 (New York: Oxford University Press, 1999), 856–57.

4. Quoted in Cohen, Consumers' Republic, 71, also 69–70.

5. Board of Governors of the Federal Reserve System, Consumer Installment Credit, part 1, vol. 1 (Washington, DC: Government Printing Office, 1957), 9–12; Cohen, Consumers' Republic, 123.

6. National Savings 7, no. 8 (1951): 4.

7. Chicago Tribune, December 22, 1963, sec. A, p. 1; "2 Providence Banks Drop School Savings Programs," New York Times, May 24, 1964, sec. F, p. 13; New York Times, August 14, 1961, p. 31; Washington Post, February 18, 1951, sec. L, p. 7; U.S.

Department of the Treasury, *Annual Report of the Secretary of the Treasury on the State of the Finances for the Fiscal Year Ended June 30, 1951* (Washington, DC: United States Government Printing Office, 1952), 166, and *Annual Report*, 1960, p. 160; U.S. Department of Treasury, Savings Bond Division, *A History of the United States Savings Bonds Program* (Washington, DC: Department of Treasury, 1991), 31, 45.

8. Hanc, *United States Savings Bond Program*, 83, also 49, 60; Thaler and Sunstein, *Nudge*, 107–11.

9. William H. Whyte, Jr., "Budgetism: Opiate of the Middle Class," *Fortune* (May 1956): 133.

10. *New York Times Magazine*, January 17, 1954, p. 108; Tucker, *Decline of Thrift*, 134, 138.

11. *Mary Poppins*, DVD, directed by Robert Stevenson (1964, Walt Disney Home Entertainment, 2004); P. L. Travers, *Mary Poppins* (New York: Reynal and Hitchcock, 1934).

12. From 1950 to 1990, rates are measured by the System of National Accounts (SNA) 93. From 1975 to 1984, according to SNA 68, net household saving rates averaged: U.S. (8.3 percent), Italy (21.4 percent) Japan (19.3 percent), Belgium (16.1 percent), West Germany (12.7 percent), France (12.6 percent), and United Kingdom (8.5 percent). Horioka, "Why Is Japan's Household Saving Rate So High?" 53.

13. Lawrence Mishel, Jared Bernstein, and Sylvia Allegretto (Economic Policy Institute), *The State of Working America 2006/2007* (Ithaca, NY: ILR Press, 2007), 48, 57.

14. Raymond W. Goldsmith, *A Study of Saving in the United States*, vol. 1 (New York: Greenwood Press, 1955), 5.

15. Harold W. Torgerson, "Developments in Savings and Loan Associations, 1945–53," *Journal of Finance* 9, no. 3 (September 1954): 285.

16. Hanc, *United States Savings Bond Program*, 5–6, 9, 36, 74–76.

17. Ibid., 27, 31, 35–36; Robert B. Avery, Gregory E. Elliehausen, Glenn B. Canner, and Thomas A. Gustafson, "Survey of Consumer Finances, 1983," *Federal Reserve Bulletin* (September 1984): 685.

18. Torgerson, "Developments in Savings and Loan Associations," 285–89.

19. *Scraps* (Farmers and Mechanics Savings Bank), no. 88 (May 1951): 2, Minnesota Historical Society, St. Paul, MN.

20. U.S. Department of Treasury, *History of the United States Savings Bond Program*, 36; U.S. Department of the Treasury, *Annual Report*, 1954, pp. 156–57.

21. *New York Times*, December 9, 1951, p. 177, November 11, 1947, p. 29, September 16, 1948, p. 33, June 1, 1958, sec. E, p. 9; *Los Angeles Times*, September 29, 1955, p. 37; *Chicago Tribune*, December 22, 1963, sec. A, p. 1.

22. George Katona, *Private Pensions and Individual Saving*, monograph no. 40, Survey Research Center, Institute for Social Research (Ann Arbor: University of Michigan, 1965), 94.

23. Lawrence B. Glickman, *A Living Wage: American Workers and the Making of Consumer Society* (Ithaca, NY: Cornell University Press, 1997), 79–82.

24. See Jackson Lears, *Fables of Abundance: A Cultural History of Advertising in America* (New York: Basic Books, 1995).

25. "The Problem of Unemployment—II," *Listener* (British Broadcasting Corporation) 5 (January 14, 1931).

26. George Soule, *A Planned Society* (New York: Macmillan, 1932), 234; see also Alan Brinkley, *The End of Reform: New Deal Liberalism in Recession and War* (New York: Knopf, 1995), chap. 4; David M. Potter, *People of Plenty: Economic Abundance and the American Character* (Chicago: University of Chicago Press, 1954), 78–90; on the late-nineteenth-century origins of the concept of underconsumption, see Rosanne Currarino, "The Politics of 'More': The Labor Question and the Idea of Economic Liberty in Industrial America," *Journal of American History* 93, no. 1 (June 2006): 17–36.

27. U.S. National Resources Committee, *Consumer Expenditures in the United States: Estimates for 1935–36* (Washington, DC: Government Printing Office, 1939), 1; on the origins of the idea of the "American standard of living," see Glickman, *Living Wage*, chap. 4.

28. Italics mine. Robert R. Nathan, *Mobilizing for Abundance* (New York: McGraw-Hill, 1944), 76, 80–82; also Cohen, *Consumers' Republic*, 115–16.

29. Quoted in Brinkley, *End of Reform*, 68.

30. Nathan, *Mobilizing for Abundance*, 70, 95, 99, 123, 150–51.

31. Brinkley, *End of Reform*, 257, 261–63.

32. January 4, 1957, quoted in Packard, *Waste Makers*, 171–72; Cohen, *Consumers' Republic*, 112–13.

33. *Proceedings of the 8th Constitutional Convention of the CIO, 1946*, quoted in Cohen, *Consumers' Republic*, 155, also 153–54.

34. Quoted in Packard, *Waste Makers*, 17.

35. Cohen, *Consumers' Republic*, 143–44.

36. See note 1, this chapter.

37. Packard, *Waste Makers*, 236, also 186; John Kenneth Galbraith, *The Affluent Society* (Boston: Houghton Mifflin, 1958), 202–207.

38. Robert M. Collins, *More: The Politics of Economic Growth in Postwar America* (Oxford: Oxford University Press), 181–83, 197, 211–12.

39. *New York Times*, November 30, 1991, sec. 1, p. 1.

40. Italics mine. "Transcript of President Clinton's Speech at Waseda University," White House Office of the Press Secretary, in U.S. Newswire, July 7, 1993.

41. "Remarks by the President to Airlines Employees," September 27, 2001, Chicago, http://www.whitehouse.gov/news/releases/2001/09/20010927-1.html, accessed January 15, 2009; on war bonds, see *New York Times*, October 26, 2001, sec. C, p. 7.

42. *Daily Telegraph* (London), November 27, 2001, p. 6.

43. The White House, Office of the Press Secretary, "Press Conference by the President," December 20, 2006; Paul Krugman, "Economic Storm Signals," *New York Times*, December 1, 2006, sec. A, p. 31.

44. Gordon, "From Singer to Shinpan," 139; Gelpi and Julien-Labruyère, *History of Consumer Credit*, 95–99.

45. Edwin R.A. Seligman, *The Economics of Instalment Selling: A Study in Consumers' Credit* (New York: Harper & Brothers, 1927), 1:48–49, 111–14, 331.

46. International Labour Office, *A Contribution to the Study of International Comparisons of Costs of Living: An Enquiry into the Cost of Living of Certain Groups of Workers*

in Detroit (U.S.A.) and Fourteen European Towns (Geneva: International Labour Office, 1932), 2–3, 17–19, 25, 105–106, 156–58, 195–98.

47. John E. Hamm, *The English Hire-Purchase Act, 1938: A Measure to Regulate Installment Selling* (New York: Russell Sage Foundation, 1940), 3; Calder, *Financing the American Dream*, 235–37.

48. *World Thrift*, 1938, no. 11: 311, 331.

49. Clyde William Phelps, *Financing the Installment Purchases of the American Family* (Baltimore: Commercial Credit Co., 1954), 14; Gelpi and Julien-Labruyère, *History of Consumer Credit*, 102–103, 135, 141–42.

50. Aylmer Vallance, *Hire-Purchase* (London: Thomas Nelson, 1939), viii, 72–73, 100–101; Hamm, *The English Hire-Purchase Act*, 7–9, 12–13, 24.

51. Louis Hyman, *Debtor Nation: The History of America in Red Ink* (Princeton: Princeton University Press, 2011), chap. 4.

52. Board of Governors, *Consumer Installment Credit*, 2, 268–69; Jan Logemann, "Different Paths to Mass Consumption: Consumer Credit in the United States and West Germany during the 1950s and '60s," *Journal of Social History* 41, no. 3 (Spring 2008): 530–31.

53. Galbraith, *Affluent Society*, 201; Board of Governors, *Consumer Installment Credit*, 21; Phelps, *Financing the Installment Purchases*, 9, 28–29, 28, n. 86.

54. Seligman, *Economics of Instalment Selling* 1:277, Board of Governors, *Consumer Installment Credit*, 15; Calder, *Financing the American Dream* 297–99.

55. Whyte, "Budgetism," 133.

56. Board of Governors, *Consumer Installment Credit*, 4; Martha L. Olney, *Buy Now, Pay Later: Advertising, Credit, and Consumer Durables in the 1920s* (Chapel Hill: University of North Carolina Press, 1991), 1–2, 52–53.

57. Logemann, "Different Paths to Mass Consumption," 537.

58. Board of Governors, *Consumer Installment Credit*, 12.

59. Isabelle Gaillard, "Selling Televisions on Credit: The Rise of Consumer Credit in Postwar France," in Jan Logemann, ed., *Cultures of Credit: Consumer Lending in Global Perspective* (New York: Palgrave Macmillan, forthcoming).

60. George Katona, Burkhard Strumpel, and Ernest Zahn, *Aspirations and Affluence: Comparative Studies in the United States and Western Europe* (New York: McGraw-Hill, 1971), 96–98; Logemann, "Different Paths," 543.

61. Hyman, *Debtor Nation*, 132–33.

62. Robert Shiller, *Irrational Exuberance*, 2nd ed. (Princeton: Princeton University Press, 2005), 13, 21.

63. Board of Governors, *Consumer Installment Credit*, 12–13; Cohen, *Consumers' Republic*, 122–23.

64. National Association of Home Builders, *Housing Facts, Figures, and Trends*, pamphlet, March 2006, p. 14; Statistics Bureau, Ministry of Internal Affairs and Communications, Japan, *Housing and Land Survey, 2003*, http://www.stat.go.jp/english/index/official/207.htm#4, accessed March 8, 2010; National Board of Housing, Building and Planning, Sweden, and Ministry for Regional Development of the Czech Republic, *Housing Statistics in the European Union 2004* (Stockholm: National Board of Housing, Building and Planning, 2005), 38.

65. Kenneth T. Jackson, *Crabgrass Frontier: The Suburbanization of the United States* (New York: Oxford University Press, 1985), 196–97, 203–205.

66. Kathleen J. Frydl, *The GI Bill* (Cambridge: Cambridge University Press, 2009), 265, 273; Jackson, *Crabgrass Frontier*, 293–95; Cohen, *Consumers' Republic*, 122–23.

67. Frydl, *GI Bill*, 280, 285, 299.

68. Herman M. Schwartz, *Subprime Nation: American Power, Global Capital, and the Housing Bubble* (Ithaca, NY: Cornell University Press, 2009), 181.

69. Employee Benefit Research Institute, *Notes* 29, no. 5 (May 2008): 9.

70. Teresa Ghilarducci, *When I'm Sixty-Four: The Plot against Pensions and the Plan to Save Them* (Princeton: Princeton University Press, 2008), 21–22, 53–54.

71. Employee Benefit Research Institute, *Fast Facts*, no. 158 (March 30, 2010); EBRI, *Notes* 29, no. 5 (May 2008): 7; "Individual Account Retirement Plans: An Analysis of the 2007 Survey of Consumer Finances, with Market Adjustments to June 2009," *EBRI Issue Brief*, no. 333 (August 2009): 1.

72. Ghilarducci, *When I'm Sixty-Four*, 91–92.

73. White House (Stuart E. Eizenstadt), "Letter to Senators," October 23, 1979, Staff Offices, Domestic Policy Staff, Eizenstadt File, Box 106, and Office of the White House Press Secretary, "Remarks of the President at the Signing Ceremony for the Depository Institutions Deregulation and Monetary Control Act of 1980," March 31, 1980, Staff Offices, Speechwriters, Chronological File, Box 66, Carter Library, Atlanta, GA. Thanks to Devin Fergus for sharing these documents. Also Joseph Nocera, *A Piece of the Action: How the Middle Class Joined the Money Class* (New York: Simon & Schuster, 1994), 77–78, 162, 207–209, 225.

74. James R. Barth, Susanne Trimbath, and Glenn Yago, eds., *The Savings and Loan Crisis: Lessons from a Regulatory Failure* (Santa Monica, CA: Milken Institute, 2004), 20–25, 50–54.

75. German figure from 1993. Pirmin Fessler and Martin Schürz, "Stock Holdings in Austria," *Monetary Policy & the Economy* (Oesterreichische Nationalbank) qtr. 2 (2008): 91; Tokuo Iwaisako, "Household Portfolios in Japan," National Bureau of Economic Research, Working Paper 9647, April 2003, p. 6; Nocera, *Piece of the Action*, 190, 219–20, 231–36, 276, 279, 286–89.

76. Lawrence Mishel, Jared Bernstein, and Heidi Shierholz, *The State of Working America 2008/2009* (Ithaca, NY: ILR Press, 2009), 274–75.

77. Nocera, *Piece of the Action*, 189–96.

78. Thomas A. Durkin, "Credit Cards: Use and Consumer Attitudes, 1970–2000," *Federal Reserve Bulletin* (September 2000): 624–25; Carol C. Bertaut and Michael Haliassos, "Credit Cards: Facts and Theories," in Giuseppe Bertola, Richard Disney, and Charles Grant, eds., *The Economics of Consumer Credit* (Cambridge: MIT Press, 2006), 182.

79. Bertaut and Haliassos, "Credit Cards," 183, 202, 226; also Hyman, *Debtor Nation*, 150, 171, 240–41.

80. José A. García, *Borrowing to Make Ends Meet: The Rapid Growth of Credit Card Debt in America* (New York: Demos, 2007), 6, 13; also Robert D. Manning, *Credit Card Nation* (New York: Basic Books, 2000).

81. Demos and Center for Responsible Lending, *The Plastic Safety Net* (New York: Demos, 2005), 7, 19.

82. García, *Borrowing*, 1; and ibid., *In the Red or in the Black? Understanding the Relationship between Household Debt and Assets* (New York: Demos, 2008), 7.

83. García, *Borrowing*, 6–7.

84. Sallie Mae, *How Undergraduate Students Use Credit Cards*, 2009, http://www.salliemae.com/NR/rdonlyres/0BD600F1-9377-46EA-AB1F-6061FC763246/10744/SLMCreditCardUsageStudy41309FINAL2.pdf, accessed May 17, 2010.

85. Martha R. Seger (Board of Governors, Federal Reserve), and Dodd, in Senate Committee on Banking, Housing, and Urban Affairs, *Home Equity Loans, Hearing before the Subcommittee on Consumer Affairs of the Committee on Banking, Housing, and Urban Affairs*, 100th Cong., 1st sess., November 18, 1987 (Washington, DC: Government Printing Office, 1988), 33, 34; Jim Luther, "Senators Outline Plans For Floor Challenges Next Week," Associated Press, June 6, 1986.

86. *Washington Post*, October 7, 1987, sec. F, p. 12; John Cunniff, "Time Bomb," Associated Press, Business Section, November 14, 1986; Chemical Bank ad, *Daily News* (New York), April 28, 1987.

87. Chet Currier, Associated Press, Business News, "Tax Law: Pluses and Minuses for Homeowners," October 23, 1986.

88. Senate Committee on Banking, Housing, and Urban Affairs, *Home Equity Loans, Hearing*, 36, 39.

89. See Richard Bourdon, *Home Equity Loans under the New Tax Reform Act*, CRS Report for Congress, Congressional Research Service, August 12, 1987, p. 8.

90. Alan Greenspan and James Kennedy, "Sources and Uses of Equity Extracted from Homes," Finance and Economics Discussion Series, Divisions of Research & Statistics and Monetary Affairs, Federal Reserve Board, March 2007, pp. 8, 27, 40; Herman M. Schwartz, "Housing, Global Finance, and American Hegemony," in Herman M. Schwartz and Leonard Seabrooke, eds., *The Politics of Housing Booms and Busts* (Basingstoke: Palgrave Macmillan, 2009), 45, 48.

91. Mishel et al., *State of Working America 2008/2009*, pp. 284, 292–95.

92. Schwartz, *Subprime Nation*, 3–7, 26–30.

93. Simon Johnson and James Kwak, *13 Bankers: The Wall Street Takeover and the Next Financial Meltdown* (New York: Pantheon, 2010), 128; Paul Krugman, *The Return of Depression Economics and the Crisis of 2008* (New York: W. W. Norton, 2009), 149–50, 157, 163; "Financial Bill Poses Big Test for Lobbyists," May 23, 2010, *New York Times*, sec. A, p. 1.

94. Hyman, *Debtor Nation*, chap. 6.

95. Greenspan, "The Crisis," 6–7; Johan Norberg, *Financial Fiasco: How America's Infatuation with Homeownership and Easy Money Created the Economic Crisis* (Washington, DC: Cato Institute, 2009), 26–43.

96. "Remarks by FDIC Chairman Sheila Bair to The New America Foundation conference: 'Did Low-Income Homeownership Go Too Far?': Washington, DC, December 17, 2008," http://www.fdic.gov/news/news/speeches/archives/2008/chairman/spdec1708.html, accessed June 19, 2010.

97. In 2008 dollars. U.S. Census Bureau, *Current Population Reports, Income, Poverty, and Health Insurance Coverage in the United States, 2008* (Washington, DC: GPO, 2009), 29; Federal Reserve Board, *2007 Survey of Consumer Finances*, http://www.federalreserve.gov/pubs/oss/oss2/2007/scf2007home.html, accessed June 23, 2010; Mishel et al., *State of Working America 2008/2009*, pp. 44–49.

98. Demos and CRL, *Plastic Safety Net*, 9–11; Commission on Thrift, *For a New Thrift: Confronting the Debt Culture* (New York: Institute for American Values, 2008), 19–24.

99. Brian K. Bucks, Arthur B. Kennickell, Traci L. Mach, and Kevin B. Moore, "Changes in U.S. Family Finances from 2004 to 2007: Evidence from the Survey of Consumer Finances," *Federal Reserve Bulletin* (February 2009): A10–11, 18–19.

100. Paul A. Volcker, "An Economy on Thin Ice," *Washington Post*, April 10, 2005, sec. B, p. 7; Tom Abate, "Americans Saving Less than Nothing," *San Francisco Chronicle*, January 8, 2006, sec. J, p. 1.

101. Testimony of Chairman Alan Greenspan, "The Economic Outlook before the Joint Economic Committee, U.S. Congress," June 9, 2005.

102. Quoted in "Rising Trouble with Mortgages Clouds Dream of Owning Home," *New York Times*, March 17, 2007, sec. A, p. 1; also Austan Goolsbee (economic adviser to presidential candidate Barack Obama), "'Irresponsible' Mortgages Have Opened Doors to Many of the Excluded," *New York Times*, March 29, 2007, sec. C, p. 3.

CHAPTER 12: KEEP ON SAVING?

1. "Remarks by President Barack Obama," Federal News Service, April 14, 2009, Georgetown University, Washington, DC, April 14, 2009.

2. According to the S&P/Case-Shiller Home Price Indices of twenty major cities as of November 2010. S&P Indices, "U.S. Home Prices Keep Weakening as Nine Cities Reach New Lows," press release, January 25, 2011; Bucks et al., "Changes in U.S. Family Finances from 2004 to 2007," A12.

3. See "The New Frugality," special report, *Time*, April 27, 2009.

4. *The Economist*, April 3, 2010; Ashoka Mody and Franziska Ohnsorge, "After the Crisis: Lower Consumption Growth but Narrower Global Imbalances," IMF Working Paper, January 2010 (Washington, DC: International Monetary Fund, 2009), 13, 30; *New York Times*, March 3, 2011, sec. A, p. 4.

5. Robert H. Frank, "Go Ahead and Save. Let the Government Spend," *New York Times*, February 15, 2009, sec. B, p. 8.

6. "Report on the Modernisation of the National Savings Movement," July 1965, Ad Hoc Committees: Sub-Committee to Investigate Decline of Savings Groups Organisation, 1966, TNA, NSC 7/260.

7. "Report of the Committee to Review National Savings," Chairman: Sir Harry Page, March 1973, 1: 31–33, 67–68, 457, NSC 306/12; "A Movement with a Future: Report of the National Savings Committee Steering Committee (Radice Report)," December 31, 1976, pp. 2–4, 13, 47, TNA, NSC 7/480.

8. Schwartz and Seabrooke, "Varieties of Residential Capitalism in the International Political Economy: Old Welfare States and the New Politics of Housing," in Schwartz and Seabrooke, Politics of Housing, 16–17; Jim Kemeny, "'The Really Big Trade-Off' between Home Ownership and Welfare: Castles' Evaluation of the 1980 Thesis, and a Reformulation 25 Years on," Housing, Theory and Society 22, no. 2 (2005): 60–66.

9. Consumption measured in U.S. dollars using purchasing power parities. Horioka, "Are the Japanese Unique?" 129–30.

10. Ministère de l'Economie, "Bilan de la réforme du livret A: Un succès confirmé" [Balance sheet of the reform of the Livret A account: A confirmed success], News Press, August 4, 2010; Le Figaro, August 2, 2010, p. 21; http://www.banque-france .fr/gb/stat_conjoncture/telechar/stat_mone/monetab1.pdf, accessed June 30, 2007.

11. Jean-Pierre Raffarin, in "French Government Not to Lower Rate on Livret A National Savings Accounts," AFX News, AFX European Focus, March 6, 2003.

12. Georges Gloukoviezoff, "De la bancarisation de masse à l'exclusion bancaire puis sociale" [From mass banking to bank exclusion followed by social exclusion], Revue Française des Affaires Sociales, 2004, no. 3: 11–38; also http://www.v4.caisse-epargne.fr, accessed August 16, 2010.

13. Sparkasse Bremen, "Die Sparkasse Bremen. Gut für Bremen," July 26, 2007; Satzung der Die Sparkasse Bremen AG [Statutes of the Bremen Savings Bank] (Bremen: Sparkasse Bremen, 2004), 3; Sparkassen-Finanzgruppe, Savings Banks Finance Group— Number One in the German Financial Market (Berlin: Sparkassen-Finanzgruppe, 2008), 8, 25; http://www.postbank.com, accessed August 18, 2010.

14. Sparkassen-Finanzgruppe, "Brief Portrait: Geld und Haushalt—Money and the Private Household—An Advisory Service of the Sparkassen-Finanzgruppe," Berlin, January 2007; also www.geldundhaushalt.de, accessed February 18, 2011.

15. Klaus Dieter Webpals, "Bankmarketing und Jugend: Marketingmassnahmen von Banken mit der Zielgruppe Jugendliche bis 28 Jahre unter besonderer Berücksichtigung der Sparkassen von Oberfranken und Mittelfranken" [Bank-marketing and youth: Marketing measures by banks directed at youth up to age 28, with emphasis on the Oberfranken and Mittelfranken Savings Banks] (PhD diss., Universität Kassel, 2004), 38, 47; Sparkassen SchulService [Savings banks' School Service], Lehrerinformation zum Foliensatz: Sparen [Teacher information on the guidelines: Saving] (Stuttgart: Deutscher Sparkassen Verlag, 2005), 2; Christine Kadolli (Deutscher Sparkassenverlag), "Sparkassen-SchulService: Schulsponsoring mit Tradition," mimeo, July 2007, Stuttgart.

16. Axel Börsch-Supan, Anette Reil-Held, and Reinhold Schnabel, "Household Saving in Germany," in Börsch-Supan, Life-Cycle Savings, 85–88; Yorck Dietrich, Eigentum für jeden: Die Vermögenspolitischen Initiativen der CDU und die Gesetzgebung 1950–1961 [Property for everyone: Wealth Formation initiative of the Christian Democratic Union and legal initiatives] (Düsseldorf: Droste, 1996).

17. Rationalisioerungskuratorium der Deutschen Wirtschaft [Committee for rationalization of the German economy], Teilzahlungsfinanzierung in den USA [Installment financing in the USA] (Munich, 1956), 38, quoted in Logemann, "Different Paths," 545.

18. Gelpi and Julien-Labruyère, *History of Consumer Credit*, 137–38, 147; Rebecca Belvederesi-Kochs, "Moral or Modern Marketing? *Sparkassen* and Consumer Credit in West Germany," in Logemann, *Cultures of Credit*.

19. Camille Selosse and Lorna Schrefler, *Consumer Credit and Lending to Households in Europe* (Brussels: European Credit Research Institute, 2005), 8, figure 6; Iain Ramsay, "Comparative Consumer Bankruptcy," *University of Illinois Law Review*, 2007, no 1: 244–45, n. 17.

20. Gunnar Trumbull, "Banking on Consumer Credit: Explaining Patterns of Household Borrowing in the United States and France," in Logemann, *Cultures of Credit*; Paul Defourney and Josette Bienfait, *Données d'image sur le credit* [Survey of attitudes toward credit] (Paris: Cetelem-BVA, 1992), 7.

21. Bank for International Settlements, *Statistics on Payment and Settlement Systems in Selected Countries: Prepared by the Committee on Payment and Settlement Systems of the Group of Ten Countries*, March 2007, pp. 6, 47, 97, 232, http://www.bis.org/publ/cpss78.pdf, accessed September 20, 2010.

22. Interview with Thomas Wersebe, Sparkasse Bremen, July 27, 2007, Bremen; also with Wolfgang Blümel, Hamburger Sparkasse, July 27, 2007, Hamburg.

23. MasterCard, "Debitnutzung in Europa: Dank den Frauen geht's voran" [Using debit in Europe: Progressing thanks to women], press release, August 1, 2006.

24. "Bahncard: Jetzt auch ohne Kredit " [The Bahncard: Now also offered without the credit function], *Taz, die Tageszeitung*, July 14, 1995; Angelika Buchholz, "Der Bahncard-Flop," *Süddeutsche Zeitung*, February 5, 1999.

25. Central Credit Register, National Bank of Belgium, http://www.nbb.be, accessed September 22, 2010.

26. Ramsay, "Comparative Consumer Bankruptcy," 250–54, 260; République Française, Conseil Économique et Social, "Endettement et surendettement des ménages" [Household debt and overindebtedness], *Journal officiel de la République Française, avis et rapports du Conseil Économique et Social*, 2000, II-74, http://lesrapports.ladocumentationfrancaise.fr/cgi-bin/brp/telestats.cgi?brp_ref=004000197&brp_file=0000.pdf; Udo Reifner and Helga Springeneer, "Die private Überschuldung im internationalen Vergleich—Trends, Probleme, Lösungsansätze" [Personal overindebtedness in international comparison: Trends, problems, solutions], in SCHUFA Holding AG, *Schulden-Kompass 2004: Empirische Indikatoren der privaten Ver- und Überschuldung in Deutschland*, 2004, pp. 164–66, 186–89, http://www.schufa-kredit-kompass.de/media/studien/pdf_1/kk04_internat_vergleich.pdf; "Bankruptcy—Austria," European Judicial Network in Civil and Commercial Matters, European Commission, April 28, 2005, http://ec.europa.eu/civiljustice/bankruptcy/bankruptcy_aus_en.htm, all accessed February 4, 2011.

27. Herman M. Schwartz and Leonard Seabrooke, "Varieties of Residential Capitalism," in Schwartz and Seabrooke, *Politics of Housing*, 16–17; Kemeny, "'The Really Big Trade-Off,'" 60–66; Katona et al., *Aspirations*, 93, 95.

28. Teresa A. Sullivan, Elizabeth Warren, and Jay Lawrence Westbrook, *The Fragile Middle Class: Americans in Debt* (New Haven: Yale University Press, 2000), 3, 75, 141–42; Charles Yuji Horioka and Ting Yin, "A Panel Analysis of the Determinants of Household Saving in the OECD Countries: The Substitutability of Social Safety Nets

and Credit Availability," unpublished paper, February 3, 2010; Logemann, "Different Paths to Mass Consumption," 546.

29. A comprehensive set of recommendations appears in New America Foundation, Assets Building Program, *The Assets Report, 2010*, April 2010, www.newamerica .net, accessed October 28, 2010; also Commission on Thrift, *For a New Thrift*; on automatic enrollment, see Thaler and Sunstein, *Nudge*.

30. Michael Sherraden and Ray Boshara, "Learning from Individual Development Accounts," in Annamaria Lusardi, ed., *Overcoming the Saving Slump: How to Increase the Effectiveness of Financial Education and Saving Programs* (Chicago: University of Chicago Press, 2008), 209–36.

31. New America Foundation, Assets Building Program, *Savings in American Households: A Collection of Facts and Statistics*, November 16, 2009.

32. World Savings Banks Institute, "A WSBI Roadmap for Postal Financial Services Reform and Development," June 2010, http://www.wsbi.org/uploadedFiles/Position _papers/0620PositionPaperEN.pdf, accessed August 2, 2010.

33. *New York Times*, November 13, 2010, sec. B, p. 1.

34. HM Treasury (United Kingdom), *Financial Inclusion: The Way Forward*, March 2007.

SELECTED BIBLIOGRAPHY

Addams, Jane. *Twenty Years at Hull-House*. Urbana: University of Illinois Press, 1990.

Alger, Horatio, Jr. *Ragged Dick and Struggling Upward*. East Rutherford, NJ: Viking Penguin, 1985.

Alter, George, Claudia Goldin, and Elyce Rotella. "The Savings of Ordinary Americans: The Philadelphia Saving Fund Society in the Mid-Nineteenth Century." *The Journal of Economic History* 54, no. 4 (December 1994): 735–67.

Alton, Thad Paul. *Polish Postwar Economy*. New York: Columbia University Press, 1955.

Ambaras, David R. "Social Knowledge, Cultural Capital, and the New Middle Class in Japan, 1895–1912." *Journal of Japanese Studies* 24, no. 1 (Winter 1998): 1–33.

American Bankers Association. *School Savings Banking*. New York: Ronald Press, 1923.

Aulich, James. *War Posters: Weapons of Mass Communication*. London: Thames & Hudson, 2007.

Balderston, T. "War Finance and Inflation in Britain and Germany, 1914–1918." *Economic History Review* 2nd ser., 42, no. 2 (May 1989): 222–44.

Bank Negara Malaysia. *The Central Bank and the Financial System in Malaysia—A Decade of Change*. Kuala Lumpur: Bank Negara Malaysia, 1999.

Beeton, Mrs. [Isabella Mary]. *Mrs. Beeton's Book of Household Management*. Ed. Nicola Humble. Oxford: Oxford University Press, 2000.

Bellah, Robert N. *Tokugawa Religion: The Values of Pre-Industrial Japan*. Glencoe, IL: Free Press, 1957.

Bentham, Jeremy. *Pauper Management Improved: Particularly by Means of an Application of the Panopticon Principle of Construction*. London: R. Baldwin, 1812.

Blank, Rebecca M., and Michael S. Barr, eds. *Insufficient Funds: Savings, Assets, Credit, and Banking among Low-Income Households*. New York: Russell Sage Foundation Press, 2009.

Blum, John Morton. *From the Morgenthau Diaries*. 3 vols. Boston: Houghton Mifflin, 1959–67.

Board of Governors of the Federal Reserve System. *Consumer Installment Credit*. Part 1, vol. 1. Washington, DC: Government Printing Office, 1957.

Börsch-Supan, Axel, ed. *Life-Cycle Savings and Public Policy: A Cross-National Study of Six Countries*. Amsterdam: Academic Press, 2003.

Brewer, John, and Frank Trentmann, eds. *Consuming Cultures, Global Perspectives: Historical Trajectories, Transnational Exchanges*. Oxford: Berg, 2006.

Brinkley, Alan. *The End of Reform: New Deal Liberalism in Recession and War*. New York: Knopf, 1995.

Bucks, Brian K., Arthur B. Kennickell, Traci L. Mach, and Kevin B. Moore, "Changes in U.S. Family Finances from 2004 to 2007: Evidence from the Survey of Consumer Finances." *Federal Reserve Bulletin* (February 2009): A1–A56.

Buyst, Erik, Martine Goossens, Leen Van Molle, and Herman Van der Wee. *Cera 1982–1998: The Power of Co-operative Solidarity.* Antwerp: Mercatorfonds, 2002.

Caisse des Dépôts et Consignations. *Le Livret A—Une histoire de l'épargne populaire* [Livret A passbook—A history of popular saving]. Paris: La documentation Française, Caisse des Dépôts et Consignations, 1999.

Caisse Générale d'Épargne et de Retraite de Belgique. *La Caisse Générale d'Épargne et de Retraite et ses différent services* [The General Savings Bank and Pension Fund and its various services]. Bruxelles: Vanbuggenhoudt, 1910.

———. *Mémorial 1865–1965 de la Caisse Générale d'Épargne et de Retraite de Belgique* [Memoirs of the General Savings Bank and Pension Fund of Belgium]. Bruxelles: CGER, 1965.

Calder, Lendol. *Financing the American Dream: A Cultural History of Consumer Credit.* Princeton: Princeton University Press, 1999.

Cargill, Thomas F., and Naoyuki Yoshino. *Postal Savings and Fiscal Investment in Japan.* Oxford: Oxford University Press, 2003.

Carson, William J. *Savings and Employee Savings Plans in Philadelphia.* Philadelphia: University of Pennsylvania Press, 1932.

Carter, Susan B., and Richard Sutch. "Myth of the Industrial Scrap Heap: A Revisionist View of Turn-of-the-Century American Retirement." *Journal of Economic History* 56, no. 1 (March 1995): 5–38.

Carver, Thomas Nixon. *War Thrift.* Preliminary Economic Studies of the War, no. 10. New York: Oxford University Press, 1919.

Cassa di Risparmio delle Provincie Lombarde. *First International Thrift Congress, Milan, 26–31 October 1924.* Milan: Organising Committee of the Congress, 1925.

Central Council for Savings Promotion. *Savings and Savings Promotion Movement in Japan.* Tokyo: Central Council for Savings Promotion, 1981.

Charities Aid Association. *Postal Savings Banks for the United States of America,* no. 41. New York: State Charities Aid Association, 1885.

Child, Lydia Maria. *The American Frugal Housewife: Dedicated to Those Who Are Not Ashamed of Economy,* 12th ed. Boston: Carter, Hendee, 1832.

Chochiku Kōdō to Chochiku Ishiki ni kansuru Chōsa Kenkyūkai. *Dai 6-kai chochiku kōdō to chochiku ishiki ni kansuru chōsa hōkokusho* [Report on 6th Survey of Savings Behavior and Savings Consciousness]. Tokyo: Chochiku Kōdō to Chochiku Ishiki ni kansuru Chōsa Kenkyūkai, 1998.

Chochiku Kōhō Chūō Iinkai [Central Council for Savings Information]. *Chochiku to shōhi ni kansuru seron chōsa* [Opinion survey on household savings and consumption]. Tokyo: Chochiku Kōhō Chūō Iinkai, 1987–96.

Chochiku Zōkyō Chūō Iinkai [Central Council for Savings Promotion]. *Chochiku hakusho* [Savings white paper]. Tokyo: Chochiku Zōkyō Chūō Iinkai, 1963.

————. *Chochiku undō: Chozōi 30 nen no ayumi* [History of savings campaigns]. Tokyo: Chochiku Zōkyō Chūō Iinkai, 1983.

Cohen, Jerome B. *Japan's Economy in War and Reconstruction.* Minneapolis: University of Minnesota Press, 1949.

Cohen, Lizabeth. *A Consumers' Republic: The Politics of Mass Consumption in Postwar America.* New York: Knopf, 2003.

————. "The Consumers' Republic: An American Model for the World?" In Garon and Maclachlan, *Ambivalent Consumer,* 45–62.

————. *Making a New Deal: Industrial Workers in Chicago, 1919–1939.* Cambridge: Cambridge University Press, 1990.

Collins, Daryl, Jonathan Morduch, Stuart Rutherford, and Orlanda Ruthven. *Portfolios of the Poor: How the World's Poor Live on $2 a Day.* Princeton: Princeton University Press, 2009.

Commission on Thrift. *For a New Thrift: Confronting the Debt Culture.* New York: Institute for American Values, 2008.

Committee on Thrift Education of the National Education Association and the National Council of Education. *Thrift Education; Being the Report of the National Conference on Thrift Education.* Washington, DC: National Education Association, 1924.

Cook, Haruko Taya, and Theodore F. Cook. *Japan at War: An Oral History.* New Press, 1992.

Currarino, Rosanne. "The Politics of 'More': The Labor Question and the Idea of Economic Liberty in Industrial America." *Journal of American History* 93, no. 1 (June 2006): 17–36.

Defoe, Daniel. *The Complete English Tradesman.* 1839 ed. Gloucester: Alan Sutton, 1987.

————. *An Essay upon Projects.* Ed. Joyce D. Kennedy et al. New York: AMS Press, 1999.

————. *The Life and Strange Surprizing Adventures of Robinson Crusoe.* 1719; rev. ed. Oxford: Oxford University Press, 1999.

De Grazia, Victoria. *Irresistible Empire: America's Advance through Twentieth-Century Europe.* Cambridge: Belknap Press of Harvard University Press, 2005.

De Grazia, Victoria, ed. *The Sex of Things: Gender and Consumption in Historical Perspective.* Berkeley: University of California Press, 1996.

Demos and Center for Responsible Lending. *The Plastic Safety Net.* New York: Demos, 2005.

Diamond, Peter, and Hannu Vartiainen, eds. *Behaviorial Economics and Its Applications.* Princeton: Princeton University Press, 2007.

Dickens, Charles. *The Life and Adventures of Martin Chuzzlewit.* London: Penguin, 1999.

————. *The Personal History of David Copperfield.* Harmondsworth, Middlesex, England: Penguin Books, 1966.

Duet, Daniel. *Les Caisses d'épargne* [Savings banks]. Paris: Presses Universitaires de France, 1991.

————. *Les Caisses d'épargne Françaises et leur activité: Tradition ou évolution (1818–1981)* [French savings banks and their activities: Tradition or evolution]. PhD diss., Paris: Les Éditions de l'épargne, 1983.

Dyer, Henry. *Dai Nippon: The Britain of the East*. London: Blackie & Son, 1904.

Fawcett, Henry. *The Post Office and Aids to Thrift*. London: G. E. Eyre and W. Spottiswoode, 1881.

Feldman, Gerald D. *The Great Disorder: Politics, Economics, and Society in the German Inflation, 1914–1924*. New York: Oxford University Press, 1993.

Feldstein, Martin. "Social Security, Induced Retirement and Aggregate Capital Accumulation." *Journal of Political Economy* 82, no. 5 (September–October 1974): 905–26.

Ferber, Katalin. "'Run the State Like a Business': The Origin of the Deposit Fund in Meiji Japan." *Japanese Studies* 22, no. 2 (2002): 131–51.

Ferguson, Niall. *The Ascent of Money: A Financial History of the World*. New York: Penguin, 2008.

————. *The World's Banker: The History of the House of Rothschild*. London: Weidenfeld & Nicolson, 1998.

Fingleton, Eamonn. *In the Jaws of the Dragon: America's Fate in the Coming Era of Chinese Hegemony*. New York: Thomas Dunne Books/St. Martin's Press, 2008.

Foucault, Michel. *Discipline and Punish: The Birth of the Prison*. Trans. Alan Sheridan. New York: Vintage Books, 1977.

Franklin, Benjamin. *The Autobiography of Benjamin Franklin*. Comp. D. H. Montgomery. Boston: Ginn and Company, 1927.

Friedman, Milton. *A Theory of the Consumption Function*. Princeton: Princeton University Press, 1957.

Frydl, Kathleen J. *The GI Bill*. Cambridge: Cambridge University Press, 2009.

Fujihira, Shinju. "Conscripting Money: Total War and Fiscal Revolution in the Twentieth Century." PhD diss., Princeton University, 2000.

Fukuzumi, Masae. *Sage Ninomiya's Evening Talks—Ninomiya-Ō Yawa*. Trans. Isoh Yamagata. In Tadaatsu Ishiguro, ed., *Ninomiya Sontoku: His Life and "Evening Talks."* Tokyo: Kenkyusha, 1955.

Galbraith, John Kenneth. *The Affluent Society*. Boston: Houghton Mifflin, 1958.

García, José A. *Borrowing to Make Ends Meet: The Rapid Growth of Credit Card Debt in America*. New York: Demos, 2007.

————. *In the Red or in the Black? Understanding the Relationship between Household Debt and Assets*. New York: Demos, 2008.

Garon, Sheldon. "Fashioning a Culture of Diligence and Thrift: Savings and Frugality Campaigns in Japan, 1900–1931." In Sharon A. Minichiello, ed., *Japan's Competing Modernities*, 312–34. Honolulu: University of Hawai'i Press, 1998.

————. "Japan's Post-War 'Consumer Revolution,' or Striking a 'Balance' between Consumption and Saving." In Brewer and Trentmann, *Consuming Cultures*, 189–217.

————. "Luxury Is the Enemy: Mobilizing Savings and Popularizing Thrift in Wartime Japan." *Journal of Japanese Studies* 26, no. 1 (Winter 2000): 41–78.

————. *Molding Japanese Minds: The State in Everyday Life*. Princeton: Princeton University Press, 1997.

————. "Saving for 'My Own Good and the Good of the Nation': Economic Nationalism in Modern Japan." In Sandra Wilson, ed., *Nation and Nationalism in Japan*, 97–114. London: RoutledgeCurzon, 2002.

————. "Savings-Promotion as Economic Knowledge: Transnational Insights from the Japanese Experience." In Martin Daunton and Frank Trentmann, eds., *Worlds of Political Economy*, 163–88. Houndmills, Basingstoke, Hampshire: Palgrave Macmillan, 2004.

Garon, Sheldon, and Patricia L. Maclachlan, eds. *The Ambivalent Consumer: Questioning Consumption in East Asia and the West*. Ithaca, NY: Cornell University Press, 2006.

Gelpi, Rosa-Maria, and François Julien-Labruyère. *The History of Consumer Credit: Doctrines and Practice*. Trans. Mn Liam Gavin. Houndsmills, Basingstoke, Hampshire: Macmillan, 2000.

Ghilarducci, Teresa. *When I'm Sixty-Four: The Plot against Pensions and the Plan to Save Them*. Princeton: Princeton University Press, 2008.

Gilbert, Charles. *American Financing of World War I*. Westport, CT: Greenwood, 1970.

Glickman, Lawrence B. *A Living Wage: American Workers and the Making of Consumer Society*. Ithaca, NY: Cornell University Press, 1997.

Goh, Keng Swee. *Wealth of East Asian Nations*. Singapore: Federal Publications, 1995.

Goldsmith. Raymond W. *A Study of Saving in the United States*. Vol. 1. New York: Greenwood Press, 1955.

Gordon, Andrew. "From Singer to Shinpan: Consumer Credit in Modern Japan." In Garon and Maclachlan, *Ambivalent Consumer*, 137–62.

————. "Managing the Japanese Household: The New Life Movement in Postwar Japan." *Social Politics* 4, no. 2 (Summer 1997): 245–83.

————. *A Modern History of Japan*. New York: Oxford University Press, 2003.

Great Britain. Post Office. *The Post Office: An Historical Summary*. London: His Majesty's Stationery Office, 1911.

Great Britain and Ireland. Post Office Savings Bank. *Report upon the Progress of Post Office Savings Banks*. London: W. P. Griffith, 1862.

————. *Reports, Minutes, and Memoranda from 30th November, 1860, to 13th September 1861*. London: W. P. Griffith, 1862.

Greenspan, Alan. "The Crisis." April 15, 2010. http://www.brookings.edu/~/media/Files/Programs/ES/BPEA/2010_spring_bpea_papers/spring2010_greenspan.pdf, accessed June 19, 2010.

Hall, Peter A., ed. *The Political Power of Economic Ideas: Keynesianism across Nations*. Princeton: Princeton University Press, 1989.

Hamilton, James Henry. *Savings and Savings Institutions*. New York: Macmillan, 1902.

Hamm, John E. *The English Hire-Purchase Act, 1938: A Measure to Regulate Installment Selling*. New York: Russell Sage Foundation, 1940.

Hanc, George. *The United States Savings Bond Program in the Postwar Period*. New York: National Bureau of Economic Research, 1962.

Hanguk Ŭnhaeng [Bank of Korea]. *Chigŭm ŭn jŏchuk I jolsil I pilyohan tae imnida* [Now is the time to save]. Seoul: Bank of Korea, 1997.

Havens, Thomas R. H. *Valley of Darkness: The Japanese People and World War Two*. New York: Norton, 1978.

Heilbroner, Robert L. *The Worldly Philosophers: The Lives, Times and Ideas of the Great Economic Thinkers*, 4th ed. New York: Simon and Schuster, 1972.

Hofheinz, Jr., Roy, and Kent E. Calder. *The Eastasia Edge*. New York: Basic Books, 1982.

Honorary Secretary of the Gloucester Penny Bank. *Penny Banks for Villages and Small Towns*. London: Longman, Green & Co., 1861.

Horioka, Charles Yuji. "Are the Japanese Unique? An Analysis of Consumption and Saving Behavior in Japan." In Garon and Maclachlan, *Ambivalent Consumer*, 113–36.

———. "The Causes of Japan's 'Lost Decade': The Role of Household Consumption." *Japan and the World Economy* 18, no. 4 (December 2006): 378–400.

———. "Consuming and Saving." In Andrew Gordon, ed. *Postwar Japan as History*, 259–92. Berkeley: University of California, 1993.

———. "Why Is Japan's Household Saving Rate So High? A Literature Survey." *Journal of the Japanese and International Economies* 4, no. 1 (March 1990): 49–92.

Horne, H. Oliver. *A History of Savings Banks*. London: Oxford University Press, 1947.

Hyman, Louis. *Debtor Nation: The History of America in Red Ink*. Princeton: Princeton University Press, 2011.

Ibrahim, Al' Alim, ed. *Generating a National Savings Movement: Proceedings of the First Malaysian National Savings Conference, Kuala Lumpur, July 8–10, 1993*. Kuala Lumpur: ISIS Malaysia, 1994.

Ihara, Saikaku. *The Japanese Family Storehouse, Or the Millionaire's Gospel Modernised*. Trans. G. W. Sargent. Cambridge: Cambridge University Press, 1959.

Ikeda Yoshimasa. *Nihon shakai fukushishi* [History of Japanese social welfare]. Kyoto: Hōritsu Bunkasha, 1986.

Inoue Tomoichi. *Kinken shōrei gyōsei oyobi hōsei* [Encouragement of diligence and thrift: administration and law]. Tokyo: Seibunkan, 1904.

International Labour Office. *A Contribution to the Study of International Comparisons of Costs of Living: An Enquiry into the Cost of Living of Certain Groups of Workers in Detroit (U.S.A.) and Fourteen European Towns*. Geneva: International Labour Office, 1932.

International Thrift Institute. *The International Thrift Institute*. Milan: Archetipografia di Milano, [1947].

———. *Third International Thrift Congress, Paris, 20th–25th May, 1935*. Milan: International Thrift Institute, 1937.

Jackson, Kenneth T. *Crabgrass Frontier: The Suburbanization of the United States*. New York: Oxford University Press, 1985.

Japan. Communications Museum [Teishin Sōgō Hakubutsukan]. Tokyo.

Japan. Ministry of Finance [Ōkurashō]. Shōwa zaiseishi shiryō [Archives of Shōwa-era financial history], and Sengo zaiseishi shiryō [Archives of postwar financial history].

Johnson, Chalmers A. MITI and the Japanese Miracle: The Growth of Industrial Policy, 1925–1975. Stanford: Stanford University Press, 1982.

Johnson, Paul. Saving and Spending: The Working-Class Economy in Britain, 1870–1939. Oxford: Clarendon Press, 1985.

Johnson, Simon, and James Kwak. 13 Bankers: The Wall Street Takeover and the Next Financial Meltdown. New York: Pantheon, 2010.

Judt, Tony. Postwar: A History of Europe Since 1945. New York: Penguin, 2005.

Kaigo Tokiomi, ed. Nihon kyōkasho taikei: Kindaihen [Anthology of Japanese textbooks in modern times]. 27 vols. Tokyo: Kōdansha, 1961–67.

Katona, George, Burkhard Strumpel, and Ernest Zahn. Aspirations and Affluence: Comparative Studies in the United States and Western Europe. New York: McGraw-Hill, 1971.

Kemmerer, Edward W. Postal Savings: A Historical and Critical Study of the Postal Savings Bank System of the United States. Princeton: Princeton University Press, 1917.

Keyes, Emerson W. A History of Savings Banks in the United States, from Their Inception in 1816 down to 1877. 2 vols. New York: Bradford Rhodes, 1876–78.

Kimble, James J. Mobilizing the Home Front: War Bonds and Domestic Propaganda. College Station: Texas A&M University Press, 2006.

Kinmonth, Earl H. The Self-Made Man in Meiji Japanese Thought: From Samurai to Salary Man. Berkeley: University of California Press, 1981.

Kokumin Chochiku Shōreikyoku [National Savings Promotion Bureau]. Kokumin Chochiku Shōrei Iinkai gijiroku. [Proceedings of National Savings Promotion Council]. Secret. 5 vols. Tokyo: Kokumin Chochiku Shōreikyoku, 1938–41.

Korea Taehakkyo Kyŭngjae Yonguso [Korea University, Economics Institute]. Kukmin jŏchuk undong banghyang gwa chujin jogik ui palchŏn bangan [Proposal for development of promotional organizations of national savings campaigns]. Seoul: Korea Taehakkyo Kyŭngjae Yonguso, 1996.

Krugman, Paul. The Return of Depression Economics and the Crisis of 2008. New York: W. W. Norton, 2009.

Kume, Kunitake. The Iwakura Embassy, 1871–73: A True Account of the Ambassador Extraordinary & Plenipotentiary's Journey of Observation through the United States of America and Europe, 5 vols. Ed. Graham Healey and Chushichi Tsuzuki. Chiba, Japan: The Japan Documents, 2002.

Labaree, Leonard W, ed. The Papers of Benjamin Franklin. Vol. 7. New Haven: Yale University Press, 1963.

Leff, Mark H. "Politics of Sacrifice on the American Home Front in World War II," Journal of American History 77, no. 4 (March 1991): 1296–1318.

Lewins, William. A History of Banks for Savings in Great Britain and Ireland. London: S. Low, Son and Marston, 1866.

Lim, Richard. Banking on a Virtue: POSBank, 1972–1997. Singapore: POSBank, 1997.

Logemann, Jan. "Different Paths to Mass Consumption: Consumer Credit in the United States and West Germany during the 1950s and '60s." *Journal of Social History* 41, no. 3 (Spring 2008): 525–59.

Logemann, Jan, ed. *Cultures of Credit: Consumer Lending in Global Perspective.* New York: Palgrave Macmillan, forthcoming.

Low, Linda, and T. C. Aw. *Housing a Healthy, Educated and Wealthy Nation through the CPF.* Singapore: Times Academic Press, 1997.

MacGregor, T. D. *The Book of Thrift: Why and How to Save and What to Do with Your Savings.* New York: Funk & Wagnalls, 1915.

Maclachlan, Patricia L. *Consumer Politics in Postwar Japan.* New York: Columbia University Press, 2002.

——. *The People's Post Office: The History and Politics of the Japanese Postal System, 1871–2010.* Cambridge: Harvard University Asia Center, forthcoming, 2011.

Mahathir Mohamad, and Shintaro Ishihara. *The Voice of Asia: Two Leaders Discuss the Coming Century.* Tokyo: Kodansha International, 1995.

Malthus, T. R. *An Essay on the Principle of Population.* Comp. Donald Winch. Cambridge: Cambridge University Press, 1992.

Mandeville, Bernard. *The Fable of the Bees.* Ed. Irwin Primer. New York: Capricorn Books, 1962.

Manning, James Hilton. *Century of American Savings Banks.* New York: B. F. Buck, 1917.

Manning, Robert D. *Credit Card Nation.* New York: Basic Books, 2000.

Mathias, Peter, and Sidney Pollard, eds. *The Cambridge Economic History of Europe.* Vol. 8. Cambridge: Cambridge University Press, 1989.

Mayet, P[aul]. *Agricultural Insurance, in Organic Connection with Savings-Banks, Land-Credit, and the Commutation of Debts.* Trans. Arthur Lloyd. London: S. Sonnenschein, 1893.

Meiji Zaiseishi Hensankai. *Meiji zaiseishi* [Meiji-era financial history]. 15 vols. Tokyo: Maruzen Kabushiki Gaisha, 1904–1905.

Mill, John Stuart. *Principles of Political Economy,* 2nd ed. London: J. W. Parker, 1849.

Mishel, Lawrence, Jared Bernstein, and Heidi Shierholz (Economic Policy Institute). *The State of Working America 2008/2009.* Ithaca, NY: ILR Press, 2009.

Mock, James R., and Cedrick Larson. *Words that Won the War: The Story of the Committee on Public Information, 1917–1919.* Princeton: Princeton University Press, 1939.

Modigliani, Franco, with Richard Brumberg. "Utility Analysis and the Consumption Function: An Interpretation of Cross-Section Data." In Kenneth K. Kurihara, ed., *Post-Keynesian Economics,* 388–436. New Brunswick, NJ: Rutgers University Press, 1954.

Morse, Jarvis M. *Paying for a World War: The United States Financing of World War II.* Washington, DC: U.S. Savings Bond Division, 1971.

Moss, Michael, and Iain Russell. *An Invaluable Treasure: A History of the TSB.* London: Weidenfeld and Nicolson, 1994.

Mura, Jürgen (Wissenschaftsförderung der Sparkassenorganisation), ed. *History of European Savings Banks*. 2 vols. Stuttgart: Deutscher Sparkassenverlag GmbH, 1996–2000.

Naimushō Shakaikyoku [Home Ministry, Social Bureau]. *Kinken shōrei undō gaikyō* [Report on campaign to encourage diligence and thrift]. Tokyo: Shakaikyoku Shakaibu, 1927.

Najita, Tetsuo. *Ordinary Economies in Japan: A Historical Perspective, 1750–1950*. Berkeley: University of California Press, 2009.

Nathan, Robert R. *Mobilizing for Abundance*. New York: McGraw-Hill, 1944.

National Archives at College Park, MD. Records of the Bureau of the Public Debt, RG 53, and Records of the Savings Bond Division, War Finance Division, General Records of the Department of the Treasury, RG 56.

National Archives of the United Kingdom: Public Record Office, Kew, Richmond. Records of the National Savings Committee (NSC), and Records of the Treasury (T).

National Monetary Commission. *Special Report from the Banks of the United States*. Washington, DC: Government Printing Office, 1909.

Nelson, Laura C. *Measured Excess: Status, Gender, and Consumer Nationalism in South Korea*. New York: Columbia University Press, 2000.

———. "South Korean Consumer Nationalism: Women, Children, Credit, and Other Perils." In Garon and Maclachlan, *Ambivalent Consumer*, 188–207.

Nitobe, Inazo. *Bushido: The Soul of Japan*, 17th ed. Tokyo: Teibi, 1911.

Nocera, Joseph. *A Piece of the Action: How the Middle Class Joined the Money Class*. New York: Simon & Schuster, 1994.

Nolan, Mary. *Visions of Modernity: American Business and the Modernization of Germany*. New York: Oxford University Press, 1994.

Oberholtzer, Sara Louisa. "School Savings Banks." *Annals of the American Academy of Political and Social Science* 3 (July 1892): 14–29.

Okada Kazunobu. *Chochiku shōrei undō no shiteki tenkai* [Historical development of savings campaigns]. Tokyo: Dōbunkan, 1996.

Okita, Saburo. *Causes and Problems of Rapid Growth in Postwar Japan and Their Implications for Newly Developing Economies*. Tokyo: Japan Economic Research Center, 1967.

Ōkurashō Zaiseishi Hensanshitsu. *Shōwa zaiseishi* [Shōwa-era financial history]. Vol. 11. Tokyo: Tōyō Keizai Shinpōsha, 1957.

Ooms, Herman. *Tokugawa Village Practice: Class, Status, Power, Law*. Berkeley: University of California Press, 1996.

Osthaus, Carl R. *Freedmen, Philanthropy, and Fraud: A History of the Freedman's Savings Bank*. Urbana: University of Illinois Press, 1976.

Overy, R. J. *War and Economy in the Third Reich*. Oxford: Clarendon Press, 1994.

Packard, Vance. *The Waste Makers*. New York: David McKay, 1960.

Park, Chung Hee. *The Country, the Revolution and I*. 2nd ed. Seoul: Hollym Corp., 1970.

Partner, Simon. *Assembled in Japan: Electrical Goods and the Making of the Japanese Consumer.* Berkeley: University of California Press, 1999.

Phelps, Clyde William. *Financing the Installment Purchases of the American Family.* Baltimore: Commercial Credit Co., 1954.

Post Office Savings Bank. *The First Hundred Years of the Post Office Savings Bank of Singapore.* Singapore: Post Office Savings Bank, 1977.

Pratt, John Tidd. *The History of Savings Banks in England, Wales, and Ireland.* London: C.J.G. & F. Rivington, 1830.

Ramsay, Iain. "Comparative Consumer Bankruptcy." *University of Illinois Law Review,* 2007, no 1: 241–74.

Roach, Stephen S. *Stephen Roach on the Next Asia.* Hoboken, NJ: Wiley, 2010.

Roberts, George E. *Objections to a Postal Savings Bank, Address by Geo. E. Roberts, President of The Commercial National Bank of Chicago, Delivered before the Minnesota State Bankers Association, at Its Annual Meeting held at Lake Minnetonka, June 15th, 1909.* [1909].

Robinson, Edward L. *One Hundred Years of Savings Banking, 1816–1916.* [New York]: Savings Bank Section, American Bankers Association, 1917.

Robinson, Howard. *The British Post Office: A History.* Princeton: Princeton University Press, 1948.

Rodgers, Daniel T. *Atlantic Crossings: Social Politics in a Progressive Age.* Cambridge: Belknap Press of Harvard University Press, 1998.

Rowntree, B. Seebohm. *Land & Labour: Lessons from Belgium.* London: Macmillan, 1910.

Rueschemeyer, Dietrich, and Theda Skocpol, eds. *States, Social Knowledge, and the Origins of Modern Social Policies.* Princeton: Princeton University Press, 1996.

Saitō Michiko. *Hani Motoko.* Tokyo: Domesu Shuppan, 1988.

———. "Senjika no josei no seikatsu to ishiki—*Shufu no tomo* ni miru" [Women's daily life and consciousness in wartime—looking at the magazine *Shufu no tomo*]. In Akazawa Shirō and Kitagawa Kenzō, eds., *Bunka to fashizumu: Senjiki Nihon ni okeru bunka no kōbō,* 285–326. Tokyo: Nihon Keizai Hyōronsha, 1993.

Samuel, Lawrence R. *Pledging Allegiance: American Identity and the Bond Drive of World War II.* Washington, DC: Smithsonian Institution Press, 1997.

Sand, Jordan. *House and Home in Modern Japan: Architecture, Domestic Space, and Bourgeois Culture, 1880–1930.* Cambridge: Harvard University Asian Center, 2003.

Scher, Mark J., and Naoyuki Yoshino, eds. *Small Savings Mobilization and Asian Economic Development: The Role of Postal Financial Services.* Armonk, NY: M.E. Sharpe, 2004.

Schewe, Donald Bruce. "A History of the Postal Savings System in America, 1910–1970." PhD diss., Ohio State University, 1971.

Schorske, Carl E. *Fin-de-siècle Vienna: Politics and Culture.* New York: Knopf, 1979.

Schreiner, Mark, and Michael Sherraden. *Can the Poor Save? Saving and Asset Building in Individual Development Accounts.* New Brunswick, NJ: Transaction, 2007.

Schwartz, Herman M. *Subprime Nation: American Power, Global Capital, and the Housing Bubble.* Ithaca, NY: Cornell University Press, 2009.

Schwartz, Herman M., and Leonard Seabrooke, eds. *The Politics of Housing Booms and Busts.* Basingstoke: Palgrave Macmillan, 2009.

Searle, G. R. *The Quest for National Efficiency: A Study in British Politics and British Political Thought, 1899–1914.* Berkeley: University of California Press, 1971.

Seligman, Edwin R.A. *The Economics of Instalment Selling: A Study in Consumers' Credit.* 2 vols. New York: Harper & Brothers, 1927.

Sham, Donald. "The Origin and Development of the United States Postal Savings System." PhD diss., University of California, Berkeley, 1942.

Sherraden, Michael, and Ray Boshara. "Learning from Individual Development Accounts." In Annamaria Lusardi, ed., *Overcoming the Saving Slump: How to Increase the Effectiveness of Financial Education and Saving Programs,* 280–97. Chicago: University of Chicago Press, 2008.

Shimizu, Hiroshi. *Japan and Singapore in the World Economy: Japan's Economic Advance into Singapore, 1870–1965.* London: Routledge, 1999.

Shin, Gi-Wook, and Michael Robinson, eds. *Colonial Modernity in Korea.* Cambridge: Harvard University Asia Center, 1999.

Shin seikatsu to chochiku: Zenkoku fujin no tsudoi kiroku [New life and saving: Records of national women's meetings]. Tokyo: Chochiku Zōkyō Chūō Iinkai, 1959–62.

Shively, Donald H. "Sumptuary Regulation and Status in Early Tokugawa Japan." *Harvard Journal of Asiatic Studies* 25 (1964–65): 123–64.

Smiles, Samuel. *The Autobiography of Samuel Smiles, LL.D.* Ed. Thomas Mackay. London: John Murray, 1905.

———. *Self-Help, with Illustrations of Character, Conduct, and Perseverance.* Oxford: Oxford University Press, 2002.

———. *Thrift.* London: John Murray, 1875.

———. *Workmen's Earnings, Strikes, and Savings.* London: John Murray, 1861.

Smith, Adam. *An Inquiry into the Nature and Causes of the Wealth of Nations.* Ed. Edwin Cannan. Chicago: University of Chicago Press, 1976.

Society for the Prevention of Pauperism in the City of New-York. *Documents Relative to Savings Banks, Intemperance, and Lotteries.* New York: E. Conrad, 1819.

———. *The Second Annual Report of the Managers of the Society for the Prevention of Pauperism, in the City of New-York.* New York: E. Conrad, 1820.

Sombart, Werner. *The Quintessence of Capitalism: A Study of the History and Psychology of the Modern Business Man.* Trans. M. Epstein. New York: E. P. Dutton, 1915.

St. Claire, Labert. *The Story of the Liberty Loans.* Washington, DC: James William Bryan Press, 1919.

Stead, Alfred. *Great Japan: A Study in National Efficiency.* London: John Lane, 1906.

Straus, S. W. *History of the Thrift Movement in America.* Philadelphia: J. B. Lippincott, 1920.

Takemura, Eiji. *The Perception of Work in Tokugawa Japan: A Study of Ishida Baigan and Ninomiya Sontoku*. Lanham, MD: University Press of America, 1997.

Talamona, Mario. *I Manifesti della giornata mondiale del risparmio, 1924–1999* [Exhibitions of World Thrift Day]. Rome: Associazione fra le Casse di Risparmio Italiane, 1999.

Thaler, Richard H., and Cass R. Sunstein. *Nudge: Improving Decisions about Health, Wealth, and Happiness*. New Haven: Yale University Press, 2008.

Thernstrom, Stephan. *Poverty and Progress: Social Mobility in a Nineteenth-Century City*. Cambridge: Harvard University Press, 1964.

Thiolon, Jean-Pierre. *Les Caisses d'épargne* [Savings banks]. Paris: Berger-Levrault, 1971.

Tomeoka Kōsuke Nikki Henshū Iinkai, ed. *Tomeoka Kōsuke nikki* [Tomeoka Kōsuke diary]. Vol. 2. Tokyo: Kyōsei Kyōkai, 1979.

Tooze, Adam. *The Wages of Destruction: The Making and Breaking of the Nazi Economy*. London: Allen Lane, 2006.

Toyama Shigeru. *Nihonjin no kinben-, chochiku-kan* [Japanese people's views of hard work and saving]. Tokyo: Tōyō Keizai Shinpōsha, 1987.

Trentmann, Frank. "The Evolution of the Consumer: Meanings, Identities, and Political Synapses before the Age of Affluence." In Garon and Maclachlan, *Ambivalent Consumer*, 21–44.

Tucker, David M. *The Decline of Thrift in America: Our Cultural Shift from Saving to Spending*. New York: Praeger, 1991.

U.S. Congress. House. *Postal Savings Banks in Foreign Countries*. 59th Cong., 2nd sess., 1907. H. Doc. 723.

———. *Postal Savings Depositories*. 47th Cong., 1st sess., 1882. H. Rep. 473.

———. Committee on the Post-Office and Post-Roads. *Postal Savings Bank: Hearings before the Committee on the Post-Office and Post-Roads*. March 1910. Washington: Government Printing Office, 1910.

U.S. Congress. Senate. *Nature and Practical Workings of Postal Telegraphs, Telephones, and Postal Savings Banks of Foreign Countries*. 55th Cong., 2nd sess., 1897. S. Doc. 39.

———. *Postal Savings Banks in Foreign Countries*. 55th Cong., 1st sess., 1897. S. Doc. 154.

———. *To Establish Postal Savings Depositories*, 60th Cong., 1st sess., 1908. S. Rep. 525.

———. Committee on the Post Offices and Post Roads. *Industrial Savings Bill: Hearing before a Subcommittee of the Committee on Post Offices and Post Roads*. 66th Cong., 1st sess., August 22, 1919. Washington: Government Printing Office, 1919.

U.S. Department of Agriculture. Bureau of Agricultural Economics. *National Survey of Liquid Asset Holdings, Spending and Saving*. Part 1. Washington, DC: U.S. Department of Agriculture, 1946.

U.S. Department of Treasury. Savings Bond Division. *A History of the United States Savings Bonds Program*. Washington, DC: Department of Treasury, 1991.

————. War Loan Organization. Savings Division. *War Savings in 1919, Second Federal Reserve District, Preliminary Report of the Director of War Savings*, mimeo. [New York, 1919].

U.S. National Resources Committee. *Consumer Expenditures in the United States: Estimates for 1935–36.* Washington, DC: United States Government Printing Office, 1939.

U.S. Office of the Comptroller of the Currency. *Annual Reports of the Comptroller of the Currency.* Washington, DC: Government Printing Office, 1900–13.

Vallance, Aylmer. *Hire-Purchase.* London: Thomas Nelson, 1939.

Van Put, August, et al., eds. *Les Banques d'épargne belges: Histoire, droit, fonction economique et institutions* [Belgian savings banks: History, law, economic function, and institutions]. Tielt: Lannoo, 1986.

Wadhwani, Rohit Daniel. "Citizen Savers: The Family Economy, Financial Institutions, and Social Policy in the Northeastern U.S. from the Market Revolution to the Great Depression." PhD diss., University of Pennsylvania, 2002.

Weber, Eugene. *Peasants into Frenchmen: The Modernization of Rural France.* Stanford: Stanford University Press, 1976.

Weber, Max. *The Protestant Ethic and the Spirit of Capitalism.* Trans. Talcott Parsons. New York: Charles Scribner's Sons, 1958.

Wells, H. G. *A Modern Utopia.* London: Chapman and Hall, 1905.

Westney, D. Eleanor. *Imitation and Innovation: The Transfer of Western Organizational Patterns to Meiji Japan.* Cambridge: Harvard University Press, 1987.

Whitney, Nathaniel R. *Sale of War Bonds in Iowa.* Iowa City: State Historical Society of Iowa, 1923.

Whyte, William H. "Budgetism: Opiate of the Middle Class." *Fortune* (May 1956): 133–37, 164–66, 172.

Winter, Jay, and Blaine Baggett. *The Great War and the Shaping of the 20th Century.* New York: Penguin Studio, 1996.

World Bank. *The East Asian Miracle: Economic Growth and Public Policy.* London: Oxford University Press, 1993.

World Savings Banks Institute. Archives of the International Savings Banks Institute, 1924–94.

Yoshimi Shun'ya, ed. *Sensō no hyōshi: Tōkyō Daigaku Jōhō Gakkan shozō dai-ichiji sekai taisenki puropaganda postaa korekushon* [World War I posters: from the collection of the University of Tokyo Interfaculty Initiative in Information Studies]. Tokyo: Tōkyō Daigaku Shuppankai, 2006.

Yoshimi Yoshiaki. *Kusa no ne no fashizumu* [Grassroots fascism]. Tokyo: Tōkyō Daigaku Shuppankai, 1987.

Yūsei Kenkyūjo Fuzoku Shiryōkan (Teishin Sōgō Hakubutsukan) [Postal Services Archive], ed. *Modanizumu no jidai to yūsei posutaa* [Age of modernism and postal posters]. Tokyo: Yūsei Kenkyūjo Fuzoku Shiryōkan, 1997.

Yūseishō [Ministry of Posts and Telecommunications]. *Yūsei hyakunenshi* (One-hundred-year history of postal services). Tokyo: Yūseishō, 1971.

Yūseishō Chokinkyoku [Postal Savings Bureau]. *Yūbin kawase chokin jigyō 80 nenshi* [Eighty-year history of postal money orders and savings activities]. Tokyo: Yūcho Kenkyūkai, 1957.

Zakaria, Fareed. "Culture Is Destiny: A Conversation with Lee Kuan Yew." *Foreign Affairs* 73, no. 2 (March/April 1994): 109–26.

Zook, George F. "Thrift in the United States." *Annals of the American Academy of Political and Social Science* 87 (January, 1920): 205–11.

INDEX

Page references followed by *fig* indicate an illustrated figure; followed by *t* indicate a table.